Valuing Emotions is the result of a uniqu
psychoanalysis, and anthropology, a
emotions.

The book places emotions at the very center of human identity, life, and value. It lays bare how our culture's idealization of rationality pervades the philosophical tradition and leads those who wrestle with serious ethical and philosophical problems into distortion and misunderstanding. The book also shows how important are the social and emotional contexts of ethical dilemmas and inner conflicts, and it challenges philosophical theories that try to overgeneralize and oversimplify by leaving out the particulars of each situation.

In offering a realistic account of emotions and an in-depth analysis of how psychological factors affect judgments of all kinds, this book will interest a broad range of readers across the disciplines of philosophy and psychology.

CAMBRIDGE STUDIES IN PHILOSOPHY

Valuing emotions

CAMBRIDGE STUDIES IN PHILOSOPHY

General editor ERNEST SOSA (Brown University)

Advisory editors JONATHAN DANCY (University of Keele), JOHN HALDANE (University of St. Andrews), GILBERT HARMAN (Princeton University), FRANK JACKSON (Australian National University), WILLIAM G. LYCAN (University of North Carolina at Chapel Hill), SYDNEY SHOEMAKER (Cornell University), JUDITH J. THOMSON (Massachusetts Institute of Technology)

JAEGWON KIM *Supervenience and mind*
WARREN QUINN *Morality and action*
MICHAEL JUBIEN *Ontology, modality, and the fallacy of reference*
JOHN W. CARROLL *Laws of nature*
HENRY S. RICHARDSON *Practical reasoning about final ends*
JOSHUA HOFFMAN & GARY S. ROSENKRANTZ *Substance among other categories*
M. J. CRESSWELL *Language in the world*
NOAH LEMOS *Intrinsic value*
PAUL HELM *Belief policies*
LYNNE RUDDER BAKER *Explaining attitudes*
ROBERT A. WILSON *Cartesian psychology and physical minds*
BARRY MAUND *Colours*
MICHAEL DEVITT *Coming to our senses*
MICHAEL ZIMMERMAN *The concept of moral obligation*

Valuing emotions

Michael Stocker
Irwin and Marjorie Guttag Professor of Ethics and Political Philosophy
Syracuse University

with

Elizabeth Hegeman
John Jay College of Criminal Justice

CAMBRIDGE UNIVERSITY PRESS

Published by the Press Syndicate of the University of Cambridge
The Pitt Building, Trumpington Street, Cambridge CB2 1RP
40 West 20th Street, New York, NY 10011-4211, USA
10 Stamford Road, Oakleigh, Melbourne 3166, Australia

© Michael Stocker and Elizabeth Hegeman 1996

First published 1996

Stocker, Michael.
Valuing emotions / Michael Stocker, with Elizabeth Hegeman.
    p.   cm. -- (Cambridge studies in philosophy)
ISBN 0-521-56110-8 (hard).—ISBN 0-521-56786-6 (pbk.)
1. Emotions (Philosophy)   2. Reason.   3. Emotions – Social aspects.
    4. Emotions and cognition.   I. Hegeman, Elizabeth.   II. Title.
III. Series.
B105.E46S76   1996
128'.3 – dc20   95-43038

A catalog record for this book is available from the British Library.

ISBN 0-521-56110-8 hardback
ISBN 0-521-56786-6 paperback

Transferred to digital printing 2001

To Sidney Morgenbesser for showing me the importance and delights of good philosophy – from my first philosophy course to now.

To Graeme Marshall for fifteen years of shared philosophical life, of sustained and sustaining interest.

Michael Stocker

To my parents Bonnie and George Hegeman and my daughter Sarah Larsen for valuing emotions.

Elizabeth Hegeman

Contents

ACKNOWLEDGMENTS — page xi
PREFACE — xiii

INTRODUCTION — 1

PART I. PRELIMINARY MATERIAL

1. THE IRREDUCIBILITY OF AFFECTIVITY — 17
   1. Emotions and affectivity — 24
   2. The content account — 26
   3. Irreducibility to desire — 28
   4. Irreducibility to reason — 38
   5. Irreducibility via more complex accounts — 51
   6. Feelings are rarely merely feelings — 53
   7. Concluding remarks — 54

2. HOW EMOTIONS REVEAL VALUE — 56
   1. A start on some issues — 56
   2. Problematic issues about the values emotions reveal — 58
   3. Whether all emotions contain or reveal value, with special focus on interest and intellectual emotions — 65
   4. Some relations between my claim and emotivism and naturalism — 73
   5. Perhaps evaluatively revealing emotions only reveal values — 82
   6. The unsavory connection between the content claim and the information claim — 86

PART II. EMOTIONS AND VALUE: SOME EPISTEMOLOGICAL
AND CONSTITUTIVE RELATIONS

3. EMOTIONAL PROBLEMS SUGGEST EPISTEMOLOGICAL
   PROBLEMS   91
   1. False truisms about reason and emotions   91
   2. Psychoanalytic connections   108
   3. Unhealthy philosophical accounts of emotions   112
   4. Ordinary ways good emotions are important for good
      evaluations   114

4. DO THESE CONNECTIONS SHOW EMOTIONS IMPORTANT
   FOR VALUE, OR DO THEY SHOW SOMETHING ELSE?   122
   1. Do emotional defects explain evaluative defects, or do
      they share a common cause?   122
   2. Is there a real or healthy distinction between emotions
      and their underlying patterns?   129
   3. Perhaps emotions are important, not for evaluations, but
      only for people as evaluators   133
   4. Is this just the information claim?   136

5. EMOTIONS ARE IMPORTANT FOR EVALUATION AND VALUE   138
   1. Medical treatment   138
   2. Justice and formalistic ethics   139
   3. The right of self-defense and emotions   150
   4. How being a good person and acting well requires emotions 152
   5. Many ordinary goods, especially interpersonal ones,
      are emotional   160

6. EMOTIONS AS CONSTITUENTS AND AS ADDED
   PERFECTIONS   169
   1. Emotions as added perfections   169
   2. Emotions as constituents   174
   3. Further issues   177
   4. A suggestion about pleasure in books VII and X of the
      Nicomachean Ethics   182
   5. How we are also Aristotelians about pleasure   184

7. SOME FURTHER WAYS EMOTIONS HELP WITH
   EVALUATIVE KNOWLEDGE 188
   1. Emotions as epistemologically useful for justifications and
      for countertransference 188
   2. Some other claims about the epistemological usefulness of
      emotions 190
   3. Some general points about emotions and practical, often
      unarticulated, evaluative knowledge 192
   4. How emotional-evaluative knowledge can be practical . . 201
   5. Emotions as important, but perhaps not necessary, for
      evaluative knowledge 203

PART III. CASE STUDIES: PHILOSOPHICAL AND OTHER COMPLEXITIES OF EMOTIONS

8. THE INTERDEPENDENCE OF EMOTIONS AND
   PSYCHOLOGY 209
   1. Killing another person – just by way of example 209
   2. Empathy and sympathy 214
   3. Shame 217
   4. Painful emotions 230

9. AFFECTIVITY AND SELF-CONCERN 243
   1. Spiritual maladies 244
   2. Anger and pride 246
   3. Harm, fear, and pity 253
   4. Fear 254
   5. Pity and self-pity 258
   6. Concluding remarks 264

10. THE COMPLEX EVALUATIVE WORLD OF ARISTOTLE'S
    ANGRY MAN 265
    1. *Orgē* and value 265
    2. Narcissism and Aristotle's angry man 268
    3. Slights, flattery, and recognition by others 286
    4. The personal and the impersonal in some emotions . . . 298
    5. Who gets angry on behalf of whom 306
    6. Closeness and identification 307
    7. Size 320
    8. Conclusion 322

11. SOME FINAL CONCLUSIONS	323
REFERENCES	327
SUBJECT INDEX	341
NAME INDEX	348
INDEX OF ARISTOTELIAN AND PLATONIC SOURCES	353

Acknowledgments

A very early version of some of this work was read to the 1991 University of Michigan Philosophy Colloquium, an occasion made especially pleasurable by the participation of Professor William Frankena in whose honor the colloquium was held. Sadly, he is no longer with us.

Another part of an early version was read to the University of Illinois at Chicago Philosophy Department as its Irving Thalberg Memorial Lecture. Professor Thalberg had done significant work on the emotions and had been a good friend. It was a considerable but melancholy honor to give a lecture honoring his memory.

For discussion of parts of this work, thanks are owed to the philosophy departments of Columbia University, New York University, the University of Adelaide, La Trobe University, and the Australian National University; the Society for Ethics and Legal Philosophy; the Department of Psychiatry, Medical School, State University of New York, Upstate; the Oxford University–University of Southern California Legal Theory Institute; and the New Jersey Regional Philosophy Association. Thanks are also owed to my 1994 and 1995 seminars on moral psychology at Syracuse University for reading and commenting on large portions of earlier drafts.

"Emotions and Ethical Knowledge: Some Naturalistic Connections," *Midwest Studies in Philosophy,* 19 (1994) 143–158, consists of an early version of some parts of this work, now mainly in Chapter 3. An early version of some parts of this work, especially from Chapter 6, forms "How Emotions Reveal Value and Help Cure the Schizophrenia of Modern Ethical Theories," in Roger Crisp, ed., *How Should One Live?* (Oxford: Oxford University Press, 1996).

Chapter 1, "The Irreducibility of Affectivity," is largely a revised version of "Psychic Feelings: Their Importance and Irreducibility," *Australasian Journal of Philosophy,* 61 (1983) 5–26. The bulk of Chapter 9, "Affectivity and Self-Concern," is a revised and abbreviated version of "Affectivity and

Self-Concern: The Assumed Psychology in Aristotle's Ethics," *Pacific Philosophical Quarterly*, 64 (1983) 211–229.

I am grateful to the many philosophers, psychoanalysts, and others who have so generously discussed this work with me. I take great pleasure in acknowledging their help – in the appropriate places and in accord with the discussion of Chapter 10, section 3, "Slights, flattery, and recognition by others." My apologies to those I have failed to acknowledge.

In addition to those thanked here, I am grateful to Lawrence Blum and Henry Richardson for discussion and for showing me unpublished work. For commenting on portions of this work, I thank Jonathan Adler, Paul Bloomfield, Jeffrey Blustein, John Deigh, Chris Gowans, Daniel Haggerty, Elijah Millgram, Richard Moran, Stuart Rachels, and Nancy Sherman.

Eugene Garver was especially helpful on Aristotle – in personal discussions, in written comments, and in unpublished works.

I am pleased to acknowledge my colleagues at Syracuse University. For help with early versions of this work, I thank Jonathan Bennett, Robert Daly, John Robertson, and Ernest Wallwork.

For both philosophical and stylistic help with an early and also a late version of this work, my warm thanks to Lynne McFall.

It is difficult to give adequate thanks to my colleague Laurence Thomas. We talked about these issues for many years – walking to the philosophy department, in long and short discussions, and in a seminar we taught together.

For discussions before the work began and for help with various drafts, I am pleased to thank one of the people to whom I dedicate this book: my companion in philosophy, now half a world away, Graeme Marshall.

My greatest debt is owed to Elizabeth Hegeman. I thank her for her help throughout this work, and for joining me in four of its chapters.

Preface

My present concerns in ethics and moral psychology are with people, their motives, purposes, and emotions, and as givers and recipients of attention, affection, and value. I have been working toward, and on, these themes for the past twenty years. During this time, my work has moved from concern with an aspect of our modern ethical theories – the absence of people from those theories – to a deepening concern with moral psychology. One way I characterize my changing focus during these twenty years is by recalling that earlier – from 1965, when I left graduate school and started teaching – I had agreed with Moore's claim in *Principia Ethica* that "conduct is undoubtedly by far the commonest and most generally interesting object of ethical judgments" (sec. 2).

My 1973 article, "Act and Agent Evaluations,"[1] criticized the view, perhaps still dominant, that there are no conceptual connections between act and agent evaluations: that, for example, there are no conceptual connections between what shows an act wrong and what shows an agent bad. (This is discussed in Chapter 5, especially section 4.) I argued that as ethicists concerned with evaluating acts, we should also be concerned with the agents of those acts. From this conjunctive view, I became more and more concerned with and interested by people, especially as understood by moral psychology. It also led to my interest in Aristotle and psychoanalysis (discussed later). During this time, I also came to the related view that many modern ethical theories are schizophrenic. As put in "Act and Agent Evaluations" (1973), "The Schizophrenia of Modern Ethical Theories" (1976), and "Values and Purposes: The Limits of Teleology and the Ends of Friendship" (1981),[2] these theories allow, even require, a split between value and motivation, holding that motivations are irrelevant to the value of what is done or even intended.

1 *Review of Metaphysics,* 27 (1973) 42–61.
2 *Journal of Philosophy,* 73 (1976) 453–466 and 78 (1981) 747–765.

Some argue for these disconnections between value and motivation: it can be "for the best" if values do not make up our motivations, are not sought directly, and perhaps are not even recognized as values. Put in terms of theoretical structure, it is held that ethical theories can be esoteric or self-effacing, to use Sidgwick's and Derek Parfit's terms.[3]

It is easy enough to see how that could be for the best in particular circumstances – say, where manipulation or instrumental effectiveness, rather than openness, is required. And if we are concerned with there being the most value in the universe, that could be for the best quite generally. So for that matter, and for the same reasons, it could be for the best that people never have existed or cease to exist soon. But whether or not for the best in that sense, none of this is best for us. None tells us how to live well, or how we should live. Whether or not those theories are right about total value in the universe, they are not right about us, nor are they right for us. They are not good ethical theories.

These theories misunderstand, and often do not even allow for, large and important parts of human life. As argued in "Schizophrenia" and in "Values and Purposes," they misunderstand, and often do not even allow for, friendship. They fail to see the role many significant values play in our lives, including the extent to which we guide and understand ourselves in terms of our values, and how what we value makes us the sorts of persons we are and societies the sorts of societies they are. Those theories thus fail to see how our values enter directly into so much of our life, and so much of moral importance for us. This, anyway, was the view I was then developing.

A correlative way I see my change of focus is that starting from a committed interest in moral theory, especially moral theory concerned with act evaluations, I came to think that our theories were too theoretical, too driven by theory and too concerned with theory, and certainly not concerned enough with people. Moral psychology was a useful corrective. But it was too often, for my taste anyway, too concerned with theory, rather than with how people are or actually can be.

Valuing Emotions, started in 1991, is a study of some relations between value and emotions. It is concerned both with theory and with how people are and can be. Among its main concerns are showing how our life, thought, and action are involved with emotion and are emotional, how emotions are important for ethical knowledge, how values are constituted by emotions, and how various relations between value and emotions are

---

3 *Methods of Ethics* (Indianapolis, Ind.: Hackett, 1981); and *Reasons and Persons* (Oxford: Oxford University Press, 1984).

mediated by psychology and culture. Because of the complexity and size of these issues, I consider only some emotions, some ethical knowledge, some values, and some relations among these. (In the body of the work, this complexity is increased by an explicit extension of my concern from emotions to all of affectivity.)

My central positive theme is that emotions are essential constituents of life, playing essential roles both in making a life good or bad and also in making it the sort of life it is, with the sort of identity it has. One of my central negative themes is that many contemporary ethicists, along with other contemporary philosophers, have lost sight of the evaluative importance of emotions and perhaps of emotions themselves. I will document these charges in the body of the work. But I now want to relate some personal experiences and anecdotes to introduce and give some support to my claims.

The first is a composite of many different experiences: it is only something of an exaggeration to say that almost every time I have discussed with other philosophers how important I think emotions are, I have been asked about Mr. Spock – one of the main characters of *Star Trek,* a popular television science fiction serial (at least in the United States). He is a half-human, half-"Vulcan" crew member of the central "star ship." Like other Vulcans, he does not have emotions, and part of the story revolves around this. He is portrayed as being able to do almost everything humans do, often better than humans, including make evaluations. In almost all respects, he is exactly like us, except that he lacks emotions. And since he is exactly or almost exactly like us, but emotionless, he is taken as presenting a serious problem for my claims about the need for or even the importance of emotions.

When raised, the issue of Spock is always immediately understood and thought important. Very often it is thought decisive: since Spock does not need emotions to live a good life, neither do we.

I think this line of thought entirely mistaken. I have no objections to using a fiction to investigate a philosophical claim. Too many philosophical arguments, examples, and counterexamples are unconvincing or problematic precisely because they are so abstract and partial, and so lacking in human detail. Thus, we could take appeals to Spock as compendious ways of giving an example with considerable, useful detail. So taken, these appeals can be seen as invitations to investigate what is right or wrong with the thought that other beings could be exactly like us, perhaps even somewhat better, even though they lack emotions, and to investigate the related thought that emotions are not essential or even important for us.

This, however, is not how I hear the use of Spock. Philosophers who use this example seem convinced that Spock is really – that is, humanly – possible. But, as it has seemed to me, they are convinced without any examination. They just easily and naturally "see" that Spock is possible. They do not query whether he is actually portrayed as lacking emotions, or whether we are only told that he lacks them. Nor do they query whether there are inconsistencies between what we are told about him and what we are "shown" about him regarding emotions.

If only we could settle philosophical debates this way. We could then conclude that thinking does not require language, after having seen a fictional character "convincingly portrayed" as thinking, but not in any language. We could conclude that there is no real problem of other minds, after having seen a fictional character "convincingly portrayed" as fully capable of acting intelligently, but without a mind; that being human does not require being embodied, after having seen a fictional character "convincingly portrayed" as just like us, but without a body; and that the argument of the *Republic* is mistaken, after having seen a fictional character "convincingly portrayed" as both evil and happy.

Many of the philosophers who accept the Spock argument see as one of their occupational tasks the questioning and investigation of even ordinary views. But as said, when thinking about Spock and emotions, they seem to accept those conclusions without examination, precisely because that character is so convincing and seems so real and plausible. It is almost as if they think about Spock, "Well, here at last is something we need not investigate, but can just accept." This may be too harsh. Perhaps their acceptance and use of Spock should be seen mainly as an expression of the ideal of unemotionality – an ideal they hold for themselves or find in philosophy. In any case, I think we must ask why Spock so easily appeals to and convinces so many philosophers. Their easy use of Spock suggests a deeply held view, a view that cannot bear examination, but is, somehow, not thought to need examination. This is or comes close to being, in psychoanalytic terms, an *idealization* of reason and a correlative *splitting off* and demonization of emotions.[4] (I will return to this.)

The second anecdote is about only one philosopher. (I think it as well

---

4 On the psychoanalytic notion of idealization and splitting off, one locus classicus is Melanie Klein, *Love, Guilt and Reparation, and Other Works, 1921–1945* (New York: Delta Books, 1977) and *Envy and Gratitude and Other Works 1946–1963* (New York: Delta Books, 1977). See also Heinz Kohut, *The Restoration of the Self* (New York: International Universities Press, 1977), and Jay Greenberg and Stephen Mitchell, eds., *Object Relations in Psychoanalytic Theory* (Cambridge, Mass.: Harvard University Press, 1983).

not to identify this person, and to say only that he, if indeed the person is a man, is a respected philosopher who has done considerable work on emotions.) In 1985, I wrote to him, sending him a copy of my "Psychic Feelings" (now Chapter 1 of this book) in reply to an article of his arguing that feelings are unimportant for emotions and for a good life. He replied that he could not see why I wanted to argue for the importance of feelings; and he offered the following to support his view. He claimed that he and many of his neighbors lived good, even if ordinary, lives. They played with their children, made love, engaged in neighborhood activities, went to work – and they did all this without feelings. Their lives, he told me, were good, and made good by these activities without feelings; and thus feelings are not necessary for a good life.

I asked him whether he meant that they did all this without momentous feelings, perhaps feelings of great ecstasy. He replied that he meant not just momentous feelings, but all feelings. I wrote back that I doubted the accuracy of his claim that they lacked all feelings. Perhaps he simply did not notice them in others or himself. I also wrote that to the extent that I accepted that claim, I could not accept his evaluation that they lived good lives, much less ordinary good lives.

My reason for mentioning this series of letters is that I find it at best strange that anyone would think it uncontroversial and ordinary that he and his neighbors lived without any feelings. I also find it strange, beyond belief really, that anyone could think that such people could have good lives.

I should add that when I met this philosopher several years later, I found him to be an ordinary, friendly person, and indeed very personable and outgoing. In no way did I find him affectless or lacking in emotionality. On the contrary. The question, thus, presents itself: how could such an affectively alive and engaged person, who was also an acute and good philosopher, claim and believe what he did? To my mind at least, this also suggests a deeply held view, an unarticulated idealization that cannot bear examination, and that is not thought to need examination.

The next anecdotes have to do with encounters I had with two friends who are psychoanalysts, who helped me with this work. While it was still in a very early stage, I asked one of them, Elizabeth Hegeman, who also has training in both clinical psychology and anthropology, how being affectless bore on evaluative ability – whether, for example, she could draw on her cases to illustrate how affectlessness is connected with evaluative mistakes. She began by discussing some ways particular neurotic patterns involve a complex interplay of emotional and evaluative distortions and other patterns. But I wanted her to tell me about affectlessness, not affective distortions. When I pressed her on this, it took her a considerable time to see that I really meant affectlessness, not just some deficit or distortion in affect. Her principles of charitable interpretation stopped her from thinking that I really meant affectlessness. When she did realize I meant this, she replied, with a tempered mixture of firmness and exasperation, that neither she nor anyone she knew in psychoanalysis or anthropology had ever met totally affectless people; and that to be affectless, in my sense, was pretty much simply not to be a person. I persisted by asking her nonetheless to join me in the philosophical thought experiment of imagining, if only for the sake of philosophy, such a person. She said she was unable to do so. She went on to suggest, again with firmness and exasperation, that she doubted whether I and other philosophers really could imagine such a person, instead of just imagining that we could imagine such a person.

Recognizing the need for help, I urged Hegeman to join me in writing on the subject. She at first demurred, disclaiming any knowledge of philosophy. I replied that she was at least as qualified there as I was in psychoanalysis, and that was not going to stop me. Upon further urging, she agreed to collaborate with me where appropriate. Chapters 3, 7, 8, and 10 are products of this collaboration. And her help with the rest of the book has been considerable.

The second psychoanalyst, Sandra Buechler, who had done considerable doctoral and postdoctoral work in academic psychology on the emotions, made many helpful suggestions about an early version of the work. At the end of our discussion, she asked, with great diplomacy and friendliness, why I was arguing for the importance of affectivity and emotions. On her understanding, both of emotions and of the academic and scientific fields concerned with them, there was no need to argue for their importance. Their importance was, at best, the starting point, and it was usually passed well before the starting point. The importance of emotions was, in short, pretty obvious to everyone – except, she was coming to suspect, perhaps to philosophers.[5]

She then proceeded to ask not only about me and why I was spending my time on those issues, but also about those I was writing for. She wondered whether, if we really did need to be told what I was saying, we would be able to hear it.

---

5 As the career of Silvan Tomkins and an article by Robert Zajonc suggest, she may have overestimated the openness of academic psychology and psychologists to emotions and affectivity. For Tomkins, see "The Quest for Primary Motives: Biography and Autobiography of an Idea," *Journal of Personality and Social Psychology,* 41 (1981) 306–329. For Zajonc, see "Feeling and Thinking," *American Psychologist,* 35 (1980) 151–175.

As to this last, I am unsure. To indicate why, I offer this final anecdote, which recounts some events that took place well before any of the others just mentioned. In about 1977, I attended a talk on Spinoza, one of the great theorists of emotions. The speaker criticized, even excoriated, his (if this person was a man) fellow writers on Spinoza for their laziness, shoddy thinking, lack of imagination, timidity, concern for reputation. Somewhat later that day, we went to another philosophy talk, this time on the ethics, emotions, and virtues of belief. He told me that he had a quick, but to his mind decisive, argument against there being any such subject: that is, against there being any emotions, virtues, or ethics of belief. The core of the argument was that we do not ascribe to beliefs or believings, or other intellectual "products," any evaluative or descriptive terms having to do with emotion, virtue, or value.

I asked him what he thought he had been doing several hours earlier. He quickly agreed that he had, indeed, been making just such ascriptions.

This, in itself, goes a long way toward making my point about the "invisibility" of emotions -- in this case, emotions about intellectual and cognitive matters. This can also be used to put the question of the second psychoanalyst: how did that philosopher not hear himself and his powerful use of emotions and evaluations of others' emotions? What was it about his and others' philosophical work that somehow placed it outside the ambit of where he saw emotions and what is emotional?

There is a final point about hearing that may also help us see the force of these last questions. A day or so after the talk on Spinoza, that philosopher, once again and without any self-consciousness, was claiming that we do not ascribe emotions and evaluations of emotions to beliefs and believings.

That encounter with the Spinoza scholar may have been the first time I was struck by the strangeness of how at least many philosophers deal with emotions. The strangeness was not so much in the content of their views on emotions. After all, I join many other philosophers in thinking that many of our fellows' views are strange, not to say mistaken. Rather, what I was struck by was the strange ways at least some philosophers think about emotions or do not think about emotions: how they find it strangely easy not to recognize emotions, either of other people or even their own, and how strangely hard they find it to remember their encounters with emotions of other people or of their own.

This strangeness is what we should expect if philosophy and philosophers do idealize reason and demonize emotions. As shown in this encounter, the refutation of an idealized view often does not result in a rejection of the view, or even putting it in question and on hold. The person holding that view may rapidly "forget" that the position has been refuted, and the idealized view may reappear, sometimes quickly and sometimes after a decent interval. (There are, of course, other possibilities. For example, the view may be given up, but only in favor of another, even a negative, idealization: the "god that fails" can easily become a demon.)

At the same time that I was struck by philosophers' strangeness about emotions, I was also struck and heartened by the explosion of philosophical works on emotions and moral psychology. Many of these works also argued against those strange philosophical treatments or lack of treatment of emotions.[6]

My thoughts at that time, including my being struck and intrigued by philosophers' strange treatment of emotions, expressed and also helped fuel my increasing interest and concern with moral psychology, the topic of many of my subsequent publications.[7] *Valuing Emotions* presents my most recent thoughts about these issues.

---

6 I am thankful that this explosion continues. Here I will list only those recent works mentioned in this book that had appeared by 1980: William Alston, "Feelings," *Philosophical Review,* 78 (1969) 3–34; Errol Bedford, "Emotions," *Aristotelian Society Proceedings,* 57 (1956–1957) 281–304; Lawrence Blum, *Friendship, Altruism, and Morality* (London: Routledge and Kegan Paul, 1980), "Compassion," in Amélie O. Rorty, ed., *Explaining Emotions* (Berkeley: University of California Press, 1980); Ronald DeSousa, "The Rationality of Emotions," *Dialogue,* 18 (1979) 41–63, and in Rorty, *Explaining Emotions;* William Gean, "Emotion, Emotional Feeling and Passive Bodily Change," *Journal for the Theory of Social Behavior,* 9 (1979) 39–51; Reynold Lawrie, "Passion," *Philosophy and Phenomenological Research,* 41 (1980) 106–126; Graeme Marshall, "On Being Affected," *Mind,* 77 (1968) 243–259; Iris Murdoch, *The Sovereignty of Good* (London: Routledge and Kegan Paul, 1970); Jerome Neu, "Jealous Thoughts," in Rorty, *Explaining Emotions;* Moreland Perkins, "Emotion and Feeling," *Philosophical Review,* 75 (1966) 139–160; George Pitcher, "Emotion," *Mind,* 74 (1965) 326–346; Georges Rey, "Functionalism and Emotions," in Rorty, *Explaining Emotions;* Amélie O. Rorty, "Explaining Emotions," *Journal of Philosophy,* 75 (1978) 139–161, *Explaining Emotions* and *Mind in Action* (Boston: Beacon Press, 1988); David Sachs, "Wittgenstein on Emotion," *Acta Philosophica Fennica,* 28 (1976) 250–285; Robert Solomon, "Emotions and Choice," *Review of Metaphysics,* 27 (1973) 20–41, and in an expanded version in Rorty, *Explaining Emotions,* and *The Passions* (New York: Doubleday, 1976); Peter Strawson, "Freedom and Resentment," *Proceedings of the British Academy,* 48 (1962) 187–211; Gabriele Taylor, "Justifying the Emotions," *Mind,* 84 (1975) 390–402.

There is, in addition, Elizabeth Anscombe's landmark "Modern Moral Philosophy," *Philosophy,* 33 (1958) 1–19. This work was not concerned directly with emotions, but it must be mentioned for what it showed both about moral psychology, itself, and also the need ethics has for moral psychology. John Rawls, *A Theory of Justice* (Cambridge, Mass.: Harvard University Press, 1971), also takes moral emotions seriously and has encouraged many others to do so, too.

7 "The Schizophrenia of Modern Ethical Theories"; "Desiring the Bad," *Journal of Philosophy,* 76 (1979) 738–753; "Intellectual Desire, Emotion, and Action," in Rorty, *Explaining Emotions;* "Values and Purposes: The Limits of Teleology and the Ends of Friendship"; "Responsibility, Especially for Beliefs," *Mind,* 91 (1982) 398–417; "Psychic Feelings: Their Importance and Irreducibility," *Australasian Journal of Philosophy,* 61 (1983) 5–26; "Affectivity

Much of *Valuing Emotions* and many of those publications are devoted to showing how contemporary ethics ignores emotions or thinks them unimportant for ethics, and showing why this is mistaken. Part of this has to do with why contemporary ethics is so concerned – in my view, by far overconcerned – with duty, where duty is understood in terms of acts we must do or must not do; and why, concomitantly, there is little concern with character and emotions. Some of those earlier publications offer accounts of that. *Valuing Emotions,* however, devotes only a little time to this – except for showing that, as played out in contemporary ethics, a concern for duty and acts coupled with a lack of concern for character and emotions is morally dangerous, misleading, and mistaken.

Valuing Emotions shares some of the concerns of *Plural and Conflicting Values,*[8] the work of, mainly, 1985–1989. However, I think of that book as less concerned with moral psychology than with modern ethical theory. The balance is reversed in *Valuing Emotions*. But as argued both there and here, I do not think ethical theory can be done well without moral psychology, or that moral psychology can be done well without ethical theory – thus, my continuing joint concern with both.

I do not think of *Valuing Emotions* as reaching any final or large-scale truths or doctrines about moral theory, moral psychology, or even about emotions, except perhaps these three methodological points. First, many "simple truths" of our theories are more simple than true. Complexity is the rule, not the exception. Second, we should keep in mind that moral theory and moral psychology are about us and that our concern with how we are should be at least as great as our concern with our theories. Third, a philosophical study that pays attention to the emotions philosophers place and do not place in their works, whether implicitly or explicitly, can show us much of importance about ethics, emotions, philosophy, and ourselves.

Some further prefatory comments on *Valuing Emotions* may be useful. This work has both positive themes and more negative, critical themes. The former are the core of this work, and can be briefly put: to show, both abstractly and concretely, both generally, theoretically, and particularly, many of the ways emotions are important for ethics and various other areas of philosophy.

The negative themes are, largely, concerned with criticizing other philosophers and their views, or lack of views, about emotions and their

and Self-Concern: The Assumed Psychology in Aristotle's Ethics," *Pacific Philosophical Quarterly,* 64 (1983) 211–229; "Emotional Thoughts," *American Philosophical Quarterly,* 24 (1987) 59–69.
8 Oxford: Oxford University Press, 1990.

importance for value. In particular, I am concerned to show how misunderstanding, or simply not focusing on, emotions is deeply implicated in serious and pervasive mistakes in ethics and other areas of philosophy. As important as these criticisms are for philosophy and for *Valuing Emotions*, the main role of these criticisms is to advance the positive themes of this work, especially to help us see the importance of emotions for ethics and other areas of philosophy.

This is to put a positive interpretation on the negative parts of the work. Some readers have suggested a more negative interpretation, holding that the importance of emotions has been recognized by most philosophers, even if only implicitly, or that philosophers would acknowledge that importance, if only they were asked; and concluding that the negative themes of *Valuing Emotions* are directed against a straw position. I have already indicated some reasons I reject this charge and I will give it further attention in the body of this work. But some brief remarks now may be useful.

To start with, I would be pleased were these more optimistic and favorable accounts of philosophers' views about emotions correct. We could all, then, be spared the need – or what I see as the need – to clear away misunderstandings. But as I will show, philosophers have offered, as full or full enough accounts of human life and value, accounts that somehow omit emotions and their importance; philosophers have also offered views that are plausible only if emotions are not important; and some philosophers have explicitly denied the importance of emotions for life and value. To be sure, were many of even these philosophers asked about emotions and their importance, they would say that of course they think emotions are important. But, as the anecdote about the Spinoza scholar suggests, after having said this, many would, undoubtedly, all too quickly and too easily take up their earlier discussions where they left off, once again not talking about emotions. Often, what they do say leaves little, if any, room for emotions and their importance. Instead of holding that philosophers think, whether explicitly or only implicitly, that emotions are important, at least often it may be more accurate to say that they only think that they think this.

In fact, this leads me to suspect that the claim that I am attacking a straw position may itself be a good illustration of the self-misunderstanding philosophers have about emotions and their recent philosophical treatment. I am, of course, alive to the possibility that I am making my position unfalsifiable, by taking any challenge as a symptom of the disease. I will, thus, take considerable care to substantiate my charges that many philosophers misunderstand, equivocate, and vacillate both about emotions and also about what they take themselves to hold about emotions. The discrepancies between what they think they think about emotions, and what their work suggests they think, show a lot about both emotions and also philosophers' attitudes toward and treatment of emotions. To mention only one point, there are many ways the discipline of philosophy is thought of as nonemotional, and is thought well of because it is thought nonemotional. This is part and parcel of philosophers not thinking about emotions, and thinking well of not thinking about emotions.

There is a further methodological reason for rejecting the charge that I am attacking a straw position. This reason, too, involves a suspicion. I think it will be agreed that many contemporary ethicists and other philosophers do not spend much, if any, time discussing the importance of emotions. Nonetheless, we are told, they implicitly do acknowledge the importance of emotions, or would acknowledge it if asked. I would like to know, and not only to help rebut this charge, why they do not discuss this explicitly. This question is made more pressing by the fact that they discuss so much else, almost "everything else," around that topic.

This helps fuel my suspicion that their lack of discussion is explained and motivated by what would be brought out in an explicit discussion. I think these philosophers would have difficulties reconciling what they do discuss explicitly with what would be brought out. For many of their views about ethics and the rest of philosophy suggest, or even require, that emotions are not important. If their silent views about emotions – their implicit views, or views they would express if asked – are that emotions really are important, then these two sets of views are in severe tension with each other. It would be difficult and troublesome to think about them together. Not thinking about one of them would help avoid this difficulty and would help avoid recognizing a need to resolve this tension.

On my view, then, *Valuing Emotions* is not criticizing a straw position when it argues that philosophers have generally not recognized *that* emotions are important for value. I do think, however, that it is possible to debate that issue in a way that diverts attention from the main issue, the core, of *Valuing Emotions: how* emotions are important.

I do not think there can be any real doubt that *how* emotions are important has not received much attention in contemporary ethics or philosophy. This is true both in general and in detail, and both abstractly and concretely. To explain this lack of attention, I will have to show *why* contemporary philosophers have not been concerned enough with this *how*. In short, then, *Valuing Emotions* is concerned with showing *that* contemporary philosophers have ignored, and often denied, or only equivocally and vacillatingly accepted, the importance of emotions. This negative part of the work is at times presented with more affect than the more positive parts, and it might thus seem the main focus of the work. But it is not. *Valuing Emotions* is concerned to show *that* emotions have not been given their due. It is far more concerned with *why* this has happened. And it is still more concerned with *how* emotions are important. This last is its core issue.

Michael Stocker

This collaboration with Michael Stocker is the natural outgrowth of certain central themes in my academic and intellectual life, as it is for him. We have both found too little interest in people and subjectivity in our fields. These interests have moved in parallel to some of the intellectual developments taking place around us: an increased interest in, and sense of the importance of, subjectivity and the self and the inner life of the self as an influence on what is known, and as a topic of importance in itself. The inner position of the observer, and his or her social situation and perspective, have come to be regarded as sources of valuable knowledge in themselves in the social sciences and in psychoanalysis, not just sources of error or distortion as they were often regarded thirty years ago. Countertransference is now an important source of information not just about the analyst, but about the object world of the patient as reproduced in the microcosm of the analytic setting.

The first anthropological field work I did, in 1962, which was my honors work at Radcliffe College, was divided into two parts: the first was a study of two squatter barrios outside Bogota, Colombia, and the second was a study of my own motivations and biases in choosing the places described, with particular attention to how my social situation affected my perceptions of the communities, the process of selecting this subject of study, and the conclusions I came to. Although now this seems like a natural and even necessary part of any field work, at the time it was considered radical, and embarrassingly self-centered. The anthropology department at Harvard rejected the thesis on the basis that the study took place in a city and culture too closely related to my own, and I would therefore not be sufficiently objective. (Fortunately for me, Leon Bramson, then the chair of the social relations department, thought well of the work and was willing to accept it.)

In 1965, after having completed all of the required course work and field study for the doctorate in anthropology, I left anthropology out of a deep sense that the very elements that were most crucial in shaping social science understanding were being left out: an awareness of the situation and subjectivity of the observer as an essential ingredient in the process of observation and documentation. Having assisted Dr. Oscar Lewis in the field in Puerto

Rico in 1963, and having studied a housing project in Cali, Colombia, in 1964 (with a grant from the Columbia University Latin American Institute, funded by the Ford Foundation), I had become convinced of the centrality of the observer's subjective experience and personal involvement in determining the substance of any study.[9]

I was especially convinced of the importance of the relationship of the field worker with the subjects of study (at that time called "informants") in determining the results of any field work, in content, in perspective, and in shaping conclusions about what is important and how it is evaluated. I came to see over and over that even "hard data," like genealogies, household censuses, and work histories of residents, the basic data on which anthropologists rely so heavily, became transformed as my relationship with my informants developed. Without recognizing it as such, I had stumbled upon what psychoanalysts already knew as transference/countertransference and the importance of the interpersonal field. I could no longer write or think as if I were an impersonal, uninvolved observer, simply recording facts.

I also found it impossible to remain uninvolved and not do something to ease the situation of those I was studying who, themselves, were suffering and raising their children in dire poverty. To refrain would have been to participate in a terrible ironic extension of the colonial economic relationship, but at the time I had to conceal my efforts. Now there is advocacy anthropology, but in 1965 this was not accepted as an appropriate role.

After completing my doctorate in clinical psychology at New York University, I was drawn to interpersonal psychoanalysis as a further exploration of the influence of the inner self on the intersubjective field. Psychology and psychoanalysis have grown in their valuing of the subjective self of the analyst as well as the analysand over the past thirty years, and this is shown by the shift in meanings of the word 'countertransference': it used to be an objectionable emotional residue in the analyst which was believed to interfere with the accurate perception of the patient's real dynamics, and it used to be thought that it should be gotten rid of as thoroughly and as quickly as possible. Since the work of Heinrich Racker and others,[10]

---

9 Discussed in Hegeman, "The Development of a Worker Elite in a Cali Barrio," in Hegeman and Leonard Kooperman, eds., *Anthropology and Community Action* (New York: Doubleday Anchor Press, 1974).
10 For Racker, see *Transference and Countertransference* (New York: International Universities Press, 1968). See also Donald W. Winnicott, "Countertransference," *British Journal of Medical Psychology*, 31 (1960) 17–21, reprinted in his *The Maturational Processes and the Facilitating Environment* (London: Hogarth Press, 1965); and Michael Gorkin, *The Uses of Countertransference* (Northvale, N.J.: Jason Aronson, 1987). Countertransference is discussed in

countertransference has been transformed and the analyst's subjective use of self-awareness is now one of the most valuable tools to understanding the patient's true emotional state. This book takes up that parallel in a different subject area: what used to be considered "interference," or error data that interfered with the kind of truth that was being sought, is now understood as a part of the truth, and indeed perhaps even a more essential and indicative kind of truth than the original subject matter! This paradigm shift in psychoanalysis was foreshadowed by Harry Stack Sullivan's 1936 call for psychiatrists and social scientists to become observers who are observant of their observing.[11]

As a part of the Western intellectual tradition, philosophy has so much distaste for nonrational aspects of experience because it works within a highly idealized model of the self, a model that excludes states that are unacceptable or repugnant to most adults, such as the states of extreme helplessness, shame, or pain. The self that is free to theorize or hypothesize, to engage in discourse, to connect freely or disconnect from other human beings, like the "free white male" Athenian citizens, represents only the sector of society privileged with the leisure or enviable jobs allowing freedom from manual labor or feeding or cleaning up after other people in a bodily way.

These excluded self-states are not merely unpleasant reminders of a distasteful reality, they may actually be incompatible with the "normal" reality of scholars in the Western tradition, because much of our "normal" reality screens out the reality that our privilege rests on the exploitation, or at least the exclusion from privilege or power over their own lives, of many fellow human beings, and that we may at least at the moment be doing absolutely nothing about it except ignoring it. It is possible that I assert this so strongly because of my psychoanalytic work with traumatized people, who feel marginalized and alienated because they believe (usually with some accuracy) that others cannot or will not share their horrible or unbearable experiences.

Dissociation, for example and in this culture at least, is the painful and inadequate best accommodation the traumatized individual can make to living in a world where no one wants to know about the trauma. It almost invariably leads to further trauma to try to make the pain and helplessness known; it may even be life-threatening to try to put it into words within the

---

Chapter 3, section 3, and in Chapter 7, section 1.
11 "A Note on the Implications of Psychiatry, The Study of Interpersonal Relations, for Investigations in the Social Sciences," in *The Fusion of Psychiatry and Social Science* (New York: Norton, 1964).

abusive situation, and considerable denigration comes to those who try to record experience that contradicts our ideas of how things are supposed to be, and especially what authorities are supposed to be like.

Dissociation is only one form of self-experience that is marginalized because it does not fit in with our ideologies of what a person is. But I would argue that our notions of what a person is are extremely fragile, tenuous constructs, more like a time- and culture-bound definition of what a person should be, or how we would like to live, or would like to think we are living, than representative of the actual range of human experience.

So this claim goes beyond the criticism that academic disciplines, as they are conducted presently, exclude the experience of many members of our own culture. I am saying that although we take it for granted, the model of the person, itself, in our ideological system – as, perhaps, in every culture – is based on many forms of denial of individual and collective experience required by our cultural system, not just the denial of irrational or excluded feelings. Although the scope of this book is valuing emotions, there are many other ways in which academic life, as well as all of our other professions and cultural institutions, rest on some faulty premises about human nature that have to do with the shaping and selectivity exerted by the process of socialization into each culture. This limitation would apply to such work whatever the culture within which we were considering the nuances and internal contradictions.

To illustrate: cross-cultural theorists such as Richard Shweder, George Devereux, and Colin Ross[12] have commented that compared with other cultures, contemporary Western society values a self with tight boundaries, that is conceptualized as separable and separate from others and is very much under the control of the will. This theme will be readily recognizable in the various doctrines based on the worth and the responsibility of the individual, ranging from capitalism to the Bill of Rights.

Another example: the Western self is also pictured as being in ultimate control of nature, rather than the other way around. This form of denial has led us into a collision course with the natural environment, as noted by Dorothy Dinerstein in *The Mermaid and the Minotaur: Sexual Arrangements and Human Malaise,*[13] and by many ecologists and feminist theorists since. The feminist criticism of the scientific pursuit of progress suggests that it

---

12 Shweder, *Thinking through Cultures: Expeditions in Cultural Psychology* (Cambridge, Mass.: Harvard University Press, 1991); Devereux, *Basic Problems of Ethnopsychiatry* (Chicago: University of Chicago Press, 1980); Ross, *Multiple Personality Disorder* (New York: John Wiley and Sons, 1989).
13 New York: Harper and Row, 1976.

may be particular to Western culture, and the result of distorted gender relations, which leave child care exclusively in the hands of women, to deny the interdependence of human beings on each other and with the natural environment. How could we not expect that some of these distortions would be found in our academic work? In this sense our effort here is not just to focus on some devalued or omitted aspects of philosophical theory, but also to bring our thinking in line with feminist thought in the broadest possible sense.

A note as to the nature of our collaboration: Stocker is interested in and familiar with both philosophy and psychoanalysis, and I in anthropology and psychoanalysis. The work originated in his seeing the philosophical implications of certain psychoanalytic issues as we discussed them. At other times, our collaboration makes it impossible to distinguish who is responsible for which part.

Although Stocker seems to be known among philosophers for his distaste for theory in philosophy, we noticed that in our discussions I was constantly asking for examples of what he meant, and indeed was unable to grasp his points fully without them. As a psychoanalyst/anthropologist, I find myself unable to feel that I understand some human event without detailed description so minute that it may seem maddeningly dense to those of a more generalizing bent.

Stocker came to see that my concreteness represents a commitment we both have to the belief that interactions between human beings can only be understood in their fullest possible context, including the internal relationship with the self and other inner loyalties and attitudes, and external social relationships that affect evaluation so profoundly.

The realization that our delineation of the assumptions of a discipline is not universally applicable to all human beings in all cultures does not, to me, diminish the value of what we are doing, just as I do not believe that my overall emphasis on what is left out, or not included, in our cultural constructions diminishes what philosophy has done and can do. We value the culture in which we live, the academy within which we teach and work, and the relationships with family, colleagues, and fellow citizens that make up our lives sufficiently to care enough to want to deepen or enlighten, rather than correct, the nature of these assumptions which underlie so much of our culture, not just philosophy.

Elizabeth Hegeman

Introduction

How important are emotions for ethics? Early in our tradition, the dominant view was that emotions have central evaluative importance. For example, Aristotle thought that to be a good person, one must have the right emotions. This includes, but goes well beyond, holding that emotions help make a life good because of the pleasure or pain they involve and because of how they help motivate us to do what is good. He also thought that having the right emotions is constitutive of virtue and of being a good person, and for knowing what to do and how to live. But during the past hundred years or so, philosophers have generally deemed emotions not all that important for ethics.

I favor a more traditional view. To show why, I will argue for two interrelated themes: that there are important constitutive connections between emotions and values, and that there are important epistemological connections between them. To show the constitutive connections, I start by showing how emotions might seem external to values: by only "pointing to" them, or by being only useful for them, or by being only added flourishes to them. I conclude by showing how emotions are internal to value, in fact so internal that they are inseparable from it or are even forms of it. To show the epistemological connections, I start by showing how emotions provide evidence for or symptoms of value. I conclude by showing how emotions are expressions of, and may even be, evaluative knowledge.

A central concern of this book, then, is to show the great human value and importance of affectivity and emotions. In saying this, I do recognize that some emotions, such as spite, and some emotional configurations, such as narcissism, are bad. Nonetheless, in ways to be detailed, affectivity and emotions have inestimable human value and evaluative importance: put briefly, without emotions it is impossible to live a good human life and it may well be impossible to live a human life, to be a person, at all. An absence or deficiency of affect is a characterizing feature of many neuroses, borderline conditions, and psychoses, as well as of such maladies of the spirit as meaninglessness, emptiness, ennui, *accidie*, spiritual weakness, and spiritual tiredness. This is also to say that accounts of people that omit the fact that we are affective beings are not accounts of healthy people, people who can and do lead good and human lives. Any theory of the person that denies, omits, or misunderstands affectivity and emotions will therefore be inadequate, both descriptively and evaluatively.

Now is not the time to stop and show which philosophers have held such a view; and, as noted in the Preface, I am far more concerned with showing how emotions are important for ethics than in discussing who failed to see this. Instead, then, of discussing which philosophers have failed to accord emotions great evaluative importance, we might note that not all philosophers see this as a failing – and this for various sorts of reasons.

For the first of these reasons, we can turn to Steven Luper-Foy who writes, "There are whole traditions – Epicureanism, Stoicism, Buddhism, etc. – that develop the suggestion that unemotionalness is crucial to happiness."[1] I will not enter into a discussion of whether those cultures do have ascetic or unemotional ideals, or whether they also hold that implementing those ideals is important for happiness. Nor will I enter into such discussions about our culture, except to say that in many ways it embraces those ideals. This, after all, was one of Nietzsche's main targets. So too, it is one of the main targets of *Valuing Emotions*.

It should be made clear, however, that I am not interested in these ideals as ideals, whether ours or other peoples'. Insofar as I am concerned with ideals, my concern is with ideals as lived and followed and the sorts of lives that result from their being lived and followed. I, further, restrict my attention to the real lives and actual possibilities of people in *our* culture(s). (Who we are will become clearer shortly.) Understanding just ourselves is difficult and complex enough. If I can help show how emotions enter into only our lives, and are involved with only our values, I will consider the work a success. It is entirely sufficient for my purposes if affect and emotions are necessary for good and healthy lives of people like us, living in the sorts of societies and cultures we live in: living, in short, the sorts of lives we live and aspire to.

I will not spend much time on direct criticisms of this first objection to

---

[1] Review of *Morality and the Emotions* by Justin Oakley, *Philosophy and Phenomenological Research,* 54 (1994) 725–728, p. 726. I should note that I had the pleasure of being one of the supervisors of Oakley's doctoral dissertation – written at La Trobe University (Melbourne, Australia) – which was the basis of Oakley's book. In another doctoral dissertation I had the pleasure of supervising – "The Joy of Torture: The Happiness of Stoic Sages" (Syracuse University, 1995) – Joseph Waligore contests the usual view that Stoic doctrine held that a lack of emotions and of emotionality is needed, or even important, for happiness.

my claim that good lives require emotions. My more indirect criticisms – given in discussions of how various goods and good lives involve emotions, and how various bads and bad lives lack emotions or the right emotions – will do all that I think need be done on this score. I will, however, devote considerable time to various other "reasons" for thinking emotions unimportant for value and valuation.

Among the main reasons considered, and rejected, by *Valuing Emotions* is the conglomerate of views recognizing emotions but downgrading them to auxiliary or instrumental status. Here we find the view that emotions provide only a nice flourish or added embellishment for ethics and ethical life – that, for example, it is a nice added touch, if in doing one's duty, one can also be cheerful or motivated by care. We also find the view that emotions can be motivationally important as causes and incentives or disincentives for moral or immoral action: for example, anger leads to unconsidered and inconsiderate action. Turning now to more epistemological concerns, we also find the view that emotions provide evidence for what one values: for example, your guilt at not paying your taxes shows that you think you should pay them. Emotions, and other forms of affectivity, do indeed play these roles. But as will be argued, they also play far more important roles – roles that place them at the very center of value and evaluation.

Another of the main targets of *Valuing Emotions* has already been mentioned in the Preface. This is the compound view that acts are the primary concern of ethics; that there are no significant conceptual connections between act evaluations and agent evaluations; that the main, or only, place emotions could be of evaluative importance is in regard to agent evaluations; and thus that there is no important reason for ethics to be concerned with emotions. This work argues that agents, character, and lives are among the primary concerns of ethics, and that emotions are central to their value, as well as to the value of acts, themselves.

A related reason for thinking emotions unimportant for value and evaluation stems from the view that ethics is mainly concerned with, or modeled on, justice and the political, especially as these are understood by liberalism. This focuses evaluative attention on what is "outer," turning away from what is "inner," even from values and desires for doing what is outer.

As I see matters, such focus on acts and the outer is somehow encouraged by the view that our morality is a guilt morality, not a shame morality. Somehow, the guilt is not understood in terms of emotions, but only or mainly in terms of duties, which, in turn, are understood in terms of acts and what is outer – and these, in turn, are seen as the main concerns of ethics. Shame morality, on the other hand, is seen as concerned with character and emotions, and ultimately with feelings about the self, the primary object of shame. This in turn is connected with liberalism. As the psychoanalyst Helen Block Lewis writes in *Shame and Guilt in Neurosis,* "The concept of guilt motivation as a higher order of morality than shame motivation is particularly congenial to an industrial society based on the autonomy or personal independence of its members (Tawney, 1926)."[2]

Unfortunately, exploring these historical and cultural issues would lead too far afield. I will have to content myself with simply claiming that whatever their origins and explanations both the overconcentration by ethicists on duty and acts and also the concomitant lack of concentration on character and emotions are serious errors. I will also argue, more indirectly and more briefly, that the contrast between guilt and shame moralities is overblown, as is the claim that our morality is a guilt morality. These arguments will also show that we are quite properly concerned with character and with feelings about character.

In their different ways, then, these last considerations emphasize the evaluative importance of acts, and may, thus, seem to agree with Moore's claim in *Principia Ethica* that "conduct is undoubtedly by far the commonest and most generally interesting object of ethical judgments" (sec. 2). I argue against this commonly held view in two ways. The first is by showing how emotions, too, have considerable evaluative importance. The second argues that this view embodies a particularly narrow conception of the nature and values of acts: that what they are and, more importantly, their value lies wholly in what they "contribute" to the world or what they are done in order to do or achieve. I argue, to the contrary, that emotions are constitutive elements of acts, what is outer, and even duties, and that emotions help give these their value. So for example, both in terms of the acts they are and their value, an act of friendship and one of keeping a promise can be quite different, even though they both help produce or constitute the very same part of the very same world: your meeting Smith at the appointed time and place.

Unless the notion of conduct is seen as including emotions and other moral-psychological elements, that notion is a barren and uninteresting one for ethics, rather than "the commonest and most generally interesting

---

2 New York: International Universities Press, 1971, p. 66. She refers us to R. H. Tawney, *Religion and the Rise of Capitalism* (New York: Harcourt, Brace, 1926). See also Bernard Williams, *Shame and Necessity* (Berkeley: University of California Press, 1993).

object of ethical judgments." Arguments for this are a central focus of many of my other works.[3] This task is continued in *Valuing Emotions,* sometimes by explicit argument and more often by illustration.

Another reason why ethicists have ignored emotions or thought them evaluatively and ethically unimportant stems from views about emotions and their place in our lives. For example, some think of emotions as abnormal, perhaps rare, events, often of considerable height or depth. Emotions thought of this way are naturally thought of as misleading, disrupting, or even overwhelming us. Emotions are also thought of as simply bodily, and thus as lacking any secure connections with reason, rationality, and value.

I can be overwhelmed by fear of the masked person who suddenly appears at my living room window. This fear can seize my total attention and paralyze me, preventing me even from calling for help. It can also have a distinct beginning and end, starting when I first see the person and lasting little longer than it takes to recognize that it is a friend, playing a joke. Insofar as emotions are like this, they had better be rare and abnormal. A life in which they were common would be a life of nightmares, dementia, and psychosis.

If emotions are thought of in terms of emotional mountains and canyons, it is natural to see them as abnormal, overwhelming, misleading, and disruptive, and certainly lacking secure and respectable connections with value. Thinking of them as bodily also aids thinking of them as lacking those connections. And thus, to show that there are secure and respectable connections between emotions and value, it will be important for me to show that emotions need not be disruptive, and that they can be normal and entirely common and ubiquitous, and also that they are not simply bodily.

I am not alone in arguing for this. Many other contemporary philosophers also argue for the respectability of emotions: showing that emotions

---

3 I include here "Intentions and Act Evaluations," *Journal of Philosophy,* 67 (1970) 589–602, "'Ought' and 'Can'," *Australasian Journal of Philosophy,* 49 (1971) 303–316, "Act and Agent Evaluations," *Review of Metaphysics,* 27 (1973) 42–61, "The Schizophrenia of Modern Ethical Theories," *Journal of Philosophy,* 73 (1976) 453–466, "Values and Purposes: The Limits of Teleology and the Ends of Friendship," *Journal of Philosophy,* 78 (1981) 747–765, *Plural and Conflicting Values* (Oxford: Oxford University Press, 1990), "Self–Other Asymmetries and Virtue Theory," *Philosophy and Phenomenological Research,* 54 (1994) 689–694, and "Abstract and Concrete Value: Plurality, Conflict, and Maximization," in Ruth Chang, ed., *Incommensurability, Comparability, and Practical Reasoning* (Cambridge, Mass.: Harvard University Press, 1997). My thoughts on this were sharpened by being on a panel with Henry Richardson and David Velleman, discussing Richardson's *Practical Reasoning about Final Ends* (Cambridge: Cambridge University Press, 1994), at the 1995 meetings of the Eastern Division of the American Philosophical Association.

have cognitive, evaluative, and desiderative content. But, as shown in Chapter 1, many of these philosophers forget about, ignore, or even deny the affectivity of emotions. In arguing for the respectability of emotions, they offer a radically deficient account of emotions. This is an account that, of all things, presents emotions as if they can lack affectivity and emotionality.

In this work, I, too, am concerned to normalize and rescue emotions, and to show that they enjoy secure and respectable connections with value, in part because of their important cognitive, evaluative, and desiderative content. But I am also concerned to emphasize the affectivity of emotions and of people. I will argue for the normalization, respectability, and the importance of emotions while, and often by, recognizing their affectivity. This will involve showing how their affectivity enters into both their value and our knowledge of their value.

I am also concerned to show the complexity of emotions. This includes, but goes beyond, showing that they involve cognitive, evaluative, and desiderative content, and are also affective. It includes showing their psychological complexity: showing how they involve and can be understood only in terms of various psychic states and structures, such as character types, neurotic formations, stances or approaches to the world, to mention only some elements. It also includes showing how emotions are interpersonally and socially complex: how, for example, to understand emotions we also have to understand the sociological and interpersonal relations of people with those emotions, and how understanding those relations involves understanding those emotions; and how, at a still greater level of generality and complexity, emotions can be understood only if we understand the worlds of people with those emotions and that understanding such worlds involves understanding those emotions.[4]

My discussions will often be presented more by illustration than by discursive argument. And they will often be presented with help from

---

4 Arguing for these various points, especially to his professional colleagues, was the life work of the psychologist Silvan Tomkins. See his "The Quest for Primary Motives: Biography and Autobiography of an Idea," *Journal of Personality and Social Psychology*, 41 (1981) 306–329. For a somewhat similar project by and for psychoanalysts, see Ernest Schachtel, *Metamorphosis* (New York: Da Capo Press, 1984), and also Charles Spezzano, *Affect in Psychoanalysis* (Hillsdale, N.J.: Analytic Press, 1993). Amélie O. Rorty has done similarly important and signal work for philosophers in writing and editing works on emotions. See her *Explaining Emotions* (Berkeley: University of California Press, 1980) for an early anthology of some of her and others' papers on emotions. See also her *Mind in Action* (Boston: Beacon Press, 1988) for a collection of many of her papers on emotions.

Aristotle and various, mainly contemporary, psychoanalysts. As I hope will be seen, we can learn much about life, emotions, and value, not just Aristotle's and psychoanalysts' views, by studying them.

The use of Aristotle or psychoanalysis may be thought controversial. I will try to counter this worry. At this stage of the book, it may be sufficient to say that I will mainly be concerned to use, not defend, those views. And in my use of them, I have tried to make my views acceptable to, and useful for, ethicists, philosophers, and others of many different schools.

Put very briefly, I use Aristotle and psychoanalysis because they offer very useful and detailed accounts and case studies of emotions, ranging from the most abstract to the most particular. These accounts and studies also help establish one of the central themes of *Valuing Emotions:* that particular emotions, and emotionality in general, can be understood philosophically only with the aid of other disciplines, including psychoanalysis, psychology, sociology, and anthropology; and that for these disciplines to succeed, they must deal with emotions.

More particularly, I use Aristotle because of the centrality of affectful emotions, to use a pleonasm, and the centrality of psychological concerns to his ethical views. I use psychoanalysis because affectivity and emotions are at the center of its theory and practice. My use of it also will allow me to present examples from life, rather than from, say, literature, while avoiding the danger Bernard Williams warns us against: "what philosophers will lay before themselves and their readers as an alternative to literature will not be life, but bad literature."[5]

I think it worth saying that I see and use psychoanalysis as an ongoing enterprise that is at the very same time both practical and theoretical, with heavy emphasis on the practical. Moreover, I mainly use more practice-oriented accounts of psychoanalysts, not their theoretical, and especially not their high theoretical, views. I take very seriously the view expressed by Nancy Chodorow, a theorist of sociology and psychoanalysis, that

psychoanalytic theory, like much academic psychology, and virtually all the popular psychology literature has tended to overgeneralize and universalize – [for example,] to oppose all men to all women and to assume that masculinity and femininity (and their expressive forms) are single rather than multiple. This is a peculiar tendency in a field whose data are by necessity so resolutely and intractably idiographic, so individual and case-based.[6]

---

5 *Shame and Necessity,* p. 13.
6 *Femininities, Masculinities, Sexualities* (Lexington: University of Kentucky Press, 1994), p. 71.

In addition to not seeing psychoanalysis primarily as a theory, much less as a settled theory, I do not see it as a theology or demonology. I especially do not see it as Freudology: a religion or cult with Freud's work as holy or unholy writ, which adherents accept with veneration, in detail and overall, and without correction; and which critics attack root and branch, in part and whole, showing how flawed it is. Some defenders and many critics of psychoanalysis do think of psychoanalysis this way. But on my view, we can no more evaluate psychoanalysis by evaluating Freud than we can evaluate contemporary medicine by evaluating the use of leeches by early doctors,[7] or than we can evaluate physics by evaluating Newton's work.

Some comments about affects and affectivity by three psychoanalysts, Ernest Schachtel, Henry Krystal, and David Rapaport are important for the general concerns of *Valuing Emotions* and also for the ways they help illustrate how this work will use psychoanalysis. These comments suggest just how common and ordinary emotions are; how they need not be eventlike or momentous; how there is far more to emotions and our emotional life than those mountains and canyons; and how emotions can be diffuse, pervasive, and long lasting, forming our background, as well as the tone, the color, the affective taste, the feel of activities, relations, and experiences. In addition to being diffuse, pervasive, and long lasting, emotions and emotionality are the rule, not the exception.

As Schachtel writes in *Metamorphosis,*

there is no action without affect, to be sure not always an intense, dramatic affect as in an action of impulsive rage, but more usually a total, sometimes quite marked, sometimes very subtle and hardly noticeable mood, which nevertheless constitutes an essential background of every action. (p. 20)

An even more widely ranging claim about action and affects is made by Krystal:

Affects are familiar to everyone. They are part of our experiences, so ordinary and common that they are equated with being human. . . . Yet their very universality and constant presence with us throughout life make them as unidentifiable as the prose in our speech.[8]

If these claims are right, as I think they are, we see how common emotions and affects are. To show this and also how various and complex they are, I

---

7 To borrow from the psychoanalysts Richard Gartner, Dodi Goldman, et al. in a letter in *New York Review of Books,* 42, no. 1 (1995) 42–43, p. 43.
8 *Integration and Self-Healing: Affect, Trauma, and Alexithymia* (Hillsdale, N.J.: Analytic Press, 1988), p. xi. A similar view is also offered by the contemporary neurologist Antonio R. Damasio in *Descartes' Error: Emotion, Reason, and the Human Brain* (New York: G. P. Putnam's Sons, 1994) under 'background feelings', pp. 150–151.

offer the following passage, along with its footnotes from Rapaport's "On The Psychoanalytic Theory of Affects":

Their central role in therapy, however, does not exhaust the clinical significance of affects. We have come to label as affect such a wide variety of phenomena that both in diagnostic and therapeutic work we are in danger of being led astray by the term, as long as we lack a systematic view of the relationships of all the phenomena to which we apply it.[ii] A brief survey will show the complexity of the situation.

We call affect not only the infant's rage (encountered later on in tantrums and in the destructive outbursts of some catatonics) and the adult's anger accompanied by the corresponding expressive movements and other physiological concomitants, but also the subjective feelings of those well-controlled adults who show little or no affect expression, as well as the anger of overcontrolling compulsive persons who just "know" that they "could be" or "should be" angry. We also call affects those displays which impress the onlooker as histrionic or as affectations, and which certain character types are prone to produce, either in exaggeration of experienced, or as substitutes for not experienced, affects. It is not quite clear how these are related to the "as if" affect of those schizoid personalities described by Helene Deutsch (1942, p. 123).[iii] Nor is their relation clear to those oversensitive incipient and ambulatory schizophrenics who appear to wallow in their affects, which on closer inspection turn out to be restitution products following a total withdrawal of object cathexes;[iv] these patients are affectively moved by anything that seems to promise them the experience of affects, because it proves to them that they are still capable of feeling.[v] Nor is there a clarity about the relations of both these latter types to those more crudely obvious schizophrenic affect phenomena termed "flat affect" and "inappropriate affect." We need not dwell on displaced affects, somatic affect equivalents without conscious affect experience, or on the relation of these to conversion symptoms and psychosomatic disorders and all the rest that belong to the chapter of "unconscious emotion"; they have been variously discussed (Fenichel, 1945; Alexander, 1943; Rapaport, 1942). But we must mention the related phenomena of "frozen affects" which find expression – without conscious affect experience – in stereotyped postures, facial expressions, tones of voice, motility, etc., to which Reich (1933) called attention. And we must take notice of such affects as anxiety, guilt, elation, depression, which – in contrast to the momentary affects so far mentioned – may take pathological chronic forms; even more important they may take characterological chronic forms, as in anxious people, gay people, gloomy people, bashful people, etc. (Landauer, 1938). Furthermore, we must mention a special group of affects, namely those grouped around the experiences of the comic, wit, humor, etc., which are apparently related to a specific kind of saving of cathectic expenditure, rather than to any specific kind of cathectic tension. It is noteworthy that a proclivity to elicit and/or experience such affects may also take a chronic form and structuralize into a character trait (Brenman, 1952). Finally we must mention such specific and complex affective states as apathy, nostalgia, boredom, etc., which are also relatively chronic affect formations (Bibring, 1953).

To make even more glaring the complexity of what a theory of affect must account for, we might add that, on the one hand, neurotic inhibition and ego limitation cuts down the range of intensity and variability of affect experiences; on the other, regression processes bring to the fore unbridled and unmodulated affective attacks in which, while the intensity is formidable, range and variability are minimal.

---

ii: While all the phenomena discussed below have to do with affects, and are time and again so referred to in the literature, my listing them here does not imply that they are correctly labeled as affects nor that the theory of affects alone must account fully for all of them. Indeed, some of the phenomena to be listed are most complex, and more than the theory of affects will have to be invoked for their explanation. What I imply by listing them here is that they constitute an important problem for the theory of affects also.

iii: ". . . outwardly he conducts his life as if he possessed a complete and sensitive emotional capacity. To him there is no difference between his empty forms and what others actually experience . . . [this] is no longer an act of repression but a real loss of object cathexis."

iv: Here the subjective experience of lack of affect in depersonalization (Schilder, 1924; Fenichel 1945) and in certain allied syndromes of organic etiology (Bürger-Prinz and Kaila, 1930; Schilder, 1924) is also relevant.

v: Compare Federn on narcissistic affect (1936, p. 336).[9]

(Before continuing, I would call attention to the fact that Rapaport uses, as will I, the terms 'schizophrenic' and 'schizoid' to label different, even if related, conditions. For our purposes, it is sufficient to say that a form of thought disorder is central to schizophrenia, and that being so detached as to be unrelated emotionally is central to being schizoid.)

Schachtel's, Krystal's, and Rapaport's claims tell against the views that emotions are always momentous, that they are rare, and that they are entirely bodily. By telling against the claim of rarity, they also tell against the view that emotions are always or generally disruptive. For that view is

---

9 *International Journal of Psycho-Analysis*, 34 (1953) 177–198; reprinted in Robert P. Knight and Cyrus Friedman, eds., *Psychoanalytic Psychiatry and Psychology: Clinical and Theoretic Papers, Austen Riggs Center*, volume 1 (New York: International Universities Press, 1954); and in *The Collected Papers of David Rapaport*, ed. Merton M. Gill (New York: Basic Books, 1967), from which this quotation is drawn, pp. 478–479. The works Rapaport refers to are: Franz Alexander, "Fundamental Concepts of Psychosomatic Research: Psychogenesis, Conversion, Specificity," *Psychosomatic Medicine*, 5 (1943) 205–210; E. Bibring, "The Mechanism of Depression," in P. Greenacre, ed., *Affective Disorders* (New York: International Universities Press, 1953); M. Brenman, "On Teasing and Being Teased: And the Problem of 'Moral Masochism'," *Psychoanalytic Study of the Child*, 7 (1952) 264–285; H. Bürger-Prinz and M. Kaila, "On the Structure of the Amnesic Syndrome," in David Rapaport, ed., *Organization and Pathology of Thought* (New York: Columbia University Press, 1951); Helene Deutsch, "Some Forms of Emotional Disturbance and Their Relationship to Schizophrenia," *Yearbook of Psychoanalysis*, 1 (1942) 121–136 (New York: International Universities Press, 1945); P. Federn, "On the Distinction between Healthy and Pathological Narcissism," 1929, in *Ego Psychology and the Psychoses* (New York: Basic Books, 1952); Otto Fenichel, *The Psychoanalytic Theory of Neurosis* (New York: Norton, 1954); K. Landauer, "Affects, Passions and Temperament," *International Journal of Psycho-Analysis*, 19 (1938) 388–415; David Rapaport, *Emotions and Memory*, 2nd unaltered edition (New York: International Universities Press, 1942); Wilhelm Reich, *Characteranalyse* (Vienna: Selbstverlag des Verfassers, 1933); Paul Schilder *Medical Psychology*, 1924, tr. and ed. David Rapaport (New York: International Universities Press, 1953).

plausible only if emotions are rare, or only if ordinary life is ordinarily disrupted.

This may answer, or help answer, a negative claim that emotions are disruptive. I am interested in answering that claim. But I am far more interested in establishing a contrary, positive claim: that emotions are not just features of everyday, healthy, and good life, but also that they help make everyday life healthy and good.

Even if the importance of emotions for life is not recognized by contemporary philosophers and by some psychologists, it is recognized by many others. A deep truth about our life is stated by Roger Angell:

> Even those of us who have not been spoiled by . . . the fulfillment of the wild expectations of our early youth are aware of a humdrum, twilight quality to all our doings in middle life, however successful they may prove to be. There is a loss of light and ease and early joy, and we look to other exemplars – mentors and philosophers . . . – to sustain us in that loss.[10]

It is unclear which philosophers, at least which modern philosophers, Angell might have in mind. But what is clear is the importance of the emotions and feelings of light and ease and early joy, as well as those of a humdrum, twilight quality.

We thus see that at least some emotions can be valuable, useful, and enabling. Here we might consider such related emotions as being *interested in*, *warmed by*, *feeling at home* with people, activities, and places. It is obvious that we are concerned that those we love and care for be interested in what they do, and that they care for those they live and work with. We are also concerned that they hold and act upon their values with care, concern, and interest. (Some philosophers have questioned my calling interest an emotion. I deal with this in Chapter 2, section 3, and Chapter 3, especially section 1.) So, I find it valuable, useful, and enabling to be interested in my professional activities, to be warmed by the attention and friendliness of my colleagues, and to feel at home in my university. Correlatively, I am saddened for those who have lost interest in the discipline, who have chilly relations with students and colleagues, and who feel out of place in their universities.

As this suggests, and as will be argued, emotions are essential for many sorts of lives, both many sorts of good lives and many sorts of bad lives. Any theory of the person or psyche that denies, omits, or misunderstands emotions will, therefore, be inadequate both descriptively and evaluatively. A primary goal of *Valuing Emotions* is to show many of the ways emotions are

---

10 "The Sporting Scene – Distance," *New Yorker,* 56 (September 22, 1980) 83–127, p. 127.

important for lives, for value, and for evaluation. The structure of this work is as follows. Chapters 1 and 2, which form Part I, set out various preliminary issues of concern throughout the work. Chapter 1 argues for the importance and irreducibility of affectivity, especially against contemporary attempts to understand affectivity in terms of desire and reason. It shows how these accounts fail, either by being circular or by giving us affectless accounts of affect and emotions. Chapter 2 makes a start on showing how emotions contain and reveal values, and how we can learn from our emotions what values we hold. It raises the worry that perhaps emotions are only external to value: mainly, only instrumentally valuable in revealing value. It discusses some ways my epistemological claims about emotions are related to emotivism and naturalism. It also shows how the worry that the only evaluative role of emotions is to reveal values fits naturally with the affectless accounts of emotions discussed in Chapter 1.

Part II, consisting of Chapters 3 through 7, is concerned with how emotions and values are deeply interrelated, both epistemologically and constitutively. Chapter 3 – written in collaboration with Elizabeth Hegeman – shows how emotions are important for evaluative knowledge: how, on both psychoanalytic and more ordinary understandings, not having emotions or not having the right emotions is deeply implicated with evaluative errors. This chapter is also concerned to show how the philosophical division of emotions into affectful and affectless elements runs the serious risk of portraying emotions in a way that is accurate only for people suffering serious psychological problems. Chapter 4 considers and rejects various worries to the effect that, although there are the sorts of connections shown in Chapter 3, they are not really with emotions, but only with various nonemotional states, or that they are not with values, but only with people as evaluators.

Chapter 5 starts the primary argument that emotions are internal to value. Its main way of doing this is by examining various cases of valuable activities and ways of living that depend on emotions. Chapter 6 borrows from Aristotle's two accounts of pleasure – pleasure is activity and pleasure perfects activity – to show two ways emotions are internal to value. Some goods, such as play, are the activities they are and are good because of the emotions they involve. Others, such as various forms of work, are made better by emotions that "accompany" them. Chapter 7 – also written in collaboration with Hegeman – returns to epistemological relations between emotions and value to show how emotions can be essential to practical, evaluative activity and knowledge, especially for the values discussed in earlier chapters.

Part III, consisting of Chapters 8 through 10, takes up some themes from the earlier chapters. The earlier seven chapters argue for the moral importance of affectivity in general and emotions in particular. They also argue that emotions can be understood only with the help of a complex psychology and moral psychology, aided by psychoanalysis, anthropology, sociology, and a host of other disciplines. Chapters 8 through 10 are case studies of these claims, and are meant to illustrate and support them.

Chapter 8 – written in collaboration with Hegeman – is a study of some current philosophical views about killing, empathy, shame, and painful emotions. Chapter 9 is a study of Aristotle on affectivity and also self-concern. It discusses the significance of the absence of spiritual maladies, such as depression, in the psychology and moral psychology Aristotle assumes and deploys, and how, therefore, that psychology and moral psychology fit us poorly. Chapter 10 – also written in collaboration with Hegeman – discusses *orgē,* anger, mainly as presented in the *Rhetoric,* and also in the *Nicomachean Ethics.* One of its main concerns is to show that such *orgē* is usefully understood as expressing and also constituting the narcissism of Aristotle's men, as narcissism is understood psychoanalytically.

To conclude the Introduction, I want to repeat a point made in the Preface about the core concerns of *Valuing Emotions* and a point made here about its focus. *Valuing Emotions* is not devoted just or even mainly to showing that philosophers have failed to give emotions their due. Nor is it devoted just or even mainly to showing that while also exhorting us to mend our ways. It is devoted to showing both of these. But it is even more devoted to several other goals: to show the effects of not giving emotions their due; to show the myriads of ways emotions are important, at all levels, for ethics and value; and to show, or make a start on showing, in both theoretical and more particularized ways, how emotions are important for ethics, for much of philosophy, and for us.

PART I

Preliminary material

1

The irreducibility of affectivity

This chapter and the next one are concerned with preliminary material. Three interrelated claims are central to this work. First, absence and deficiency of affect and emotionality are characterizing features of dissociation, depersonalization, and of various neuroses, borderline conditions, and psychoses. Second, without affectivity it is impossible to live a good human life and it may well be impossible to live a human life, to be a person, at all. Third, accounts of people that deny or omit the fact that people are affective beings are not accounts of healthy people, who can and do lead good and human lives. Putting these together, to accept such accounts is to accept accounts of beings who are, at best, unhealthy, who suffer from these maladies, and who may well not even be people.

In this chapter, I am concerned to show how, and if possible why, recent philosophical accounts of people and even of emotions have ignored or misunderstood affectivity. Much of what I say about these philosophical accounts involves issues that are at something of a remove from the more strictly evaluative concerns central to this work. I return to these in the following chapters and readers interested only in those evaluative concerns might want to move directly to Chapter 2. But I think that to understand the evaluative issues, it is useful to work through these other issues.

The anthropologist Richard Shweder writes, "Three-year olds, Ifaluk

This is largely a revised version of "Psychic Feelings: Their Importance and Irreducibility," *Australasian Journal of Philosophy,* 61 (1983) 5–26. Special thanks are owed to Kent Bach and Michael Bratman for many discussions on these issues. I would also like to thank Annette Baier, Sylvain Bromberger, Christopher Cordner, Michael Devitt, Bert Dreyfus, Mark Johnston, L. A. Kosman, Genevieve Lloyd, Kimon Lycos, Gareth Matthews, Amélie O. Rorty, Robert Shope, Irving Thalberg, John Taurek, and an anonymous referee for the *Australasian Journal of Philosophy.* Versions of the article were read to various philosophy department seminars. For help with revising the article, my thanks are owed to Jonathan Adler and Elijah Millgram. Similar views are found in Graeme Marshall, "On Being Affected," *Mind,* 77 (1968) 243–259, and Stephen Leighton, "A New View of Emotion," *American Philosophical Quarterly,* 22 (1985) 133–141.

islanders, and psychoanalysts (in other words, almost everyone, except perhaps the staunchest of positivists) recognize that emotions are *feelings.*"[1] Whether or not philosophers show themselves given to positivism, their treatment of feelings is remarkable. When feelings are discussed at all, they are often radically misunderstood. What is at least as remarkable is their absence as serious topics in philosophical psychology or even moral psychology. Often, they are not even treated as unimportant topics, and are just not examined at all.

There are, of course, some exceptions to this.[2] But, it must be emphasized, these are exceptions to the way feeling and affectivity are treated – that is, are mostly *not* treated – by contemporary philosophers. Feeling and affectivity enjoy the same lack of importance and lack of attention in cognitive psychology, an area of psychology very closely allied with various contemporary philosophical currents. As the academic, research psychologist Robert Zajonc writes, "Contemporary cognitive psychology simply ignores affect. The words *affect, attitude, emotion, feeling,* and *sentiment* do not appear in the indexes of any of the major works on cognition . . ."[3]

Before examining some current philosophical views about emotions and affectivity, I should explain why I consider affectivity to be psychic, not or

---

1 *Thinking through Cultures: Expeditions in Cultural Psychology* (Cambridge, Mass.: Harvard University Press, 1991), ch. 6, "Menstrual Pollution, Soul Loss, and the Comparative Study of Emotions," p. 241.
2 Among these, we find Max Scheler, *Formalism in Ethics and Nonformal Ethics of Values* (Evanston, Ill.: Northwestern University Press, 1973) especially pp. 256–264 and 332–344; Stephen Strasser, *Phenomenology of Feeling* (Pittsburgh: Duquesne University Press, 1980); William Alston, "Feelings," *Philosophical Review,* 78 (1969) 3–34; Amélie O. Rorty, "Explaining Emotions," *Journal of Philosophy,* 75 (1978) 139–161, reprinted in her *Explaining Emotions* (Berkeley: University of California Press, 1980) and *Mind in Action* (Boston: Beacon Press, 1988); Georges Rey, "Functionalism and Emotions," in Rorty, *Explaining Emotions,* especially pp. 176–180, under 'the qualitative'; John Haugeland, "Understanding Natural Language," *Journal of Philosophy,* 76 (1979) 619–632, especially section 5; R. Lawrie, "Passion," *Philosophy and Phenomenological Research,* 41 (1980) 106–126; Graeme Marshall, "On Being Affected," *Mind,* 77 (1968) 241–259; Iris Murdoch, *The Sovereignty of Good* (London: Routledge and Kegan Paul, 1970); Jerome Neu, "Jealous Thoughts," in Rorty, *Explaining Emotions;* Moreland Perkins, "Emotion and Feeling," *Philosophical Review,* 75 (1966) 139–160; George Pitcher, "Emotion," *Mind,* 74 (1965) 326–346; Robert Solomon, "Emotions and Choice," *Review of Metaphysics,* 27 (1973) 20–41, and, in an expanded version, in Rorty, *Explaining Emotions,* and his *The Passions* (New York: Doubleday, 1976); Peter Strawson, "Freedom and Resentment," *Proceedings of the British Academy,* 48 (1962) 187–211; Gabriele Taylor, "Justifying the Emotions," *Mind,* 84 (1975) 390–402.
3 "Feeling and Thinking," *American Psychologist,* 35 (1980) 151–175, p. 152, n. 3. He proceeds to list many works that ignore affect and several that do mention or discuss it. The academic psychologists Rainer Reisenzein and Wolfgang Schönpflug discuss these issues in "Stumpf's Cognitive–Evaluative Theory of Emotion," *American Psychologist,* 47 (1992) 34–45.

not just bodily. I should also explain why I talk about feelings, in addition to emotions, moods, attitudes, and interests.

Psychic, not bodily: My main explanation of why I place affectivity in the psyche and not, or not just, in the body is put nicely by Descartes. Talking of emotions or passions, he writes, "we feel as though they were in the soul itself."[4] This is to contrast those feelings with bodily feelings, which he says, "we relate to our body or some of its parts . . . which we perceive as though they were in our members." This, of course, would have to be amplified in terms of what the different feelings are about and what we must understand in order to understand the content and the genesis of the feelings or of the activity giving rise to them.

There are undoubtedly many connections between psychic and bodily feelings. Some emotions and feelings are most naturally, and perhaps even necessarily, expressed by bodily means. Further, various feelings seem at once bodily and psychic: for example, some that are involved in sexual desire and sexual activity, in the exultation of climbing a difficult cliff, and in certain forms of disorientation and tension. On the other hand, various feelings do not seem to require any bodily feeling, or, for that matter, any bodily expression: for example, being interested in a philosophy problem one is working on or excited by a movie one is watching.[5] (Chapter 2, section 3, argues that intellectual interest can be an emotion or emotionlike.)

Notwithstanding the sometimes important relations between psychic and bodily feelings, I will concentrate on psychic feelings. One reason I focus on psychic, nonbodily feelings is to counter the view of many contemporary philosophers that all feelings are nothing but, or at least always involve, bodily feelings. This, especially the former, may explain a theme found in various of the philosophers discussed here: that since bodily

---

4 *The Passions of the Soul* I.25, as translated by E. S. Haldane and G. R. T. Ross in *The Philosophical Works of Descartes* (New York: Dover, 1931). The next quotation is from I.24. See also I.27–29.

5 Discussion of whether the body or bodily feelings are essential to emotions are found in ancient, medieval, and contemporary philosophical works. See, for example, Aristotle, *De Anima* I.1, and the *Nicomachean Ethics* III.10; Aquinas, *Summa Theologica* 1–2, Q. 22; John Dewey, "The Theory of Emotion," *The Early Works (1882–98),* volume 4 (Carbondale: Southern Illinois University Press, 1971), especially pp. 152–188, originally in the *Psychological Review,* 1 (1894) 553–569 and 2 (1895) 13–32; Perkins, "Emotion and Feeling"; and William Gean, "Emotion, Emotional Feeling and Passive Bodily Change," *Journal for the Theory of Social Behavior,* 9 (1979) 39–51. See also Nicholas J. H. Dent, "Varieties of Desire," *Aristotelian Society Proceedings,* supplementary volume 50 (1976) 152–176, and J. Benson, "Varieties of Desire," *Aristotelian Society Proceedings,* supplementary volume 50 (1976) 177–192.

feelings are conceptually irrelevant to emotions, feelings are conceptually irrelevant to them. On my view, the premise is true of some emotions, but the conclusion is false.

Feelings, not just emotions, moods, interests, and attitudes: I now turn to why I talk about feelings, not just emotions, moods, interests, and attitudes. (Henceforth, by 'feeling' I mean *psychic* feeling, unless otherwise made clear.) One reason is that it allows us an easy way to refer to the characterizing feature of Plato's and others' middle part of the soul, *thumos,* spirit, distinguishing it from reason and desire. Turning now to a different triad, it is also useful to have a term for what is common to these following three sorts of (if I may) feelings: feelings had by the person, such as being full of interest; feelings about the world, such as being interested in some particular thing; and feelings in the world, such as finding a particular thing interesting.[6] I do not think 'emotions', 'moods', 'interests', or 'attitudes', or any combination of them, is adequate for this.

So too, it is useful to have a common term for the affectivity common to emotions, moods, interests, and attitudes. A further reason to distinguish feelings from emotions, moods, interests, and attitudes has to do with intensity. The intensity of feelings is at least one of the important differentiating factors between anger and rage, between fear and terror, and between many other emotions. It is also one of the important determinants of the waxing or waning of the one into the other.

In the rest of this book, I am not as careful as I could be in distinguishing among emotions, moods, interests, and attitudes, nor among them and feelings. My arguments are usually cast in terms of *emotions,* but they also are, or can easily be made into, arguments about feelings, moods, attitudes, and interests. Some of what I say about emotions, including some examples I offer as examples of emotions, would undoubtedly be better put in other terms, such as feelings, or moods, or interests, or attitudes. It will, thus, often be useful to read 'emotions' as 'feelings, emotions, moods, interests, or attitudes'.

My overuse of 'emotion' may be distracting. But apart from this, I do not think it is harmful. I focus on emotions for mainly strategic reasons: emotions are prominent, both in life and the literature. Further, philosophers have thought emotions problematic and also unimportant for value and evaluation largely because emotions are affective – and affective in the same ways feelings, moods, interests, and attitudes are affective. Thus, if bothered

---

6 I am here indebted to Scheler, *Formalism in Ethics and Nonformal Ethics of Values,* especially pp. 256–264 and 332–344.

by emotions, philosophers should also be bothered, and for the same reasons, by feelings, moods, interests, and attitudes.

One further point should be made about my understanding of feeling and affectivity. It is often held that part of the *esse* of affectivity is *percipi:* that feelings must be felt, and part of what it is to be felt involves awareness of the feeling. Many philosophers take this to be Freud's view. And it is indeed a view Freud held early in his career. Giving an account of Freud's "pure discharge" theory of affect, as found in his 1915 paper, "The Unconscious," David Rapaport writes,

ideas when repressed – when their cathexis is withdrawn, or when they are countercathected – persist as actualities (as memory traces) while affects when repressed (decathected or countercathected) persist only as potentialities.[7]

But as Rapaport also writes, this was problematic even for the early Freud:

I believe that here Freud as yet lacked the observations which could have indicated to him (as they did to him as well as to Brierley and Jacobson later) that discharge thresholds of drives and affects are indispensable concepts of an affect theory. But such thresholds heightened (presumably by countercathexes) to attain repression of affect would render the repressed "affect charge" just as actual as memory traces render unconscious ideas. Freud's conception here shows the limitation of a pure discharge theory of affects which has no place in it for threshold structures.[8]

As indicated by Rapaport's "as they did to him . . . *later,*" Freud went on to give up his view that affects require awareness, and came to allow for unconscious affects, as do most, if not all, contemporary psychoanalytic schools and psychoanalysts.[9]

We might note that this is not the only occasion where philosophers have thought of Freudian theory, and indeed of psychoanalytic theory quite

---

7 "On The Psychoanalytic Theory of Affects," *International Journal of Psycho-Analysis,* 34 (1953), 177–198; reprinted in Robert P. Knight and Cyrus Friedman, eds., *Psychoanalytic Psychiatry and Psychology: Clinical and Theoretic Papers, Austen Riggs Center,* volume 1 (New York: International Universities Press, 1954); and in *The Collected Papers of David Rapaport,* ed. Merton M. Gill (New York: Basic Books, 1967), from which this and following quotations are drawn. This one is from p. 484.
8 P. 484. Rapaport is referring to M. Brierley, "Affects in Theory and Practice," *International Journal of Psycho-Analysis,* 18 (1937) 256–268, and to one or both of Edith Jacobson's, "The Psychoanalytic Theory of Affects," 1951, unpublished manuscript, and "The Affects and Their Pleasure-Unpleasure Qualities in Relation to the Psychic Discharge Processes," in R. M. Lowenstein, ed., *Drives, Affects, Behavior* (New York: International Universities Press, 1953).
9 For example, see Henry Krystal, *Integration and Self-Healing: Affect, Trauma, and Alexithymia* (Hillsdale, N.J.: Analytic Press, 1988); Joyce McDougall, *Theaters of the Mind: Illusion and Truth on the Psychoanalytic Stage* (New York: Brunner Mazel, 1991); and Charles Spezzano, *Affect in Psychoanalysis* (Hillsdale, N.J.: Analytic Press, 1993).

generally, in terms of *early* Freudian theory. In *Being and Nothingness,* Sartre argues that Freud's account of repression involves a mutually inconsistent triad of views all endorsed by Freud: repression involves ego processes; all ego processes are conscious; repression and what is repressed are not conscious. In early works, Freud did hold that ego processes are entirely conscious. But he later came to hold what now goes without saying in psychoanalytic theory and practice: that many ego processes are not conscious, but are unconscious or preconscious.

I agree with the later Freud and contemporary psychoanalysis about the "location" or "nature" of feelings. I do not think that we must be aware of the feelings we are having, or even that we must be aware of having them. As I see matters, awareness of one's feelings can range from full reflective and attentive awareness, through dim and confused awareness, to total or almost total unawareness, including what in psychoanalytic terms is said to be preconscious or even unconscious. But to show the irreducibility of feelings, and to show at least many of the important connections between value and emotions, these issues need not be settled; nor need it even be allowed that we can be less than fully aware of our feelings.

Nonetheless, some brief comments on these issues should be useful. One can feel shame without having any idea why one is feeling shame. Further, one can feel shame without being able to identify one's emotion or emotional state as shame. As Helen Block Lewis writes in *Shame and Guilt in Neurosis,*

> Although the level of shame affect was often quite strong, the patients themselves did not identify their own psychological state as shame. Rather, they said they felt "depressed," or "lousy" or "blank." I have tentatively called this phenomenon "overt, unidentified shame" and have traced sequences from it into depressions, diffuse anxiety and obsessive ruminations about shameful events, and about guilt.[10]

So too, one can be angry about something without recognizing what one is angry about. I might recognize that I am angry, but fail to see that I am angry at you, or at you for insulting me. I might be angry without realizing it. I might, instead, misidentify my emotional state as anxiety or boredom. Or I might mistakenly think that I am in no emotional or affective state at all.

Much the same holds for many other emotions. (I say "many" simply to avoid the need to discuss whether it holds for all.) I think all of the following can make perfectly good sense and can be true: "For many years I was unaware that I was resentful at all, much less resentful of you"; "For many

---

10 New York: International Universities Press, 1971, p. 53.

years, I was unaware that I was in love with you"; "For many years, I was unaware that I was depressed." One strong piece of evidence for this possibility is that when we learn what emotions we have been having without noticing them, we often learn why we had what had seemed to us inappropriate and unmotivated thoughts and fantasies, as well as previously inexplicable anxiety and tension.

Some theorists – perhaps because they hold that the *esse* of emotions is *percipi* – tell us that these phenomena we are not aware of are dispositional, not occurrent. And some tell us that these phenomena are attitudes and moods, not emotions. I disagree with both.

Before showing why, I want to emphasize that here, as so often, the distinction between the occurrent and the dispositional is important. To mention only one point, it gives one of the central explanatory and classificatory categories for various tendencies and pronenesses: for example, my proneness to getting angry at you far more easily than I get angry at others. I also want to emphasize that such long-term anger might be purely dispositional. Even while I have this proneness, it is possible that until I feel myself provoked by you, I am thoroughly and through-and-through calm and in an entirely equable mood. We might, thus, agree with Antonio R. Damasio in *Descartes' Error: Emotion, Reason, and the Human Brain* and think of these times of calmness as times "between emotions," as times when there are only "background feelings."[11]

I do not want to enter into issues about whether we are always in some emotional state or other, or if there are times between emotions, how extensive are those times. But, by continuing with the story just given, I want to emphasize a third point: that even between times of out-and-out anger toward you, I can still be angry at you where this anger is not merely dispositional anger. My anger might only occasionally rise to the surface. When it does, it might not be fully formed as anger at you or even as anger at all. It might be felt simply as a general sourness or a more particular sourness directed especially at you. And when below the surface, it can be there simmering away, troubling the waters. It can serve as part of my standing emotional, background conditions, often unattended to, but fully there as part of my world.

This makes two points of importance for us. First, there may be fewer and shorter times between emotions than is thought. In any case, how much time there is will certainly be a matter of particular circumstances, and individual and social difference – for example, how given a person or

---

11 New York: G. P. Putnam's Sons, 1994, p. 150.

people are to emotionality. Second, these forms of anger that are other than out-and-out anger cannot be understood in terms of dispositional anger or some other dispositional emotion. They are there occurrently.

What I have just claimed about emotions is commonplace in regard to beliefs and thoughts, where we distinguish between the occurrent and the dispositional, between the foreground and the background, between what is used and what is attended to; and where we also distinguish among differing degrees of clarity or inchoateness; and where we question how often and how long, or even whether, we can be between all beliefs or thoughts. These, then, are some reasons why we cannot divide all emotions into those that are fully present to us and those that are only dispositional. They are reasons why we cannot understand as dispositional many emotions that are not fully present to us. These reasons can be easily modified, and many require no modification, to show why it is also a mistake to think that all such "feelings" are not feelings, but only moods, attitudes, or interests.

1   Emotions and affectivity

We might expect philosophers who pay attention to emotions also to pay attention to affectivity. This expectation, however, is often not met. Many contemporary philosophers think that in the bad old days theorists held that emotions were, more or less, nothing but bodily feelings, much on the order of a stomachache or a burn.

This account of history is more fanciful than real. One of our earliest theorists of emotions, Aristotle, stresses the cognitive content of emotions. To take an example that comes up many times in this work, in *Rhetoric* II.2, Aristotle characterizes anger, *orgē*, in terms of the rational, the conative, and also the affective: "Anger [*orgē*] may be defined as a desire accompanied by pain, for a conspicuous revenge for a conspicuous slight at the hands of men who have no call to slight oneself or one's friends" (II.2, 1378a31 ff., tr. Roberts).[12] To have such anger, I must have certain thoughts, including

[12] I will usually give Aristotle references to the *Rhetoric* and the *Nicomachean Ethics* in the text as just done. Bekker page numbers are generally estimated from English translations. For the *Rhetoric* (*Rht*), I use the translations by John Henry Freese (Loeb Library, London: Heinemann, 1926) and by W. Rhys Roberts, in Jonathan Barnes, ed., *The Complete Works of Aristotle*, volume 2 (Princeton: Princeton University Press, 1984). For the *Nicomachean Ethics* (*NE*), I use the translations by W. D. Ross (London: Oxford University Press, 1925), by Harris Rackham (Loeb Library, Cambridge, Mass.: Harvard University Press, 1947), and by W. D. Ross and J. O. Urmson, in Barnes, ed., *The Complete Works of Aristotle*, volume 2. Different translations are used mainly because I did not always have the same translation at hand. I note

evaluative thoughts, I must have certain desires, and I must also experience pain: I must be pained by the thought of a conspicuous slight, and I must intend to retaliate for the slight.

Jumping more than two millennia, William James did hold that emotions *are* bodily feelings or awareness of them. But even he attached considerable importance to the thoughts, desires, and values of, or attendant on, emotions. This raises a serious problem for those who hold that James thought of emotions *just as* bodily feelings: what role, on their view, can those thoughts, desires, and values play? They are not simply causes of the bodily feelings – if to be *simply* a cause is to be, *as it happens*, a cause that plays no further conceptual role. As I read James, those thoughts, desires, and values can cause those feelings, but feelings do not just, as it happens, have those causes. Rather, it is conceptual of those feelings, when they are emotions, that they have those causes.[13]

One of the best accounts of James on these issues was given recently by Charles Young.[14] He argues that James does not ignore or dismiss thoughts, desires, and values. Instead, he sees them as necessary, but insufficient, for emotions – an insufficiency made good by the presence and awareness of those goings-on. On Young's view, James does not hold that emotions simply are bodily feelings, but only that such feelings are a *differentiating* feature of emotions. In this sense, they make emotions emotional. Briefly put, James's reasons are, first, that we can have the very same thoughts, desires, and values when we do not have an emotion as when we do have it; and second, that the agent's awareness of those physiological goings-on is what differentiates between an affectless complex and its corresponding emotion.

I do not agree with James on the second point: that all emotions are differentiated from their corresponding affectless complexes by awareness of physiological goings-on or bodily feelings. Nor do I think it conceptually true that all emotions even involve *bodily* feelings. But I do agree with

in the text the few times a point depends on using one translation rather than another. Changes from one translation to another are noted in the reference.
13 On one way to understand this, see Donald Davidson, "Hume's Cognitive Theory of Pride," *Journal of Philosophy*, 73 (1976) 733–757, reprinted in *Essays on Action and Events* (Oxford: Oxford University Press, 1980). For problems with such an account, see Annette Baier, "Hume's Analysis of Pride," *Journal of Philosophy*, 75 (1978) 27–40.
14 In his review of *Ethics with Aristotle* by Sarah Broadie, *Journal of the History of Philosophy*, 31 (1993) 625–627, p. 625. My thanks are owed Young for discussion of this and related issues. My thanks are also owed to John Deigh for discussion. For a recent work at once critical of, but favorable to, a more standard account of James, see Damasio, *Descartes' Error: Emotion, Reason, and the Human Brain*.

him on the first point: that without *feelings*, there is no outrage or even anger, but only "some cold-blooded and dispassionate judicial sentence confined entirely to the intellectual realm, to the effect that a certain person or persons deserve chastisement for their sins."[15] And I also agree with him in holding that there is far more to emotions than what is bodily, and that this "more" involves thoughts, desires, and values or evaluations. Perhaps in *Language, Truth, and Logic,* A. J. Ayer depicted emotions as contentless feelings, perhaps even bodily feelings. (And there is good reason for emotivists to rely on such a conception of emotions, lest their accounts of values in terms of emotions suffer circularity. But not all emotivists heeded this reason. This is shown in William Alston's argument that Charles Stevenson's emotivism was circular precisely this way, because of the role of *approval* – that is, thinking *well* of – in the "reducing" emotion.[16])

2 The content account

During the 1950s, inspired to some extent and in different ways by Wittgenstein, Ryle, Heidegger, and Sartre, there emerged what was announced as a new account of emotions – which I will call the *content* account of emotions. It went beyond a rediscovery of what was generally held from Plato through, on my view, at least James: that emotions have, indeed are in part constituted by, cognitive, desiderative, and evaluative content. With these earlier philosophers, it held that content is of central importance to emotions and that such content is what distinguishes emotions from other states. But it went beyond this to hold that there is nothing more to emotions or emotionality than such affectless content.

Content theorists, thus, hold that once questions about content are resolved, there is no further question about affectivity, precisely because such content *is* affectivity. Not only is such content necessary and sufficient for affectivity, it is all there is to affectivity. As I shall argue, the content account fails as an account of affectivity. It ends just as it starts: without affectivity. It is unable even to distinguish between what is and what is not affective. Its conditions are not even sufficient for affectivity, much less an account of it.

I am uncertain why content theorists went beyond the traditional view that content helps constitute emotions to hold that emotions are nothing

---

15 "What Is an Emotion?" in K. Dunlap, ed., *The Emotions* (New York: Hafner, 1967), p. 17, originally in *Mind,* 9 (1884) 188–205. See also p. 103 of *The Emotions* for a relevant passage from ch. 25 of James's *The Principles of Psychology* (New York: Holt, 1896).
16 "Moral Attitudes and Moral Judgments," *Nous,* 2 (1968) 1–23.

but content. Perhaps these theorists found affectivity difficult or even unacceptable, perhaps because they were unable to understand or explain it; or perhaps they thought of it as mere feeling, perhaps even mere bodily feeling. If any of these speculations is right, we may be able to see why these theorists could not accept the traditional view that emotions are only in part constituted by content. For if content is only part of emotions, emotions are more than content. Affectivity is an obvious candidate for what else is needed. And this, if my speculations are sound, is unacceptable for content theorists.

Content theorists face a somewhat similar, perhaps smaller, problem, were they to hold that *only some* emotions are reducible to affectless content. They would, then, have to tell us which emotions their account is about and which it is not about. Once again, they would have to do this without invoking affectivity – which again seems the most natural feature of emotions that explains why they are not reducible to affectless content.

In any case, I think these theorists have to tell us which emotions and which forms of affectivity they are concerned with. It would be wonderful beyond belief if there were exactly one account of all emotions, or all forms of affectivity, including all the complex and variegated forms of affectivity mentioned by Rapaport in the Introduction. As I trust this makes clear, *Valuing Emotions* does not hold that there is only one sort of affectivity or only one characterization or account of it. As just said, that would be wonderful beyond belief. It would be even more wonderful and still more beyond belief if this one account could be given in terms of the affectless elements of the content account.

A central theme of this chapter is that psychic feelings cannot be understood just in terms of desire and reason – at least not in the affectless ways desire and reason are commonly understood. The chapter will also sketch some reasons to think that at least some important forms of desire and reason, themselves, involve feelings. My goal here is not simply to refute other and mistaken views. It is also, by means of these other views, to show why philosophers have had such trouble with, and perhaps reluctance to deal with, affectivity. And it is also, again by means of these other views, to help give a better account of both the importance and nature of affectivity. I will first consider some simple attempts to understand feeling in terms of desire and reason. Those reductions are, in section 3, a reduction of feeling to desire; and in section 4, a reduction of feeling to reason. These reductions fail in one of two ways. They fail by not giving an account of emotions that guarantees that emotions have affect. Thus, even when the conditions of these accounts are satisfied, we may still not have an emotion – unless, as I am unwilling to do, we countenance "affectless emotions." Alternatively, these accounts fail by circularly invoking feeling in their account of feeling – for example, by invoking affectively laden desire or affectively laden reason.

3 Irreducibility to desire

Let us now turn to attempts to understand affectivity in terms of desire. Desire is intimately connected with feeling and emotion. One way to recognize this is that emotions often figure in, perhaps even are in whole or part, motives and motivations. Indeed, in his recent book, *Emotional Intelligence,* Daniel Goleman, psychologist and writer on behavioral and brain sciences for the *New York Times,* writes that "All emotions are, in essence, impulses to act."[17] Emotions are often like this. For example, to love and care for someone typically involves a desire to be with and benefit that person. To fear something typically involves a desire to avoid it. So too, at least some objectless forms of feeling might seem understandable in terms of desire. High spiritedness and excitement might be understandable in terms of the quantity and quality of desires, such as a strong desire to be active, to be on the move and just doing something. More particular excitement might be thought to be the desire to be doing some particular thing.

Desire might also be thought to enter into many emotions in a different way, via pleasure or pain. Many, if not most, emotions – or even, according to Aristotle, all emotions (*NE* II.5, 1105b21 ff.) – involve pleasure or pain. Pleasure and pain might, in turn, be thought characterizable in terms of desire: for example, in terms of what we desire to get or avoid, or in terms of the getting or avoiding. And thus, the affectivity of the hedonic aspects of emotions might be thought to be reducible, at least in part, to these desires. I will discuss such desire at the end of this section.

---

17 New York: Bantam Books, 1995, p. 6. Goleman's book appeared too late for a thorough study. But I have been able to note several places where we agree or disagree. For other expositions of such a view, discussed in Rainer Reisenzein, "Emotional Action Generation," in Wolfgang Battmann and Stephan Dutke, eds., *Processes of Molar Action Regulation,* forthcoming, see Magda Arnold, *Emotion and Personality* (New York: Columbia University Press, 1960), N. H. Fridja, *The Emotions* (Cambridge: Cambridge University Press, 1986), W. McDougall, *An Outline of Psychology* (London: Methuen, 1923), R. S. Lazarus, *Emotion and Adaptation* (New York: Oxford University Press, 1991), and Lazarus, A. D. Kanner, and S. Folkman, "Emotions: A Cognitive–Phenomenological Perspective," in R. Plutchik and H. Kellerman, eds., *Emotion: Theory, Research, and Experience* (New York: Academic Press, 1980).

From the outset of our tradition, philosophers have described emotions in ways acknowledging that some emotions do and some do not involve desire, and that some emotions do and some do not help constitute motives. Here we could look at the characterizations of emotions in Aristotle's *Rhetoric*, book II, chapters 2–11.[18] Desire (*orexis*) and wish (*boulēsis*) do *not* figure in this characterization of fear, which "may be defined as a pain or disturbance due to imagining some destructive or painful evil in the future" (II.4, 1382a22 ff.). Nor is it found in the characterizations of shame and shamelessness (ch. 6) or pity (ch. 8) or, I think, indignation and envy.

It might be suggested that we can account for these absences of desire by noting that the *Rhetoric* is concerned with emotions only insofar as they are useful for persuasion, especially in public assemblies. As Aristotle writes in the opening chapter of book II of the *Rhetoric*, "The emotions are those things that change people so as to affect their judgments, and that are attended by pleasure and pain" (1378a20 ff.). In light of such concerns, what is important to mention about emotions is that they can, and can be used to, change or maintain people's views. It might, thus, be thought that it is simply left unsaid, but not denied, that emotions also involve desire.

I am not persuaded by this. To note only one point, desire or wish does figure in the characterizations of some other emotions also discussed in the *Rhetoric*. As already seen, it is a feature of *orgē*: "Anger may be defined as a desire . . ." Growing calm, discussed in II.3, is characterized in terms of anger and in terms of desire. Desire is also found in the characterizations of friendship and enmity (ch. 4) and, I think, kindness (ch. 7) and emulation (ch. 11).

We should have no trouble in seeing that some of our emotions also "lack" desire. Consider the following example of what we might call *intellectual* or *aesthetic interest*. One afternoon during my last year at college, I walked along Broadway, on the upper west side of Manhattan, with an artist I was very fond of. (I leave open the relative importance of her being an artist and my being fond of her.) The street was absolutely familiar to me: I walked down it everyday. It was also the usual sort of city street around city campuses, with ordinary fruit and vegetable stands, clothing, hardware, and stationery stores, restaurants, and bars. Following her comments on what she saw and her "directions" on how to see the street, I saw and felt it in a new way. It was now vivid, exciting, and alive, with wonderful colors,

---

18 My thanks are owed to Gisela Striker's discussion of the *Rhetoric* treatment of emotions in her "Emotions in Context," delivered to the panel on "The Emotions in Greek and Hellenistic Ethics," the 1995 Pacific Division of the American Philosophical Association.

shapes, variety, and form. I saw and felt the street emotionally, and with emotions that were *not* constituted by desire.

Here we might also consider the object relations account of shame presented by the psychoanalyst Andrew Morrison:

> an object relations orientation introduces concerns with introjects and split-object representations, and unstable self–other boundaries. The shame-prone self (or ego) is seen as unstable, archaic, and undifferentiated with regards to objects, maintaining symbiotic, stilted, or indifferent or unsatisfactory relationships. Shame, then, is seen as a manifestation of painful and incomplete autonomy and identity, reflected in a vulnerability to hostile and rejecting significant (internal and external) objects.[19]

Such shame need not involve any desire – not even the desire to hide, or to be rid of one's vulnerability, or to be protected or stronger. It can simply be a way of experiencing the world and oneself, a way of living out one's felt vulnerability.

To be sure, we can easily imagine why I might have wanted to continue seeing and feeling that afternoon street scene: precisely because it is vivid and exciting. And we can easily imagine how its being seen as vivid and exciting could enter into motives for continuing to see it. So too, for wanting to avoid feelings of shame. Nonetheless, desire need not be part of what it is for a scene to be vivid and exciting, or to be seen and felt as vivid; or part of what it is to feel shame. Thus, at least these emotions and the ones Aristotle discusses are not to be understood as involving desire, much less as being constituted by desire.

The existence of these two sorts of emotions – those with and those without desire – raises many questions. Can the same emotion come in both varieties, one with and the other without desire? Are emotions essentially ways of seeing and feeling, with desire an occasional, inessential addition? Are emotions without desire somehow deficient or impoverished?

I am unsure how to answer these questions either in general or in many particular cases. I am unsure whether we could be dealing with the same sort of interest, say, or only a closely related sort, in the case where someone merely sees and feels a situation as interesting and the "nearest" possible case where the person also wants to continue seeing it on account of the felt interest. Perhaps they are instances of different emotions; or perhaps the differences do not show different emotions, but only whether the person is more passive or more active. (These notions of activity and passivity are taken up later, especially in Chapter 9.)

19 *Shame: The Underside of Narcissism* (Hillsdale, N.J.: Analytic Press, 1989), p. 46.

We do not need to pursue these issues. It is sufficient to have seen that some instances of emotions, and perhaps also some types of emotions, do not involve desire and are merely ways of seeing and feeling. We should, however, consider how, if at all, the existence of two sorts of emotions, and especially emotions without desire, affects the content claim. Such emotions clearly show that the affectivity of emotions cannot always be reduced to desire – if, that is, the reducing desire must be part of the content of the emotion. Nonetheless, it may still be possible to reduce affectivity to content – if, for these desireless emotions, their affectivity can be reduced to reason or value or the sorts of desire connected with pleasure or pain.

Even if some instances of affectivity cannot be reduced to desire, because the emotions lack desire, it may be possible to reduce other instances to desire. So, it could be held that where fear does involve a desire – for example, the desire to flee – the affectivity of fear is nothing but this desire. To allow that the affectivity of fear may, at least in part, also come from its more cognitive side, we might make the more modest claim: that only some of the affectivity of fear is nothing but that desire. Once it is seen how important desire is in other accounts of the mental and of human life and action – for example, in belief–desire psychologies – some such reductive move might seem irresistible, not just attractive.

However, no matter how attractive this move seems, it does not succeed. As I now want to argue, where desire does provide some or all of the affectivity of an emotion, such desire is, itself, affective. Thus, any attempted reduction of affectivity to desire either simply fails or fails by being circular. To show this, I will sketch a general, current view of desire. I shall argue that precisely because it does not hold that feeling is an irreducible element of desire, we cannot understand feeling in terms of such desire. As I shall also argue, this view of desire may well be inadequate as an understanding of desire, itself – again, precisely because it does not hold that feeling is an irreducible part of desire.

I call this the *functional* or the *explanatory-theoretical* account of desire. It understands desire just as what, along with belief, explains or gives direction to or energy for action.[20] In calling my target the functional or explanatory account of desire, I do not intend to suggest that my arguments are

20 Among theorists who advance or use this account of desire we find Hilary Putnam in "The Mental Life of Some Machines," *Mind, Language, and Reality* (Cambridge: Cambridge University Press, 1975), volume 2, pp. 410–411; David Armstrong in *A Materialist Theory of the Mind* (New York: Routledge and Kegan Paul, 1968), p. 152; Donald Davidson in "Belief and the Basis of Meaning," *Synthèse*, 27 (1974) 309–323, pp. 313–314; and Bruce Aune in *Reason and Action* (Dordrecht: Reidel, 1977), pp. 57–58.

directed against only contemporary functionalist accounts of the mind, or that my arguments for the irreducibility of affectivity are just other arguments for the existence of *qualia*.[21] To mention one point, I do not think that the *esse* of affectivity is *percipi*.

Nor do I know whether my arguments should be taken as criticizing belief–desire accounts of explanation of action. For I do not know how, or even whether, affectivity figures in the explanation of action. Further, belief–desire accounts of action explanation can be limited to just what is needed to explain action. They need not be concerned to give full accounts of the mind. Thus, insofar as these accounts do not hold that affectivity is relevant to action explanations, they could consistently allow, or at least be explicitly neutral about, the existence and importance of such affectivity.

My target, then, is this functional or explanatory account of desire. To show this account of desire inadequate, both for an understanding of feelings and also for an understanding of desire itself, I will focus on a special case of that account, which I call the *biological–functional* account. It can be most easily understood as holding that we are to understand desire in terms of its biological function. Various such accounts are offered by contemporary theorists. But it will be useful – if only to show that not only we moderns make errors about desire – to use Spinoza's account. In the *Ethics,* he writes that the mind

> endeavors to persist in its own being, and that for an indefinite time. . . . This endeavor when referred solely to the mind is called *will,* when referred to the mind and body in conjunction it is called appetite. . . . Further . . . desire is generally applied to men, in so far as they are conscious of their appetites, and may accordingly be thus defined: *Desire is appetite with consciousness thereof.* (III.ix, tr. R. H. M. Elwes, emphases in original)

Why I call this a biological–functional account should be clear enough. Putting it briefly, of natural necessity, people desire their own self-preservation or perfection. Indeed, this might seem to explain both what desire is and why we have it. The connections between feelings and self-preservation and perfection seem obvious. What could be felt as more important, more moving, more of concern, and more interesting for people than their own existence and well-being? What could be more vivid than what conduces, or what one takes to conduce, to one's own existence or well-being?

---

21 See, for example, Ned Block, "Troubles with Functionalism," in Wade Savage, ed., *Minnesota Studies in the Philosophy of Science,* volume 9 (Minneapolis: University of Minnesota, 1979).

I agree that there are such connections. But they are not given by, or even understandable in terms of, the biological–functional account of desire. For it does seem that we can easily conceive of people who do not care for or about their own existence and well-being, who do not find objects and activities that preserve or improve life interesting, or even among their objects of concern or care or desire.

It could be objected that these people are not really conceivable, or that they may be conceivable only as terribly unhealthy or terribly deformed people, as monsters or pathological beings. And just as it is unclear what we can learn about the nature of food by examining the nature of poisonous food, or even simply unwholesome or unhealthy food, it is unclear what we can learn about the nature of people by examining such unhealthy or deformed people. This is an important point. But it is not available to those who want to reduce feeling to desire. As argued throughout this work, the relevant notion of health is, itself, feeling-laden. To be a healthy person, one must have feelings.

Proponents of reducing feeling to desire have another way to object to my conceivability claim. They can note that even if it is right, all that is shown is that self-preservation and self-perfection need not interest a person, need not evoke or be the object of desire. For all that, they can point out, interest in something could still simply be a desire, so long as it is some other desire. However, that claim also is mistaken. A being can seek things, including its own well-being and existence, without feeling. It need not be interested in, moved by, care for or about, or be concerned with either the things it seeks or in the seeking of them.

To avoid a suggestion of contradiction, my point might be better put this way: simply seeking one's own well-being might be held to be, as such, a sort of care, concern, and interest. Machines such as lathes that look after themselves, monitoring and tending to their supply of lubricating oil, might in this sense be called self-tending machines and be said to care for, be interested in, concerned about, their own well-being. Nonetheless, we can hold – and I think we must hold – that these machines need not have feeling-laden care, concern, and interest. We can hold that these machines serve their interests with great success and assiduity, but that nonetheless their interests do not interest them. So too, lower animals such as protozoa can be said to care for themselves, in the sense that they seek food, avoid certain harms, and the like. But we need not ascribe feeling-laden interest, care, or concern to them. If this is right, we cannot understand feelings in terms of such functionally characterized "desires."

I am not concerned to question whether these states or activities of these machines and lower animals are properly said to involve care, concern, and interest. After all, these notions are very elastic. 'Care' can be used where there is affectivity, as in such full-blown emotional states as love. It can also cover caring activities expressive of such emotions. And it can also cover routinized and institutionalized activities, which may even be feelingless, as suggested by the terms 'the caring professions' or 'day care'. 'Concern' and 'interest' are elastic in these ways, too. Thus, it may be perfectly acceptable to ascribe some form of care, concern, and interest to those lower animals and machines.[22]

So far from harming my claim, this helps it. It shows that there are both feelingless and also feeling-laden forms or instances of care, concern, and interest. But, the biological–functional account cannot distinguish between feeling-laden and feelingless instances of care. It cannot distinguish between the feeling-laden interest, care, or concern of love and the feelingless sorts of care, concern, and interest that we can ascribe to those machines and very low forms of animal life. We thus see that it gives a radically inadequate characterization of feelings.

It might be objected that these examples work in my favor only because they are devoid of awareness. The thought here is that if, perhaps *per impossibile*, a machine or lower animal were aware of seeking its own enhancement or preservation, then that seeking, or the complex of the seeking and awareness of it, would be feeling-laden. I see no reason to accept this claim, and not just because of the difficulty in assessing such a counterimpossible.

Let us, therefore, turn to people. Here we might be asked to remember Spinoza's characterizations of desire in terms of awareness of preserving oneself, or his account of pleasure and pain in terms of transitions to greater or lesser perfection, and awareness of these transitions (*Ethics,* III.xi). Once again, I see no reason to think that desire, understood in terms of the functional or the explanatory–theoretical, now conjoined with awareness of this, is even sufficient for, much less is the same as, affectivity. People can seek their own enhancement and preservation, be aware that they are doing this, but nonetheless lack feelings. More strongly, the prospect, the seeking, and the attainment of their own enhancement and preservation, even with full awareness, can be feelingless.

My last claim might seem to contradict claims of Schachtel, Krystal, and other psychoanalysts I use, who hold that human life is through-and-

---

22 My thanks are owed Jenny Teichman for discussion here.

through affective. If these theorists are right, then all people must have feelings, quite generally and, thus, also about their life-enhancing activities. I am inclined to agree with those theorists about the generally affective nature of human life. And indeed, for many of the same reasons that I am inclined to do that, I reject the biological–functional account of affectivity. If there is a contradiction here, it is in reductionists using psychoanalytic theory against my claim. Insofar as psychoanalytic theory holds that even seemingly feelingless people really do have feelings – feelings they are not fully or even partially aware of – that theory will also hold that these people have, say, dissociated from, blocked, or repressed these feelings. But reductionists will be unable to give any reason to distinguish between such people's forms of care, concern, and interest from healthy people's forms of care, concern, and interest.

Further, if psychoanalytic theorists hold that feelingless self-enhancing activity is impossible, they do not hold this because they think that feeling is to be understood in terms of seeking what is self-enhancing. Rather, they hold this because they see people and all human activity as essentially affective. Further, they see such affectivity as sui generis and irreducible. Thus, if proponents of those reductive accounts of desire invoke those psychoanalytic theories to object to my claim that such activity can be feelingless, they have already abandoned their own reductive claims.

Let us now turn to another way to see that feeling is not reducible to desire: by drawing on the quotation from Roger Angell's "The Sporting Scene – Distance,"

> Even those of us who have not been spoiled by . . . the fulfillment of the wild expectations of our early youth are aware of a humdrum, twilight quality to all our doings in middle life, however successful they may prove to be. There is a loss of light and ease and early joy, and we look to other exemplars – mentors and philosophers . . . – to sustain us in that loss.[23]

On the accounts that would reduce feeling to desire, there would be no reason to think that Angell's people of middle life do not still have, and do not have in the very same ways, the desires and goals they had when young. But, it is clear that even if they still have the same goals and desires, they have them in importantly different ways. The desires have altered in their feelings, perhaps even to the point of there being no feelings in those desires or for those desired objects. I can see no coherent way to put these vital points in terms of the biological–functional or explanatory–theoretical accounts of desire and feelings.

23 *New Yorker,* 56 (September 22, 1980) 83–127, p. 127.

In summary, then, I have claimed that desires can be had with any number of different feelings, or with no feelings at all. Thus, those attempted reductions of feeling to desire fail even in giving what is extensionally sufficient for feelings.

Further, such accounts of desire are inadequate even as accounts of at least many forms of desire, in particular those we might call full-blooded, feeling-laden forms of desire – of *really* wanting something.[24] The evaluative importance of such desire is similar to that of feelings. As with feelings, so with such desire: we are concerned that the people we care for have such desire, that their activities evoke and merit such desire, that they hold and enact their values with such desire. Any adequate theory of desire must allow for such desire. Whether it should also allow for feelingless desire is not an issue we need pursue here.

Let us now turn briefly to the connections, mentioned earlier, among pleasure and pain, desire, and affectivity. This will allow an extension of the irreducibility argument to particular feelings, not just feelings in general. It will also help show that there are various, mutually irreducible feelings.

Spinoza's account of pleasure does not strike me as even a plausible conceptual account of pleasure, much less an accurate one. We may often be pleased by noting that we have made a transition to a better state. But this is a highly contingent matter. It is not only conceptually possible, but also psychologically and actually possible, not to take pleasure in this.

Now for some more modern accounts. Richard Warner offers one in "Enjoyment," holding that a person takes pleasure in or enjoys something, S – an experience or activity, say – if and only if the person desires to have or do S for its own sake, and certain belief or awareness conditions are satisfied.[25] Second, some pleasures or enjoyments might be characterized by the fulfilling of desire. Third, they might be characterized in terms of an effect, especially a psychic effect or affect, of fulfilling desire or awareness of fulfilling it. Fourth, they might be characterized in terms of what is sought

---

24 See Karl Duncker, "On Pleasure, Emotion, and Striving," *Philosophy and Phenomenological Research*, 1 (1940) 391–430. (Duncker is important also for the accounts of the hedonic, discussed later.) See also Brian O'Shaughnessy, *The Will* (Cambridge: Cambridge University Press, 1980) under 'act-desire', for example, volume 1, p. li. My thanks are owed to Graeme Marshall for discussing with me this notion of desire and much else in this chapter.
25 *Philosophical Review*, 89 (1980) 507–526. His exact formulation is given on p. 518. His *Freedom, Enjoyment and Happiness* (Ithaca, N.Y.: Cornell University Press, 1987) treatment of these issues requires felt desires: see pp. 82 and 131–136. This avoids the problem of affectlessness, but it may have trouble with the problem of the heterogeneity of pleasures and desires, discussed several paragraphs below. My thanks are owed to Warner for discussion of these issues.

in seeking such fulfillment. These four accounts are nonexclusive, and a further account employing two, three, or all of them might be the best of all such accounts.

The argument that feeling cannot be understood in terms of feelingless desire can be easily modified to show that pleasure and pain, too, cannot be understood in terms of feelingless desire. Here we could focus on the feelingless desire or on the being with such a desire. Considerations that allow us to hold that there can be such a desire or such a being should also allow us to hold that fulfilling such a desire need involve no feeling at all, much less hedonic feeling.

If this extremely brief argument-sketch is well taken, we see that accounts of the hedonic in terms of the conative must use a notion of feeling-laden desire. This need not be circular, since there are other feelings than pleasure, enjoyment, and the like.

But because of the heterogeneity of feeling, such an account is likely to be inadequate, unless it is circular. Briefly put, that heterogeneity shows that to be able to understand the hedonic in terms of desire, desire cannot be laden with just any feeling. For example, interest and fascination, or the feelings they involve, often do not fit the bill. People can be interested in, even morbidly fascinated by, what they find repulsive, disgusting, horrible, or evil precisely because of what makes it such. Consider the tale in Plato's *Republic* (439) about Leontius's, or his eyes', desire to see the corpses. Or consider how some physical deformities seize attention. Any of these can give us feeling-laden desire – even, I think, desire to see or continue to see something for its own sake. But there need be no pleasure or enjoyment in the seeing or in what is seen. So too, one may without any enjoyment or pleasure, but with interest, want to do and do for its own sake what one believes to be one's duty, such as caring for the wounded.

Claims that if there is desire, there must be pleasure or enjoyment seem, then, to be expressions of dogmatic psychological hedonism. So, of course, does the correlative suggestion that whatever one finds or believes pleasurable or enjoyable must motivate one to seek or maintain it.[26]

Without continuing the argument, I want simply to suggest that similar considerations may show that if having or satisfying such a feeling-laden desire is to be sufficient for pleasure or enjoyment, pleasure or enjoyment may have to be the feeling with which the feeling is laden. But even if desire

---

26 On these claims and a discussion of the example of aiding the wounded, see Justin Gosling, *Pleasure and Desire* (Oxford: Oxford University Press, 1969), ch. 5, especially pp. 70–71. See also Duncker, "On Pleasure, Emotion, and Striving."

is laden with pleasure or enjoyment, there are still problems: for example, one can look forward with pleasure to what turns to ashes in one's mouth. So perhaps it is best simply to conclude this section by summing it up as having argued for two claims: first, feelings, including hedonic ones, are irreducible to desire; second, there are various, mutually irreducible feelings.[27]

4 Irreducibility to reason

Let us now turn to attempts to understand feelings in terms of reason. I will examine two interrelated sorts of attempts. The first takes feelings to be understandable in terms of how we see or understand the world. The second takes feelings to be judgments, questions, imagined scenes, and the like. I will argue that these attempted reductions either simply fail or, by invoking feeling-laden concepts, are circular.

When it is claimed that emotions involve cognitive content, and are reducible to such content, perhaps along with desire, what is the nature of that content? I have already suggested that it need not be content we are aware of. But this still leaves almost entirely open what sort of content it is. *Beliefs* are the cognitive content favored by many theorists. They, thus, hold that to be afraid of a snake over there, I must *believe* something to the effect that there is a snake over there and that it is dangerous.

But not all theorists of emotions require belief. Aristotle, for one, does not. To have *orgē*, I need not believe that I have been slighted; to be afraid I need not believe that I am endangered. What is sufficient, he holds, is that I have the relevant *phantasia,* thought or mental image. Our understanding of *phantasia* must be slanted more to imaging and accepting, than merely entertaining. So taken, for me to be afraid that the plane will crash, I need not believe that it will. I might know that this is monumentally unlikely, and be willing to bet at huge odds that it will not. We might note that the plane's crashing is almost as fictional an object for me as Anna Karenina's death, which, despite being wholly fictional, saddens me.[28]

We might say that all that is needed is that I am frightened by the thought that the plane might crash. But 'the thought' cannot refer just to the content, understood as the Meinongian object, "the plane's crashing." That is not frightening. It may even be of the wrong ontological sort to be frightening or comforting. I must "take up" that content. But it is insuffi-

---

[27] My thanks are owed to Kent Bach for discussion here.
[28] On emotions about fictional objects, see Richard Moran, "The Expression of Feeling in Imagination," *Philosophical Review,* 103 (1994) 75–106.

cient for me to take it up and hold it in just any way. I need to get caught up in it and take it seriously, and with fear.[29]

An even weaker, or at least a very different, way that emotions might have cognitive content is by involving ways of experiencing and feeling the world or oneself. We have already read something along these lines, in the psychoanalytic, object relations account of shame presented by Andrew Morrison in *Shame: The Underside of Narcissism:*

> An object relations orientation introduces concerns with introjects and split-object representations, and unstable self-other boundaries. The shame-prone self (or ego) is seen as unstable, archaic, and undifferentiated with regards to objects, maintaining symbiotic, stilted, or indifferent or unsatisfactory relationships. Shame, then, is seen as a manifestation of painful and incomplete autonomy and identity, reflected in a vulnerability to hostile and rejecting significant (internal and external) objects. (p. 46)

I understand this as saying that emotions of shame can manifest those states without containing any such beliefs or thoughts as "I have done something bad or shameful." One can simply experience, see and feel, the world or oneself with shame.

Much else needs to be said about the exact nature of the cognitive elements of emotions – whether these are beliefs, thoughts, pictures, ways of experiencing the world or oneself – and indeed (as discussed in the next chapter) whether some emotions lack even the least of these elements. But let us now turn our attention to cases where feelings do involve beliefs and their close relatives.

Such involvement shows, first, that psychic feelings need not be totally arational, the way, say, a muscle ache is. Second, they show that feelings need not be simply a matter of desire. So, I do agree with the content claim that there are important connections between feeling and reason. But the question at hand is not whether there are connections, not even what they are like. It is whether feeling is reducible to reason.

---

29 For argument that only thoughts, rather than beliefs, are needed for emotions, see Patricia S. Greenspan, "A Case of Mixed Feelings: Ambivalence and the Logic of Emotion," in Rorty, *Explaining Emotions* and her *Emotions and Reasons* (New York: Routledge, 1988), especially ch. 2, "Emotions without Essences" (presented, in an earlier version, at the University of Cincinnati Philosophy Colloquium, March 1985); and my "Emotional Thoughts," *American Philosophical Quarterly,* 24 (1987) 59–69 (also presented at that colloquium). For argument that not even thoughts may be needed, see John Deigh, "Cognitivism in the Theory of Emotions," *Ethics,* 104 (1994) 824–854, and Jenefer Robinson, "Startle," *Journal of Philosophy,* 92 (1995) 53–74. On Aristotle's understanding of *phantasia,* see Franz Brentano, *The Psychology of Aristotle* (Berkeley: University of California Press, 1977); Kimon Lycos, "Aristotle and Plato on 'Appearing'," *Mind,* 73 (1964) 496–514; and Martha Nussbaum, *Aristotle's De Motu Animalium* (Princeton: Princeton University Press, 1978), essay 5.

To examine that issue, let us consider some cases. When one is concerned to get somewhere in a hurry, slow drivers by the dozens may seem to vie with each other to block the way. When in a bad mood, many ordinarily unnoticed things come to the fore with insistent irksomeness. When one is interested in something, its presence or absence may be especially vivid: at a party, the hungry person's eye may be captured by the food, the collector's by the antiques, the lubricious person's by sexual possibilities. And for someone possessed by universal enthusiasm, as children and mystics from time to time are, just everything can be seen vividly, and can capture one's attention and imagination. In short, then, attention and interest have very strong conceptual interconnections.[30]

Some theorists, such as S. Alexander, even identify interest and attention.[31] He holds that feeling is not only "not independent of conation" (p. 242) but "If the name 'attention' be preferred to conation, I have no objection" (p. 243). Frederick Olafson writes, "attention has, as Husserl points out, an especially personal character since shifts of attention express the interests of the ego in a uniquely direct way."[32] Gabriele Taylor, too, can be taken as suggesting that attention – her "thought concentration" – is interest, care, or concern.[33]

Further, as argued by Heidegger, Sartre, and others, various features we see in the world are "created" by our interests. So a mountain is, or is seen as, an *obstacle* only for someone wanting to get beyond it. For someone enjoying the scenery, it may be only an object of magnificent beauty. A piece of metal is a screw driver because of its uses. And uses have importantly to do with interests.

Sartre's general account of emotions in his *Sketch for a Theory of the Emotions*[34] and also in *Being and Nothingness* is couched in terms of the world's being seen in various ways. For example, depression is typified by seeing the world as "not for you," "not available." Jealousy involves interpreting incidents jealously. Sartre also characterizes emotions and emo-

---

30 See Alan R. White, "The Notion of Interest," *Philosophical Quarterly*, 14 (1964) 319–327, p. 320. See also Aristotle, *On Dreams*, I.2, 460b1 for an account of this in terms of deception, caused by interest.
31 See his "Foundations and Sketch-Plan of a Conational Psychology," *British Journal of Psychology* (1911).
32 "Consciousness and Intentionality in Heidegger's Thought," *American Philosophical Quarterly*, 12 (1975) 91–103, p. 92, discussing Husserl's *Ideas* (New York: Humanities Press, 1967), part 3, ch. 9 of the English edition.
33 "Justifying the Emotions," *Mind*, 84 (1975) 390–402. She can also be taken as suggesting that attention is only a precondition for, or sign of, them.
34 London: Methuen, 1971. Page references below are to this edition.

tionality in general in terms of a way of seeing the world. He characterizes this way as magical, contrasting it with a scientific, causal way of viewing the world.

Various recent philosophers have held that the feelings of emotions, and emotions themselves, are to be understood in terms of more discursive or propositional forms of reason. At various places in his *Sketch* Sartre suggests this. So do Bedford in "Emotions,"[35] Pitcher in "Emotion," Solomon in "Emotions and Choice," and Neu in "Jealous Thoughts."

Bedford denies the importance, indeed the role, of feelings in emotions. He argues that emotions are, instead, to be understood as complexes of belief, evaluation, and action.

Pitcher argues similarly. He explicitly denies that emotions require, or often even have, feelings – or sensations, as he calls physical or mental sensations or feelings. Giving an account of hope, he writes:

> If P hopes that she will come today, he simply believes that she might come and considers that her coming would be a good thing. He may also experience one or more sensations, but he need not; and even if he does it is doubtful that they will be part of his *hope*. (p. 338, emphasis in original)

Solomon claims that "My anger [at John for stealing my car] *is* my judgment" that John has wronged me (p. 257, emphasis in original).

Neu makes a similar point about jealousy, writing that "Jealousy is not a sensation or a headache, it is in essence a set of thoughts and questions, doubts, and fears" (p. 432). This is preceded by his claim that "the lover of a patient of a psychoanalyst may always raise the questions: 'What is missing?,' 'What is the analyst providing that I cannot?,' 'Are there things that my lover can say to her analyst that she cannot say to me?,' and so on." He then adds what is here of importance to us, "To imagine the elimination of jealousy is to imagine the elimination of the possibility of these questions, for these questions *are* jealousy" (pp. 431–432, emphasis in original).

I certainly agree that making certain judgments, asking certain questions, having certain thoughts, seeing the world certain ways are all importantly connected with various feelings, emotions, moods, and attitudes. Indeed, the connections here are constitutive. Thus, these accounts are certainly right in claiming that emotions have important, constitutive, cognitive content, along with evaluative and desiderative content. But they are wrong insofar as they restrict their account of emotions to such content. They are wrong precisely because in doing so, they disregard affect: thus giving, of all things, accounts of emotions as lacking emotionality. Alter-

---

35 *Aristotelian Society Proceedings*, 57 (1956–57) 281–304.

natively, these accounts are circular, because the forms of reason they deploy are, themselves, feeling-laden. I will show this by taking Sartre, Pitcher, Solomon, and Neu in turn.

Sartre characterizes emotions and emotionality in terms of seeing the world, or its relevant parts, as magical versus seeing it as instrumental, causal, and scientific. However, one can see the world as magical but have no emotions or feelings on account of that. The magical might be so commonplace, or one might be so phlegmatic and stolid or so played out that one is in no way moved by what is or is seen as magical. So too, the world seen as instrumental might be seen with, or seen as having, various sorts of emotions and associated feelings. It may be seen with loneliness or awe, and seen as being hard and inhuman.

Some other points about Sartre should be made. The first is more about Sartre the person and philosopher than about the content of his philosophy. It is that his problematic and inadequate treatment of affectivity is especially noteworthy, if not astonishing, given the important roles played by emotions in his writings, and the emotionality of his writings.[36]

The second point is about the content of Sartre's philosophy. I can only speculate on why he failed to see the gap between reason and feeling – how the magical might not be emotional and how the causal can be emotional: it is that he thought of these issues in terms of a specific sort of people. As I imagine such people, they are modern, rationalistic, well educated, who will be moved in the appropriate ways by magic. They are people who are at home in a technical, modern form of life. For such people, the magical may well be moving, perhaps frightening, even terrifying. But for those whose culture is more "traditional" or animistic the magical may be ordinary and nonemotional. Indeed, the combined instrumental, causal, and scientific world may be emotional, at least in the sense of being experienced with, and arousing, feelings of being foreign, distant, lonely, and inaccessible.

It might be objected on Sartre's behalf and against me that his account of affectivity is given in terms, not only of reason, but also of ways of "living a world," which world has, or upon which we have projected, affective meanings (see pp. 77–78 of his *Sketch*). But he often does attempt to characterize emotionality and affective meanings in feelingless ways. Further, obvious extensions of my argument show that for the notion of "living a world" to be adequate for affectivity, that notion, itself, must be feeling-laden. For as my arguments show, there are any number of feeling-

---

36 My thanks are owed to Max Deutscher for discussion here.

laden and feelingless ways of living a world – the very same world – whether or not it, itself, is feeling-laden or feelingless.

This last claim about the very same world might be contested by arguing that the world or world-view of the judgmental person is different from that of the nonjudgmental person; so too for the worlds of an optimist and pessimist; and so on. The argument would be that such worlds cannot be adequately described just in terms of emotionally and affectively neutral facts, judgments, and the like. But, in fact, this argument tells in my favor. It helps show that affectivity cannot be explained away, accounted for, or described just in terms of nonaffective worlds and nonaffective judgments. Although Sartre did not say that this is what he was doing, and much of what he said suggests that he would deny trying to do this, I see no other way to interpret his claims that emotions and affect are ways – just like any interpretive way – of seeing the world.

Contrary to what he claimed, it is one thing for something to be seen as having an affective quality or warranting an affect and another for us to have that affect: we can, for example, see that something is interesting without being interested in it, and we can be interested in something even if we see that it is not interesting. Affective meanings are and must be in us, not just in the world. We can fail to be interested in a world seen to be interesting. Interest in a world requires that we be interested in a world, whether or not it is seen as interesting.

Let us now turn to Pitcher. He held that to believe that something that might come about would be good is – is exactly what it is – to hope that it will. I will start my argument against his account of hope with a different example. A company in a distant city sends me a package, wrapped in their local newspaper. It describes an impending marriage in that city in terms suggesting that it will be a good marriage, and good for all concerned. I would find it strange to be told, much less told as a matter of conceptual truth, that if I believe the newspaper account, then I must hope that those people will marry.

It might be replied that I need not hope for that since I do not care for those people, and am in no way emotionally engaged with them. This may be a good reply, but it is unavailable to Pitcher. He wanted to reduce hope to what is affectless.

Let us suppose that we can, somehow, get around this issue; or let us simply consider another case, where I do care about and am emotionally engaged with the people. Suppose that I believe that my friends Jane and Jim will or may well marry each other and also that this would be a good thing. Even here I see no reason why – much less why as a matter of conceptual truth – I need hope that they marry each other. I might hope that if they marry each other or other people, their marriage or marriages are good. But apart from that and similar concerns, I need not care whom they marry or even whether they marry. I may not consider it my business to engage emotionally with their more intimate life and concerns. I might, in fact, find the thought that it would be good if they married each other too intrusive and not of my concern.

To guarantee that if I think that their impending marriage would be good, then I hope they do get married, we require, at the very least, the addition of something else. One of the more likely additions is that I have a personal or emotional involvement with one or both of them. But I do not see how such involvement, or other likely candidate conditions, can be understood in nonaffective terms.

Similarly, a person might make the judgments Pitcher says are sufficient for hope – "If P hopes that she will come today, he simply believes that she might come and considers that her coming would be a good thing" – but still not hope. So person P might make those judgments, but because P does not care whether she comes, not hope that she comes. P might be a parent coolly contemplating the arrival of a child's friend. It cannot be objected on Pitcher's behalf that hope also involves evaluations such as "her coming would be a good thing" and that evaluations are feeling-laden. For that, instead of saving his account, would show clearly that hope cannot be characterized nonaffectively. So far as I can see, then, Pitcher's account of hope fails by leaving out the affectivity of hope, or even that hope is affective.

Let us now turn to Solomon. I might see that John has wronged me by stealing my car but not be angry at him – perhaps because I take such wrongs with shame, not anger, or perhaps because I do not mind his having wronged me. In any case, affect, not simply judgment, is needed. If I do not have affect, I cannot be angry at John but, as William James said, at most make "some cold-blooded and dispassionate judicial sentence confined entirely to the intellectual realm, to the effect that some person or persons deserve chastisement for their sins."

Solomon is aware of this problem. In the appendix to "Emotions and Choice," added for *Explaining Emotions,* he writes:

One might make a judgment – even much of a set of judgments – in an impersonal and uninvolved way, without caring one way or the other. But an emotional (set of) judgment(s) is necessarily personal and involved. Compare "What he said to me was offensive" (but I don't care what he thinks) and "He offended me!" Only the latter is constitutive of anger (. . . the latter is, in part, a judgment about my own self-esteem). (p. 276)

If this says that emotions involve feeling-laden judgments, then I agree. But I take it as saying something else: perhaps that by conjoining enough feelingless judgments – perhaps "the full set" of judgments – emotion is guaranteed. Or perhaps it is saying that there are certain judgments, such as "He offended me!" that must be personal and involved, and thus that guarantee emotion.

I think that the latter is the more probable interpretation. I also think that there is no need to go into this. For neither interpretation helps Solomon. Both can be taken in ways that do not guarantee affectivity. After all, I might well note that my self-esteem is attacked, but not care about that. So understood, that judgment need not be feeling-laden or express or report on a feeling. To be sure, that judgment can also be taken as saying that I *felt* the attack, that it struck home, and that my self-esteem was wounded. This, I think, is what Solomon requires. But it is either feeling-laden, itself, or alternatively, it is a report of my affectful state, of how I feel. Thus, it cannot help account for emotionality in terms of affectless judgments.

Further, whether or not it is affectively laden or, in other ways, sufficient for affectivity, it is insufficient for anger. I may not care about being wounded in that way, just as I may not care about suffering a physical wound. So, in order for "He offended me!" to come close even to guaranteeing anger – which is far less than constituting anger – it must state or guarantee that, in the proper and feeling-laden ways, I care about what was done to me.

Let us now turn to Neu. The lover of the analyst's patient might ask those questions merely to get information, perhaps about the differences between what is shared in a love relation and what is shared in an analytic relation, or perhaps out of a lifeless curiosity that was originally generated by jealousy. This is to say that a person may make the judgment "I have been betrayed" or ask the question "Have I been betrayed?" or have the vision of a betrayal clearly in mind, but nonetheless not be jealous. Each of these cognitive goings-on is compatible with not caring about, and also not being concerned with or interested by, being betrayed.

To be sure, judgments, questions, and scenes can be taken as essentially involving feeling. Judgments can be made, questions asked, scenes imagined, with and out of care, concern, and interest, and with and out of jealousy, hope, or anger. Only when feeling-laden do these judgments, questions, and scenes come even close to being jealousy, hope, or anger.

For these related reasons, then, I think these content theorists mistaken. I say this while agreeing that their accounts are right about many of the constituents of emotions, and while also agreeing that those constituents, or their being held in the appropriate ways, typically account for having the emotion. But these relations between content and emotions are not identity, nor are they entailment, nor do they guarantee the emotion. Content simply does not give all there is to affectivity, nor is it even sufficient for affectivity.

We can also show in ways not tied to these specific philosophers why reductions of feeling to reason fail. To do so, it will be useful to remember the three sorts of psychic feelings mentioned earlier: feelings of the person, such as being full of interest; feelings about the world, such as being interested in some particular thing; and feelings in the world, such as finding a particular thing interesting. I concentrate on the second and third, since the first is least likely to be understandable in terms of reason.

The second and third are naturally allied with different forms of reason. Put in terms of seeing, feelings about the world are naturally allied with ways of seeing the world, such as seeing it with interest. Feelings in the world are naturally allied with ways the world is seen to be, such as seeing it to be interesting. However, since I am equally concerned with both sorts of feelings, there is no need to distinguish between them or between those forms of reason.

Let us start with some relations between interest and attention, as shown in a supposedly hungry person's attention to, vivid seeing of, the food. Certainly, if a person did not notice the food or, having noticed it, did not pay attention to it, that would raise a rebuttable presumption that the person is not hungry or, for other reasons, is not interested in food.

But, the feeling is not reducible to feelingless reason. I may pay attention to something – indeed, it can fill up my whole field of attention without my being interested in it or finding it interesting. Here we might think of what one may do when bored: for example, pass or kill time by watching a wretched and thoroughly uninteresting program on television, if only to keep one's mind off how boring everything is. But, also, a person can become through-and-through occupied with details of a job, or whatever, in ways that merit calling the involvement and the details merely mechanical or habitual. The details may well fill one's attention without one's being interested in or by them or what they are details of. Perhaps they were once interesting, and perhaps that accounted for their then filling one's attention. But now, all that remains is that they fill one's attention.

This point can also be put in a way that emphasizes "categories" of understanding rather than beliefs and objects of attention. A person can continue to use categories of understanding and perception, even after interest, care, and concern have gone. Jaded aesthetes, now uninterested in matters of taste and beauty, may still note the things they used to, and may still see, categorize, and understand the world in the ways they did when passionately interested and caught up in the aesthetic. One natural way to put this is that although they still see the same things and in the same ways, they are no longer touched or moved by them, no longer open to them.

Shifts in ways of seeing also go the other way. Before I slipped on the ice, I believed it was dangerous to walk on ice and I wanted to avoid these dangers. But I had only an intellectual appreciation of those dangers and a pro forma desire to avoid them. Having slipped, and without any change of beliefs or desires or values, I am afraid. It cannot be held that I have new beliefs, such as "I *really* could slip; it could *now* happen to *me*." For I already believed that. To be sure, I did not take it *seriously,* in the sense of taking it with fear. But this is just my point. This shift from not being afraid to being afraid is not given by a change in beliefs, but by a change in the emotional ways the beliefs are taken. When I am afraid, the beliefs are emotionally present, emotionally charged, and feeling-laden; when they are not, I am not afraid.

In addition to shifts between emotions and what are not emotions, there are shifts between emotions. Changing the story, we may suppose that before slipping on the ice, I felt only a general wariness and perhaps some general concern about the dangers people face walking on the icy sidewalk. Just after slipping, I was afraid of walking on the ice. After a while, I was no longer afraid, but again only somewhat wary and generally concerned. But throughout, my beliefs, and also my desires and values, stayed the same. So too, the very same "jealous" questions, imagined scenes and details can help constitute jealousy or only sadness about one's wayward partner. (Later chapters will take up some factors that may account for whether such content yields jealousy or sadness.)

We should note that this last point shows that it is not sufficient for fear of slipping on the ice that one has the relevant beliefs, desires, and values and that one takes these seriously. As just shown, there are any number of ways of taking these seriously: for example, with fear; as a matter of serious personal or intellectual concern, informing a desire to know why I get so easily and deeply "spooked" by such things; or even with amusement.

It may seem strange to say that when amused by those matters, I take them seriously. But this simply helps make my point. We naturally take the seriousness of taking slipping seriously as the seriousness of fear, as fearing-seriousness. But as shown by the contrast between being amused and not being amused by what one recognizes as a good joke, we see that "solemn" seriousness, as shown in fear, is not the only sort of seriousness shown by emotions.

These last comments may suggest that on my view beliefs, desires, and values engender fear (or some other emotion) only if the person is somehow already given to fear, perhaps by being prone to or all set to being afraid. This could quickly lead to a charge of circularity or at least of uninformativeness: that I hold that such content engenders fear only in someone all set to be fearful.

That such specificity may, in fact, be required will be seen later, especially in the discussions of the extensive detail needed for understanding emotions. (See, for example, Chapter 8, section 2, on sympathy and empathy; Chapter 8, section 3, on shame; Chapter 9, section 2, on pride; and Chapter 10 on what Aristotle discussed under the heading of *orgē,* anger.) Here I will simply make two related claims: first, as will be seen, such specificity is highly informative; and second, since I am not trying to give anything like a reductive account of these emotions, any real or seeming circularity is no problem for me – although it is a severe one for those who would understand emotions just in terms of their content.

In saying this, I do not deny the importance of beliefs, desires, and values for emotions, nor do I deny the importance of changes in beliefs, desires, and values for changes in and of emotions. (I do deny something like this in Chapter 2, section 3.) I hold only that these are insufficient to account for, much less constitute, emotions and changes in emotions.

My arguments for this, even if accepted, might be faulted for employing too "dry" an account of understanding: an account given solely in terms of the intellect and, in particular, in terms of what the agent holds true, or probable, the implications seen and accepted, and the like.

I will briefly discuss two somewhat different varieties of this objection. First, some philosophers have argued that if one *really* understands, if one has *real* understanding, then in at least certain cases, one will be moved in the appropriate ways. So, it is claimed that if you really understand what it means, especially what it means to you, for your spouse to be deceiving you, if you really see that person in the bed or even the arms of a rival, you will be jealous; if you really understand what it is for others to be in pain, you will feel for them and be moved to help them; if you really see that a given act is right, you will be moved to pursue it.[37]

37 My thanks are owed to Elijah Millgram for discussion here. See, for example, Richard M.

I am dubious about these claims. I certainly see why the fact that a deceived person, knowing of the deception, is not jealous strongly suggests, perhaps even shows, a lack of emotionality. But I do not see that it goes any way toward even suggesting a lack of intellectual understanding. Perhaps this just shows that I endorse the common philosophical view that intellectual understanding is, in this sense, dry.

No matter how important this issue about understanding, I do not think we need pursue it. Those claims about nondry understanding do urge a difference between intellectual understanding and emotional understanding, or at least what in popular terms is called emotional understanding.[38] But arguments calculated to show that understanding, including knowledge, belief, and judgment, should be understood as affectively laden are very similar to my arguments that feelings – and also emotions, attitudes, interests, and moods – must be understood as affectively laden. And in any case, arguments that the cognitive content of emotions is nondry and affectively laden are not arguments in favor of the content claim. They are arguments against that claim.

The second objection to the dry conception of understanding can be put in the following way (which is like the point about seriousness just made). We might say that when focused on reason, as differentiated from desire, the content claim identifies emotions and feelings with propositional content. But to say this is not to say enough. That propositional content must be *held* by the person in question. However, there are any number of different ways the content can be held: for example, with certainty, with doubt, or as a hypothesis. Only some of these have any chance of allowing the content claim to be plausible. To take an extreme case, my thinking that there is no real possibility that there is a snake in the bushes is consistent with my nonetheless fearing that there is one there. But it does not reach even the status of being an extremely poor reduction candidate for that fear.

Hare, "What Makes Choices Rational?" *Review of Metaphysics,* 32 (1979) 623–637; Timothy Sprigge, "Metaphysics, Physicalism, and Animal Rights," *Inquiry,* 22 (1979) 101–143; John McDowell, "Are Moral Requirements Hypothetical Imperatives?" *Aristotelian Society Proceedings,* 52 (1978) 13–29, and also "Virtue and Reason," *Monist,* 62 (1979) 331–350, especially his objections to noncognitivism in sections 3, 6, and 7.

38 My thanks are owed to Joseph Waligore for arguing that the Stoic understanding of belief and judgment was of this nondry sort – in his Syracuse University, 1995, doctoral dissertation, "The Joy of Torture: The Happiness of Stoic Sages." Among the main citations Waligore offers for this are Seneca, *De Ira,* II.5–6; Epictetus, *Discourses,* I.28; Cicero, *Tusculan Disputations,* III.74–75; Antony C. Lloyd, "Emotion and Decision in Stoic Philosophy," in John Rist, ed., *The Stoics* (Berkeley: University of California Press, 1978); and Martha Nussbaum, *The Therapy of Desire* (Princeton: Princeton University Press, 1994).

Content theorists, thus, owe us an account or characterization, or at least a list, of ways of holding propositional content: ways that allow for their reductions. They must also show us that there are nonaffective and nonemotional ways to characterize those holdings.

As the latter makes clear, I remain to be convinced that we can characterize *belief* just in terms of *holding true,* and do not need, in addition, some notion like *trust.* I also remain to be convinced that we can characterize either *holding true* or *trust* in nonaffective and nonemotional ways. At least many cases or senses of belief *that* and trust are emotional or affective, and indeed share some emotional or affective features of belief *in.*

Hume and the problems of distinguishing between entertaining and believing come to mind here. So do many questions about the possibility of nonaffective characterizations of modalities of knowledge, such as the differences between seeing a tree, and thus knowing that it is there, and knowing by nonperceptual means that it is there; or the differences between seeing the greenness of the tree's leaves and thus seeing and knowing that it has green leaves and knowing this latter by nonperceptual means; or the differences between seeing the greenness and knowing what that is like and (if this is even possible) knowing this not only by nonperceptual means but also in nonaffective ways. So too, there are questions about the possibility of nonaffective characterizations of *presence* and other differences between seeing something and just hearing or reading a "fully detailed" report about it. Here we might also think of the differences between what is shown and what is presupposed. We might agree with Aristotle's claim that it makes a difference "whether lawless and terrible deeds are presupposed in a tragedy or done on the stage" (*NE* I.11, 1101a32 ff.).

I think that these are serious issues for attempts to understand understanding, belief, and the like in dry, nonaffective ways.[39] But in much of what follows, I nonetheless write as if there are dry, nonaffective ways to characterize them: in terms of just *neutrally* and nonaffectively holding the relevant content. I am unsure whether there can be such neutral holding. Put another way, I am unsure whether *dry* holding is simply holding without any affect, or instead whether it involves a special sort of affect.

But for present purposes, there should be no need to enter that dispute. If there is such nonaffective holding, it is inadequate for understanding emotion and affect. And if all forms of holding content are affective, content

---

39 On this, see William Charlton, "Force, Form, and Content in Linguistic Expression," *Aristotelian Society Proceedings,* 84 (1983–1984) 123–143, and *Weakness of Will* (Oxford: Blackwell, 1988), especially p. 55.

theorists will be unable even to begin their claims. They will simply have no way to state the content claim coherently enough to allow it to be examined and accepted or, as I think far more likely, rejected.

5 Irreducibility via more complex accounts

My arguments so far have been directed against relatively simple and briefly sketched reductive accounts of feeling. A natural question in regard to what has been argued so far is whether fuller and more complex accounts might allow for reduction. As is now commonplace, thanks in part to psychoanalysis, to understand emotions and feelings we must study the history of those who have them. Correlatively, we can make good hypotheses about, and even discern and understand, people's feelings and emotions by taking note of "a large enough slice" of their desires, beliefs, and evaluations, especially when conjoined with their bodily and behavioral goings-on.

Since the more complex accounts – including those that might make use of the history or large-scale descriptions of people – have yet to be propounded, it is difficult to assess them. Thus, the following are meant only as some reasons why I think my arguments, or easy modifications of them, would also tell against more complex reductive attempts. (In Chapter 9, I discuss a complex account of emotions in terms of structural-cognitive relations, showing that it fails, precisely because it is nonaffective.)

I do recognize that, say, psychoanalytic accounts of emotions and feelings make much of infantile and other early precursors, including archetypal or infantile scenes and scenarios. But, for good reason, this is not the whole of those accounts. Those theories also hold that those emotions and feelings as had by adults are typically affectful, barring dissociation and the like, and also that their infantile origins were affectful. Thus, even if an adult's jealousy is explained by its being like, or its being a descendant of, some earlier emotion -- whether fully formed jealousy, protojealousy, or some other emotion – we still need an account of what it is for either adult jealousy or the earlier emotion to be feeling-laden and to have emotional "charge."[40]

So too, I agree that we can discern what feelings people have by noting a large enough slice of their lives, even if the descriptions and the like are feelingless. I also agree that it is difficult to imagine a person with no feelings, or feelings quite different from ours, if that person has, or is seen as

---

40 I do not think adequate attention is paid to this by many philosophers, for example, Neu, "Jealous Thoughts"; and Ronald DeSousa, "The Rationality of Emotions," *Dialogue,* 18 (1979) 41–63, and in Rorty, *Explaining Emotions.*

having, the same interwoven myriads of beliefs, desires, evaluations, values, and bodily and behavioral goings-on as we do. I further agree that it can be difficult to imagine how someone without certain feelings and emotions would have the very same myriads of beliefs, desires, and the like that we do when we have those feelings and emotions. For instance, I find it difficult to imagine someone who is *not* angry, but who is constantly looking for and seeing signs of disrespect, is all too ready to retaliate for any believed wrong, always says harsh things, and is constantly getting into arguments, disputes, and fights.

I agree that this would be very difficult to understand. Nonetheless, I do not see this as in any way sustaining the possibility of a reduction. We impute those feelings to that person on those grounds because we understand that person as an affective being with psychic feelings. Perhaps this is part and parcel of our understanding people in terms of a psychological theory that sees people as affective beings. But whether or not based on anything like a theory, I suggest we think that just in virtue of being a person, that person has feelings; and because of those grounds, that person has those particular feelings. It is for some such reasons that we find it hard, if not impossible, to imagine that the person described earlier is not angry. But then, that difficulty in no way suggests, much less sustains, the possibility of a reduction of feeling to what is nonaffective. For that whole train of thought is about people as affective beings.

A correlative way to put this point is that our understanding, and the understanding of those theories, of healthy people is of people who are affective beings. Moreover, our conception of health involves taking up emotionally the desires, beliefs, and values put forward by content theorists as what emotions are. At its strongest, this is to say that it is conceptual of healthy people that – at least typically and failing certain conditions – if they hold such content, they will have emotions. But even if this is right, this is no support for the content claim. For the content claim is about what is conceptual of that content, and not about what is conceptual of that content when held by healthy, affective beings: that is, beings who are affectively healthy and healthily affective.

Second, I do not think that complexity is what is lacking from the simple feelingless accounts. I do not think that the lack could be made good by adding still other feelingless states or feelingless goings-on. This can be seen, I think, by considering the notion of "interest in some object." At least certain forms of such interest are preeminently ways of desiring that object. Here we might think of a hungry person's hungry interest in some food. Reason, behavior, functional states, and bodily states are relatively unimportant compared with desire, even though they, too, are clearly bound up in such interest. Thus, if my claim of irreducibility is mistaken in regard to such interest – that is, interest understood largely as desire – a reduction in terms of feelingless desire should at least come close to working. But if my arguments are right, that reduction not only fails, it fails miserably.

My argument might be faulted for using too simple an understanding of desire. It might be held that the relevant desires are, or involve, hierarchies of and about the desire. So, it might be held that to be interested in some object O_1, one must desire to have O_1, but in addition one must also desire to have that desire, one must see one's desire for O_1 in a certain light, and so on. I do not think we need investigate the plausibility of this claim as a claim about desire. For a feelingless desire for O_1 is not even close to giving a correct understanding of interest in O_1. I cannot see how any progress is made by augmenting that feelingless desire with feelingless hierarchies of or about desire -- for example, with a feelingless desire that one have a desire for O_1 and a feelingless way of seeing what such a desire is like.

What might well help is an understanding of what it is to have such an interest in O_1, where this understanding is put in terms of desiring with interest, or perhaps pleasure, that one desire O_1, or seeing with interest or pleasure that one desires O_1. But these higher-order elements are feeling-laden. And if we can recur to higher-order feeling-laden elements, there should be no reason not to start with them at the ground level – for example, with desiring O_1 with interest or pleasure.

6 Feelings are rarely merely feelings

The arguments just given are clearly insufficient to still all doubts about more complex reductive accounts. Perhaps, then, it would be useful to sketch a consideration that might incline people to think that some reductive account must be possible. Suppose it is agreed that we cannot get an account of care or interest in terms of desire and reason. How, it might nonetheless be asked, could those or similar accounts be improved, much less made successful, by the incorporation of feeling? How would the addition of some inner pang, say, improve the account? The thought here is that feelings are too much inner phenomena and conceptually too poor to bolster up accounts of care, concern, and interest.

A variant of this thought has immediate application to my claims that, because they are affective, at least some emotions have significant evaluative and even moral importance. How, it will be asked, can feelings – mere feelings, inner pangs or other conceptually poor inner phenomena – have such evaluative and moral importance?[41]

A complete reply would involve an account of the nature of psychic feelings, and especially how, like other psychic elements, they are connected with the inner and the outer. Here it should be sufficient to note the following. Undoubtedly, some psychic feelings are panglike. A momentary tingle of psychic tension or excitement might be panglike. It might also provide an example of an entirely inner goings-on. Whether it is panglike or entirely inner may well be interesting, but not for our present concerns. Indeed, for present purposes the present objection is beside the point and misguided.

It must be remembered that the psychic feelings with which I have been concerned – care, concern, and interest – have been shown to have conceptual complexity. Just consider their relations with reasons and content-laden objects. Further, those psychic feelings often should be thought of not merely as connected with, but as "modes" of, action, reason, or desire: for example, one can act, see, or desire *with* interest. These psychic feelings are not conceptually impoverished the ways pangs are supposed to be. Nor are they any more objectionably inner than are desire and reason.[42]

In other chapters, we will see that feelings are complex, intrapersonal and interpersonal, social, and also that they are evaluatively and morally important. In caring about emotions one is caring about what is complex, intrapersonal and interpersonal, social, and valuable, and also affective. In short, feelings are not mere feelings; there is little that is mere about them; and this helps explain how what is mistakenly thought of as mere feelings can be of vital evaluative and moral importance.

7 Concluding remarks

In this chapter, I have argued that emotions involve affectivity, indeed that they are affective. I have argued that this is at least very close to being a tautology, and a fairly shallow one at that. If an excuse is needed for arguing for such a claim, perhaps it can be found in the fact that my arguments for the affectivity of emotions were far less for the affectivity of emotions than they were for the irreducibility of such affectivity. In what follows, I will

---

41 My thanks are owed to Richard Moran for discussion here.
42 For discussion of issues concerning the inner and outer natures of such feelings, see Gareth Matthews, "Ritual and Religious Feelings," in Rorty, *Explaining Emotions,* and, in an earlier version, "Bodily Motions and Religious Feelings," *Canadian Journal of Philosophy,* 1 (1971) 75–86.

argue for the evaluative and indeed the moral importance of emotions, at least in part because of their affectivity. I will not argue for the evaluative and moral importance just of emotions. That could be argued for by showing that emotions have such importance in virtue of their nonaffective content, and not in virtue of their affectivity. What I want to argue is that at least part of the evaluative and moral importance of emotions has, precisely, to do with their affectivity.

Put briefly, I will argue that psychic feelings have vital evaluative and moral importance. To take up a point mentioned in the previous section, some philosophers might find this claim troublesome, if not provocative, precisely because it is put in terms of feelings. While they can, perhaps, see how emotions, moods, and attitudes have evaluative importance, they might wonder how mere feelings can have such importance.

My main response is given in the body of this book. But an important start has been made in this chapter. My claim may sound troublesome and provocative, especially to those who think of affectivity and psychic feelings in terms of mere feelings, especially where these are understood as panglike, often bodily, inner sensations. But this is not my understanding of feelings.

Some might think it would have been better for me to put my goal in other and more acceptable terms. Instead of saying that I will argue for the evaluative and moral importance of feelings, I might be urged to say that I will argue for the evaluative and moral importance of emotions, moods, attitudes, and interests. But had I put it that way, then in order to avoid misunderstanding I would have had to add that I attribute at least part of the importance of emotions, moods, attitudes, and interests, not just to their nonaffective content, but also to their affectivity: that is, to feelings.

2

How emotions reveal value

This chapter continues presenting preliminary material, but now of a more evaluative nature. It focuses on how affective entities and states such as emotions, moods, interests, and attitudes reveal value, and do so at least in part as affective entities and states. Section 1 makes a start on showing how they reveal value. Section 2 raises some issues about the sorts of values they reveal. Section 3 discusses whether they all reveal values. Section 4 shows why the fact that they reveal value supports neither emotivism nor naturalism. Section 5 raises the worry that perhaps these affective states are valuable, but only instrumentally so. Section 6 shows how that worry is closely allied to the content account of affectivity, considered in Chapter 1.

1 A start on some issues

During the past one hundred years, many philosophers and other theorists have likened psychic feelings, including emotions and other affective entities and states, to bodily feelings, and thus as lacking any complexity or conceptual content. (I concentrate on emotions, but much the same holds for moods, attitudes, interests, and other affective states and entities.) But as is now generally recognized, they have considerable conceptual complexity and content, in part made up by values. For example, part of what it is to be proud about something is to think it good. Emotions can also *reveal* values: the values they contain and that help make them up. My pride in what I did reveals that I think it good.

Here are some other examples, starting with a case that does not involve serious values. I found out that I was still a fan of a team, and not just interested in watching a football game, by finding myself annoyed at that team's failures and pleased by its successes. Turning to a serious matter, I found out part of how very bad I thought the start of a recent war was by finding myself very upset and saddened almost to distraction upon hearing that it had begun. Before hearing of the outbreak, and before reacting emotionally to it, I thought I would see the war simply as yet another of those geopolitical happenings, yet another merely very unfortunate international affair, but nothing really serious, nothing really terrible. After hearing of the start of the bombing and reacting as I did, I no longer had that evaluative view at all.

Aristotle's *Rhetoric* account of anger provides another illustration of how emotions can aid in the discovery of values: "Anger [*orgē*] may be defined as a desire accompanied by pain, for a conspicuous revenge for a conspicuous slight at the hands of men who have no call to slight oneself or one's friends" (*Rht* II.2, 1378a31 ff., tr. Roberts). *Orgē* thus involves value or evaluation in at least three ways. Its cause or ground must be seen and evaluated as a conspicuous slight. The slight must be seen and evaluated as uncalled for. And the target of the slight, oneself or one's friends, must be cared about. So, if someone has not even acknowledged your presence and that arouses *orgē* in me, or has called you a pompous prig and that arouses *orgē* in me, that can show that I take doing that or saying that to you to be a slight, that I take the slight to be conspicuous and unjustified, and that I care about you.

It can reveal these evaluative facts even if, before experiencing that episode of *orgē*, I would not have taken them to be facts. Beforehand I might have thought that I did not take those people's ignoring you or calling you a pompous prig to be a slight; or that it was at most a minor slight or one you had coming to you; or that I did not care what others did or said to you, or even that I did not care much, if at all, for or about you. My *orgē* shows that each of these evaluative beliefs is mistaken. Similarly, my getting angry at someone who makes a slighting reference to my nationality or religion can show me, even contrary to what I thought, that I do care about that.

So far I have suggested that emotions can reveal value that they contain. But in addition, people's characters and their values can be revealed by emotions. The difference between the way discussed so far and this way is that if you have such *orgē* – more so if you are given to such *orgē*, and especially if you qualify as an angry or *orgē*-filled person (as discussed in Chapter 10 below) – you can show yourself to be a person who cares about and values honor and standing, especially your honor and standing. We might call these values general characterological values. For they are "in" and help make up one's character and this is shown by the emotion, even if they are not in the emotion.

In what follows, I will show still other ways emotions reveal values. I will also show that not all emotions have the same relations with value; that emotions reveal not just our values and evaluations but much of our interior and exterior worlds; and that these various relations are often very complex.

We might note that emotions reveal far more than just values and evaluations. They can also reveal their other "components." If I am angry at you for saying that my country exploits even those countries it claims to help, my anger can show that, contrary to what I thought, I do not hold hardheaded, *Realpolitik* views about international relations. So too, if I am annoyed at John's borrowing my car without permission, this can show that I was mistaken in thinking that I now accept whatever my friends do to me.

Emotions can also play various revelatory roles in psychoanalysis. It is a commonplace there – and in many other places, too – that changes in affect can indicate many other changes and that to discover the truth one should trust and follow the affect. Many examples bearing this out occur when working with patients with dissociated material – due to trauma, say. This material might be recovered or reconstructed only through emotional enactments or reenactments of a highly charged nature – enactments that collapse the present and past as if the trauma were then and there happening again. The psychoanalysts Ethel Spector Person and Howard Klar discuss a case where the analyst dropped a pen and stooped to pick it up, whereupon the previously complacent patient said, "If you touch me, I'll kill you." It hardly needs saying that, for the patient, this "triggering" event – this "danger signal" which makes the patient relive the past as if it were present – was or instantaneously became highly emotional.[1]

2   Problematic issues about the values emotions reveal

I now want to introduce some issues about value that is or may be revealed by emotions. In this section, I will consider which values are revealed by emotions; the "ontological" status of these values; whether all emotions reveal values; and some epistemological roles of emotions in revealing emotions. Section 3 discusses whether all emotions reveal values.

I will start with the issue of *which values are revealed by emotions*. It may be difficult to know which values are revealed by the emotions. My anger at the slights mentioned earlier need not show that I care for you, my nationality, or religion. It could instead show that I care for myself or my standing with others. I could be angered by others' thinking so little of me that they feel free to say whatever they might like in front of me, without any need to pay attention to how I might feel.

[1] My thanks are owed to Elizabeth Hegeman for discussion here. The example is drawn from Ethel Spector Person and Howard Klar, "Establishing Trauma: The Difficulty Distinguishing between Memories and Fantasies," *Journal of the American Psychoanalytic Association*, 42 (1994) 1055–1081.

This difficulty in discovering the values an emotion contains may tell against claims that emotions contain and reveal values and that they help us discover what we value. Or, as I think, it may only show the need for accurate attention to our emotions. (I will return to this.)

Let us now turn to some issues about *the "ontological" nature of the values revealed by emotions*. Emotions may show *valuings* rather than value: how a person values something, not the value something has or the value the person takes it to have. Sometimes people have emotions that contain and reveal valuings, not values; and sometimes people have emotions that reveal a lack of valuing, even in the face of acknowledged value.

To put the first, we can use an example that calls into question the philosophical claim that emotions contain and reveal values, and that is also very worrying for what it shows about the dangers of the world, including the world of emotions. Sartre writes that anti-Semites often think and say things like, " 'You see, there must be *something* about the Jews; they upset me physically.' " He continues, "This argument, which I have heard a hundred times, is worth examining. First of all, it derives from the logic of passion. For, really, now, can we imagine anyone's saying seriously: 'There must be something about tomatoes, for I have a horror of eating them'?"[2]

The philosophical questions raised by this are clear enough. It forces us to ask whether an anti-Semite's emotions, and of course the horror of eating tomatoes, reveal values or just valuings. Indeed, do emotions ever reveal values that are not just valuings?

Theorists partial to emotivism might take Sartre's examples as showing that valuings have primacy over values, or at least that emotions show only valuings not value. But others might ask us to see what is going on here as similar to what goes on in regard to belief: that we can have false, pernicious, and ridiculous beliefs is no objection to the claim that belief is "of" what is true, nor does it show that the object of belief is only what is believed true. (This issue will be taken up in different ways, especially in later chapters.)

Now to the second way emotions might show only valuings not values: I may not value, or may barely value, what I know has very great value. For example, I may not value or may barely value a given school of music, even though I know – and know directly, for myself, not just by being told by those I know do know – that it is of the very highest value. If I do not already know that I value the music little, I might discover this by finding myself uneager to attend concerts of that music, and bored and restless

---

2 *Anti-Semite and Jew* (New York: Schocken Books, 1976), p. 10, emphasis in original.

when I hear it performed. Once again the generalization is clear: can emotions reveal values or a lack of values or do they simply reveal valuings?

We have just considered some examples of emotions with questionable relations between valuings and values. Let us now turn to some other emotions that involve valuings, and perhaps also values, the agent does not really make or hold.

Some emotions involve what I will call *fantasy* valuings; and, inspired by the *Philebus, false* valuings. I will call the related emotions, fantasy or false emotions.[3] Here is an example: some friends, just back from Spain, regale me with tales of their travels, including the intensity of the sun, the blueness of the sky, the spirit of bull fights. Their emotions show how much they liked and valued their trip and those aspects of Spain. I get caught up in their enthusiasm and start imagining and fantasizing myself back in Spain, having a wonderful time, being thrilled by the bull ring. My emotions are very similar to those of my friends, showing – if emotions do show valuings and value – that I, too, value those aspects of Spain. After my friends leave, my enthusiasm wanes, and I regain my equilibrium. I remember just how much I disliked the heat, the crowds, and especially the bull fights. And, somewhat sadly, I quickly see that were I to go back to Spain, I would undoubtedly still dislike them even were I to go with my friends. I come to see that I do not really value what my emotions "showed" I value. I was somehow just swept up by and into my friends' enthusiasm, and for a while imagined and fantasized myself enjoying what I in no way do enjoy, neither in aspect nor on the whole and overall.

It might be held that even if I do not value being in Spain, I must really value being like my friends or being caught up in their enthusiasm. I do not agree. But even if I am wrong, that would only force a modification, not a retraction, of my claim about the possibility of false or fantasy emotions and correlatively of false or fantasy values and valuings. I would be wrong in the letter of the claim – that is, in the literal and exact meaning of the claim that some emotions reveal no real values or valuings at all. But I could still maintain what is very close to the spirit of that claim: that we can seriously misidentify our emotions and what values and valuings they show.

In effect, we have already seen this. As noted earlier, I might think that I was angry on account of how you were treated, when I was really angry

---

3 The next several paragraphs recapitulate an argument from "Emotional Thoughts," *American Philosophical Quarterly*, 24 (1987) 59–69, and take into account some objections Joseph Waligore made to that argument. See also R. Jay Wallace, *Responsibility and the Moral Sentiments* (Cambridge, Mass.: Harvard University Press, 1994), section 2.4, "Irrational Guilt," especially pp. 45–46.

only because those mistreating you had no compunction about doing this in my presence. In the case at hand, instead of valuing *what* my friends did, it is said that I value what my *friends* did. Instead of valuing visiting Spain, seeing the sights, attending bull fights, I value being like my friends. Perhaps I value being like my friends, not in their valuing visiting Spain, but in being like them, pretty much however they might be and whatever they are doing. Putting the matter in terms of desires, I do not want to visit Spain, I somehow want to want to visit Spain or want to be a person who wants to visit Spain or to be like my friends.

The cases I have presented of false or fantasy emotions are examples of somewhat short-lived emotions. For a time, perhaps a very short time, the person is caught up in an emotion, and then leaves it. There are other cases of emotions, and also of moods, interests, and attitudes, that are quite similar to these emotions, but which are long-lived. I will focus on a special case of these: emotions of someone else that the person has caught, taken up, and carries. I will call these *other-induced* emotions.[4] A good example is the sadness of a son of a depressed mother, a sadness he finds himself having from time to time, but having in a strange way – a way that, as he feels, is not really his way. As we and he could say, he is then and there living, not just experiencing, his mother's sadness: he slips into or takes on her sadness, rather than sadness of his own.

For another case, consider a family feud that proceeds mainly by reviling Uncle Jack, especially at holiday parties from which he is ostentatiously excluded. For a time, whenever Jack was mentioned, Jill joined the rest of her family in reviling him. But she now has come to realize that for a long time she was not "really there," not really joined with the others in reviling him. She also came to realize that for a long time, well before this realization, she had not really thought badly of him, but had really liked and admired him; and that she had, if only as a nagging, unarticulated, background worry, found the family feud petty, lacking grounds, and ridiculous. Upon realizing all this, she might recognize that those feelings she had experienced and accepted were not really hers, but were only caught from, or induced by, the rest of her family.

These cases of other-induced emotions are somewhat like cases of role playing. But they are only somewhat like it. They are also somewhat like my taking up my friends' enthusiasm for Spain. But again, they are only somewhat like it. One significant difference is that they are more a part of the person than those other emotions. But even though they are more a

---

4 My thanks are owed to the psychiatrist Dr. Lleni Pach for discussion here.

part of that person, they may well not really be part – or may not be a real part – of that person. These cases raise issues about authenticity, now focusing on feelings and their authenticity.

To the extent that we think that large portions of a life, even an entire life, can be inauthentic, we should have little trouble in allowing that false or fantasy emotions can be more pervasive, affecting more of a person for longer periods of time and in more ways, than even these last cases. This, I think, is one way to understand Ivan Illych's "disquiet" about his whole life, and about the truth or falsity of his leading values and emotions.[5]

In their different ways, then, these various affective states, whether emotions, moods, interests, or attitudes, all raise serious questions about the status of the values and valuings they show, and thus about the status of the claim that emotions and other affective states always contain and reveal value and valuings. There are still other sorts of emotions and other affective states that raise many of these questions. I will mention only two of these, which I will call *evaluatively mistaken* emotions and *leftover* emotions.

We are all familiar with factually mistaken emotions, emotions that involve mistaken facts or factual beliefs: for example, I mistakenly think that John has stolen my car and I am angry at him for stealing my car, until I find out that he did not steal it. Similarly, emotions can involve values people are mistaken in thinking they hold. This was shown above by means of false or fantasy emotions.

There is another, and perhaps simpler and less controversial, way to illustrate such evaluatively mistaken emotions: by invoking mistakes in evaluative reasoning that show up in emotions. Suppose that I hold a certain principle of justice, J_1, and mistakenly think that since I hold J_1, I am committed to hold another one, J_2, which I do hold for that reason. Suppose, further, that I correctly think you have violated J_2, and, on account of that, I am indignant. Or suppose that I accept the authority of a given religion and mistakenly think that it disapproves of a certain sort of act; and thinking that, I am indignant over your doing such an act.

In these and many other, similar cases, there is a real question whether I really do hold the values, and really do make the valuings, involved in the emotions. At the least, there is some reason to think that those emotions reveal my holding the first principle of justice or the authority of that religion, rather than the second principle or my religion's condemnation of that act.

5 I am grateful here to Pauline Chazan, "Self-Esteem, Self-Respect, and Love of Self: Ways of Valuing the Self," forthcoming in *Philosophia*.

To describe *leftover emotions*, I will make use of Helen Block Lewis's instructive *Shame and Guilt in Neurosis*.[6] She suggests that we should understood both guilt and shame as stemming from the superego, but from different "parts" of it. (Her characterization in terms of the superego will strike many as outmoded, but it can be easily recast in more contemporary terms.) Guilt is presented as coming from the fear that one has failed to follow internalized requirements and prohibitions, which are felt as issuing from authority figures, especially such loved ones as one's parents. Shame, on the other hand, is presented as coming from the fear that one has failed to live up to ego ideals, which are internalized "imagos" of, typically, loved care-givers, such as one's parents. (Imagos are somewhat inchoate, not fully formed, indeterminate "pictures" or "understandings" of idealizations, especially of idealized people.)

People can feel guilt over not meeting requirements they no longer accept or even reject – indeed which they no longer accept precisely because of the values contained in and sustained by those requirements. So too, people can feel shame on account of not living up to ego ideals and imagos they no longer accept or even reject – again, precisely because of the values involved. I call these emotions leftover emotions, and their values, leftover values.

It might be held that people with such emotions still do accept, even if only in part, those leftover values and the authority of those leftover requirements and ideals. Or it might be held that, even though the leftover values contained in or sustained by the requirements and ideals are no longer accepted, the value or authority *of* or *behind* them has, somehow, been maintained: what these people now feel guilt or shame about is not violating those requirements and ideals, but violating their *parents'* requirements and ideals, say, or even disobeying or disappointing their parents, themselves.

For reasons sketched already, this latter position would be enough to sustain at least the spirit of the claim that there are serious questions about how some emotions reveal value or valuing. I am inclined to hold that there are some emotions that reveal absolutely no real values or valuings at all. But I see no reason to argue for this.

Indeed, I see some reason *not* to argue for this. As I see matters, much of the difficulty we would have in settling this issue has to do with independent and more general difficulties we have in knowing what it is really and

---

6 New York: International Universities Press, 1971. See especially chs. 1 and 2. See also Wallace, *Responsibility and the Moral Sentiments,* section 2.4, "Irrational Guilt."

63

truly to have or accept a value or engage in a valuing, as contrasted with doing so in a false, fantasy, evaluatively mistaken, or leftover way. There are many cases of varying unclarity. I take some comfort, however, from what also seems generally true: the unclarities about real and true values and valuings correspond to and vary with unclarities about real and true emotions. Where we have clearly real emotions, we have clearly real values or valuings or both, and where we have clearly false, fantasy, evaluatively mistaken, or leftover emotions, we have clearly false, fantasy, evaluatively mistaken, or leftover values or valuings or both.

Let us now turn to *some epistemological roles of emotions in revealing values*. The opposition between "cool reason" and studied beliefs, on the one hand, and emotions, on the other, is common enough. In Chapter 3, it will be shown how this opposition is problematic, misleading, and mistaken. Nonetheless, it can be used now to start putting a central claim about the epistemological role of emotions in revealing values.

What we learn from our cool reason and studied beliefs about value and evaluation often conflicts with what we learn from emotions. Values claimed by the one are not claimed, and may even be denied, by the other. Before the war started, I firmly believed that I would not find it all that bad; and before I heard you being slighted, I thought I no longer cared much for you.

So far as value and evaluative knowledge are concerned, philosophy has generally favored cool reason and studied beliefs while rejecting, or at least mistrusting, emotions. In typical confrontations between belief and emotion – for example, as expressed by the often discussed "I know that I should do ———, but I just cannot help feeling that I shouldn't" – we have been told that respect for truth or epistemology requires us to side with belief and reason against the emotions. But as my examples were meant to show, and as this work will show in various other ways, our emotions can reveal evaluative information that must be taken seriously. Emotions can be evaluatively accurate and informative, and indeed more accurate and informative than reason and belief, as in the war case. As will be shown, this is so for deep, systematic, and epistemologically compelling reasons.

I am in no way claiming that emotions are always to be trusted over belief and reason. It goes without saying that belief and reason may be accurate; that emotions can be inaccurate and misleading; and that belief and reason can be more accurate and more trustworthy than emotions. So too, of course, one's true position might be found only by discovering and overcoming distortions and other errors on both sides. This may lead to a compromise or to some entirely new position. We might note that this last takes the evaluative information given by the original emotions seriously, even though in need of correction. In addition, the corrected evaluative view might be shown by the emotions one comes to only after discovering and overcoming errors both in one's earlier beliefs and reason and also in one's earlier emotions.

Further, I am not claiming that in all cases having emotions is necessary for discovering one's values. I see no reason to think that it was in principle impossible for me to have discovered my values about the team or the war in nonemotional ways. After all, I often know or discover what I value just by asking myself "What do I value in this?" or "Do I value this?" or by noting what in fact I pursue and what I do. There may be no need to examine emotions. But in the team and war cases, as a matter of fact I did learn what I valued by means of my emotions. And in these cases at those times, there might have been no other ways that were then and there accessible to me and that I knew how to deploy to discover those values. So, even if the necessity is less than necessity in principle, emotions can be necessary for evaluative knowledge.

3 Whether all emotions contain or reveal value, with special focus on interest and intellectual emotions

Do all affective states reveal value? I will approach this, mainly, through the more specific question, Do all *emotions* reveal value? *Orgē* both contains and reveals value: only if I take it that you have been unjustifiably slighted can I have *orgē* on account of how you were treated. Some desires are also like this: I might want to eat this banana because I think that it contains potassium, which I think is good for me. A gourmet might want to eat this particular dish because it is prepared to perfection. These contrast with an infant's wanting milk, not on the basis of some evaluation, but "naturally," just as a matter of natural appetite.

In the cases of *orgē*, my desire for the banana, and the gourmet's desire for that dish, evaluations play a central role. This is to be expected, at least for adults. Part of maturation involves coming to have and act and feel on account of evaluations, not just direct and natural appetite. It also involves learning to have correct evaluations and to act and feel appropriately on account of those correct evaluations. Maturation, thus, involves acquiring a repertoire of desires based on evaluation and replacing some desires based on appetite with desires based on evaluation. In these ways, maturation involves learning to be good.[7]

7 On this, see Myles Burnyeat, "Aristotle on Learning to be Good," in Amélie O. Rorty, ed.,

Maturation does not require replacing all appetite-based desires with desires containing or depending on evaluations in this way. Nor does it require desires being directed at the good in proportion to its goodness. I mention these two things maturation does *not* require for several reasons, both philosophical and psychoanalytic. The philosophical reason is that the underpinning of at least two influential philosophical themes about conflict is precisely what I claim maturation does not require. One theme is that weakness of will is problematic, even impossible – because the good must attract in proportion to how good it is or is taken to be. The second theme is that conflict and nonmaximization require plural values, since if there is only one value, and one always wants the good, there just will be no nonmaximizing goal to pursue. I have argued elsewhere that conflict requires only plural goals, not plural values; that it is a serious error to think that desire is always even of the good, much less always in proportion to how good it is; and that these errors carry over to and explains the errors of the views about weakness of will and conflict and nonmaximization.[8]

I turn now to a psychoanalytic reason for rejecting the claim, or something very much like the claim, that desire, or the desires of mature and rational people are always for the good and proportioned to the good. Some people do live and think they should live that way, seeking only the good and in proportion to how good it is. They decide what to do or deliberate without any recourse to desires, or at least nothing they recognize as desires. But as psychoanalysis recognizes, this is a central, characterizing feature of rigidity, compulsiveness, and obsessive compulsiveness. People with these neurotic deformations are "always" concerned with what they should do, what is required, or what is best, not with what they want to do.[9]

If desires, at least of mature and rational adults, always did contain or depend on evaluations in this way, a desire to eat some food would be on account of, say, its being prepared well, its being healthful, or that politeness requires it. So too, sexual desire would be on such bases as "intercourse is good

Essays on Aristotle's Ethics (Berkeley: University of California Press, 1980).
8 In regard to whether desire must be of or directed at the good, see "The Schizophrenia of Modern Ethical Theories," *Journal of Philosophy*, 73 (1976) 453–466, and "Values and Purposes: The Limits of Teleology and the Ends of Friendship," *Journal of Philosophy*, 78 (1981) 747–765. In regard to whether desire must always be of the good in proportion to how good it is, see "Desiring the Bad," *Journal of Philosophy*, 76 (1979) 738–753. In regard to whether conflict and nonmaximization require plural values, see *Plural and Conflicting Values* (Oxford: Oxford University Press, 1990), especially ch. 7, "Akrasia: The Unity of the Good, Commensurability, and Comparability," and ch. 8, "Monism, Pluralism, and Conflict."
9 See, for example, David Shapiro, *Neurotic Styles* (New York: Basic Books, 1965), *Autonomy and Rigid Character* (New York: Basic Books, 1981), and *Psychotherapy of Neurotic Character* (New York: Basic Books, 1989), under 'obsessive'.

for me" or "this person satisfies my idea of an ideal sexual partner." If the relevant evaluative considerations are moral ones, the desires would be on account of, perhaps for the sake of, the right or the good. Such people would want food, drink, sex, or whatever only on account of its being good or right. Such people would never desire something just because they liked it.[10]

But, as I hope is clear without any further argument, even many mature, rational, and good people have desires that are more loosely informed by values and valuations. And, second, many such people have many desires just on account of likings. We might take either of these claims, especially the second, as indicating that some desires and some related emotions of mature and good people do not contain values as constituent parts.

Nonetheless, even such desires and emotions can reveal value: general characterological values, as mentioned previously. We might hold, with Aristotle, that good people will not let themselves have or act on desires if they think these are bad or unacceptable: that they will have overcome and extirpated certain appetitive desires, and they will not be, or let themselves be, improperly affected by "nonapproved" appetitive desires. (See, for example, *NE* III.11, 1119a12 ff.)

Values can play many of these roles in people who are not so good. Gluttons and other self-indulgent people can have desires for and emotions about excess food that do not contain evaluations – at least not of the sort signaled by "this food in this amount is good."

Some might say that all desires, or all desires of adults anyway, show such characterologically held values: values located in the character that help form or at least filter all desires. This, however, runs the risk of simply assuming that desires always do show value: perhaps by assuming that the process of maturation is so thoroughgoing and that values play such a large role in maturation that by the time we are mature, all our desires will have been evaluated and, if found wanting, will have been reformed or extirpated. It does not allow, for example, that instead of the values extirpating or correcting certain desires, those desires weaken or do away with those values, perhaps replacing them with more accommodating values or perhaps replacing them with no values at all.

Perhaps instead of being question-begging, this claim sets out the anticipated results of a research program, designed to see what happens in maturation. Or perhaps its claim is not only about the values of the person in

---

10 See David Wiggins, "Truth, Invention, and the Meaning of Life," and "A Sensible Subjectivism?" in his *Needs, Values, and Truth* (Oxford: Blackwell, 1991). Here and elsewhere, I have benefited from these papers.

question, but also about what others and that person can use to evaluate that person. So, it might hold that an adult's having crude and untrammeled desires that are simply taken as natural and thus to be satisfied shows that the person is crude and unthinking.

Even those who agree with me that we have spent enough time on this issue might wonder about the usefulness, or even the soundness, of the distinction between desires and emotions that both contain and reveal value and those that only reveal value: between desires and emotions that contain value within themselves and also show the values of the character they express, and those that do not contain values but do show values of the character. It might be suggested that these related distinctions between containing and revealing and only revealing are no better than ones between what is explicit and what is implicit, or between foreground and background. We might be asked to consider connoisseurs liking a Rembrandt without noting or saying to themselves "this is good." Surely, we will be urged, the liking of this Rembrandt by such people, exercising their connoisseurship, is as value-laden as it would be if they explicitly said "this is good."

For my part, however, I think that such distinctions as those between the explicit and the implicit, or the foreground and background, are useful and often important. In this case, they allow us to hold that even if all emotions that reveal value also contain it, there is a distinction between the values an *emotion* contains and what is shown evaluatively about a *person* – what values the person is shown to contain – by having that emotion. This is so even if all that is shown about the person is that this is a person who cares about the values contained in the emotion. This is not trivial – provided that, as I think, there is more to caring about such values than simply having emotions that contain and reveal them.

So far I have only alluded to the possibility of desires, emotions, and other affective states that do not contain or reveal values. I now want to show these can and do exist. I will start with some found in infants and animals that are simply about what is good or bad. I use infants and animals because it is implausible to ascribe evaluative thoughts or evaluative ways of taking matters to them.

For an example of emotions – or perhaps moods or simply affective states – that are not based on values or evaluations, we could consider the rage of very young infants who are in pain or are hungry. To ascribe such rage to them, we do not also have to ascribe to them thoughts such as "this pain or hunger is bad." Nor do we have to hold that they take the pain or hunger to be bad – at least not in any other way than simply being enraged at and by it. It is sufficient that we hold that their pain or discomfort is unpleasant or bad; that their rage is occasioned by this unpleasant or bad state; and that in an age-appropriate way, their rage "takes up" this state. I would make similar claims about the contentment of infants when well fed, warm, clean, and held in a loving way; and also for many of the feelings, moods, emotions, or other affective states we ascribe to pets, such as the contentment of one's favorite cat that has just been well fed, had its back scratched, and is curled up, purring, on its favorite cushion.

Various other affective states, such as excitement and interest, also have some instances that do contain values and others that do not. I will focus on interest and excitement to illustrate the distinction. I focus on them also to help dispel, or at least lessen, a worry that some philosophers have expressed to me: that interest and excitement are not emotions and are not even affective states. As is sometimes put, interest, such as interest in mathematics, is just an interest, not an emotion.

The goals of *Valuing Emotions* are adequately served by showing that interest and excitement are affective, whether or not they are also emotions – if, as argued, the troubles philosophers have had with emotions are really troubles with affectivity. (See Chapter 1, especially its opening paragraphs.) And we have seen that both interest and excitement are irreducibly affective. (Again, see Chapter 1, especially sections 3 and 4.) Nonetheless, I think it will be useful to show how interest and excitement are emotions or at least emotionlike.

Let us start with *intellectual* interest and *intellectual* excitement. We should note that many instances of intellectual interest and excitement depend on evaluations and are about what is good, intellectually or otherwise. We could not understand Watson and Crick and their inquiries into DNA if we did not see this. And clearly, a central part of education and maturation – both in general and also in particular activities and disciplines – involves learning to be interested in what is relevant, important, useful, and beautiful.

This learning involves developing interest and excitement, and developing the ability to mobilize and direct them. It also involves developing an ability to master them and not to be overwhelmed or disrupted by them. We learn both where to direct our interest and excitement, and also how to modulate them in relation to the value, often the intellectual value, of what does or should interest or excite us. For just as intellectual interest and excitement are important and often essential for good intellectual activity, unmodulated and undirected interest and excitement can impede or harm, even preclude, good intellectual activity.

It is clear, then, that many instances of intellectual interest and excitement are about what is intellectually or otherwise good. But it is also clear that many instances of them are *not* about what is good. I am here not thinking about what is morally bad, such as sadism, or aesthetically bad, such as kitsch. These can be intellectually interesting, at least as objects of study.

I am thinking, rather, about interest in what has no interest at all. Here we might consider cases where people have "a bee in their bonnet," an obsession, an *idée fixe*. Sometimes this is said about something that would be interesting, if only it were true or even plausible or possible: for example, squaring the circle with only a straight edge and a compass. It is also said about matters that are of no interest at all: for example, someone's "interest" in how many times the letter *e* occurs in the first edition of Hume's *Treatise*. But even here, we may be able to find a view, albeit a wildly mistaken one, that would make this interesting. Perhaps the person thinks, on numerological grounds, that Hume is to be believed only if that number is prime. If we cannot find even such a view, we might think that instead of showing interest in that issue, that person's activity is an expression of, say, obsessional disorder. If this is right, these forms of interest and excitement require a connection – whether plausible or implausible, perhaps only a deformed connection or parody of a connection – between them and what is interesting or what is intellectually or otherwise good.

Nonetheless, there are instances of interest and excitement that do not have even such a weak connection with what is intellectually or otherwise good. Here we might think of the interest or excitement infants have toward moving lights or mobiles. As I see matters, the closest we can connect this with value and evaluation is by holding that it is an age-appropriate and developmentally useful activity or protoactivity that deploys and engages what will be so vital later on in life: it is an awakening of consciousness and a beginning of engagement and activity. And these certainly are good.

Some instances of interest and excitement are still more removed from evaluative thoughts. Here we can consider the excitement of infants and toddlers during roughhousing with their parents, being tossed up and caught, or being spun around. So too, we can think of the excitement of dogs when they are playing or hunting. We can also consider the excitement of children and adults during roller coaster rides, parachuting, bungee jumping, and the like.

To be sure, in some of these last cases, there is excitement over mastering what is taken as dangerous – and this can be clearly evaluative. But there are also instances of such interest and excitement that are not based on value or evaluation – again, for example, the excitement of toddlers being tossed up and caught, and children and adults on roller coaster rides.[11] I am not denying that goods and bads are involved here. To do that would require denying the goodness of a healthy being's engagement in naturally and healthily engaging activity. But the ways such engagement can make excitement and interest good are significantly different from the ways that the goodness of finding out about DNA grounded Watson's and Crick's interest and excitement.

As noted, it has been suggested to me that interest and excitement are not emotions. This might also be urged for those instances of rage and contentment, mentioned earlier, which do not involve evaluations. As noted, I do think of them all as emotions or as other, similar affective states. But this disagreement can be a matter of unimportant classification. What is important for my concerns is that interest and excitement be seen to be connected with value and evaluation in many different ways – ways that are importantly like, whether or not exactly like, those of such clear emotions as *orgē* and anger as we experience it. What is also important for my concerns is that interest and excitement be recognized as affective.

I hope I have shown enough to sustain the first point, the one about value and evaluation. If anyone still doubts the second point, about affectivity, I do not know what to do. I do not see how to reach those who fail to see the affectivity in, say, Watson's and Crick's interest and excitement or in infants' gazing raptly at mobiles or joy at being spun around.

At this point, I might be invited to offer a characterization of emotions: a characterization showing that interest and excitement, and also infants' rage and contentment, are emotions. But as throughout, I will decline. If asked for a reason, I would invoke David Rapaport's comments:

> We have come to label as affect such a wide variety of phenomena that both in diagnostic and therapeutic work we are in danger of being led astray by the term, as long as we lack a systematic view of the relationships of all the phenomena to which we apply it.[ii]

---

11 For a discussion of near constitutional character differences, which are not based on values or evaluations and which center around liking and disliking such activities, see Michael Balint, *Thrills and Regressions* (Madison, Conn.: International Universities Press, 1987). Contrary views, suggesting the need for evaluations in emotions, are presented in Rainer Reisenzein and Wolfgang Schönpflug, "Stumpf's Cognitive–Evaluative Theory of Emotion," *American Psychologist,* 47 (1992) 34–45, and by Patricia S. Greenspan, *Emotions and Reasons* (New York: Routledge, 1988).

ii While all the phenomena discussed [above and] below have to do with affects, and are time and again referred to in the literature, my listing them here does not imply that they are correctly labeled as affects nor that the theory of affects almost must account fully for all of them. Indeed, some of the phenomena to be listed are most complex, and more than the theory of affects will have to be invoked for their explanation. What I imply by listing them here is that they constitute an important problem for the theory of affects also.[12]

What I trust will be sufficient for my concerns is to present and work with clear enough examples of emotions and much else that is affectively-charged. I am not concerned to claim, much less offer an argument, that since interest and excitement, or rage and contentment, involve values in those ways, and since they are also affective, therefore they are emotions. It is enough for my purposes that in these two important ways they be recognized as sufficiently like various emotions and such other well-recognized affective states as moods, attitudes, and, of course, interests.

This, however, presents us with the following issue. Warnings against emotions have been part and parcel of our tradition. But our tradition does not warn against intellectual interest and intellectual excitement; and given its emphasis on the intellect and rationality, it could hardly warn against them. It might, thus, be concluded that intellectual interest and excitement are not emotions, or at least are not taken as such in our tradition.

I want to turn this back either on itself or on our tradition. We do have reason to be wary of intellectual interest and excitement. They can be dangerous for moral and intellectual concerns. They can be dangerous in the ways they get us to attend to intellectual matters when we should, instead, be working in nonintellectual areas. So too, they can be dangerous in the ways they get us to work in the wrong intellectual area or too much in one area. Here we need only think of the dangers of overinterest or overexcitement, or interest and excitement about the wrong facts, and the like.

Let us now consider what follows if interest and excitement, including intellectual interest and excitement, are recognized as emotions. Since they are not among the emotions our tradition warns against, we can no longer characterize our tradition as warning against emotions as such. We will have to take our tradition as warning against only certain emotions. For much the same reasons that I will not offer a characterization of emotions, I will

---

[12] "On The Psychoanalytic Theory of Affects," *International Journal of Psycho-Analysis,* 34 (1953), 177–198; reprinted in Robert P. Knight and Cyrus Friedman, eds., *Psychoanalytic Psychiatry and Psychology: Clinical and Theoretic Papers, Austen Riggs Center,* volume 1 (New York: International Universities Press, 1954); and in *The Collected Papers of David Rapaport,* ed. Merton M. Gill (New York: Basic Books, 1967), from which this quotation is drawn (p. 478). I have added 'above and' to make clearer the reference to the long quotation given in my Introduction.

not offer a characterization of the difference between those emotions our tradition finds dangerous and those it does not. But I will offer this speculation: that difference is connected with the view that emotions, or the emotions we are warned against, are bodily, primitive, and essentially arational.

These last views about emotions – whether about emotions quite generally or only those we are warned against – are rapidly losing credit. This book is intended to speed these views on their way.

4 Some relations between my claim and emotivism and naturalism

In this section, I will discuss some links emotivism and naturalism claim between value and emotions. My main purpose here is to show, by questioning these claims, that those links are not the ones I am urging.

In earlier sections I showed some ways emotions can play epistemological roles for value and evaluation: in particular, how emotions reveal and aid in the discovery of values. For example, I found out how very bad I thought the war was by seeing how upset I was when I heard that it started. By this means, I found I had strongly underestimated both how I would evaluate the war and also the value I really did think it would have. Similarly, I found out how much I valued you, my nationality, or religion by seeing how angry undeserved slights made me.

It might seem that, if emotions do reveal value, this lends support to emotivism. I do agree with emotivists that emotions and values are closely intertwined. Indeed, as argued in later chapters, I hold that some values are constituted by emotions. However, I do not think that what I argue supports emotivism more than various competing views. Indeed, I am unsure whether what I argue is even consistent with emotivism. For much of what I argue shows how emotions involve and depend on value, rather than value on emotions. And, so far as I can see, nothing I say shows that values and judgments of value have a different sort of truth or ontological status than "ordinary" facts and factual judgments. The materials for this will be developed later, and so any conclusions about the connections between my claims and emotivism should be postponed until then.

Some might say that so far from supporting emotivism, I have given the materials for a naturalist argument: for a derivation of a moral or evaluative claim from purely factual ones. Let us recall Aristotle's characterization of *orgē:* "Anger may be defined as a desire accompanied by pain, for a conspicuous revenge for a conspicuous slight at the hands of men who have no call to slight oneself or one's friends." If I have *orgē*, I can conclude that someone has unjustifiably slighted me or mine. Thus, it might seem that I have shown how knowing that an emotion was experienced – a fact that certainly seems to be within the ambit of naturalism – can be used to prove that a wrong was done.

But that was not my claim nor do I think that the argument I gave supports that claim about naturalism. To use the claim that I was angry to show that I was wronged, we need the further claim that I was slighted without justification. And I do not think I have given any reason to think that either the slight or its being unjustified admits of a naturalistic understanding or derivation. (Some of my arguments for this will also show why I do not think I give any support for emotivism.)

This last does raise problems for the emotivist hope that moral claims admit of an analysis or explanation in terms of emotions. It shows that emotivists will need to exercise care in their choice of reducing emotions. Aristotelian *orgē*, to mention one emotion, depends on, and makes or contains, moral claims: for me to have *orgē*, I must take myself or someone close to me to have been *unjustifiably* slighted. Thus, emotivists cannot use this emotion as a reducing emotion.

But even though such anger may not lend itself to emotivism, it may also not support naturalism. For it does not follow from the fact that one is angry that one has, in fact, suffered a wrong. At most, it follows that, as one takes things, one has suffered a wrong. And it remains to be seen whether that supports naturalism.

The relations between emotions and naturalism are complex and important enough for further discussion and illustration. To this end, let us examine some claims made by Philippa Foot in her important "Moral Arguments" and "Moral Beliefs."[13] She opens "Moral Beliefs" by saying,

To many people it seems that the most notable advance in moral philosophy during the past fifty years or so has been the refutation of naturalism; and they are a little shocked that at this late date such an issue should be reopened. (p. 110)

And much of what she says about rudeness in "Moral Arguments" suggests, and has been taken as, an argument for naturalism, with rudeness as an example of an evaluative notion which admits of a naturalistic account. In "Moral Arguments" she offers what might seem to be such an account: "The right account of the situation in which it is correct to say that a piece

---

13 "Moral Arguments," *Mind*, 67 (1958) 502–513; and "Moral Beliefs," *Aristotelian Society Proceedings*, 59 (1958–1959) 83–104. Both are reprinted in *Virtues and Vices* (Oxford: Blackwell, 1978) from which the following quotations are drawn.

of behaviour is rude is, I think, that such behaviour causes offence by indicating lack of respect" (p. 102). Let us use 'the *offense-rudeness* claim' as the name for the claim that a piece of behavior is rude if it causes offense by indicating lack of respect.

As argued at the end of this section, I do not think we should take Foot as offering the offense-rudeness claim as an argument for naturalism. We should take it as an argument only against various antinaturalistic arguments. However, my main concern now is with the relations between naturalism and emotions, and I leave any interpretive discussions of Foot to the end of this section. Until then, I will examine the offense-rudeness claim in a way I do not think Foot intended it, but in a way it is often taken: as a claim offered in support of naturalism.

Let us start by asking how good an account of rudeness – whether or not the account is naturalistic – is given by the offense-rudeness claim. Is an act rude if and only if it causes offense by indicating lack of respect? I do not think so. First of all, there is this minor issue. If to be caused offense, one must *take* offense and *feel* offended, the offense-rudeness claim does not give an account, whether naturalistic or not, of rudeness. People can be treated rudely, but nonetheless not feel offended or take offense. They might not notice the act of rudeness; they might not think it rude; they might think they deserved it; they might not take the rude person seriously and might not care what that person does.

Suppose, then, that one can be caused offense without feeling offended. Or, suppose that the offense-rudeness claim is taken as giving only something like sufficient, naturalistic conditions for rudeness.

But even here there are problems. There are acts that are not rude, but that are bad and owe at least some of their badness to offense caused by lack of respect.[14] A rape victim, or a victim of some other form of assault, may be caused offense, feeling offended, by being treated merely "as a thing," as a plaything. Or the victim may be caused offense by being treated as a particular kind of person – a person to be degraded, and not a person deserving and accorded even the minimum of ordinary human respect. Some might say that such acts go far beyond rudeness. I see little reason to disagree, provided that this is not taken as saying that they are rude and a whole lot more.

Some might also say that the matter is misstated, not understated, if it is said that the rape victim is caused offense by what was done and the attitude with which it was done. Rape, it might be held, goes well beyond causing

14 My thanks are owed to Laurence Thomas here.

offense. To be raped is to be caused a whole lot more and a whole lot worse than offense. But it is not to be caused offense and also a whole lot more and a whole lot worse.[15] I think there is something to this last objection, although I am unsure whether "rape causes offense" simply suggests something mistaken or instead misstates the issue.

But I think it uncontroversial that there are some acts that are not rude but which do cause offense by lack of respect. Your not taking my feelings or position into account may well have caused me offense by indicating lack of respect. And, indeed, you may have acted wrongly and you may have wronged me by the way you treated or failed to treat me. Nonetheless, at least some acts fitting this description are not rude. They are merely inconsiderate or unduly inattentive, and those who do them may be merely inconsiderate or unduly inattentive.

To give a naturalistic account of rudeness, we need a naturalistic way to avoid these problems. We would need, for example, naturalistic accounts of the particular ways rudeness shows lack of respect. These accounts would explicitly or implicitly differentiate these ways from, say, ways of showing lack of respect that are inconsiderate but not rude. Perhaps there is a naturalistic way to do this.

But even if we can give a naturalistic account of rudeness, we may not be able to give one of 'wrong' or 'wrong, because rude'. As Foot points out, there can be good moral reasons not to show respect, and even to be rude. An emergency can make it impossible for you to pay "respectful" or indeed any attention to me; or I may have forfeited my right to be treated with respect by you. Thus, it does not follow from an act's being rude that it is wrong. Naturalists must be able to give an account of rudeness that, by naturalistic means, separates those acts of rudeness that are wrong from those that are not.

The problem here might be thought due to being concerned, not with wrongness, but with *overall* wrongness. It might, thus, be thought that the problem could be solved by focusing also on prima facie wrongness. We might, therefore, use the offense-rudeness claim to hold that in certain circumstances, causing offense is prima facie wrong. For this to support naturalism, however, there must also be a naturalistic account of those circumstances. This might include a naturalistic account of circumstances in which it is not overall wrong to treat someone rudely, and also a naturalistic account of how to balance the prima facie wrongness of rudeness in those circumstances and the wrongness of some incompossible act.

15 My thanks are owed to Robert S. Fudge for discussion here.

Even more weakly, it could be held that there is no naturalistic account of those circumstances in which the naturalistic considerations deployed by the offense-rudeness claim ground 'wrong' or 'wrong, because rude'. Thus, we could not give a naturalistic account of either in terms of the offense-rudeness claim. But it could nonetheless be held that in certain circumstances that cannot be characterized naturalistically, those naturalistic considerations do ground 'wrong' or 'wrong, because rude'. It could also be held that where they do this, the grounding has the force of necessity. So, it might be held that in certain irreducibly moral situations – situations that are not characterizable naturalistically – certain naturalistic facts guarantee new moral facts: facts that would not hold, but for those naturalistic ones, and that hold with the force of necessity. This would not be an argument for naturalism. It would, however, be an argument against the very strong antinaturalist claim that naturalistic considerations are never morally relevant or that they never hold with the force of moral necessity.

We have distinguished different sorts or strengths of naturalistic positions that the offense-rudeness claim might be used to establish: that there are naturalistic conditions for 'overall wrong', or for 'overall wrong, because rude', or for 'prima facie wrong', or for 'prima facie wrong, because rude'. However, the offense-rudeness claim does not support any of these.

My reason for holding this is that if that claim is to have any of these four moral implications, it must be changed so that it talks about, not just respect, but *deserved* respect. It must read something like: behavior is rude if it causes offense by indicating a lack of deserved respect. But even if this does not tell against naturalism, it clearly offers naturalism no support – except by telling against that very strong antinaturalism.

Let me state briefly why the offense-rudeness claim needs to be made explicitly moral by the addition of deserved respect. (In the discussion of Foot, I will show another way that claim must be made explicitly moral.) I will start by repeating some claims made earlier. It is not always wrong not to show respect. Nor is it always wrong not to show respect by being rude. There may be no time or way to show respect; or I may have forfeited my right to respect. An account of respect such that not showing it is wrong, thus, must be an account of respect that is then and there deserved. How will naturalists give an account of such deserved respect?

It might be thought that naturalists can give such an account. Alternatively, it might be thought that they can avoid the need to do so by talking about forms of common, ordinary respect owed in general to just anyone, absent any contrary reasons. Or perhaps naturalists can be satisfied by a disjunction of those sorts of respect and the sorts of respect particular people can owe to other people, either in general or more particularly, such as students to teachers and young people to their elders.

These last suggestions run into the problem of acts that are offensive because they involve lack of respect, but are nonetheless not rude: because, like rape, they are far more than rude, or, like mere inconsiderateness, are simply other than rude. However, naturalists face at least as serious a problem in characterizing common, ordinary respect. This is the same problem, or at least a very similar one, they have in characterizing offensive lack of respect that is rude.

For your act to be offensive to me, it need not cause me offense and I need not feel offended. Nor is your act shown offensive by my feeling offended. I could be too full of myself and thus mistakenly think I was entitled to what, in fact, would be an extra special show of respect. Or I could be too touchy and thus mistakenly take your show of what in fact is ordinary respect as showing lack of respect. In these cases there is no failure of respect. I am not entitled to the respect the absence of which occasions my feeling offended. Despite my feeling offended, there is no rudeness, nor is anything wrong done.

There may be a naturalistic way to describe those general sorts of circumstances in which not showing respect is rude. And even if there is no naturalistic description or account of those general circumstances, there might still be naturalistic descriptions of particular circumstances in which causing offense is rude. The following two sketches might be good starts. First, we are in a moderately crowded elevator, you realize that you have kicked my ankle, but do not apologize. Second, we are discussing a philosophical issue we have each worked on both alone and together, and despite my asking you to let me finish putting my views, you keep interrupting.

It is easy to see how in either of these circumstances, I might be offended by your lack of respect. And we can easily imagine that in these cases, there is a lack of ordinary respect owed quite generally. We can also easily imagine that there is no good reason for you then and there not to accord me such respect. And, finally, it does seem that the circumstances are characterized naturalistically.

But this is still inadequate for naturalism. Naturalism about rudeness must give a naturalistic account of rudeness, including the conditions and circumstances in which, and perhaps also the reasons why, ordinary, general respect is deserved and owed and in which not showing such respect is offensive. It is not enough to be able to point to an example of rudeness, and to describe or locate that example naturalistically.

If that were enough, we could conclude that naturalism is sustained if we can simply locate, even just point to, wrong-making characteristics by naturalistic means. And naturalistic means often do seem sufficient for this. Various instances of pain it is wrong to bring about can be located naturalistically or can even admit of a naturalistic account – as instances of pain, that is. For example, 'Jones suffering pain in his ribs from ten o'clock through noon from being hit' or 'the act of assault and battery committed on Jones, as detailed on page twenty of the police blotter'.

But that is not enough to secure naturalism. Nonnaturalists can allow that there are naturalistic means sufficient to locate those wrong-making features and facts. They can allow this while also denying that we can give naturalistic accounts of the wrongness of those features either in general or in these cases. They can claim that there is no naturalistic account of the circumstances, or ways, in which these wrong-making characteristics ground 'wrong, because rude', or of how causing such suffering, in general or just here, is overall or even prima facie wrong. On their view, to account for these moral facts and conclusions, we must make recourse to explicitly moral facts: for example, hitting Jones was a violation of his rights; he did not pose a threat that would justify his being hit as a matter of self-defense; he did not deserve to be hit, much less hurt.

Nonnaturalists can hold that, at best, it remains to be seen whether there is a naturalistic account of 'overall wrong, because rude' or 'prima facie wrong, because rude', and, more generally, of 'overall wrong' or 'prima facie wrong'. Whether or not nonnaturalists are right that there are no naturalistic accounts of what is needed here, I do not know of any such account. Thus it seems to me that naturalists have not yet given a naturalistic account of general, ordinary, respect or, more minimally, a naturalistic account or description of particular acts and circumstances which establish that in those cases, such respect is owed.

My conclusion, then, is that the case for naturalism has not been made by use of the offense-rudeness claim. It remains to be seen whether it can be made at all.[16] I am dubious about its possibility. But now is not the time to

16 For another attempt to do something along these lines – now in terms of conventions – see John Searle, "How to Derive 'Ought' from 'Is'," *Philosophical Review*, 73 (1964) 43–58. For an argument that his attempt fails, because of its problems with "other things being equal," see Judith Jarvis Thomson and James Thomson, "How Not to Derive 'Ought' from 'Is'," *Philosophical Review*, 73 (1964) 512–516. For an argument – somewhat like mine about the difficulties in giving a naturalistic account of value in terms of emotions – directed against the norm expressivism of Allan Gibbard's *Wise Choices, Apt Feelings* (Cambridge, Mass.: Harvard University Press, 1990), see Justin D'Arms and Daniel Jacobson, "Expressivism, Morality, and the Emotions," *Ethics*, 104 (1994) 739–763, especially p. 751. See also Wallace, *Responsibility and the Moral Sentiments*, pp. 48–50.

argue for this. It is sufficient for us to have seen that emotions do reveal value and evaluations in various ways, but not in the ways discussed by naturalism and emotivism. Far more remains to be shown about how emotions do reveal value and evaluations, and about the nature of such value and evaluation. These are among the central themes of the rest of this work.

An interpretation of Foot

I will close this section with a few comments on how we might interpret Foot and her use of the offense-rudeness claim.[17] I shall simply present this interpretation without trying to show whether it is her view or is only a view she gave all the materials for holding, but did not hold. As noted already, in "Moral Arguments" she points out that certain acts of rudeness are *not* wrong, even where the act is rude because it shows the lack of respect required by the offense-rudeness claim. This is to say that she allows that in some cases where rudeness is secured by the considerations found in the offense-rudeness claim, it can, nonetheless, be morally all right to do that piece of rude behavior. Thus, unless we ascribe clear inconsistency to her, we cannot take her as offering a simple naturalistic account of 'overall wrong' or 'overall wrong, because rude' in terms of caused offense.

We could take her as being interested in prima facie wrongness, in the manner sketched previously. This would leave her open to the objections also sketched previously. I think, however, that there is a way to take her as recognizing that although rudeness gives conditions for wrongness, prima facie and sometimes overall, and although such rudeness can be characterized in terms of offense, she is not arguing for naturalism, but only against various antinaturalisms.

Consider again her claim, "The right account of the situation in which it is correct to say that a piece of behaviour is rude is, I think, that such behaviour causes offence by indicating lack of respect." I have given reasons why we must understand 'respect' as '*deserved* respect' for this to come even close to being a good account of rudeness. For similar reasons, in order for Foot's account to have much chance of being correct, it must understand offense evaluatively, that is, as *undeserved* offense.

Further, offense cannot be understood as just any sort of hurt or pain or wound. It must be understood as conceptually involving an injury, insult, or affront that strikes at one's moral status or one's moral self. To be caused

---

17 My thanks are owed to Jonathan Adler and Barbara Herman for discussion here.

offense, to be offended, is thus very like being demeaned. It is to be ill treated in a way that involves not only such evaluative notions as well-being, but also such moral notions as deserved respect.

If the offense of rudeness must be understood morally, not just evaluatively, rudeness and its offense are even more strongly evaluative than pride. I mention pride because of what Foot writes in "Moral Beliefs": "The characteristic object of pride is something seen . . . as some sort of *achievement or advantage*" (pp. 113–114, emphasis added). It hardly needs saying that achievement and advantage are evaluative notions, even if they need not be moral notions.

My suggestion, then, is that the offense-rudeness claim advances Foot's purposes only if 'offense' is evaluative and perhaps also moral. If we suppose that Foot used the offense-rudeness claim to give a naturalistic account of 'overall or prima facie rude' or 'overall or prima facie wrong, because rude', we are faced with two alternatives: either she did not see that 'offense' is evaluative, or alternatively she thought that there is a naturalistic account of 'offense'. Each has severe difficulties.

It is hard to see how, having seen that pride is evaluative, she could fail to see that 'offense' is evaluative. And if she was using the offense-rudeness claim in support of naturalism, and she also did see that 'offense' is evaluative, it is hard to see why she did not make any gestures toward showing that it, too, admits of a naturalistic account.

The best interpretation, I suggest, is that her intention was not to support naturalism, but to show that extreme antinaturalism is mistaken: that it is a mistake to hold that value and such evaluations as 'achievement', 'advantage', 'wrong', 'rude', 'offensive', 'wrong, because rude' and 'rude, because offensive' are somehow "up to us," just a matter of free choice, just a matter of choosing or committing oneself. She writes in "Moral Beliefs" that,

There are here two assumptions about "evaluations," which I will call assumption (1) and assumption (2).

Assumption (1) is that some individual may, without logical error, base his beliefs about matters of value entirely on premises which no one else would recognize as giving evidence at all. Assumption (2) is that, given the kind of statement which other people regard as evidence for an evaluative conclusion, he may refuse to draw the conclusion because *this* does not count as evidence for *him*. (p. 111, emphases in original)

Clearly, one can reject naturalism even if one also rejects these two assumptions. And this double rejection – both of naturalism and also of those two assumptions – is the interpretation I urge for Foot. Although she does not argue for naturalism, she rejects various strong versions of antinaturalism. Moreover, she rejects these strong antinaturalisms because their argument that ethics is nonnatural relies on thinking of the natural just in terms given by physical science. But traditional naturalisms also do this. And, thus, both are to be rejected.

As I read Foot, she holds that the "world" can determine much of what is evaluative, including achievements, advantage, and often what is morally the case. But the world in question is the human and social world, not the world of physics or (and it may well be different) a reductive, neo-Humean naturalism. This is to say that it is not the natural, or the naturalism, that figures in current debates over naturalism and ethics.[18]

Much that I will argue for is also an argument that our world is shot through with value and also with emotion, and indeed the one because of the other. Whether, as I think, this tells against our current versions of naturalism is not one of my concerns, nor was it what I wanted to show in this section. What I wanted to show was that the relations between value and emotions I am concerned with are not those that figure in current debates over naturalism, nor are my arguments offered in order to support or attack either that naturalism or its rejection.

5 Perhaps evaluatively revealing emotions only reveal values

I have said that one of my concerns with the relations between emotions and value, or ethics, is epistemological. In particular, I have claimed that emotions reveal value. These claims about emotions revealing value might be accepted in a way that plays down, or even dismisses, the deep and intrinsic evaluative importance of emotions – precisely by emphasizing their revelatory function. One way to do this is by making what I will call the *information claim*.

The information claim is that emotions are ethically important because, and to the extent that, they reveal information about value, either value as the agents take things or value in the world. Such information is clearly important. To mention only some points, coming to know, and knowing, one's own values are essential for self-development and self-understanding,

---

18 My interpretation of Foot's negative position is similar to one urged by John McDowell in *Mind and World* (Cambridge, Mass.: Harvard University Press, 1994), especially lecture 4, with special attention to n. 12, p. 80. For an account of a naturalism that is not a neo-Humean empiricism, and an argument that Aristotle offers such a naturalism, see McDowell's *Mind and World* and also "Two Sorts of Naturalism," in Rosalind Hursthouse, Gavin Lawrence, and Warren Quinn, eds., *Virtues and Reasons,* a Festschrift for Foot (Oxford: Oxford University Press, 1995).

as well as for integrity, commitment, and much else of moral importance. In addition, to understand people and cultures, whether ourselves and ours or others, such as classical Greece, we need to know their values. Critiques of one's own or other people's lives – whether personal, social, or political lives – rely heavily on knowing what values these involve. To criticize such a way of life, it is vital to see the values it involves. Thus, for example, to know whether a person has integrity, and what the shape and focus of the integrity are, we need to know that person's values, how they are held and regarded, and the like. And we are given considerable information about this by that person's emotions. Emotions, then, are signs of or sources of vitally important evaluative information.

Emotions are thus seen as evaluatively informative and as such important: important as a means of revealing value, which, in itself, is important. In short, emotions are useful for revealing value; but what is really and in itself important is the value they reveal.

Emotions have been thought useful in other ways, too. As many philosophers hold, they help motivate us.[19] As Daniel Goleman holds, recognition of them in ourselves and in others helps us modulate and civilize behavior.[20] As Ronald DeSousa holds, they embody scenarios and patterns of salience, which allow us to move from one set of facts to another, where we do not have sufficient time or evidence to do this by nonemotional inferences or arguments.[21] As Patricia Greenspan holds, they are "adaptive" by being good guides to important information we need quickly: for example, our feeling uneasy at the used-car salesman's pitch is a good guide that we should be wary.[22] As Iris Murdoch, Martha Nussbaum, Lawrence Blum, and Margaret Walker hold, they help us notice value, for example by helping us pick values out from the welter of possible objects of attention.[23]

---

19 See, for example, Patricia S. Greenspan, *Practical Guilt* (New York: Oxford University Press, 1995), especially ch. 3.
20 *Emotional Intelligence* (New York: Bantam Books, 1995).
21 *The Rationality of Emotion* (Cambridge, Mass.: MIT Press, 1987).
22 *Emotions and Reasons,* for example, p. 11. I have benefited greatly from this work and from discussion with Greenspan.
23 Murdoch, *The Sovereignty of Good* (London: Routledge and Kegan Paul, 1970); Blum, *Friendship, Altruism, and Morality* (London: Routledge and Kegan Paul, 1980), "Iris Murdoch and the Domain of the Moral," *Philosophical Studies,* 50 (1986) 343–368, and "Particularity and Responsiveness," in Jerome Kagan and Sharon Lamb, eds., *The Emergence of Morality in Young Children* (Chicago: University of Chicago Press, 1987); Walker, "Moral Understandings: Alternative 'Epistemology' for a Feminist Ethics," *Hypatia,* 4 (1989) 15–28; Nussbaum, *Love's Knowledge* (Oxford: Oxford University Press, 1990), and "Equity and Mercy," *Philosophy and Public Affairs,* 22 (1993) 83–125. Walker's work situates this debate within a similar debate in feminist ethics: whether, as suggested by Carol Gilligan's *In a Different Voice* (Cambridge, Mass.: Harvard University Press, 1982), emotions, especially those having to do with

And as Andrew Morrison holds, they can serve as psychic defenses or as symptoms – as shame can serve in regard to sexual feelings.[24]

Not all philosophers agree that emotions are useful in these ways. Taking up some of these claims, Steven Luper-Foy writes,

> Extreme compassion and kindness may well motivate people whose lives are characterized by many acts of supererogation. But it is easy to exaggerate the emotional resources that must be available to people if those people are to meet their obligations. . . . consider three points. First, it is worth repeating that Kant himself was an extremely reserved individual. . . . In spite of his detachment, it would be silly to portray Kant as morally defective.
>
> Second, . . . on some widespread conceptions of duty we may meet our obligations without being driven to do so out of a sense of compassion or kindliness [or any other emotion]. Our motive for not interfering with the projects of others might simply be that doing so would be wrong.
>
> Third, consider cultures (such as ones heavily immersed in Buddhism) that downplay the importance of emotions in life. It is not obvious that people who are influenced by such cultures need fail to meet their responsibilities.[25]

These worries about compassion and kindness can easily be extended to all emotions, to hold that no emotions are needed for acting well or, for that matter, poorly. I will address this worry in later chapters. But I think it useful to make several brief points here about its bearing on my claims. As said earlier, my claims are about us, not people of other cultures. Further, my claims about the importance of emotions for us are not offered as necessary or even universal truths about us, but "only" as important, often or generally true, claims about us.

There are other problems with these claims of usefulness and also with the information claim. One problem is that these claims have greatest plausibility in regard to more or less *discrete* emotions: for example, my fear that John will damage my car, or my worry that this salesman is not to be trusted. These are emotions that, although they need not be emotional mountains or canyons, are eventlike: they are noticeable deviations from the ordinary flow of ordinary life.

However, if Schachtel, Krystal, Rapaport, and Tomkins are right, emotions and affectivity are found throughout much if not all of our life, not just in more or less discrete and eventlike emotional goings-on. Emotions and

---

care, community, and nurturing, are central to a desirable feminist ethics. My thanks are owed Walker for discussion of these and other issues. See also Gerald Gaus, *Value and Justification* (Cambridge: Cambridge University Press, 1990).
24 *Shame: The Underside of Narcissism* (Hillsdale, N.J.: Analytic Press, 1989), especially p. 23.
25 Review of *Morality and the Emotions* by Justin Oakley, *Philosophy and Phenomenological Research*, 54 (1994) 725–728, p. 727.

affectivity are found in the backgrounds, the tones and tastes of and in life. Here we might think of various forms and levels of interest, concern, and liveliness. These noneventlike features characterize and help make up the ordinary, often unremarkable and often unnoticed, flow of life.

I find it difficult to see how these various claims of usefulness are to be applied to these forms and instances of emotions and affectivity. How, for example, do general interest and liveliness figure in the motivation of good action, as differentiated from a general motivation to act, whether for good or ill? And how do general, background emotions embody scenes and scenarios, or serve as unarticulated guides to action, or help the agent see values? And what values do they help reveal?

Whatever the problems with these claims, however, I think we must acknowledge that emotions are useful in these ways. So, for example, having emotions and noticing and attending are closely interrelated. Those who are completely lacking in jealousy are too likely not to notice even clear evidence of infidelity, whereas those who are too given to jealousy are too likely to see evidence where there is none. Those who are "properly" given to jealousy can be expected to see facts for what they are, or at least more accurately than people of those other two sorts.

Nonetheless, I do not think we can accept these claims of usefulness if the usefulness is only *instrumental* usefulness, whether for life, value, or evaluation. And this is what the information claim holds, as do at least many versions of those other claims of usefulness.

My reason for rejecting these claims when they are taken as instrumental claims is, thus, not that I deny the instrumental usefulness of emotions for life and value. My reason is that emotions are also essential constituents of life and value. Life like ours would be impossible without emotions. And we have no idea what any human life without emotions would be like or even whether it would be possible. This is well argued by many psychological theorists such as Krystal, Tomkins, and Schachtel, and many philosophers such as Aristotle, Peter Strawson, and Charles Taylor.[26]

Holding that emotions are only instrumentally useful for human life is about as senseless as holding that belief and desire are only instrumentally useful for human life. There is no human life, or none we can imagine,

---

26 I am greatly indebted to Strawson's "Freedom and Resentment," *Proceedings of the British Academy*, 48 (1962) 187–211, and, as used here, reprinted in Gary Watson, ed., *Free Will* (Oxford: Oxford University Press, 1982); and to Taylor's "Self-Interpreting Animals," in his *Human Agency and Language, Philosophical Papers*, volume 1 (Cambridge: Cambridge University Press, 1985).

without belief, desire, and emotion; and thus no human life, or none we can imagine, for which they are only instrumentally useful.

The problem here comes from understanding usefulness as usefulness for life or value, taken quite generally and as a whole. It also comes from understanding usefulness as instrumental usefulness. Emotions can be instrumentally useful for life and value. But emotions also help constitute and are essential to what they are useful for. Indeed, a major concern of this work is to show how emotions are functionally and constitutively important and, often, vital for life and value, both in many particular cases and also for life and value taken generally and as a whole.

Showing this involves two correlative and complementary stages. The first is to show how very much of our life involves emotions and is emotional. The second is to show how life is emotional: for example, how values and knowledge of value are interconnected with, revealed by, constituted by, emotions.

6 The unsavory connection between the content claim and the information claim

The content claim (discussed in Chapter 1) holds that emotions lack affect. The information claim holds that what is evaluatively important about emotions is that they reveal value, perhaps more exactly that emotions show that the agent has detected or engaged with value. According to the information claim, what is evaluatively important about emotions is the value that is detected or revealed, not the value as engaged with, the emotionally engaged value.

Although both claims neglect affect, they do so in different ways and places. And neither claim entails the other. One can hold the information claim about the value of emotions while also holding that emotions are affective, thus rejecting the content claim. So too, one can hold that emotions are affective, denying the content claim, while holding also that what is of evaluative importance in emotions is found only in their nonaffective content. One can, further, hold that the content claim gives the correct conceptual account of emotions, while also holding that emotions are valuable in themselves, and not just for the information they provide, thus rejecting the information claim.

Nonetheless, these claims are mutually supporting. This can be seen by noting how a theorist who endorses either one could naturally and easily find materials for the other. A theorist who endorsed a content claim would need very little further material to go on to the information claim. For emotions, on the content view, are little more than the information, or the mere neutral holding of it. One way to put this is to imagine Pitcher's man P saying or thinking in a completely flat and affectless way, "I think that she might come and that it would be a good thing if she did," and to ask what we are given other than the information about that good thing, and the fact that P accepts that information.

PART II

Emotions and value: Some epistemological and constitutive relations

3

Emotional problems suggest epistemological problems

Part II, consisting of Chapters 3–7, is devoted to showing deep and systematic epistemological and evaluative connections between affective states and value and evaluation. As is generally the case in this work, emotions are the main examples of affectivity considered here. This chapter is concerned to show both that emotions as such are not harmful for reasoning and knowledge and also and far more significantly that emotions are often enough useful, even needed, for reasoning and knowledge. These connections of usefulness are not matters of entailment, nor are they even conceptual. But they are important and typical connections between having or lacking emotions and evaluative judgments. We will not be concerned to argue that these connections hold for all people or for all cultures. It is enough if we succeed in showing that they hold for us.

Chapter 4 considers and rejects various worries to the effect that although there are the sorts of connections shown in Chapter 3, they are not really with emotions, but only with various nonemotional states, or that they are not with values, but only with people as evaluators. Chapters 5 and 6 take up more strictly evaluative connections between emotions and value. Chapter 5 argues against various misconceptions about the evaluative roles of emotions, showing that they have evaluative importance even where many have suggested they play no such role. Chapter 6 presents a schematic way to categorize how some emotions do have value. Drawing on Chapters 3 through 6, Chapter 7 returns to more epistemological issues to show how emotions are important in still other ways for evaluative knowledge and for moral reasoning.

1   False truisms about reason and emotions

It is common, and not only in philosophy, to characterize people in terms of rationality. It is even a commonplace to characterize us as, in essence, rational beings. On such a view, the more rational we are, the better people we are; and perhaps, the more rational we are, the better or better off we are. Further, what is not part of rationality or does not contribute to rationality is unimportant, if not harmful, for us.[1] It is also a commonplace that emotions put us in a bad position to conduct inquiries and make sound decisions and judgments. Correlatively, it is a commonplace that cool rationality is the best standpoint for inquiry and knowledge, including evaluative inquiry and knowledge. Somewhat more modestly, it is something of a commonplace that unless emotions are under the control of reason, they are all too likely to get out of hand and interfere with our life, especially our intellectual life; and, correlatively, that if emotions are in control, that is not conducive to flourishing, especially not intellectual flourishing.[2]

We, however, think that these commonplaces are *false truisms*. Not only are they often mistaken, they also rest on and give expression to tendentious views of both emotions and cool rationality. They are part and parcel of philosophers' overvaluation of rationality – which, in psychoanalytic terms, is an *idealization* of rationality. As is so often the case with idealizations, this one involves serious interrelated misunderstandings about what is idealized – in this case, rationality – and also about what is split off and demonized or is simply not included in the idealization – in this case, emotions.

To see this, let us turn to those commonplaces about reason and emotion. They invite us to compare the usefulness and dangers of reason and emotions. But these comparisons had better not be based on an attempt to count the number of errors each might or has engendered, conjoined with an attempt to evaluate the seriousness of the various errors, or the proportion of errors to what is correct when each is in play, or some function of the number, proportion, and seriousness.

The reason we warn against making comparisons is not that they are exceedingly complex. Complexity does not stop theorists from making meaningful and reasoned claims about, say, the comparative dangers of influenza, breast cancer, and AIDS. These comparisons involve complex balancing of such facts as how common each disease is, the proportion of those afflicted who die or are seriously debilitated, the age distribution of the diseases, profiles of typical sufferers, the courses of the diseases, how the

---

[1] See Thomas Hurka, *Perfectionism* (New York: Oxford University Press, 1993), and Stocker, "Some Comments on *Perfectionism*," *Ethics,* 105 (1995) 386–400. Thanks are owed to Jonathan Adler, Samuel Levey, and Laurence Thomas for discussion.
[2] Thanks are owed to Graeme Marshall for these suggestions.

diseases are contracted and how they can be avoided, the cure or prevention rate per unit of time and money.

But when it comes to reason and emotion and their comparative dangers, it is at best fanciful to think that we have much, if any, idea how we might even start making assessments. To be sure, some emotions are dangerous, for, say, social or personal life or for intellectual or other work. But cool rationality, too, can often be dangerous and is often enough implicated in serious errors of rationality, knowledge, evaluation, and decision making. Cool beliefs and views are frequently mistaken and misleading, as are instances of cool reasoning about what the facts are, how to gather and appreciate additional facts, what to do, and how to decide what to do. As William Brennan, former Justice of the United States Supreme Court, says:

The framers [of the United States Constitution] operated within a political and moral universe that had experienced arbitrary passion as the greatest affront to the dignity of the citizen. . . . In our own time, attention to experience may signal that the greatest threat is formal reason severed from the insights of passion.[3]

Perhaps then, the commonplace should be understood as holding that emotions are typically, or too often, dangerous, but that only some instances of cool rationality are. Or perhaps it should be understood as holding that cool belief and cool rationality are not dangerous when, as is possible, the facts and procedures they involve are correct; but that emotions are always likely to be dangerous. Put in terms of people, the claim might be that inquirers who are emotional are likely to go wrong; that their being emotional typically raises questions about their reliability; but that coolly rational inquirers need not go wrong and do not, as such, raise questions about their reliability.

Here we might be reminded of the ways people's personalities and preoccupations can influence their emotions, and whatever is in turn influenced by those emotions. Various of these ways will be discussed later. For present purposes, it is enough to note the ways angry or self-pitying people are all too likely to be preoccupied by their own grievances and their own status, to be too harsh on others' views, especially views of those they feel have wronged them. These emotions and emotional states are, in short, moodlike: they seek out and collect, even create, sustaining or concordant

---

3 "Reason, Passion, and 'The Progress of the Law'," *Cardozo Law Review*, 10 (1988) 3–23, p. 17; quoted in Eugene Garver, *Aristotle's Rhetoric: An Art of Character* (Chicago: University of Chicago Press, 1994), p. 105.

facts (or "facts"), which they then use to justify and sustain that emotion, which then leads to further seeking, collecting, creating, and coloring.

Put in a related way, emotions can have a life of their own. When people are angry, especially when caught up in and controlled by anger, they are all too likely to think, feel, and act in certain distinctive ways: that is, angry ways. Such angry people are not just people who, as it happens, are angry but are in all other ways just as they would be were they not angry. They do not just feel, think, and act *with* anger, they feel, think, and act *from* and *because of* anger.

It is, however, tendentious to use these claims to show that emotions are more dangerous than cool rationality. First, these claims use emotions that mislead or overwhelm us, perhaps even emotional mountains or canyons, as their paradigm of emotions. But not all emotions, and certainly not all typical emotions, are like this.

These claims are also tendentious about rationality. To say the least, they express an exceptionally optimistic trust in rationality. Here we would do well to remember that there are many different cognitive personalities, styles, preoccupations, and indeed many different sorts of rational lives or lives of rationality. At least some, perhaps many, of these different cognitive personalities, styles, preoccupations, and lives can be cognitively harmful. To name only a few of these: undue credulity or undue skepticism;[4] undue acceptance or undue rejection of tradition and authority; undue acceptance or undue rejection of traditional ways of working with or acquiring data. In addition, there are dangers of coolly misestimating the importance of, or the evidence for or probability of, both particular and general beliefs and theories. There are also dangers of coolly working with coolly held mistaken beliefs and theories – ranging from more ordinary ones, such as phlogiston theory in the 1800s, to extraordinary ones, such as holding in the late 1900s that the universe was created only 200 years ago. The same also holds for coolly held mistaken theories, techniques, beliefs about procedures.

In all of these and still other sorts of cases, cool rationality can get out of hand. If control is what would help us avoid such getting out of hand, then just as emotions are supposed to need control, cool rationality, too, needs to be controlled.

It has been replied to us that these and the other problems and dangers of facts and rationality are really not aspects of rationality, but only of

---

4 See Jonathan Adler, "Testimony, Trust, Knowing," *Journal of Philosophy*, 91 (1994) 264–275.

deformed or distorted rationality, or even irrationality. However, this helps sustain our charge of tendentiousness by showing that the comparison between emotions and cool rationality starts off by understanding cool rationality as rationality that is not only cool, but is also cognitively accurate and beneficial. This complements its choice of cognitively disruptive and harmful emotions.

Its comparison, then, is not between emotions and rationality, but between cognitively disruptive emotions or forms of emotionality and cognitively beneficial rationality. Rather than investigating the comparative dangers and usefulness of emotions and rationality for, say, cognitive enterprises, it starts off by thinking well of cool rationality and poorly of emotionality. This colors its reasoning, suggests its examples, and leads it to find or create sustaining facts. It is no wonder that it reaches the conclusion it does, which is hardly any different from its starting point.

We want to show in a related, somewhat different way how emotions are improperly stigmatized and come to get "a bum rap." To do this we will examine such admonitions as "Don't be emotional" or "You are being emotional." These are often used as warnings or objections against being too boisterous, loud, and exuberant. As such, they express worries about taste, manners, and modes of self-presentation: how, for example, philosophers and other intellectuals should feel and should behave. Putting the matter in terms of stereotypes of European character, we could here think about preferences for what is cool, unflappable, northern over what is hot, excited, southern. We can see how some find emotionality distasteful, but we cannot see any connection between that, or between emotionality itself, and intellectual error and danger.

These admonitions can also be used to say that on account of emotions one has gone astray or is running the risk of going astray. The fact that we do issue such admonitions, and as frequently as we do, is some evidence that emotions are thought of as dangerous. And we do agree that our use of those admonitions may show what we think about emotions. But if these admonitions do show this, a closer look at them will also show that we are mistaken in what we think. That closer look will show that those admonitions express an already formed complaint, a complaint that is expressed by invoking emotionality, not a complaint that is grounded by faults of emotionality. That look will show that 'emotional' is used because the activity is independently thought bad: it is not thought bad because it is emotional.

Our diagnosis has two main parts. The first has to do with the lack of any intrinsic and common feature of acts of *going astray*. 'Going astray' is to be understood in terms of going away from and interfering with the goal that *happens* to be the goal at hand, or that should be at hand. We say "happens" to call attention to the fact that although it is the goal at hand, one could have another goal. The other goal that interferes with what happens to be the goal at hand can in other circumstances – say, with other desires – be the goal that would then happen to be the one at hand. If that other goal is the one at hand, the first goal can interfere with it, and pursuing it might then be warned against, by telling the agent not to be emotional. This is part of our account of what "Don't be emotional" means.

Another part of our argument is that emotionality does not have much, if anything, to do with the act that happens to be the act of going astray. Nothing having to do with emotions and emotionality distinguishes what is going astray from what is not. Emotions can play the very same roles in regard to the act of *not* going astray, as they do in regard to the act of going astray. No matter which of these acts is done, emotions help in the very same ways to make the act attractive, and they enter in the very same ways into desires and motives for doing the act.

This is not to deny all differences, and in fact there is this difference: when one pursues a goal that is or should be at hand, and does so on account of emotions, that does not get *called* 'being emotional'. But, as just said, the reason for this is not that emotions play no role in making the act attractive or in making up the motive for doing it. They clearly can play such roles. The reason, rather, is that when things go as they should, that just does *not get called* 'being emotional'. But when things go awry – and when, as is usual, there are emotions involved – that may well be *called* 'being emotional'. Something's being emotional does not account for its going awry, but going awry does account for its being *called* 'being emotional'.

Put in terms of our admonition "Don't be emotional," this is to say that this is a warning, perhaps even an epithet, that matters are going awry. But the warning is not justified by the presence, much less by the role, of emotions. Rather, emotionality is cited as a warning and epithet because things have gone awry or are likely to do so. Our claim, then, is that "Don't be emotional" involves a claim about what the goal at hand is or should be; a warning or complaint that some other and interfering goal is or is likely to be pursued; and a claim that emotions are among the motives and attractions for pursuing this latter goal.

For an illustration of what we mean, consider the case where one brother is buying out another brother's share in a company they have long owned together. The buyer's advisor may recommend making a certain offer: somewhat less than he is willing to pay, but not so much less as one might offer a stranger. We can easily imagine the buyer replying to the advisor,

But that will let him sell the company at current prices, without making him pay for his having made me pass up a better offer several years back, when I wanted to sell the company. It will simply be another time that he has gotten his way with me, as he has ever since we were boys.

To this, the advisor might reply,

> You're getting emotional. You asked me to help you buy the company and I am telling you how to do that. But you keep bringing up personalities and past issues. You seem more interested in settling old grievances than you do in buying at all or in buying at a good price.

We can easily understand what the advisor is saying. The buyer is going astray and what leads him astray is emotional. But buying a company, or buying it at the right price, or not wasting one's money can all be emotional. And motives involving those emotions can be among the main motives for buying a company, or buying it at the right price, or for not wasting money. Companies, money, and not paying too much are hardly matters of indifference. Nor need they be any less emotional than settling grievances with relatives.

In these ways, then, there is no difference in emotionality between settling the grievances and buying a company at the right price. That is, there is no difference in the presence, intensity, or causal powers of the emotions involved. What distinguishes them is that, as understood by the advisor, the matter at hand is buying the company at the right price, not settling grievances. To be sure, getting caught up in the latter does distract from the former. But the reverse can also be true. Suppose, for a different case, that one brother is buying out the other brother precisely to get even with him – or, more grandly, to mete out justice – but gets caught up in the question of whether the company could be bought more cheaply. This too is a distraction from what is there the matter at hand; and if there is "too much" emotional involvement in not paying too much, he might be advised not to be distracted by letting emotions get in the way of the enterprise of settling scores.

Several additional points should be noted. "Don't get emotional about money" might sound odd much as "Don't get emotional about happiness" might sound odd. But this cannot be due to money or happiness not involving emotions. For of course they do. On our view, the oddness is due to the thought that it is always rational to be concerned to be careful with money or about happiness. To the extent that being concerned with them is rational, to be concerned with them will not be to go astray.

On this supposition, if money or happiness is one's goal, there will be no *being emotional* to warn or complain about. There will be no going astray in that there will be no other goal one should have instead. If "Don't be emotional" does require going astray – pursuing a goal that one should not be pursuing – then where money or happiness is the goal in question, there is no going astray. There can be some other goal that is interfered with by pursuing money or happiness. But if pursuing either goal is going astray, it will be pursuing that other goal. For if pursuing it does interfere with money or happiness, it should not be pursued.

This clearly allows, and may even depend on, there being emotions that involve money or happiness, and which lead to their pursuit rather than the pursuit of some other goal. But since pursuing money or happiness is not an act of going astray, it does not merit the epithet 'emotional' as that figures in "Don't be emotional."

It might be objected that we have put the case for money, and perhaps even about happiness, too strongly. After all there are many cultures, religions, philosophies that do not accord paramount importance to money or even happiness. From these standpoints, the objection proceeds, such admonitions as "You are getting emotional about money" or "You are getting emotional about happiness" do make perfectly good sense and are seen as having considerable force. And even in our culture, we recognize that some appeals to money are, at best, inappropriate. Here we might think of Mr. Collins's marriage proposal in *Pride and Prejudice,* couched in terms of how financially advantageous a marriage to him would be.[5]

But this is no objection to our claim. On the contrary. It helps show that in "Don't be emotional," 'emotional' is used as an epithet, characterizing what is not of proper concern and not to be pursued. For this objection gives us a way to think of money or happiness as something that, there and then, is not to be pursued. Further, it helps show that a concern gets called 'emotional' because it is not a proper concern, rather than not being a proper concern because it is emotional. We have already seen this. For we have already seen that what is distracting is called emotional, not because it is emotional but because it is distracting. And we have also seen both that something is distracting not because of what it, itself, is, but because of how it distracts from what is or should be the matter at hand; and also that what is or should be the matter at hand at one time can be a distraction from what is or should be the matter at hand at another time.

To bring this phase of the argument to a close, we want to emphasize that we, of course, agree that emotions can lead astray. Nonetheless, we reject the claim that this is what "Don't be emotional" shows. What has to be

---

5 This is discussed in Garver, *Aristotle's Rhetoric: An Art of Character,* pp. 286–287.

explained is how emotions came to get the bum rap: how emotions came to be identified with going astray and how emotionality came to be a term of disgrace.

Part of our answer consists in pointing out how we find these questions at best misleading, suggesting that there is something about *emotions* and *emotionality* that does this. Those last questions are structurally very similar to the issue about the epithet 'woman driver' and how women come to get the bum rap of driving poorly, and what is it about women that suits them for this. So far as we know, women drivers are not worse, or markedly worse, than men drivers; nor can acts or forms of bad driving be isolated that are wholly or largely peculiar to women; nor can acts or forms of good driving be isolated that are wholly or largely peculiar to men. Put epistemologically, we doubt that those who use 'woman driver' as an epithet have any evidence to the contrary.

So, the question is, How does 'woman driver' come to be an epithet? What is it about women drivers so that their category term becomes a term of disgrace? Our answer is that there is nothing about women drivers or women, but only something about "society's" views about women, that accounts for this. Correlatively, our answer about emotions is that there is nothing about emotions, but only "society's" views about emotions, that accounts for the use of 'emotional' as an epithet.

Much, if not all, of this might be agreed to for the generality of cases. But it might, nonetheless, be held that at least in intellectual matters, emotional concerns differ in kind from nonemotional ones. So, when we tell scientists not to be emotional, but to let the facts guide them, we are contrasting emotionally laden motives and goals, such as a desire for fame, with nonemotional ones, such as desire for truth. There is something to this, but far less than seems to meet the eye. (This will be discussed later in this and other chapters.)

To see this, we must examine cool rationality to see just how nonemotional it really is, and to see, also, whether cool reason, on its own, can have such dangers. The first asks about the extent to which cool reason and cool reasoning involve emotion – for example, the extent to which they are done from emotion. It also asks about the extent to which they are characterized by emotion and are even done with emotion.

It might be thought that we can give a quick proof that reason and reasoning are nonemotional by considering "Don't get rational about this." That – unlike its contrary "Don't get emotional about this" – is often something of a joke. It warns against becoming too cool and dry. And it does this in conjunction with warning that now is the time for emotionality, perhaps play and letting go, not for rational, perhaps discursive, thinking. Here we might think again of Mr. Collins's marriage proposal in *Pride and Prejudice,* extolling the financial advantages of marrying him. Or we might think of the centipede who had no trouble walking until it tried to explain how it managed all those legs. So understood, "Don't get rational about this" would serve to tell us that reason and reasoning have their limits and are not to be used everywhere. But in no way, it might be held, does it tell us that where they are to be used, they are lacking in any way. Thus, "Don't get rational about this" might be thought to support the claim that where the matter at hand is an intellectual matter, reason has no need of emotions.

But whether or not "Don't get rational about this" does have that implication, reason does need emotions. One way to start showing this would be to examine claims made by Plato in the *Phaedrus* (253 ff.) and the *Republic* (580 ff.) that reason has, and requires for its perfection, its own proper pleasures and desires, and thus, we might also say, its own proper emotions.

So too, we might consider some claims by Ernest Schachtel and Henry Krystal. As Schachtel writes,

there is no action without affect, to be sure not always an intense, dramatic affect as in an action of impulsive rage, but more usually a total, sometimes quite marked, sometimes very subtle and hardly noticeable mood, which nevertheless constitutes an essential background of every action.[6]

And as Krystal writes,

Affects are familiar to everyone. They are part of our experiences, so ordinary and common that they are equated with being human. . . . Yet their very universality and constant presence with us throughout life make them as unidentifiable as the prose in our speech.[7]

To the extent that Plato, Schachtel, and Krystal come even close to being right, the ideal of emotionless reason or emotionless reasoning is completely unrealizable. Indeed, it is so unrealizable that it must be summarily rejected. What should, instead, be investigated is why and how it could have been put forward as an ideal.

But even if Plato, Schachtel, and Krystal are far from being right, there is the argument of Chapter 2, section 3, that intellectual interest is an emo-

---

6 Schachtel, *Metamorphosis* (New York: Da Capo Press, 1984), p. 20.
7 Krystal, *Integration and Self-Healing: Affect, Trauma, and Alexithymia* (Hillsdale, N.J.: Analytic Press, 1988), p. xi.

tion. The question now would be whether, as proponents of cool reason might be taken as advocating, the absence of intellectual interest and related emotions aids rational enterprises.

Lack of interest or its manifestations come in different varieties. Here are some of them. A person can find a problem or a topic "dead," boring, or not worth attending to: "If I have to do another of these problem sets, run another of these tests, I will scream!" One can be in the combined intellectual–emotional state of "burn out." One can simply be indifferent to the issue. We find it hard to imagine how any of these forms or states of lack of interest could be thought better for intellectual progress in general or on a particular issue than well-modulated, properly directed, intellectual interest.[8]

One way to put this last point starts by agreeing with something just said: that people led by anger may well be in a bad position for good intellectual work. Their anger may all too likely find or create "sustaining" facts, thus distorting and hiding what is really the case. This can be generalized to put the danger of emotions for intellectual work: when emotions lead, facts and truth take a back seat, facts (or "facts") are found or created in light of, or even just to sustain, that emotion.

However, any number of cool, perhaps nonemotional, states, such as a cool intellectual commitment to a mistaken theory, can also have a disruptive life of their own. Not everyone committed to save a theory, come what may, is moved to do so by emotions, much less by disruptive emotions. But more can be said in favor of the role of emotions in and for good intellectual work than that some nonemotional states are also harmful, perhaps as harmful as emotions are, for intellectual work.

To start putting this "more," we could note what many of us know, perhaps all too well: that steely, cold anger can be excruciatingly accurate and relentless. And, indeed, this anger and even far hotter anger can also help us keep our mind on the task at hand, even when it is an intellectual task, such as proving the guilt or errors of the person who has so angered us.

Further, people who think and act with proper intellectual interest – interest that is properly directed and properly modulated – are likely to be in a good position for good intellectual work. Correlatively, those without such interest, such as those who are bored or burned out, are all too likely to

---

8 This is discussed in Stocker, "Intellectual Desire, Emotion, and Action," in Amélie O. Rorty, ed., *Explaining Emotions* (Berkeley: University of California Press, 1980). For a different approach, see John Deigh's review of Douglas Walton, *The Place of Emotion in Argument*, forthcoming in *Informal Logic*.

be in a bad position for good intellectual work. Thus, even from the point of view of intellectual work and enterprises of rationality, the contrast between emotionality and cool rationality is misleading and tendentious, if not spurious. Even if cool rationality is a feature of the best intellectual approaches, so is intellectual interest.

To be sure, this allows for contrasts between those intellectual approaches which involve emotions that enhance intellectual work and those which do not enhance such work, and perhaps detract from it. But in allowing for such contrasts, this also holds that emotions are involved in the best approaches to intellectual work. And this shows not only that, but also why, there can be no accurate contrast between approaches to intellectual work that involve emotions and the best approaches to intellectual work: the best approaches involve emotions.

We might take the claim that emotions are not useful for intellectual work, and are perhaps even dangerous for it, as a way of affirming allegiance to an ideal of the *primacy of rationality*. There may be a way to continue to affirm that ideal even while accepting many of the claims made here. For example, one could hold that emotions are epistemologically and cognitively useful, but only when they are *controlled* by rationality; and that the epistemologically and cognitively best rationality requires the *cooperation* of emotions, but only those that are controlled by reason.

However, it is unclear how this supposed primacy works, when the relations involved also require cooperation. Put in terms of people, rather than forms of mental activity, to the extent that I must cooperate with you and must secure your cooperation, I do not seem in control of you; indeed you could be seen as being in control of me or at least of our joint enterprises. And if we must both cooperate with each other, neither seems to control the other. (This is reminiscent of Hegel's master–slave dialectic and Sartre's claims about the impossibility of love.)

Perhaps, then, the claim about the relations between reason and emotion would be further modified to hold that for good intellectual work reason must play the *leading* role. Whether or not this is right, we see no need to pursue the matter. Our concern was to show that emotions are not always dangerous for good, or even the best, intellectual work, and more strongly that they are often important for such work. And we have shown that.

These various points can be put in a closely related way. Throughout this work, there is mention of the neurotic defense of *intellectualization:* briefly, retaining the thoughts, considered as proposition-like, while repressing or dissociating from the affect of emotions and emotionally charged situations.[9] We would point out that the very term 'intellectualization' gives important information about what it describes. Intellectualization involves dividing emotions, and other affectively laden elements, into two parts, one with affect and the other just with proposition-like content. It then involves repressing, dissociating from, or otherwise ignoring, those affective elements, while keeping accessible what is "of the intellect," the nonaffective content, such as thoughts as propositional content and the neutral, nonaffective, holding of this content. (On neutral holding, see Chapter 1, section 4.) It is, we might say, an attempt to avoid the emotional in favor of the intellectual.

One problem for intellectualization is that there are important emotional "aspects" of the intellect, such as intellectual interest and excitement. There are also the intellectual emotions, or emotions about intellectual matters. This is a problem because, as it shows, to think that one can avoid affect and emotion by "living in the intellect" requires an idealization of the intellect. Like other idealizations, this one idealizes and distorts its object, intellect. Correlatively, it involves a negative idealization, a demonization and distortion of its split-off "negative object," emotions and affectivity. Intellectualization, thus, involves an endorsement of a distorted intellect, thinking of intellect only in terms of intellectual, proposition-like content and not in terms of how the content is held and pursued. To put this in terms of our claim about the term 'intellectualization': this distortion is a motivated and indeed a principled distortion, giving expression to the fears, hopes, and goals that lead to, and characterize, intellectualization.

This requires only a slight modification to make a parallel point about philosophy. By somehow not seeing how important intellectual emotions are for good intellectual work including good work in philosophy, and indeed by not seeing that there are intellectual emotions, philosophers make it possible for themselves to hold and espouse an idealized and distorted view of reason and of philosophy. Correlatively, to hold that view of reason, it is essential not to see that there are intellectual emotions, much less how important they are for good philosophical and other intellectual work.

In something of the same vein, some people think that rationality destroys affectivity, by making nonaffective whatever it considers and understands. Some people welcome this, because it makes tolerable or safe

---

9 See, for example, Anna Freud, *The Ego and the Mechanisms of Defense* (London: Hogarth Press, 1937).

what was so troublesome. Some fear and dislike it, because they do not want to give up affectivity. And some merely take note of this "corrosive" effect of rationality. Various of these possibilities are suggested by the joke about two people about to part company: one says to the other, "This was the most horrible, disgusting, degrading, demeaning relationship I have ever had" and the other replies, "Don't spoil it by talking about it."

For our part, we do not think that rationality, as such, dries things out. We do think, however, that, as shown by intellectualization, it is often used to get rid of the affective. We also think that because ours is a culture that idealizes rationality and devalues emotion, many of us quite naturally recoil from the awareness and felt experience of emotions. Feelings we become aware of can be so alien and disruptive that we flee from the experience and devalue the feeling even further. Here, as with intellectualization, there is a destructive route starting with feelings, moving to a jarring emotional recognition of the feelings, and then to the use of rationality to be rid of feelings.

So far, then, we have seen two ways to understand, and to reject, the claim that the best forms of rationality are nonemotional. The first and "strict" way denies that any emotion or affect, intellectual or otherwise, is important for rationality and for the work and workings of rationality. The second, and perhaps more everyday and popular, way denies this role only to such emotions as those of anger and self-aggrandizement.

This latter, we think, is the understanding of 'emotionally' in admonitions to theorists not to be emotionally involved in their work. They are being admonished, for example, not to be swayed by the fact that a theory is *theirs,* or by the hope that if it is sustained they will be richly rewarded. This second understanding is silent about the existence and importance of intellectual emotion. And we see no reason why it cannot allow for such emotion.

In any case, our view is that the claim about the epistemological superiority of emotionless, cool rationality must be taken in terms of the looser understanding, not the strict one. Taking it this way captures the worry that emotional concerns outside the intellectual area might improperly affect intellectual work. Taking it this way avoids the need to deny what is undeniable: that there are intellectual emotions and that they are important for good intellectual work.

However, taking it this way also shows that the strict and categorical contrast between rationality and emotionality is misleading and tendentious. This complements our earlier argument that this contrast is tendentious in the ways it picks examples of both emotions and cool reason –

examples that seem chosen in order to show that emotions not controlled by reason are too likely to be pathological and dangerous, but that rationality is completely safe and needs no control.

This contrast loses all interest once its tendentiousness is seen. What then becomes interesting is why so many philosophers and others have used this contrast. Why have they not seen its tendentiousness? Why do they start with such a distrust of emotions and such a trust of cool rationality? Perhaps they think of emotions in terms of disruptive emotional mountains and canyons, and cool rationality in terms of cognitively accurate and beneficial rationality. But, once again, this simply poses the question of why they do this. These questions are especially relevant about philosophers who, with obvious and serious interest, devote so much time to diagnosing many and various cognitive errors.

Whatever the reason, the cognitive usefulness and importance of emotions have often not even been noticed, and generally have not been given enough attention. To help correct this, we will continue to argue that emotions are often useful and important, and even essential, for rationality, knowledge, value, and evaluation, and thus for being a person, indeed a rational person. In this chapter, we will argue that having certain emotions is often systematically connected with being epistemologically well placed to make good evaluative judgments; and more strongly, that not having certain emotions is often systematically connected with being epistemologically ill placed to make good judgments. As we have seen and will see further, the contrast between cool rationality and emotionality is, itself, misleading, if not spurious. But, to make our points, it will be useful to continue to use it.

One way to put the claim of this chapter is that people who lack emotions are not only cold – "unnervingly cold, indeed eerie"[10] – or uninvolved or distant, but also that they are also epistemologically ill placed to make evaluative judgments. Another way to put our claim is that for quite systematic reasons, emotionally hot, or at least emotionally warm, judgments are often epistemologically better than cool ones. There are correlative claims about acknowledgment and recognition of one's emotions and emotional lacks: those who are unaware of their emotions or of their emotional lacks will, therefore, be ill placed to see which values they hold and deploy, and how they hold and deploy these values in their judgments, decisions, or wherever. There is a corresponding more positive claim: those

---

10 David Charles, "Aristotle and Modern Realism," in Robert Heinaman, ed., *Aristotle and Moral Realism* (London: University College of London Press, 1995), p. 154.

who are aware of their emotions and emotional lacks are therefore not only better placed, but are well placed, to see which values they hold and deploy, and how they hold and deploy these values.[11]

Others have made such claims, too. We take Aristotle as making them in the *Rhetoric,* for example, when he argues that to secure an acquittal it is important to gain the jurors' friendliness toward a defendant by convincing them of his good character. We do not take Aristotle as simply telling how jurors think, and thus how they can be led or misled. He is also reminding us that belief in another person and acceptance of what that person says is properly proportioned to how trustworthy we find that person. This is a way of putting his claims that we should trust and act from good character and wisdom (*phronēsis*), not cleverness, and that trustworthiness runs in tandem with good character and wisdom. As he writes,

[There is persuasion] through character [*ēthos*] whenever the speech is spoken in a way to make the speaker worthy of credence [*axiopiston*] . . . in cases where there is not exact knowledge [*akribes*] but room for doubt . . . character is almost, so to speak, the controlling factor in persuasion.[12]

As Sartre similarly notes in his discussion of bad faith in *Being and Nothingness,* we are often epistemically lax in assessing views or people we like, and demanding in assessing views or people we dislike.

To judge on the basis of evidence offered by someone, you must assign weight to the evidence. One factor for this assignment is how trustworthy you find the person to be. The proper response to someone properly found trustworthy is, after all, trust; and to someone properly found untrustworthy, a lack of trust. And friendliness – both yours toward the person in question and your assessment of that person's general friendliness and "qualifications" for being a friend – are clearly important here. This is to say that to some extent, anyway, if a witness is of good character, trust and its attendant friendliness are proper. It also helps us see that without proper trust and friendliness, judgment will likely go astray and decisions are likely to be made badly.

In many different ways, various contemporary philosophers have also argued that emotions are important for evaluation. In "Freedom and Resentment," Strawson writes that "The existence of the general framework

---

11 Thanks are owed to the philosopher and psychoanalyst Ernest Wallwork for discussions of his work in progress on this issue.
12 *Rht* I.2, 1356a5–13. The connection between trust and character is stressed by Garver, *Aristotle's Rhetoric: The Art of Character,* ch. 5, especially pp. 146–148. The quotation appears on p. 176.

of attitudes is something we are given with the fact of human society."[13] As he argues, having and being the subject of reactive attitudes is central to being and being recognized as a person; and having shared reactive attitudes is central to being a community. Indeed, it is unclear what a human community that lacked reactive attitudes would be like, or even whether it would be possible. Moreover, having such attitudes is central to understanding much of evaluative importance, and much of importance for making evaluations, about people and communities.

In "Self-Interpreting Animals," Charles Taylor argues that the concepts essential to, and constitutive of, self-understanding are emotionally laden. To understand what it is for me to experience shame, we are referred to what "shows me up to be base, or to have some unavowable and degrading property, or to be dishonorable. In this account, however long we carry it on, . . . we cannot escape from these terms into an objective [nonemotional] account."[14]

W. D. Falk, a strong opponent of emotivism, also gives an account of value in terms of affectivity:

That something has the power to evoke favor on a true comprehension of what it is like [i.e., is good] would depend partly on what it is like and partly on the affectivity of those who experience it or contemplate it for what it is like. . . . Nothing could conceivably have value except for those who can love or hate.[15]

Later we will consider still other arguments made by John McDowell, Iris Murdoch, Lawrence Blum, Margaret Walker, and Martha Nussbaum.[16]

---

13 In Gary Watson, ed., *Free Will* (Oxford: Oxford University Press, 1982), p. 78.
14 *Human Agency and Language, Philosophical Papers,* volume 1, p. 55. We are grateful to Laurence Thomas for discussion here, especially on Strawson.
15 "Fact, Value and Non-natural Predication," in *Ought, Reasons, and Morality* (Ithaca, N.Y.: Cornell University Press, 1986), p. 120. See also Franz Brentano, *The Origin of Our Knowledge of Right and Wrong* (New York: Humanities Press, 1969).
16 McDowell, "Virtue and Reason," *Monist,* 62 (1979), 331–350; Murdoch, *The Sovereignty of Good* (London: Routledge and Kegan Paul, 1970); Blum, *Friendship, Altruism, and Morality* (London: Routledge and Kegan Paul, 1980), "Iris Murdoch and the Domain of the Moral," *Philosophical Studies,* 50 (1986) 343–368, and "Particularity and Responsiveness," in Jerome Kagan and Sharon Lamb, eds., *The Emergence of Morality in Young Children* (Chicago: University of Chicago Press, 1987); Walker, "Moral Understandings: Alternative 'Epistemology' for a Feminist Ethics," *Hypatia,* 4 (1989) 15–28, and "Morality and the Emotions: Getting Things Right," unpublished manuscript; and Nussbaum, *Love's Knowledge* (Oxford: Oxford University Press, 1990), and "Equity and Mercy," *Philosophy and Public Affairs,* 22 (1993) 83–125.

2 Psychoanalytic connections

Rather than examine these philosophical positions now, we want to turn to some claims made by various psychoanalysts. This is not an unmotivated choice on our part. One of the central tenets of psychoanalysis is that there are systematic connections between emotions and epistemology, especially evaluative epistemology.[17]

Let us start with some neuroses and neurotic formations, and their attendant distortions. As the psychoanalyst Anna Freud shows in *The Ego and the Mechanisms of Defense*, and as David Shapiro shows in *Neurotic Styles, Autonomy and Rigid Character,* and *Psychotherapy of Neurotic Character,* these have interconnected constitutive and typical forms of emotions and epistemic-evaluative distortions. Drawing on them and other work, we here list in brief form some very simple examples – examples of, at once, neurotic and also epistemic-evaluative distortions.

1. A depressed man who, suffused by feelings of not being good or lovable, for that reason consistently does not even notice the ways his marriage is overall a source of suffering for both him and his wife; and, indeed, when asked, sincerely claims that he is happy and that, generally, the marriage is going well.
2. A man in a manic state who feels invulnerable, denies his need of money, and gives away a considerable part of his savings.
3. A woman who because of grandiosity feels responsible for the well-being of the entire family to such an extent that she feels guilty for all unhappinesses suffered by her children or that occur between family members.
4. A man who was beaten as a child and now, identifying with the aggressor, thinks that physical violence is the proper way to settle family problems: for example, that his eight-year-old son is "asking for a beating" when disobedient. (Identification with the aggressor is discussed in Chapter 7, section 2.)
5. A woman who was sexually abused as a child, accepted her abuser's account that this was done to her because she was bad, and now continues to think and feel that she deserves whatever harm and ill fortune, especially bad treatment from her husband, that happen to her.

---

17 Of the numerous works on this, we have found the following especially useful: Anna Freud, *The Ego and the Mechanisms of Defense*; David Shapiro, *Neurotic Styles* (New York: Basic Books, 1965), *Autonomy and Rigid Character* (New York: Basic Books, 1981), *Psychotherapy of Neurotic Character* (New York: Basic Books, 1989); Harry Guntrip, *Schizoid Phenomena, Object Relations, and the Self* (New York: International Universities Press, 1969); Joyce McDougall, *Theaters of the Mind: Illusion and Truth on the Psychoanalytic Stage* (New York: Brunner Mazel, 1991), especially ch. 7, "Reflections on Affect: A Psychoanalytic View of Alexithymia"; and also Henry Krystal, "Aspects of Affect Theory," *Bulletin of the Menninger Clinic*, 41 (1977) 1–26, "Trauma and Affect," *Psychoanalytic Study of the Child*, 36 (1978) 81–116, and "The Hedonic Element in Affectivity," *Annual of Psychoanalysis*, 9 (1981) 93–113, all collected in his *Integration and Self-healing: Affect, Trauma, and Alexithymia*.

6. The somewhat paranoid person who often sees and feels the world as beyond her control, and pictures and feels herself as a victim of others and of circumstance; and sees other people's not liking what she likes as showing slighting contempt or unconcern for her, rather than different tastes.
7. A man who is overinvolved, perhaps enmeshed, with his daughter, who tells him as they are setting off on a car trip with a friend of hers that she has decided not to bring her music tapes because her friend does not like the music; he then gets angry at the friend, condemning her presumptuousness and her musical tastes, rather than even noting, much less being pleased at, how considerate his daughter is. (Enmeshment is discussed in section 4.)
8. A woman who intellectualizes, forgetting how difficult it is to spend time with her parents, and thus subjects herself and her family to unpleasant, anxiety-filled visits.
9. The man described by the psychoanalyst Clara M. Thompson, who has a "markedly detached personality" and is "unaware of any personal emotional contact with other human beings. He is an onlooker at life,"[18] who constantly misinterprets and misunderstands others, finding them hostile or indifferent when they are not, and judges and acts accordingly.
10. People who get intellectually fussy and demanding and thus manage to see no need to deal seriously with devastating issues: for example, people who focus on the supposed exaggeration of how many United States women in general, or while university students, have been raped; and who spend a lot of time arguing, often vehemently, "just for the sake of accuracy" that it is only about 5 or 10 percent rather than 25 percent, instead of, or also, thinking how serious an epidemic even the lowest number shows and what it also shows about relations between men and women.

We have already encountered other examples, and still others will be given. What is important for us about these examples is why so naturally, even if not inevitably, the people they describe fail to notice important values and evaluative considerations, fail to make accurate assessments, misunderstand themselves and others, have inappropriate emotions, act poorly, if not wrongly.

Turning to far more serious disorders, Harry Guntrip and Joyce McDougall graphically describe two extreme ways of being affectless: being schizoid and being alexithymic. We quote at length to bring out various ways affectlessness is interconnected with moral epistemology.

In *Schizoid Phenomena, Object Relations, and the Self,* Guntrip writes, "the ego of the schizoid person in consciousness and in the outer world is delibidinized and feels no interest in objects" (p. 30). And also,

---

[18] "Development of Awareness of Transference in a Markedly Detached Personality," ch. 13 of *Interpersonal Psychoanalysis: The Selected Papers of Clara M. Thompson,* ed. Maurice R. Green (New York: Basic Books, 1964), p. 111. Originally published with the same title in *International Journal of Psycho-Analysis,* 19 (1938) 299–309.

This state of emotional apathy, of not suffering any feeling, excitement or enthusiasm, not experiencing either affection or anger, can be very successfully masked. If feeling is repressed, it is often possible to build up a kind of mechanized, robot personality. The ego that operates consciously becomes more a system than a person, a trained and disciplined instrument for "doing the right and necessary thing" without any real feeling entering in. Fairbairn made the highly important distinction between "helping people without feeling" and "love." Duty rather than affection becomes the key word. (pp. 37–38)

And finally, "As a result of this lack of feeling, schizoid people can be cynical, callous, and cruel, having no sensitive appreciation of the way they hurt other people" (p. 44). (The similarity between what Guntrip and Falk say is striking.)

A significant portion of McDougall's *Theaters of the Mind: Illusion and Truth on the Psychoanalytic Stage* is devoted to alexithymia – literally, lacking words for emotions and, less literally, being unable to recognize that one is there and then having emotions or which emotions one is having. Leading up to this discussion, she writes,

> Freud came to refer to the *repression* of ideas and the *suppression* of affects. These metaphors suggest two quite different mental processes: ideas are said to be *pushed back* from consciousness and affects to be *squashed out* of the psyche.
>   Where does affect go when it is rejected from the consciousness of the person in whom it has, if only momentarily, been mobilized? Freud provided a partial clue to the fate of unavailable affects. In *Studies on Hysteria* (Breuer and Freud 1895) as well as the papers on *Repression* (Freud 1915) and *The Unconscious* (1915), he speaks of the autonomous quality of affects and of their subsequent "transformations." The latter falls into three categories: the conversion of affects into hysterical symptoms; the displacement of an affect from its original representation onto another representation or set of representations, as in obsessional neurosis; and the transformation expressed in the actual neuroses, that is, anxiety neurosis, neurasthenia, and hypochondria.
>   . . . It appears to me that we might also posit other transformations of the vicissitudes of affective experience. Certain people are capable of disavowing their affective experience, or segments of it, in such a way that it is radically repudiated or foreclosed from consciousness. . . .[19]

Of people who are alexithymic, McDougall writes, "Instead of mentally elaborating their emotional states, they tended to discharge their feelings . . . often in inappropriate ways: through disputes, ill considered decisions, or a series of accidents" (p. 155). And also, "It is evident . . . that an inability

---

19 *Theaters of the Mind: Illusion and Truth on the Psychoanalytic Stage*, pp. 152–153, emphases in original. The works by Freud, including *Studies on Hysteria*, by Freud and Josef Breuer, are found in *The Standard Edition of the Complete Psychological Works of Sigmund Freud*, ed. James Strachey (London: Hogarth Press, 1986). *Studies on Hysteria* was also published on its own (New York: Basic Books, 1957).

to capture and become aware of one's own emotional experience must be accompanied by an equally great difficulty in understanding other people's emotional states and wishes" (p. 160).

Suggesting a comparison between alexithymics and psychotics, including schizophrenics, she says:

> This comparison may seem incongruous: few individuals appear more bizarre in public than those dominated by psychotic thought processes, while few seem so well adapted to external reality, and to comply so readily with what the world demands, as those who suffer from alexithymic . . . symptoms. The latter have created a *false self-adaptation* to others and this wall of pseudonormality enables them to face the world in spite of the grave inner distress concerning contact with others. (p. 167, emphasis in original)

And also,

> Psychotics attribute to others their overwhelming affective pain and intolerable anxiety and proceed to create a neoreality in order to make continued existence tolerable and understandable. With the same aim in mind, alexithymics attack their psychological capacity to capture affect and use it for thought or as a signal to themselves. But instead of creating a neoreality, they simply drain external reality and object relationships of their meaning. (p. 168)

At these extremes of affective pathology, there are clear, and clearly disastrous, connections between lack of emotions and affectlessness and evaluative epistemology. This holds especially in regard to the values involved in the experiences and relations that these very unfortunate people find so difficult.

To summarize some points discussed here: schizoids and alexithymics have great difficulties in understanding other people, in seeing and appreciating the value and values of other people, and thus the evaluative nature of their own situations and acts especially insofar as these involve other people. Second, schizoids and alexithymics lack a relationship with others because they lack an internal model based on emotional identification with others. They are deprived of the informative feedback from that model and they are painfully aware of their lack of information and relationship. Third, to the extent that alexithymics, and perhaps schizoids, are unable to recognize and differentiate their emotions, they are cut off from important sources of knowledge of what they value and how they value what they value.

Before continuing, we must stress that our claim here is not that an inability to have and know one's own emotions always impedes, much less always precludes, knowledge of other people and their emotions. As the psychoanalyst Otto Kernberg writes in "Factors in the Treatment of Narcissistic Personalities,"[20] "[people with] obsessive personalities . . . may develop a surprising understanding of emotional depth in others while being apparently so 'cold' themselves." And as David Shapiro writes in *Neurotic Styles,* describing how a psychopath sized up and manipulated a prison psychologist, "His awareness and his interest [in the prison psychologist] were probably limited essentially to what was immediately relevant to his own current requirements, but it was sensitive awareness nonetheless" (p. 153). Indeed, this sensitive awareness allowed him to manipulate others with remarkable success.

Our claim, then, is not that these emotional inabilities are always linked with evaluative-epistemological inabilities. Our claim is only – but this is a very important 'only' – that for systematic reasons, these inabilities often, if not typically, go hand in hand, the one explaining the other, or both having a common explanation.

3   Unhealthy philosophical accounts of emotions

In addition to suggesting deep connections between emotions and evaluative knowledge, these psychoanalytic claims about affectlessness and defects of affect raise very serious questions about those affectless philosophical accounts of emotions, discussed in Chapter 1. It was shown there that those accounts fail because they are affectless. But now, having read those psychoanalysts, we must ask what led so many recent philosophers to offer such affectless accounts of emotions. This, we now see, is to ask what led them to present as conceptually true of people and emotions what typifies various neuroses, such as intellectualization, and various borderline conditions and psychoses, such as dissociation, schizoid states, or alexithymia.

There is a simple, but to our mind unsatisfying, answer to this. It is that Pitcher and other philosophers influenced by Wittgenstein were opposed to treating emotions as mental entities, especially private mental entities. And Solomon and other philosophers influenced by Sartre were opposed to treating affectivity as bodily, and wanted to treat it as having cognitively accessible and cognitively assessable meaning.

We find this answer unsatisfying because it simply raises the same question once again, but now about feelings: what led philosophers to misunderstand feelings to such an extent? Why has it been thought that unless feelings are understood just in terms of beliefs, desires, and values, they must

---

[20] *Journal of the American Psychoanalytic Association,* 18 (1970) 51–85, reprinted in Andrew P. Morrison, ed., *Essential Papers on Narcissism* (New York: New York University Press, 1986). This quotation is from the latter, p. 218.

be understood as private entities or as bodily? Perhaps this is simply a philosophical mistake, a failure of philosophical imagination.

Addressing these issues, Graeme Marshall wrote to us that,

> often two quite different issues have been confused by those [followers of Wittgenstein and Ryle] who would make the content claim. One concerns the meaning of emotion words and the other the state one is in when one is correctly described by such words. Wittgenstein for one didn't think for a moment that we didn't *feel* hope, anger, etc.; he only thought that *what* we feel, as distinct from *that* we feel, could not be part of the meaning of the words in question. The states themselves, unlike their perhaps primitive expressions, are not sufficiently on the surface for them to contribute to what we know when we know the meaning of the words. But to deny them meaning-content is not to deny them psychological-content. . . . [So too for Ryle,] though he drifts further in the direction of behaviorism.

Marshall may well be right. If he is, we may need an account of how so many philosophers so misunderstood Wittgenstein and Ryle. Whether or not Marshall is right, we may be able to explain those misunderstandings, and also give an explanation of the attraction of the content claim, by noting that the content claim is in remarkable agreement with our philosophical mistrust of emotions and feelings. To repeat, this is a mistrust that goes so far as having less trust in emotions than in what is central to dissociation and intellectualization, and even alexithymic and schizoid conditions.

This mistrust, we might note, is found not only in philosophy. It is found even in psychoanalysis, of all places. We are thinking here of the view of many early psychoanalysts that *countertransference* – the analyst's emotional reaction to the analysand – interfered with the analysis. It was held that these emotional reactions show only problems of the analyst – typically, unresolved conflicts indicating the analyst's need of further analysis – rather than an accurate, informed, and informative reaction to the patient. The ideal analyst was seen as a blank screen and emotionally detached, not an emotionally engaged person.[21]

Some claims of Nancy Chodorow may be useful in seeing how contemporary philosophers' mistrust of emotions expresses a deep aspect of our culture. She argues that in our culture the moral world of boys, and subse-

---

21 Two important and originating works on this topic are D. W. Winnicott, "Countertransference," *British Journal of Medical Psychology*, 33 (1960) 17–21, reprinted in his *The Maturational Processes and the Facilitating Environment* (London: Hogarth Press, 1965), and Heinrich Racker, *Transference and Countertransference* (New York: International Universities Press, 1968). See also Michael Gorkin, *The Uses of Countertransference* (Northvale, N.J.: Jason Aronson, 1987) for a useful discussion and bibliography.

quently men, tends to be at once and for the same reasons lacking in affect and also abstract, categorical, and positional:

> For boys, identification processes and masculine role learning are not likely to be embedded in relationships with their fathers or men but rather to involve the denial of affective relationship to their mothers. These processes tend to be more role-defined and cultural, to consist in abstract or categorical role learning rather than in personal identification.[22]

And,

> Men, moreover, do not define themselves in relationship and have come to suppress relational capacities and repress relational needs. This prepares them to participate in the affect-denying world of alienated work. (p. 207)

Chodorow raises many issues, such as the connections between relational, that is, interpersonal capacities and emotions; and also about the role and priority of these emotions. For even if men in our society are typically deficient in interpersonal emotions, they are not deficient in all emotions and emotional engagements, such as those concerning sports and professional success.[23] Nor are men in our society typically deficient in intellectual interest and excitement. But, for the moment, we will not pursue these issues. Nor will we discuss how easy it is to parody or mischaracterize – or, what may be worse, correctly characterize – certain ethical views by showing how these views incorporate into their associated philosophical accounts of thought and feeling intellectualizing, or dissociative, or alexithymic, or schizoid forms of thought and feeling.

4 Ordinary ways good emotions are important for good evaluations

In this section, we will show some common, everyday, and well-known ways in which features of our emotional life, especially our not having emotions, are intertwined with our being epistemologically ill placed to make good evaluative judgments. To this end, let us return to Pitcher's man P who hopes or does not hope that the visitor will come.

We can start by looking at someone whose "having of the emotion" is correctly described by one of the affectless accounts of emotions mentioned earlier. We will focus on someone whose "hoping that she will come" is correctly characterized by Pitcher:

---

22 *The Reproduction of Mothering* (Berkeley: University of California Press, 1978), p. 177.
23 Thanks are owed to Laurence Thomas for discussion here.

If P hopes that she will come today, he simply believes that she might come and considers that her coming would be a good thing. He may also experience one or more sensations, but he need not; and even if he does it is doubtful that they will be part of his *hope*.[24]

Because this characterization does not include affect, despite knowing that it is satisfied, we still do not know whether P hopes that she will come. Indeed, if the full, relevant description of P is given by "P thinks that she might come and that her coming would be a good thing," then, because P lacks affect, P does not hope that she will come. P's thinking that she might come and that this would be good need not "move" P to care whether or not she comes, nor be pleased by the thought of her coming -- in short, need not move P to hope that she does.

These thoughts need not move P to hope that she will come if P is not concerned with her coming, for example, because as P sees and feels matters, it is not his business whether she comes or not. Here we might imagine that P has been told by neighbors that someone might be coming to visit them and that this will be good. Why, unless moved by concern for them, must P hope that she does come? Why must he take up any attitude toward his neighbors, even on their behalf?

Let us change the story and say explicitly that P is involved with the coming of this person, since she is coming to visit someone in his family. Even so, despite thinking that she might come and that it would be good if she does, he still might not hope she does. Explanations for this are readily available: P is physically or emotionally tired, worn out; P has lost hope in good things happening; he does not like her; he is ambivalent about her coming; although thinking it overall good if she comes, her coming fits poorly with what he would really like to do: spend time alone; he thinks it would be good for the family if she came, but would be "too much" for him; he is suffering from depression; he is bitter at the world; he has little heart for company now.

These are just some nonexclusive and nonexhaustive reasons why, despite satisfying the proposition-like content-account of hoping, P does not hope that she will come. It should be noted that only some of these reasons have to do with P's being affectively flat or more or less affectless. Others have to do with P's having the wrong sort of affect. As this should help make clear, our concern is with how various sorts of emotional problems, not just lack of affect, are connected with epistemological problems.

---

24 "Emotion," *Mind*, 74 (1965) 326–346, p. 338, emphasis in original.

If P is suffering any of these emotional problems, then for systematic reasons, he may well be – indeed, he is likely to be – ill placed to make evaluations, including about her coming. One explanation, mentioned already, of P's not hoping that she will come is that P is only an acquaintance of the people she is coming to visit. And being such a neighbor typically involves not being well positioned to see various evaluatively important details. This can be easily seen if we consider the case where P, despite being only a neighbor, does hope that their visitor will come.

Our case has it that P is told by his neighbors that a visitor may be coming to visit them, and that it would be good if she does. We will suppose that P does not merely say, sincerely and politely, "I do hope for your sake that she comes"; "Well then, let us hope that she does come"; or even "I do hope she comes." Rather, P has a hope that "puts" him right into that family. This is a hope that expresses his having obtruded into the family. This is a hope such that if the visitor does not come, P, too, can sincerely say that what he had hoped for, too, did not come about; perhaps that his hopes were not satisfied, even that they were dashed.

Here we might compare the assumptions – perhaps the presumptions and presumptuousness – of a man who says to a neighboring woman he knows only by sight, "You know, when I saw you go out last night with that person, I was afraid for you." A gentle, friendly reply might be, "Thank you for caring about me." A somewhat less gentle reply, by way of reproof perhaps, might be "I didn't know you cared so much for me." In certain cases, the rebuffing and chastising, "Who are you to care for me, to occupy yourself with me, to judge me and my situation?" might also be completely justified.

Some hopings, then, suggest that P has obtruded himself into the affairs of his neighbors, and has concerned or engaged himself with a family with which he has only a nodding acquaintance. We would draw three conclusions from these cases. First, that P believes that a visitor might come and that it would be good if she did is not sufficient to guarantee that P hopes she comes. Second, this may be a good thing, since it may well be wrong for P to hope that she comes. The third conclusion is explicitly epistemological. It concerns the epistemological state of P who hopes improperly. We do not think it is simply harsh and moralistic to think that the way he obtrudes into others' affairs, without being actively involved with them, suggests a willingness to make judgments without knowing the facts.

Somewhat similar situations of improper care also arise in families and other close relations. Spouses and other family members may be *enmeshed* with each other: that is, boundaries between them are too porous or nonexistent, each is too caught up in the life of the other, too involved and overly concerned with that person. That people are enmeshed, and how enmeshment is constituted by particular sorts of moral concern, attention, and understanding, explain how such people are typically epistemologically ill-placed or ill-equipped to make good evaluative judgments of their situations.[25]

Here, as earlier, our point is not just a moral point: here, that enmeshing people intrude into, even violate, others' privacy and autonomy. But this moral point is of some use in securing our epistemological claim. It is reasonable to wonder whether those enmeshing people's moral judgment about other people can be trusted, since they evidently lack good moral judgment about others' privacy and autonomy.

To be sure, this question can be answered in favor of such people and their judgment. A person can be lacking in one area of moral judgment without being lacking in all, and one's moral-epistemic judgment may be good even where one's behavior belies this. Our epistemological claim could, thus, use further support. We will not offer – and, for reasons that will be sketched, we do not think there could be – an argument showing a necessary connection between the moral failure of being improperly concerned with others' affairs and making moral-epistemological errors about those affairs. But we do have some more particular considerations, having to do with characteristics of those who are enmeshed or otherwise over-concerned with others.

Frequently, even typically and characteristically, enmeshment involves a failure of empathy at a deep evaluative level. Such failure is consistent with a full and fine-grained knowledge of the facts. It is a failure to appreciate the moral-emotional meaning of these facts. It is a failure to appreciate them from the standpoint of the other, to appreciate them in the way they are experienced by the other. Instead of appreciating them that way, the enmeshing person interposes or imposes a form of appreciation and evaluation something like "In those circumstances, *I* would be ———," or "That would make *me* feel ———," or "The *normal* way to feel here is ———" and then to take those meanings and ways of feeling as how it is or should be for that person.

Here we might look at a parent who is embarrassed not only by, but also for, a child who, as the parent sees it, fails to marry or to pursue a good profession, or in some other way violates family norms. To make the case

---

25 Thanks are owed to Ernest Wallwork for many of the following points about enmeshment and for other help with this work.

clearer, we would add that as is obvious – even if the parent refuses to see it – the child is fully and reflectively content with that part of life. Often, the enmeshing person acts and thinks as if the enmeshed-upon person had not made those contrary judgments and had those contrary experiences.

This failure may be clearest in regard to the enmeshment itself. The enmeshing person often, even typically, fails to see how annoyed, even resentful, the enmeshed-upon person finds the intrusiveness and the intrusions. Indeed, the enmeshing person may often believe that both the intrusiveness and intrusions – of course, not seen as such – are perfectly proper and even welcomed by the other: "Of course my children want to know what I think; I am their parent, after all." Even if the enmeshing person accurately sees how the other person feels, that feeling is, somehow, not taken seriously, not taken as giving a "proper," "correct," or "adequate" way to feel, or perhaps not even as how that person *really* feels.

Enmeshment, then, involves a failure to take the other person seriously: that is, seriously as another and separate person, who has independent and separate forms of judgment, appreciation, and feeling. We should here note that these failures – which are importantly other-regarding – are like some self-regarding failures characteristic of failures or lack of self-respect: for example, not taking oneself seriously as a moral agent, turning over to others the power to make judgments, even about how things are for oneself.

If these brief descriptions of enmeshment are right, we see how the enmeshing person's moral failure of not respecting privacy and autonomy is deeply connected with moral-epistemological failures – so too, for the moral and moral-epistemic failures characteristic of lack of self-respect.

Our claim here is not that there must always be these connections. It is certainly possible to violate another's autonomy and privacy in systematic ways and yet, in moral-epistemic ways, take them seriously as separate people. Indeed, this is necessary to do really well as a scam artist or police interrogator. And even when we restrict attention to those who improperly judge for or about others, enmeshment with its dual moral and moral-epistemic failures is not the only explanation. The man who improperly cared for his neighbor need not be enmeshed with her. The person who obtrudes into his neighbors' lives by hoping with them need not be enmeshed with them. So too, political, religious, or family leaders who would arrogate moral decisions to themselves need not be enmeshed with those they would control.

So, our claim is not that where there are moral failures, like invasion of privacy and obtruding into others' affairs, there must also be moral-epistemic failures. Nor is our claim that where there is such invasion or obtruding, there is always enmeshment. Our claim is that, as in the case of enmeshment, these moral failures are often deeply and systematically connected with moral-epistemic failures.

Let us move from these more *inter*personal defects to more *intra*personal ones. We start with a summary of some of the typical and noncontroversial reasons, mentioned previously, why P might not hope that the visitor comes, despite thinking that she might and that it would be a good thing if she does: P is physically or emotionally tired; P does not like her; P is ambivalent about her coming; P wants to be alone; P is depressed or bitter. These "emotion-defeating" conditions often, even typically, put us in poor evaluative-epistemological positions. After all, tiredness often, perhaps typically, decreases one's perceptiveness, as do ambivalence, depression, and bitterness.

It should be clear that, instead of describing generalities holding for all people, we are here describing generalities about certain sorts of people, or only certain sorts of people in certain sorts of conditions. Bitterness and ambivalence can dull attentiveness and perceptiveness. But they can do just the reverse. Indeed, they do the reverse for many people given to resentment or revenge – as some people are quite generally, and as many people are from time to time. And those who suffer from borderline personality conditions are famous for their ability, especially when motivated by hate, to know just how to wound others.[26]

So too, fear and anxiety can engender epistemic failures. But they can also engender epistemic success. Some people fail under stress because they cannot think clearly when afraid or anxious. But others respond well to stress, and some even need it to pay attention and succeed. For some people at certain times, danger and need can inhibit accuracy. But for other people or at other times, danger and need can aid accuracy. Here we might note that there is strong evidence that people in certain marginalized groups – such as women and Blacks in the contemporary United States, along with servants and salespeople – are generally better at reading moods and interpreting facial expressions than are those in power, even when those in power are the very people being interpreted.

Our point, then, is not that for all people there are general relations between emotion-defeating and emotion-engendering conditions, on the one hand, and epistemic failure and success, on the other. It is that there are such connections, and that they are systematic and typical, even if this is so only when relativized to personality, character, social group, culture, and

---

26 Thanks are owed to the psychoanalyst Elsa First here.

circumstances. Thus, in describing conditions that aid or hinder a given person's understanding, we may well be describing not people as such, but only a particular epistemic personality.

Philosophers have always had the materials to recognize this combination of systematic connections and lack of universality, even if we have failed to draw the conclusion. For even among philosophers – not to mention between philosophers and nonphilosophers – there are many intellectual styles, temperaments, and personalities.[27]

So far we have presented some aspects of P's epistemic personality by giving conditions that may account for P's not hoping that the visitor will come, despite believing that she might and that it would be good if she did. These and similar conditions may also account for P's not even noting that she might come or that it would be good if she did. So, if P is very played out, or very bitter or depressed, or generally unable to make and sustain emotional connections, P may not even see that it would be good if she came. It may simply pass him by. These emotion-defeating conditions may, thus, explain a failure to see what is good or bad. They can also lead to mistaken evaluations. P may be so "turned around" by those conditions, so filled with general, free-floating hostility, or with hostility to her or to others who would benefit from her coming, that he thinks that her coming will, in fact, be bad.

In many of these cases, P's concern is with value for this person or value for these people, not just value. As this illustrates, emotions often involve a focus or emphasis on what is good or bad for only certain people, not all people. For example, following Aristotle's account of *orgē*, anger, if an unjustified slight is to get people angry, they must take it to be directed at them or theirs. This is so even though they see that undeserved slights are bad no matter to whom they are directed.

Not surprisingly, then, some evaluative errors can be traced to focus. Let us return to P. He may be so self-absorbed that he does not hope that the visitor will come. For although he thinks that it would be good on balance if she comes, he does not think it would be good for him if she does. His self-absorption, in addition to explaining his lack of hope that she will come, could also explain how he fails to see that her coming would be good on balance where it would be good on balance primarily because of the way it would be good for his wife. Similarly P may be so concerned for his wife's welfare that he hopes the visitor does come, because it will be so good for his wife. His overconcern for his wife might at the same time also explain

---

27 This is discussed in Stocker, "Intellectual Desire, Emotion, and Action."

why he fails to note – or, having noted, fails to be moved by – how disastrous on balance the person's coming will be because of the harm it will do his daughter. Here, we might say he is looking in the wrong places, or not looking at all the right places, for value. Here too, issues of enmeshment are to the point.

Aristotle held that danger evokes fear if you or someone very close to you is endangered and that it evokes pity if the person at risk is not so close but still close enough. (This is discussed in Chapter 8, section 4.) We would extend this to hold that we typically feel only sadness, not fear or pity, for those who are very far from us. And just as they are far from us, we know less about them, both quantitatively and qualitatively. Indeed, this is one of the ways they are far from us. Similarly, we can distance ourselves from someone by not finding out about, not thinking about, and generally not attending to that person.

Now, our claim is not that if one is emotionally distant, or has defective or distorted emotions, or at an extreme if one is affectless, one must make errors about value. Nor is our claim nearly so strong as David Rapaport's, made at the end of "On the Psychoanalytic Theory of Affects":[28]

> Affects . . . are just as indispensable a means of reality testing as thoughts. Indeed, they are more indispensable for reality testing in all except successfully intellectualizing and obsessional characters. Reality testing without the contribution of affect . . . readily changes into obsessional or paranoid magic.

Our claim is only that there are deep and systematic connections between emotional, affective, and evaluative defects and errors, and also between emotional, affective, and evaluative strengths and abilities.

These and other epistemological issues are pursued further in Chapter 7. The intervening chapters focus more on evaluative issues, important both in their own right and also for what they show about evaluative epistemology.

---

28 *International Journal of Psycho-Analysis,* 34 (1953) 177–198; reprinted in Robert P. Knight and Cyrus Friedman, eds., *Psychoanalytic Psychiatry and Psychology: Clinical and Theoretic Papers, Austen Riggs Center,* volume 1 (New York: International Universities Press, 1954); and in *The Collected Papers of David Rapaport,* ed. Merton M. Gill (New York: Basic Books, 1967), from which this quotation is drawn, p. 508.

4

Do these connections show emotions important for value, or do they show something else?

It is a truism that emotions put us in a bad epistemological position for evaluation. Much of this work, however, is concerned to show that this is, often, a false truism; and that lacking, rather than having, emotions puts us in bad epistemological positions. More positively, this work argues that emotions are epistemologically important for evaluations and evaluative knowledge. This chapter considers some worries about these connections between emotions and evaluations and evaluative knowledge.

These worries, though different, share a common theme. They accept the existence of important connections between emotions and evaluations, but they suggest that I have failed to locate the right terms of the connections. Sections 1 and 2 discuss whether emotional defects really do explain evaluative defects, or whether, instead, they share a common cause. They also discuss whether what really accounts for evaluative defects are the nonemotional aspects or the nonemotional underlying conditions of emotions. Section 3 considers and rejects the claim that, instead of showing that emotions are essential for value and evaluation, what has been shown is only that emotions are essential for people as evaluators. Section 4 considers and also rejects the claim that the argument so far adds up to nothing more than an enlarged form of the information claim.

1 Do emotional defects explain evaluative defects, or do they share a common cause?

To accept that emotions and some emotional lacks and defects are typically and naturally connected with evaluative defects is not yet to accept that these connections are important. They might even be thought unimportant since, at least often, we can correct for those conditions. For example, knowing that I am played out, I can pay special attention to sources of value that, in my state, I might otherwise be inclined to overlook. Or knowing that I do not care much for you, I can take special pains to make sure that I give your interests due weight.

Now, I do agree that at least sometimes and to some degree, we can correct for our emotions and emotional lacks. It is, however, difficult to know how well, how easily, and how long we can correct for those conditions which at once impair our emotions and also our epistemological, judging relations with value. Our will, our attention, our vigilance are sooner or later all too likely to fail.

But even if they are all too likely to fail, this might not be thought to show the evaluative-epistemological importance of emotions. It might, rather, be taken as showing that the epistemological relations emotions have with value and evaluation are only external or indirect. For it might suggest that what helps or hinders the epistemological work is not emotions, but rather their various affectless "elements" – to use one term to cover content, preconditions, and underlying patterns – that figure in having or not having emotions. If this is right, we might be able to argue for a variant of the content claim discussed in Chapter 1. The new claim is not that emotions are nothing but affectless content. It is that the evaluative and epistemological work done by emotions is done only by their affectless elements.

To hold that it is not emotions as affective, but their affectless elements, that do the work gives a way to reject the spirit, while accepting the words, of claims made by Lawrence Blum, John McDowell, Martha Nussbaum, and other contemporary philosophers that emotions, themselves, are essential for moral knowledge.

Consider, for example, McDowell's claim that, "Perhaps with Aristotle's notion of practical wisdom in mind, one might ask why a training of the feelings . . . cannot *be* the cultivation of an ability – utterly unmysterious just because of its connections with feelings – to spot (if you like) the fitnesses of things."[1] Or consider the related claim that emotions can be "organizationally dominant," helping constitute central "thoughts and categorical preoccupations," "interpretations of situations," and that "[T]hey focus attention and define what is salient."[2]

---

1 "Values and Secondary Qualities," in Ted Honderich, ed., *Morality and Objectivity* (London: Routledge and Kegan Paul, 1985), reprinted in Geoffrey Sayre-McCord, ed., *Essays on Moral Realism* (Ithaca, N.Y.: Cornell University Press, 1988). The quotation is from the latter, p. 178; emphasis in original.
2 Amélie O. Rorty, "The Two Faces of Courage," in her *Mind in Action* (Boston: Beacon Press, 1988), pp. 300–301. She is there talking about virtues, not emotions. But it also holds true for emotions – and not only because they are so important for virtues.

Those claiming that the evaluative work done by emotions is done only by their nonaffective elements could accept the words of those claims, while rejecting their spirit. They can certainly agree that training of feelings can lead to an increased ability to spot the fitnesses of things. Indeed, they can hold that training of the feelings is one of the best ways, perhaps the very best way, to increase that ability. But they can also hold that this is because the training of feelings involves the training and improvement of those nonaffective elements. In regard to fear, one of McDowell's examples, they can hold that training feelings of fear can lead to a greater ability to spot what is and what is not dangerous: to be able to tell, for example, whether a snake is poisonous or aggressive. They can also hold that on their view, too, the evaluative work of emotions is done by their organizational dominance, their associated thoughts, categorical preoccupations, and interpretations, and the ways they help focus attention and define what is salient – provided, of course, that these are all understood as nonaffective.

So too, they can acknowledge the instrumental importance of knowing one's own emotions and emotional lacks. After all, to be able to correct for one's emotions or emotional lacks requires awareness of what they are and how they work, which values they deploy or avoid deploying, how they do this, and so on. Along these lines, it could be held that if a self-absorbed person fails to see others' interests, or if having seen them fails to be moved by them, the real account would lie not in the emotions of self-absorption, but in self-absorption's nonaffective elements. A similar claim would be made about explaining the father's mistaken and inappropriate evaluations of thinking poorly of his daughter's friend for "imposing" her musical tastes on his daughter and his failing to see his daughter's consideration. The claim would be that we should not invoke his emotions, but rather his seeing the world from an enmeshed standpoint – where, of course, this is understood as nonaffective.

If the nonaffective elements – again, content, preconditions, and underlying patterns – do the evaluative work, the conclusion would not be that correct evaluative understanding comes from or even really depends on correct emotions. Nor would it be that incorrect evaluative understanding comes from incorrect emotions. It would be that typically and for systematic reasons, correct evaluative understanding and correct emotions come together as a package, as do incorrect evaluative understanding and incorrect emotions.

I do agree that there are good reasons to focus on those nonaffective elements. But we must also focus on the emotions – on, that is, the emotions as affective, as emotional. The argument for this runs throughout the work. In the remainder of this chapter, I give two particular pieces of this argument. In this section, I argue that, instead of the nonaffective elements always explaining emotions and their evaluative work, emotions often explain and do the evaluative work of those nonaffective elements. In the next section, I argue that often there is no real distinction between what is emotional and what is nonemotional.

I start this two-part argument with Sartre's *Anti-Semite and Jew*,[3] and then move to some psychoanalytic considerations. Sartre's work is a compelling account of anti-Semitism, as found in France and other parts of Europe during the first forty or so years of this century. He characterizes anti-Semites of this time and place in terms of their highly specific patterns of thought and attention, which involve serious intellectual errors. To mention three features of these patterns, anti-Semites are on the lookout for, and pay great attention to, wrongs done by Jews, which they notice and characterize as 'wrongs done by a Jew' or even 'Jewish wrongs'. In contrast, they are not on the lookout for wrongs done by French Catholics, which in any case they would never describe as 'wrongs done by a Catholic', much less 'Catholic wrongs'.

Second, anti-Semites, correlatively, find strange "confirmations" for their views. As Sartre writes,

> A young woman said to me: "I have had the most horrible experiences with furriers; they robbed me, they burned the fur I entrusted to them. Well, they were all Jews." But why did she choose to hate Jews rather than furriers? Why Jews or furriers rather than such and such a Jew or such and such a furrier? (pp. 11–12)

We might wonder how many of her fur coats were stolen or burned, and how many by Jewish furriers. We might also wonder why, if she had such trouble with all Jews or even just Jewish furriers, she continued to patronize them. But perhaps we should simply end our questioning by agreeing with Sartre's answer to his own questions, "Because she had in her a predisposition toward anti-Semitism" (p. 12).

There is, third, the anti-Semites' taking *being Jewish* as a "magical" essence, had by all and only Jews. This essence infects the acts of Jews – pretty much all the acts of all Jews, and certainly only Jews – making their wrongs Jewish wrongs, and justifying and explaining why Jews are to be mistrusted, held in contempt, hated, treated harshly, even exiled, imprisoned, or killed.

---

3 New York: Schocken Books, 1976. For a similar, but more general, treatment of discrimination, see Adrian Piper, "Higher Order Discrimination," in Owen Flanagan and Amélie O. Rorty, eds., *Identity, Character, and Morality* (Cambridge, Mass.: MIT Press, 1990).

It is important to see that such anti-Semitism does involve these and other intellectual errors – errors that may well be understood as nonemotional. But it is also important to see how such emotions as hatred, contempt, loathing, and disgust are foundational in creating and sustaining anti-Semitism – including those erring patterns of thought and attention. So for example, even if anti-Semites acknowledge the falsity of a certain piece of "evidence" they had thought sustains their anti-Semitism – perhaps they are brought to acknowledge that, both by absolute number and percentage, far fewer Jewish furriers damage coats left with them than do non-Jewish furriers – and even if they thus cease using that "evidence," another piece of "evidence," another rationalization, is almost immediately on the scene to take its place. Their hatred, contempt, loathing, and disgust for Jews demands a rationalization, and a new rationalization is soon at hand to take the place of the old one.

So, anti-Semitic emotions do have important nonaffective elements. But these nonaffective elements do not always explain the emotions or their evaluative work. Things are often the other way around. Often, the loathing and hatred directly explain why anti-Semites have (seemingly) nonaffective views about Jews. The explanation can be somewhat less direct: as just suggested, anti-Semitic emotions can need rationalizations – anti-Semites can feel a need to "back" even their anti-Semitic emotions with views that, if right, might be seen as justifying the emotions. In this indirect way, emotions can explain their nonaffective elements.

Psychoanalysis offers us complementary arguments that show how emotions – emotions as affective – explain their nonaffective elements. In *Neurotic Styles,* Shapiro writes,

paranoid people rarely laugh . . . they do not seem to feel amused.
Such a loss of affective experience cannot be regarded as a result of inner surveillance or as an intentional act of suppression. The paranoid person may steer and direct his behavior meticulously, but he is no more able than anyone else to make a feeling disappear. While the loss of affective experience is not a result of an intention or a direction, it is a result of the state of rigid directedness and intentionality. It is impossible to be as mobilized as he is – alert, watching himself, rigidly steering every gesture and expression – and at the same time be amused. (pp. 77–78)

Suppose, then, that we want to explain why paranoid people do not understand jokes – why, in this limited evaluative area, they make mistakes. Following Shapiro, we might not appeal to their emotional and affective lacks, but to their "state of rigid directedness and intentionality." This latter explains both their lacks and also their not understanding jokes.

Although this state might not "contain" emotions, emotions play a central role in Shapiro's account of paranoia and that "state of rigid directedness and intentionality" – and not just because there is an absence, even a "precise absence," of emotions and affectivity. As he characterizes this state, attention is directed away from areas that arouse certain emotions to other, far less dangerous areas. For present purposes, this can be seen as simply an illustration of a central and common psychoanalytic tenet: such emotions and emotional states as fear, anxiety, and distress explain many instances of seeming affectlessness – both many cases of selective inattention and many cases of repression and dissociation.[4]

For another illustration of this, let us move away from psychoses. Suppose we have a normal case of someone's not paying attention to you. There are any number of possible explanations of this, some emotionless and some emotional. The person may not have paid attention to you because of an unwillingness to engage emotionally with you, perhaps because such engagement is felt to be too dangerous. In simple and straightforward ways, emotions explain this lack of attention.[5]

Similarly, in many cases where there seems to be only affectless patterns of thought, the affectlessness is to be explained in terms of repression and dissociation. And, in many cases, what is repressed or dissociated is affect, not just affectless content. Indeed, the repression or dissociation involved in intellectualization, for example, would fail from the outset were it to work only on what is affectless. Stressing the point, intellectualization starts with what is affectively laden, "gets rid" of the affect, and ends by producing something that is affectless. Understressing the point, in intellectualization and in many other neurotic formations, the repressed or dissociated affect is inadequately characterized as "simply not being there." At the least, it is absent affect that should be and would be there but for the repression or dissociation. And often, even though it is not there in usual ways, it is still there, but in special ways, such as in anxiety.

I am not arguing that all, or even all morally significant, patterns of emotionless thought, desire, and attention are really emotionally moti-

---

[4] See, for example, "'Speak! That I May See You': Some Reflections on Dissociation, Reality, and Psychoanalytic Listening," by the psychoanalyst Philip Bromberg in *Psychoanalytic Dialogues*, 4 (1994) 517–547. See also the long quotation from David Rapaport in the Introduction.

[5] Thanks are owed to the psychoanalyst Sandra Buechler for stressing the importance of being unwilling to experience certain emotions, in addition to the importance of not experiencing them. I am also grateful to her for general discussion on emotions and for showing me her chapter "Emotions," in Donnel Stern, John Fiscalini, Carola Mann, and Mary Lou Lionells, eds., *The Handbook of Interpersonal Psychoanalysis* (Hillsdale, N.J.: Analytic Press, 1995).

vated. Mere "innocent" inattention is a possibility. Nor, therefore, am I suggesting that wherever those patterns are affectless, there is intellectualization or some other neurosis or unhealthy split.[6] Emotional, affectful engagement is essential for being a healthy, well-functioning person. But concomitantly, it is also essential to be able to focus and limit one's affective concerns.

This last involves being able to change the focus and intensity of those concerns. It also involves being able to engage affectfully with only some of what there and then one could engage with. This is to say that it also involves being able to limit engagement, to make sure that much else that one could feel is there and then unfelt or barely felt. In these ways, affectivity is like more cognitive forms of attention. In both, it is essential to have flexibility and control in regard to the extent and sorts of engagement.

I would also stress that in some cases, dissociation and other forms of not being emotionally engaged are exactly the states people should be in. As Philip Bromberg writes in "'Speak! That I May See You': Some Reflections on Dissociation, Reality, and Psychoanalytic Listening," "When ordinary adaptational adjustment to the task at hand is not possible, dissociation comes into play" (p. 520). The importance of this – both for philosophical understanding of the issues and for more ordinary understanding of the pressures and dangers of life that lead to "strange" forms of thought and feeling – warrants presenting the text surrounding that quotation:

> Where drastically incompatible emotions or perceptions [such as abuse by a loved parent] are required to be cognitively processed within the same relationship and such processing is adaptationally beyond the capacity of the individual to contain this disjunction within a unitary self-experience, one of the . . . [usual modes of understanding these experiences] is hypnoidally denied access to consciousness to preserve sanity and survival. When ordinary adaptational adjustment to the task at hand is not possible, dissociation comes into play. The experience that is causing the incompatible perception and emotions is "unhooked" from the cognitive processing system and remains raw data that is cognitively unsymbolized within that particular self–other representation.
>
> Dissociation is not inherently pathological, but it can become so. The process of dissociation is basic to human mental functioning and is central to the stability and growth of personality. It is intrinsically an adaptational talent that represents the very nature of what we call "consciousness." Dissociation is not fragmentation. In fact, it may be reasonably seen as a defense against fragmentation, and in this regard, Ferenczi's (1930a, p. 230) struggle with whether fragmentation is merely a mechan-

---

6 Thanks are owed to Julia Driver for discussion here.

ical consequence of trauma or may actually be a form of adaptation to it was brilliantly ahead of its time. (pp. 520–521)[7]

2 Is there a real or healthy distinction between emotions and their underlying patterns?

One of the claims argued for in the preceding section is that the evaluative work of some emotions may be, or may be thought to be, explained by their nonemotional components or underlying, nonemotional patterns of thought, attention, value, and desire; but in turn, the evaluative work of many of these nonemotional features can be explained in terms of emotions. So, for example, Sartre held that anti-Semitic emotions are to be explained in terms of their underlying patterns. He also held that those patterns are to be explained in terms of emotions: in terms of the anti-Semite's ontological or existential fear "of himself, of his own consciousness, of his own liberty, of his own instincts, of his own responsibilities, of solitariness, of change, of society, and of the world" (p. 53).

This still leaves open the possibility that explanations in terms of what is nonemotional go further back and go deeper than those in terms of what is emotional. So, we could hold that Sartre's account of anti-Semites' patterns of thought in terms of fear only postpones the issue. We can still ask about the new and explanatorily prior emotion: here, fear. Perhaps this emotion is to be explained in terms of nonemotional patterns of thought, attention, and desire, which in turn are not to be explained in terms of still other emotions.

There may well be some value to the general quest for what is further back and deeper. But I think that there is little to be gained by trying to answer the question, "Which is deeper, thoughts or emotions?" To be sure, in explaining human phenomena, we often think that what is earlier is deeper or at least more explanatory. But if we are concerned with what is earlier or earliest, we should note that in infants and very young children, emotions and their nonemotional components and underlying patterns, or precursors of both, are inextricably interconnected and interdependent –

---

[7] He is referring to the early and pioneering psychoanalyst Sandor Ferenczi, "Notes and Fragments II," in Michael Balint, ed., *Final Contributions to the Problems and Methods of Psychoanalysis* (New York: Brunner Mazel, 1980). For more on healthy dissociation (which he calls "decoupling"), see Richard A. Shweder, *Thinking through Cultures: Expeditions in Cultural Psychology* (Cambridge, Mass.: Harvard University Press, 1991), ch. 6, "Menstrual Pollution, Soul Loss, and the Comparative Study of Emotions," especially pp. 260ff.

or, better, exist only in states having features of both. It is not just that these states are in part constituted by emotions or protoemotions, and also by thoughts or protothoughts. It is that those emotional aspects are also and at the same time and in the same ways thought aspects; and those thought aspects are also and at the same time and in the same ways emotional aspects. There is no real division that can be made here. Any philosophical analytic division will be, at best, an artifact of a theory, and runs the risk of being highly misleading.[8]

To be sure, what is developmentally true may not be true later on. But my claim does not rely just on what happens at the outset of people's lives, when infants or young children. I think it is quite generally reasonable to see emotions and their nonemotional elements as interconnected and interdependent at all levels of explanatory depth. Let us look again to Shapiro's *Neurotic Styles*. He argues that we can understand the nature of particular neuroses, and why particular people have one rather than another, only by seeing how the neuroses are bound up in a style that encompasses affect, thought, forms of attention, desire, and much else. Part of his argument for this is an argument that any attempt to explain the one in terms of the others is, necessarily, doomed to failure.

This was shown in his discussion of paranoid emotional responses or lack of responses, especially those centering around amusement. It is brought out perhaps even more clearly and more explicitly in what he writes about the neurotic style of impulsiveness:

The [impulsive] mode of cognition and the mode of affective functioning fit or mesh . . . and it is virtually impossible to separate them. It would be possible to argue for the psychological primacy of either of them. One could argue, in other words, that the impulsive person does not search beyond the immediately relevant present because his interests and emotional involvements are limited to immediate gains and satisfactions. Or one could equally well argue that the limitations of his cognition and the domination of his awareness by the immediately striking, concrete, and personally relevant interferes with the development of long-range interests or enduring values and aims. Such arguments would, I believe, be specious. Both areas of functioning and the modes that respectively characterize them exist together, each is hardly imaginable without the other, and, in all likelihood, they develop together. The two modes share essential features: immediacy of experience and expression of impulse is paralleled by immediacy of cognitive response. The

---

8 See, for example, the psychoanalytic works of Daniel Stern, *The Interpersonal World of the Infant* (New York: Basic Books, 1985), and especially *Diary of an Infant* (New York: Basic Books, 1990). The latter has a good, analytic bibliography. See also Melanie Klein's discussions of the depressive, schizoid, and paranoid stances of infants, in her *Love, Guilt and Reparation, and Other Works, 1921–1945* (New York: Delta Books, 1977), and *Envy and Gratitude and Other Works 1946–1963* (New York: Delta Books, 1977).

insufficiency of basic affective structures that are essential equipment for integrative development of a given whim or impulse may well be paralleled by an insufficiency of basic cognitive equipment. (pp. 154–155)

If Shapiro is right, not just about impulsiveness but more generally about the interdependence of emotions and nonemotional patterns, we would make theoretical mistakes by attempting to understand emotions in terms of their underlying nonemotional patterns or those nonemotional patterns in terms of their underlying emotions. So too, we would be led to make serious practical errors about how to correct those emotions that lead to evaluative errors. For if emotions are explained in terms of their nonemotional elements, but not vice versa, it will naturally seem that we can correct "mistaken" emotions by correcting their nonemotional elements: that, so to speak, emotional defects can be cured just by "cognitive therapy."

But first, we must be able to get the corrected beliefs and desires *to take,* to matter, to be moving. It would not be enough that anti-Semites come to see that a particular act by a particular Jew is an everyday, ordinary act, or is even a fine act. That thought must also be integrated into, and seen to conflict with, their anti-Semitism. And further, this conflict must matter to them. It cannot be seen just as a puzzling anomaly, of the sort that besets many, if not most, theories and generalizations. Nor can it be defended against in ways that stop it from mattering to them or moving them. They must be – and this means that almost certainly *they* must make themselves be – emotionally available and open to that thought and (what we see as) its obvious implications.

Saying this is little more than saying what we have just seen in regard to anti-Semitism: to improve some nonemotional elements, we must also, or even first, correct the emotions that explain or underlie those elements. As we have just read from Shapiro's *Neurotic Styles,* much the same holds for the amelioration of paranoia.

Further, some emotions and nonemotional patterns can be made epistemologically more useful for value and evaluation by improving the emotions and nonemotional patterns in tandem. As David Wiggins writes in "A Sensible Subjectivism?":

Finer perceptions can both intensify and refine [emotional] responses. Intenser responses can further heighten and refine perceptions. And more and more refined responses can lead to the further and finer and more variegated or more intense responses *and* perceptions.[9]

---

9 In his *Needs, Values, and Truth* (Oxford: Blackwell, 1991), p. 196; emphasis in original.

It might, thus, be agreed that we should take care not to suggest the wrong explanatory relations between emotions and their nonemotional aspects and underlying patterns of thought, attention, and desire. But, if we do take such care, it might then be thought that there is no good reason not to make, and many good reasons to make, the philosophical analytic distinction between emotions and those nonemotional aspects and underlying patterns. After all, we know that an emotion is not the same as those aspects and patterns, and indeed we know that they are not even coextensive: a person can have such thought, attention, and desire without having the emotion.

But we should ask what sort of distinction this is. I think that in making this distinction, we may well have carried philosophical analysis too far, to the point of misleading artificiality, or at least a mistaken psychology. Indeed, as we have indicated, this distinction provides a central, characterizing feature of intellectualization and other neurotic states.

None of this is intended to suggest that quite generally, or quite generally in healthy people, there is no distance between emotions and those nonemotional aspects and patterns of thought, desire, and attention. It is, however, to question the nature of that distance. It also is to suggest that it may not be the right sort of distance to sustain the claim that it is what is nonemotional, rather than emotions, that is epistemologically relevant.

As noted, absence of affect can be entirely healthy and unproblematic, epistemologically and in other ways. But, as shown throughout this work, it is easy for there to be too great an absence of affect, for there to be too much affectlessness. And this, along with being unhealthy, also engenders many evaluative-epistemological problems. To put again the concluding words of the previous section, one can lack too much affect, one can have affectless patterns to too great an extent. Such affectlessness typifies and is constitutively central to the "affect-denying world of alienated work," repression, other neurotic defenses, and also delibidinization, dissociation, alexithymia, and more severe schizoid phenomena.

Thus, as just said, if we rely on that distinction and the distance between emotions and affectless components and nonemotional patterns of thought, desire, and value, we run the very serious risk of having carried philosophical analysis too far, to the point of misleading artificiality, or at least a mistaken psychology. Even though there can be distance between emotions and those aspects patterns, it is not the right sort of distance to sustain the claim that what is nonemotional, rather than emotions, is epistemologically relevant.

3 Perhaps emotions are important, not for evaluations, but only for people as evaluators

Much of what has been argued so far focuses on the person: showing that by having correct emotions, a person is well placed to make good evaluative judgments; and that by having no emotions or by not having correct emotions, a person is ill placed to make good evaluative judgments. Some of the reasons advanced for this had to do with affectless people and the moral and epistemological problems they suffer.

These reasons might seem to undercut my argument. For as argued by the psychological theories invoked by that argument, people without emotions are not just ill placed to make evaluative judgments. If such people are even possible, they are so utterly maimed and ill that they would have to be institutionalized and might, despite this, still not survive. Further, and more generally, we should be very reluctant to draw conclusions about what is generally the case for normal and healthy beings from what holds in abnormal or deformed lives. Just as we should be reluctant to draw conclusions about how normal people think from the thinking of people with thought disorders, such as schizophrenia, we should be reluctant to draw conclusions about the evaluative capacities of normal people from those of affectless people.

However, many of these arguments were not concerned with total or even serious affectlessness, but only with such defects as emotional distortions and lacks of only certain emotions. Where more thoroughgoing affectlessness was used, its primary role, and often its only role, was to show the deficiencies of other philosophical views – views that, intentionally or not, depicted people or their emotions in ways that allow, or even require, that they be affectless.

There is a closely related worry about the argument given to show that emotions are important for evaluative abilities and sensitivities: even if it did not focus too much on abnormal people, it focused too much on people, rather than values. The claim is that, at best, those arguments show only something about us as beings who evaluate and act on our evaluations, and not about value.

This claim starts off by accepting, or at least using, a contention of the Introduction: that instead of being rare and unusual, emotions are part and parcel of our everyday life, and that, as held by Schachtel, Krystal, and Tomkins, our lives are through-and-through emotional. The claim continues, however, that showing this does not show that emotions are directly important for value and evaluation. It might show only that they are important for aspects of our lives that, although important for value and evaluations, are themselves completely outside the ambit of value and evaluation.

Some examples may help here. Adequate nutrition is essential for living and, in this way, for making and acting on evaluative judgments. So too, to make and act on evaluative judgments, one must be able to think well. This, in turn, requires not having thought disorders, not suffering from severe problems with long- or short-term memory, not experiencing real or imaginary overwhelming terrors, being able to make and sustain connections with reality and other people, being able to direct and control one's attention, having sufficient energy to think and act on one's decisions, and so on. Those who see a tight connection between motives and emotions could make much the same claim, now directly about emotions. They could hold that without emotions there is no motivation; that without motivation there is no action or thinking, including evaluative thinking: and thus that without emotions, there is no action or thinking, including evaluative thinking.

These, then, are all conditions for being able to evaluate well and act on our evaluations: beings who evaluate and act on evaluations must have those features. This may show that they are essential to us as evaluators. But it does not show that they are internal to or directly important for value or evaluation.

To solidify the point, we might be asked to consider an analogy with mathematics. Many of the claims made about emotion and value can be made about emotion and mathematics: when they lack certain emotions, people are likely to be less inclined to engage in mathematics, and less likely and even less able to appreciate and do mathematics. This could be due to general liveliness and interest: people without these general emotional qualities of life are unlikely to do mathematics, and even less likely to do it well. Or it could be due to matters more tied to mathematics: interest in mathematics is at least generally needed to do well in it. We might thus conclude that, considered as beings who do mathematics, we can make good use of, and may even need, certain emotions. Thus, emotions are useful, even essential, for mathematicians doing mathematics. But this does not show that those emotions are internal to or essential or even important for mathematics. (As made clear in Chapter 6, section 2, I am not suggesting that mathematics is emotional, but only that the doing of it can be.)

In short, then, it is not enough for my claims about the importance of emotions for value that the psychoanalysts we read – Guntrip, McDougall,

Shapiro, and others – are right in claiming that a person without emotions, or without a large enough range of adequate emotions, will be unable to make and act on evaluations. Emotions must also be directly essential for evaluation, not just essential for it in the sense that those lacking emotions suffer from some condition or other which makes evaluation and acting on evaluations difficult or impossible.

Before replying to these arguments, I want to note that, pretty much as it stands, it can be used against a claim frequently made to cast suspicion on the possibility of ethical knowledge. This claim agrees that emotions are important for being good at recognizing and acting on value. But it takes this as showing value to be epistemically suspect. My reply proceeds by way of the analogy with mathematics. Emotions are important for mathematicians, but that does not show mathematics epistemically suspect. Even more generally, emotions are important for people considered as beings who think and act, but that does not show the generality of human thinking and acting epistemically suspect.

Let us return to the worry whether emotions are important, not for value, but only for people who evaluate and act on evaluations. I am dubious about the extent or strength of the distinction between value, on the one hand, and people who evaluate and act on evaluations, on the other. Ethics is concerned with value understood ontologically. But it is also concerned with moral epistemology and moral practice. Being a good moral judge and being able to act on moral judgments is constitutive of being a good person. Thus, to show that emotions are important for making and acting on moral judgments is to show much of ethical importance.

Further, we would need some explanation of how emotions could be important in the ways shown for judgment and action but not also for value. In particular, we would need an explanation of how such judgment and action is not about, and does not concern, value. After all, the judgment is moral judgment and the action is action consequent on such judgment.

To summarize, the worry was that I showed only that emotions are important for our dealings with value – for example, our moral judgment and action – but not also for value, itself. But, even if this is all that has been shown, that 'only' is hardly grounds for dismissiveness. For emotions will have been shown to have considerable, vital importance for ethics.

I see no need to go further into these tangled and complex issues now. We have seen that emotions and their components and underlying patterns play significant epistemological roles in helping and hindering us in noticing and appreciating value. Other chapters (especially 7) will continue the discussion of the conceptual relations between affect and those components and patterns, and also the nature of the relations between evaluative understanding and emotions. Nonetheless, I think that we have already seen enough to conclude that people who have correct emotions, because they are such people, are typically well placed to make correct evaluations, and people who have incorrect emotions are, because they are such people, typically poorly placed to make correct evaluations.

4 Is this just the information claim?

It might seem that my arguments of the preceding section have done little more than extend the information claim – the claim that emotions reveal value and thus have instrumental, not intrinsic, value. Those arguments might seem just to extend their instrumental value to their helping us notice and appreciate value.

But I think that my position gives us two interrelated and very strong reasons to reevaluate the claim that emotions have only instrumental, and not also intrinsic, value. First, it is a well-established part of our ethical tradition, and of many if not most others, that being good at noticing and appreciating value – and, more widely, being a good judge – has instrumental value, but not only instrumental value. To be able to judge well and to be a good judge are, themselves, important internal parts of what it is to live well and to be good.

Second, much the same holds for being alive to value: having the sorts of attention, concern, and desire that are essential for inquiring about and noticing value, how these can be helped or harmed by various policies, plans, and acts. Such attentiveness is part of what it is to hold a value, or more clearly to love a value or indeed a person. To the extent that we are not attentive, the nature of our love, perhaps even the existence of our supposed love, is called into question. Without attentive care, there is strong reason to think that the love of that object is deficient, or that something else is loved, such as the *thought* of loving that object. Whether or not these were among Aristotle's reasons, they give us some reason to say with him that morally virtuous people are lovers of virtue and that moral virtue involves a love of virtue (*NE* I.8., 1099a5 ff.). Thus, love of value has both considerable instrumental and intrinsic value: instrumentally, it aids our attentiveness to value; intrinsically, it is part of what it is to be a morally good person.

This second point should be generalized. As argued in Chapter 1, the content claim – the claim that emotions are nothing but their cognitive, desiderative, or evaluative content – is mistaken. But as also noted there, a more modest variant of its claims is correct and was absolutely standard fare for classical philosophers: nonaffective content is important and often essential for various emotions.

This provides a good place to conclude this section and chapter. For it is undeniable that such content is epistemologically useful for value and evaluation. And as argued here, people who lack or are deficient in the relevant emotions are likely to lack or be deficient in that content. As also argued, emotions must be seen as not merely instrumentally useful for value, but also as internal to value. Emotions are part and parcel of, not merely useful for, being a good evaluative judge, being able and willing to act on those judgments, and also being a lover of value.

5

Emotions are important for evaluation and value

In this chapter, I start some new lines of argument to show how emotions and other affective states are deeply interrelated with values and evaluations: in particular that emotions are constituents of various goods, that emotions are grounds of evaluations of people, actions, and practices, and that emotions figure in making moral evaluations.[1] The arguments and cases I present are a heterodox lot; but they cover a lot of ground and are good representatives of values and valuations that involve emotions. They are especially useful in the ways they show the importance of emotions where this has been ignored or denied.

Section 1 briefly examines medical treatment. Section 2 discusses justice and formalistic ethics. Section 3 considers the right of self-defense and some other rights. The fourth section shows that what we must do to be moral and act morally has essential connections with emotions. The fifth section shows how our life, even at its most ordinary, involves emotions; that much of the value of our life involves emotions; and, making much the same point, that many goods, especially interpersonal ones, are emotional.

1 Medical treatment

Medical treatment can give us a sort of case showing that not all relations between people need have emotions as constituents. I find nothing inconsistent in the thought that patients with cancer might judge a surgeon in just the ways they would judge a drug or a computer-driven, automated laser: not in terms of emotional involvement, but simply in terms of costs and

---

This chapter benefited from discussion at the Oxford University–University of Southern California Legal Theory Institute, July 1995, with a wonderful collection of philosophers, professors of law, and psychoanalysts. My very warmest thanks are given to the organizers, Martin Levine and Joseph Raz, and to the other members, Marshall Cohen, Jonathan Dancy, John Finnis, Samuel Freeman, John Gardner, Grant Lamond, Brian Leiter, Dan Ortiz, David Slawson, Jonathan Wolff, and Richard Warner.

1 My thanks are owed to Brian Leiter for help here and elsewhere in this chapter.

benefits, as determined by survival rates, gain or loss of functions, pain. The thought here might be put that where some end E can be achieved either by a mechanism or a person, there is no difference between E as done by a mechanism and E as done by a person.

Some cancer patients do have that view, but many do not.[2] Many complain that their surgeons are too technocratic, too concerned with mere effectiveness and survival rates. These patients, thus, do not view their surgeons as mere means, mere mechanisms for ridding them of cancer. This is a correlative of how they want their surgeons to view them. They want their surgeons to be concerned and involved with them as people, not just as sites for operations. And they want this, not because, or not just because, they think that doctors give better care to those they care about personally.

In these cases, then, medical patients do not see what their doctors do to them just in terms of what this does. They also see their doctors' acts as human acts, with emphasis on both 'human' and 'acts'. That is, they come at least close to seeing them as Aristotelian activities, *praxeis,* rather than as means, *kinēseis* or *poiēseis*. For the acts, themselves, not just their outcomes, are valued.

2 Justice and formalistic ethics

It has long been recognized that certain forms or instances of justice are problems – some see them as counterexamples – for claims that emotions and virtues are necessary for morally correct judgment and action. I say *"certain* forms or instances of justice," since certain others – including the following two from Aristotle and one each from Strawson and Nussbaum[3] – have not been thought problematic for that relation. In book V of the *Nicomachean Ethics,* we read that *pleonaxia,* graspingness, is one of the root causes of injustice. Further, sociable, civic emotions are necessary for justice. In "Freedom and Resentment," we read that reactive attitudes are through-and-through emotional, and that they are also at the heart of

---

2 My thanks are owed here to the medical educator and psychiatrist Dr. Robert W. Daly for discussion of this and other issues, and for discussing with me his "Schizoid Rule-Following," *Psychoanalytic Review,* 55 (1968) 400–414, and "The Specters of Technicism," *Psychiatry,* 33 (1970) 417–432.

3 Aristotle, *The Nicomachean Ethics.* The second Aristotelian point is drawn from Eugene Garver, *Aristotle's Rhetoric: The Art of Character* (Chicago: University of Chicago Press, 1994), pp. 130–135. Strawson, "Freedom and Resentment," *Proceedings of the British Academy,* 48 (1962) 187–211. In this work, I use the reprint, in Gary Watson, ed., *Free Will* (Oxford: Oxford University Press, 1982); Nussbaum, "Equity and Mercy," *Philosophy and Public Affairs,* 22 (1993) 83–125.

many forms of justice – for example, criminal justice and also noninstitutional retributive justice including indignation and remorse. And in "Equity and Mercy," we read that proper judicial equity requires full empathic understanding of the criminal by the judge, and that proper judicial mercy requires full empathic and sympathetic understanding of the defendant by the judge. (Chapter 8, section 3, presents some reservations about Nussbaum's claims.)

But some other forms of justice seem to have far less, perhaps nothing, to do with emotions. Among those that come readily to mind are certain issues of distributive justice, such as income taxes and the setting of income tax rates. I doubt if there would be much support for income tax laws taking emotions into account in any simple way, such as "income between $50,000 and $100,000 is taxable at a marginal rate of 35 percent unless this angers the taxpayer, in which case it is 30 percent, to encourage better feelings."

So too, emotions may seem irrelevant to administrative or bureaucratic justice, such as promotions in civil service jobs. Emotions may also seem irrelevant for those aspects of justice, and related areas of morality, understood in terms of universalizability and noncontradiction. In these cases and areas, it might be thought that reaching certain economic levels or following certain procedures, all of which seem clearly nonemotional, is necessary and sufficient for justice.

The claim of *Valuing Emotions* is that emotions and other affective states are important for value and valuation. (Following my usual practice, I put the case mainly in terms of emotions, not all affective states.) Its claim is not that *all* emotions are important for *all* values and evaluations. Thus, there is no strict need to show emotions important for these cases of justice. It is sufficient that they are important elsewhere. But – especially because of the importance of justice and other aspects of morality modeled on justice – I want to suggest some ways emotions are important for justice and related values and evaluations.

Let us start from the outside, showing how emotions can be externally connected with justice. Even where there can be just judgments and just actions without emotions, emotions can be important in helping constitute the respect proper to various sorts of encounters that involve justice. For example, it may well be that distributive justice, administrative justice, and various other forms of justice do not require emotions: such justice can be achieved without involving anyone's emotions. But a person's encounters with these forms of justice, and with people engaged in regulating and dispensing it, can be made better or worse by the emotions of those people.

People caught up in the toils of administrative justice can quite properly want to be taken seriously and personally, rather than in a technical or administrative way, like a number. They can also want not to be caught up in someone else's emotional life, especially where that life proceeds on its own, without reference to them and their emotional life. Here we could think of having to deal with an administrator who is indiscriminately and generally angry.

Some might think that what is relevant here is that an administrator's being indiscriminately angry is all too likely to interfere with the process, not only with the outcome, of the administrative goings-on. Focusing on this, they might hold that, for all I have shown, emotions are only instrumentally important for justice. This objection has two parts: first, certain emotions, such as generalized anger, can cause bad judicial outcomes, but are not part of such outcomes; second, the route of this causation is via processes: emotions may compromise processes of judgment, and compromised processes are likely to engender incorrect decisions.

But both parts of this objection fail.[4] Often and quite properly, we are concerned with correct processes of judgment, not just with correct judgments, considered in terms of correctness of outcome. The reason for this is not just that the better the process of judgment, the better the judgment. It also has to do with the nature of the value of the process, itself. To have to deal with an angry administrator is, itself, to have the process of adjudication called into question, if not compromised. The absence of certain emotions, and perhaps the presence of certain others, are constituents, not just causes, of a just process -- or at least of this process being both just and good.

There are other, more internal ways emotions are important for justice and for areas of value conceived of in terms of justice. I restrict myself to simply giving a list of a few of these that bear directly on income taxes. Emotions are important for whether taxation is seen more as theft or as one's contribution to the community; for whether tax compliance is more voluntary or more adversarial; for how balances are to be struck between self-reliance and a more communitarian stance for tax differentials and rates taking or not taking into account needs for medical care, pensions, housing; for whether there should be special exemptions for dependents, the elderly, or the blind. Even in these restricted cases, trust, fellow feeling, solidarity, empathy, care, and concern are important factors.

---

4 My thanks are owed to the psychoanalyst and legal theorist Martin Levine for help here and in the subsequent discussion of empathy and tax rates.

There is another, related way emotions can be important for taxes and administrative procedures, as well as for evaluative thought about them. Thinking about tax rates and collection procedures, and about other administrative procedures, is often relativized to different economic or administrative targets. This relativization may be necessary, if only because there are so many different possible targets. I do not think we need examine examples to see that some of these have special appeal, and perhaps would appeal only, to those who are very hardhearted, uncaring, punitive, judgmental, or even sadistic; others appeal to, or only to, those who are masochistic, too softhearted, overcaring, too accepting, too unwilling to make judgments. I would mistrust the choice of economic or administrative targets or procedures that appeal to people with any of these emotional configurations. So even here, not having certain emotions and not being of certain emotional sorts is important for value and evaluation.

It must be remembered that these are only some of the ways emotions are important for both value and evaluation in a very restricted area: some issues about taxation and a few administrative procedures. If emotions are evaluatively important even here, we should expect in other areas of justice, and in still other areas of evaluative concern, there can be far more important and more internal connections with emotions.

Let us now turn more explicitly to moral reasoning – an area, many philosophers are convinced, where emotions should play no role. I will argue that, on the contrary, they do and should play a role even here. To start on this, I will make some points about that most austere sort of moral reasoning: the sort involved in universalization, noncontradiction, and similar formal tests.[5] I will indicate some ways that even some of these formal procedures must make assumptions about what people are like emotionally and that at least some formal procedures must involve emotions. By 'must' in this last sentence, I do not mean that this is logically or conceptually necessary for, say, consistency. I mean that this is necessary for those tests to be attractive or even plausible.

Consider one of the usual test cases: asking for money with a promise to repay it. What will be of importance for us are the conditions, if any, under which the promiser intends to repay or not repay: that is, what goes in the

---

[5] My thanks are owed to Barbara Herman for discussion here. She argued that Kant has deep reasons for excluding considerations of emotions from universalizability tests and would thus find much of the following irrelevant. There is no reason to question this here, since neither she nor I think that all universalization tests have such reasons. For a related discussion of universalizability, see John Deigh, "Empathy and Universalizability," *Ethics*, 105 (1995) 743–763.

blank in 'I promise to repay the money ———'. We should consider this in terms of a series of maxims (or act sorts): to repay the money if I judge I *should;* to repay but only if I think it *convenient;* to repay but only if I *want* to; to repay but only if I think doing so is in my *immediate interests;* or to repay unless I have a *whim* not to.

According to many universalizability tests, none of these maxims is universalizable. A typical argument that each of these universalizations is contradictory runs that if any such maxim were thought to be the one in play, no one would lend money on a promise to repay it. The argument concludes that these maxims, thus, undercut themselves: that they are self-destructive and contradictory.

I think such claims of self-destructiveness are overblown. Harry Frankfurt makes a similar claim, "The actual quantity of lying is enormous after all, yet social life goes on. That people often lie hardly renders it impossible to benefit from being with them. It only means that we have to be careful."[6] And indeed, many of us are willing to lend money to family members, friends, charitable organizations, and others even when we know that there is a good chance that they will not keep their promise to repay it. This willingness can be reasonable and even commendable. Some of what I say bears on this. But I am far more concerned to show that whether or not these universalized maxims are, or are found to be, contradictory can depend on the emotional configurations of the person who has the maxim or of others judging it.

To show this, let us turn to various forms of rigidity – even forms that are far less rigid than those discussed in Chapter 4, section 1. I suggest that whether you find those universalized maxims contradictory can depend on how willing you are to enter into what I will call uncertain arrangements. By this, I mean arrangements where there is a good chance that the agent will mislead or disappoint others, such as the promisee, involved in the arrangement; and where, on account of this, there is likely to be contention and disagreement about what is to be done about repaying the money. To the extent that people are rigid and cannot bear uncertainty, they may well find it difficult or even intolerable to allow judgment and discretion a significant role in determining whether a promise is to be kept. They will find the relevant universalizations intolerable, and even impossible and contradictory – precisely because these universalizations violate their re-

---

6 "The Faintest Passion," Presidential Address to the Eastern Division of the American Philosophical Association, 1991, *Proceedings and Addresses of the American Philosophical Association,* 66 (1992) 5–16, p. 6.

quirements of certainty. (The issues over rigidity are similar to issues about different attitudes to risk, as discussed in regard to Rawls's original position.)

Rigidity is not the only explanation for finding uncertain arrangements intolerable and impossible. Another explanation is fear or mistrust of what people will do when not bound by strict rules and when judging their own case. This fear or mistrust can include thinking that, if given a chance, people will willfully withhold repayments. It can also include thinking, somewhat more benignly, that people are all too prone to make mistakes when judging their own case – perhaps mistakes favoring themselves or mistakes favoring others. These fearful or mistrustful people need not be bothered by uncertainty. Indeed, they may think it all too certain what will happen, if people are allowed to judge when to keep promises.

Another example of promising might be useful. Despite having promised to attend a departmental meeting, you extend your vacation and spend an extra day at the beach, simply to enjoy the sun. How people evaluate this can depend on their character and emotional configuration. (Of course, it can also depend on many other factors, such as how well you typically do your part in the running of the department.)

Those who are "understanding" and "easygoing" may excuse you and what you did. They might simply envy you for having something so much more enjoyable to do, and for being committed enough to your own enjoyment to pursue this even in the face of departmental demands. Such people might find little problem in what you did, and certainly no problem approaching a contradiction even in a universalization of your maxim. The worst they imagine happening is that the business of the department could be slowed down. But those who are more rigid may condemn you and what you did, seeing intolerable problems for the department, perhaps even the university, if everyone did that. They, thus, might well find what you did inexcusable and intolerable and its universalization contradictory. As counterparts to these rigid people, there may also be people who have such formless or indeterminate goals – or are so willing to go wherever the flow might take them, perhaps because they see themselves more as onlookers than agents – that hardly any universalized maxim strikes them as contradictory.

My goal here is simply to point out how different emotional configurations can lead to different judgments. It is not to use the possibility of different judgments – and the difficulty, if not the impossibility, of singling out which single one is correct – to fault moral theories that use universalizability tests. I am not convinced that it is always a defect of a theory to allow for various different, even conflicting, correct or at least acceptable evaluations. (In this, I may strongly disagree with those theories.)

I want now to consider three worries that have been raised about my claim: that I have used only nonformal understandings of contradictoriness; that I have used only portions of maxims; and that I slide between what a maxim is and what it is interpreted to be.

The first worry is that I have been working with a nonformal understanding of contradictoriness, taking it simply in terms of what is found emotionally intolerable or difficult to accept. But this is mistaken in several ways. That a person would *find* a universalization intolerable is sufficient for some, even though not all, such tests. Some, even if not all, contradiction tests do use a nonformal understanding of contradictoriness. And some others which do not, are unattractive or have problems precisely because they do not. (I will return to this.)

Further, many of these cases of claimed contradictoriness can be shown formally contradictory. (I make no claim, one way or the other, whether this is the sense required by all formalistic ethics, including Kant's.) Here we should note that a goal of avoiding uncertainty and "living by the rules" is an overarching thematic goal of at least many sorts of rigid people. (This does not require that they articulate or even recognize this as one of their goals.) Many of those maxims of promising are formally inconsistent with this thematic, overarching goal.

To see this, suppose that a person acts with the maxim to repay borrowed money, but only if there is no contrary desire. And suppose further that the person does so because having the money under those extremely favorable conditions will, the person thinks, help keep anxiety at bay. But the universalization of this maxim involves uncertainty and anxiety of exactly the sort that this person wants to avoid. It is, thus, possible to understand a universalization of this maxim in some such way as, "I make a promise to repay money, which depends on people lending (me) money on promises, in a world where no one lends (me) money on promises."

All of this applies to both others and oneself. *Others:* If you find uncertainty difficult or think poorly of people or just of me, you may naturally describe or interpret my not keeping a promise as my not keeping it just because I do not want to, or as acting willfully, or on a whim, or simply because I do not think it convenient for me. But if you are less rigid and more convinced of my general goodwill and good judgment, you might interpret my not keeping my promise as an expression of my good judgment – whether or not you agree with the judgment I made, or even see how I made it.

Let us now turn to *oneself*: Suppose that very reluctantly and only after serious deliberation, you decide not to keep a particular promise. You might misunderstand the basis of your decision and mischaracterize it as just doing what is convenient, or as what you want, or as acting on whim, or just for short-term self-interest. And you can misunderstand yourself in this way because of your rigidity, your finding uncertainty so intolerable, or because of your lack of trust in yourself.

To give a more particular explanation of this self-misunderstanding, you may find it so intolerable to rely on your own judgment that you should violate that rule that you find it far easier to believe that you must have made some sort of moral error in your deliberation. You would rather see yourself as having made a mistake than as having made, or having to make, such judgments. Or perhaps more generally, as a Sartrian might put it, you find freedom and responsibility so difficult to bear that you would rather think that you had made a moral error in deciding not to keep the promise than to have rules that require judgment.

One conclusion to draw here is that the fact that people find certain universalized maxims contradictory can show a lot about those people, their character, and their emotions, not just the maxims. Moreover, it can show that a test of noncontradiction, at least when deployed by or applied to certain people, is unattractive and unworthy of being followed. This goes some way toward showing that such a test is a plausible moral test only when it is isolated from certain emotional configurations and allied with certain others. And this, in turn, goes some way toward showing that for us to be reasonable in finding such a test reasonable and attractive, we must make significant inquiries or assumptions about emotional configurations.

The second worry is that I have considered only portions of maxims, and that the ones I offered do not show anything like the full *meaning* of the maxim to the agent. I think, however, that my discussion goes some way toward doing this, by indicating that our rigid person's overarching goal is to avoid anxiety, and by at least intimating that this person borrows the money intending to repay it on such favorable terms precisely to have enough money to keep anxiety at bay. Further, and far more important, this objection undercuts itself and misunderstands my goal. My goal was never to offer a thorough account of maxims and universalizability. It was to offer an account that is thorough enough to show the importance of emotions in the use and assessment of maxims. And this present objection, on its own, affirms that – precisely by its complaint about meaning. Part of what a maxim means to the agent involves emotional meaning.

A correlative way to put this second worry is that I have omitted much of the character "behind" the maxims: what people show themselves to be in their acts and maxims. I have not discussed how intending to keep a promise to repay money only if no contrary whim intervenes gives strong evidence of taking oneself to be specially privileged and specially entitled to make an exception for oneself. Or perhaps such promisers see their dealings with other people as games in which they occupy the role of trickster, Puck, a king, or even a god – once again, seeing themselves as exceptions and as having special entitlements.

However, at least many of these ways of taking onself involve particular emotional configurations, thus sustaining my claim. For example (as discussed later, especially in Chapter 10), seeing oneself as especially entitled is central to the emotional configurations of narcissism. (Whatever we might say in criticism of Kant's ethics, we must acknowledge it as a resolute enemy of narcissism.)

The third worry is that my discussion of the role of emotions in consistency tests moves too easily, and certainly without enough discussion, between what a maxim is and what it is interpreted to be. But unless one takes maxims as, somehow, clear and present to mind – perhaps fully articulated intentions coupled with fully articulated background assumptions – I find this movement hard to stop. I do not mean that so far as interpretation is concerned, anything goes – perhaps provided only that the theory and theoretician are clever or convincing enough. Nor do I mean that one can pick and choose what one's (or another's) maxim is – fiddling around, so to speak, until one gets a maxim that will or will not pass a test of noncontradiction. I mean that instead of the fixity and clarity suggested by 'what a maxim *is*', what is available may be more dependent on interpretation than is often acknowledged. We might once again consider the person who deliberates seriously about whether to keep a promise and decides reluctantly not to, but who mischaracterizes this deliberation as nothing more than window dressing or rationalization for acting on a whim.

In addition, I sometimes wonder whether we should be concerned with what a maxim is, or instead with what "it" could have been. What I mean can be put in terms of development. Earlier I suggested that because you mistrust yourself, you can misinterpret yourself, failing to see that you, after due thought, have and are acting on good reasons. You might instead think that you are acting willfully. It is also possible that by living in ways that encourage or embody this form of self-misinterpretation, you change yourself: now, your reasons, at least those running counter to rules, lack force. Indeed, you may now no longer have those reasons. At the least, you may no longer feel their force *as reasons* and they may be inaccessible to you *as reasons*. Willfulness is all you experience as running counter to rules, at least in yourself. Indeed, that may be all there now is in you for you to experience as running counter to rules. This is to describe you as a person who does not see yourself as morally autonomous, and who thinks that whenever you disagree with the rules, you are in the wrong, having been moved only by whim and willfulness. Only through a change in yourself, perhaps a gain in self-confidence and trust in yourself, will you be able to regain those reasons as reasons.

I hasten to add that I am not saying what is clearly false: that if you look to rules, you therefore show that you are rigid or lacking in autonomy; or that if you see what comes from yourself as willful, you show yourself to be lacking in autonomy. Rather, I was concerned to describe some ways of looking to rules and interpreting and understanding oneself. People who are both autonomous and nonrigid can certainly look to rules in autonomous, nonrigid ways. And people who are neither rigid nor lacking in autonomy can recognize that some of their desires, including some that run counter to rules, really are expressions of whim and willfulness.

Thus, to characterize rigid people or autonomous people, we need to say more than that they do or do not recur to rules. We need, also, to describe their *attitude* to rules, *how* they do or do not look to them. This is to say that the contrast between "deciding on one's own" and "relying on rigid rules," as well as the notions of rigidity and autonomy, cannot be understood without understanding the emotional configurations of the people in question.

To turn now to a related point: I have not been concerned to suggest that rigid people, say, need be mistaken about contradictoriness. They can certainly be right in thinking that they have the maxim they think they do. These people's lives and moral worlds may be constructed from, and understood in terms of, the categories used in those maxims. Those people can also be right in thinking that they find those universalized maxims contradictory. And they can further be right in finding those universalized maxims contradictory. In short, they can be right in thinking that, as they correctly understand those universalized maxims, they are contradictory.

Further, my claim is not that if I see why such people find those universalized maxims contradictory, I will have to downgrade, or even reassess, the probative force I think that such contradictoriness should have for them in making or judging their own decisions, or the probativeness it should have for me in assessing those people, their decisions, and their actions. Nor does my claim bear on whether or not it is best or even, somehow, morally necessary for them to be guided by contradiction tests. There may be no better moral test for them. Perhaps this last should read: or at least there may be no better moral test that they can use. This allows that there could be a better moral test, but that it is impossible for them to use it. For characterological reasons, say, such as their rigidity, they find it impossible.

There may now be a danger that useful conclusions could disappear in a sea of concessiveness. To counter this, I want to emphasize two points. First, any hesitancy I have about the probative force of contradictions found by rigid or mistrustful people concerns moderate rigidity or mistrust. Matters seem far clearer, and thus quite different, in regard to severe or pathological rigidity, including fanaticism. For example, we might attach absolutely no probative weight to anti-Semites finding a universalized maxim contradictory if the impossibility is due to a conflict between a particular maxim and their thematic, overarching anti-Semitism. And we might also think that these anti-Semites also should attach no weight to such contradictions.

Second, I also want to emphasize that I take my hesitancy about moderately rigid and moderately mistrustful people to be significant. I do find it very unclear how and to what extent contradictions due to moderate rigidity are morally probative. But – and this is the crux – while this is unclear, I find no unclarity about the fact of contradictoriness. At the very same time that I find it unclear what moderately rigid people should do and how they should determine this in light of those contradictions, I can join them in finding absolutely clear what would be contradictory by their own lights.[7]

This casts serious doubts on the role those tests can or should play, at least under some emotional conditions. It supports my claim that in order for noncontradiction tests to be attractive and plausible as moral tests, they will have to be isolated from some emotional configurations and conjoined with other emotional configurations. It also supports my claim that we should demand more of tests of noncontradiction than simply that they are tests for contradiction.

My claims about how emotions and emotional configurations are important even for formal tests of consistency are, of course, not just about rigid or mistrustful people. Much the same holds in regard to the many emotional problems, especially the neuroses and psychoses, discussed elsewhere in this work (especially Chapter 3, section 2).

---

7 Some similar problems in applying contradictory, even countermoral, rules are discussed in *Plural and Conflicting Values* (Oxford: Oxford University Press, 1990), pp. 96–105.

3 The right of self-defense and emotions

This section looks at the right of self-defense, another area in which emotions might seem unimportant for value and evaluation. Consider the following sort of case:[8] I am on a small ledge, barely large enough for me, hundreds of feet up a sheer cliff; you are falling toward me and, unless I do something, will land on me in a way that will push me off the cliff to my death. Many hold that I have the right to save myself by deflecting you, thus resulting in your death; and that I have this right no matter whether you launched yourself at me to knock me to my death, were launched at me by someone else with that goal, or merely slipped while innocently walking along the top of the cliff.

For those who hold this, it is only a small move to hold that I also have this right of self-defense no matter what your motives and emotions before or during the fall: no matter whether you launched yourself at me out of murderous hatred or out of a well-intentioned and beneficent thought that ending my life at that time would be doing me a favor; whether or not you are pleased or dismayed at the thought of doing me in; pleased or dismayed at the thought of taking me with you. Perhaps this is right. But I do not think we can – and I know we cannot simply – extend this to other cases of the right to self-defense. Even if emotions play no role in the right to self-defense against being killed, this does not show that they play no role in the right to self-defense, quite generally.

As will be discussed in Chapter 8, section 1, I have serious worries about using the example of killing another person as just an example, just to make a general point. I will therefore not discuss how, or whether, this case generalizes to other cases involving the right of self-defense to kill another person or allow another to die – except to make a very brief claim, for which some support is given later. I think that emotions often can make a difference, perhaps not so much whether, but at least how, you may defend yourself in ways that guarantee or run the risk of killing another person or allowing another person to die. I think a case could be made that you owe different amounts of care and kindness in how you defend yourself depending on whether the person endangering you is doing so out of hate or as a matter of unintended and strongly regretted accident.

---

[8] This example borrows from Judith Jarvis Thomson, "Self-Defense," *Philosophy and Public Affairs,* 20 (1991) 283–310. She is concerned with intentions, not emotions. My thanks are owed John Finnis for discussion. See also his "Intention and Side-Effects," in R. G. Frey and Christopher W. Morris, eds., *Liability and Responsibility* (Cambridge: Cambridge University Press, 1991), and "*Bland:* Crossing the Rubicon?" *Law Quarterly Review,* 109 (1993) 329–337.

This is all I will say about the bearing of emotions on the right to kill another person, or let another person die, in self-defense. I do, however, want to show that emotions are important for other rights of self-defense, when matters of life and death are not involved. Suppose that I am on a moderately crowded bus and someone comes lurching toward me in a manner that is likely to cause me some minor pain unless I get out of the way or deflect that person. Perhaps I will be heavily jostled, or have my painfully swollen feet trodden on, or I will be knocked against the side of the bus. I think that what I may do in such a case depends in part on why that person is lurching toward me. If the person is using the swaying of the bus as a welcome excuse to bang into one person after another, or just into me, then I think I owe him very little consideration. I can protect myself, even if this will hurt him. I can step aside or deflect him, even if this will cause him to bang heavily into the side of the bus or to fall down the step well. Exaggerating the possibility of calculation, I can cause him at least the amount of pain he would have caused me, or perhaps a fair amount more, as exemplary and immediate justice.

But suppose that this person, coming down upon me, was feeling and acting in a thoroughly civil way, trying to keep his balance and trying not to inconvenience, much less hurt, any other passenger, and is simply thrown off balance by the swerving of the bus. In this case, I think I owe him a lot of consideration. In a small way and for a short time, we are a community of people, sharing risks, who owe each other common decency and courtesy. In this case, this includes accepting minor harms or injuries rather than protecting ourselves at the serious expense of another innocent member of the community. In this case, I may well have no right to protect myself in a way that causes that innocent projectile of a person serious harm. And it might well be wrong for me to do so.

This is to speak directly of the bearing of intentions, motives, and the like on rights and what I may do. Much the same holds for emotions, and not only those figuring in those motives. I think I owe the person lurching toward me far less consideration if he is pleased at the prospect of hurting me; or if he took little care not to endanger others; or if he set himself loose out of hatred or contempt for me or for others. On the other hand, if, even while lurching toward me, he is unhappy and apologetic, perhaps even dismayed, about the hurt or injury he may cause, then, again, I think I owe him a lot of consideration. His fellow feeling establishes a fellowship between us and entitles him to some considerable care and consideration.

I want to end this section with a note about another set of cases. Suppose a woman is deciding how to deal with a man who is telling her that he thinks the proper place for women is at home, not out in the workplace. The emotions and emotional configuration of the man can certainly be important considerations for her in assessing what he is saying, what he means by it, how serious and insulting a matter it is, and also for deciding what she might say or do in reply. There is a considerable difference, including one of emotional configuration, between a man who says these things out of hatred and contempt for women, and a man who, perhaps in a grandfatherly way – he may be of that age – "simply" wants to protect women from the rough and tumble and the nastiness of business life.

4 How being a good person and acting well requires emotions

Let us now turn from rights to other moral concerns with being a good person and acting well and ask how emotions stand to them. According to many contemporary ethical theories, there is an unbridgeable divide between act evaluations and agent evaluations. Many of my early writings argued against this.[9] So, for example, "Act and Agent Evaluations" showed four different patterns of connections between act and agent evaluations. First, the agent evaluation is simply transferable to the act: for example, to act with malice is to act maliciously. Second, and in a very similar way, an act can be wrong to do simply because it involves acting on a morally bad intention. Third, the grounds for both evaluations are the same: for example, driving while drunk makes the driving wrong and shows the drivers to be uncaring, even bad, people. Fourth, some evaluations are conjointly act evaluations and agent evaluations: for example, to act supererogatorily is at once to do more than is morally required and to do so with morally good intentions.

As noted in the Preface, those early works eventually led to *Valuing Emotions*. This chapter, and much else in the book, return the compliment, by using the moral importance of emotions to show once again – and

---

[9] "Intentions and Act Evaluations," *Journal of Philosophy*, 67 (1970) 589–602; "'Ought' and 'Can'," *Australasian Journal of Philosophy*, 49, (1971) 303–316; "Act and Agent Evaluations," *Review of Metaphysics*, (1973) 42–61; "Agent and Other: Against Ethical Universalism," *Australasian Journal of Philosophy*, 54 (1976) 206–220; "The Schizophrenia of Modern Ethical Theories," *Journal of Philosophy*, 73 (1976) 453–466; "Desiring the Bad," *Journal of Philosophy*, 76 (1979) 738–753; "Intellectual Desire, Emotion, and Action," in Amélie O. Rorty, ed., *Explaining Emotions* (Berkeley: University of California Press, 1980); "Values and Purposes: The Limits of Teleology and the Ends of Friendship," *Journal of Philosophy*, 78 (1981) 747–765; "Affectivity and Self-Concern: The Assumed Psychology in Aristotle's Ethics," *Pacific Philosophical Quarterly*, 64 (1983) 211–229. The four patterns mentioned later are set out on p. 43 of "Act and Agent Evaluations."

indeed in many of the same ways, but now focused more directly on emotions – those interconnections. My early articles also argued against a related theme of many contemporary ethical theories: that duties are what have real ethical importance and that emotions are irrelevant to this and other matters of moral importance. Only slightly tempering this, it was allowed that emotions can modulate or nuance duties and other matters of moral importance. On this view, emotions are, at best, only evaluative frills.

To assess the plausibility of this claim, we could reconsider some of the cases discussed previously, such as wanting the cancer surgeon to be interested in you as a person, not merely as a site for an operation, or having to deal with an angry administrator. But rather than go over those cases, let us consider the following story, told to me by a student.

My sister (call her S for short) felt, perhaps recognized, a duty to help the very elderly widow, Mrs. W, next door. So S went several times a week to help W with her washing. Although S frequently told W not to fill the washing machine more than halfway, otherwise it washes the clothes poorly, W would just as frequently fill it to the brim. So S usually had to unload the machine. When this happened – sometimes even when it did not – S would come back home exasperated, muttering about how inconsiderate, and really how ungrateful, W was, causing her all that extra trouble, when she was, after all, going out of her way to be kind to her. Nonetheless, S persevered, albeit often grudgingly and with bad grace. Of course, it would have been better had she not begrudged helping W. But at least she did her duty, and that's what really matters.

I do not want to discuss the comparative question of how to rank doing one's duty, doing one's duty with kindness, and expressing one's kindness by means of a kind act. My concern here is simply to take issue with the suggestion that enacted kindness – kindness as felt and expressed – and other enacted emotions are only evaluative frills. In regard to this case, I see little room for argument. I find it hard not to see S as lacking in moral character and as showing moral failings by lacking kindness. I do not see these failings as failings of, or in regard to, moral frills.

For other cases which show that having or lacking certain emotions can be and show a moral failure, we might consider people who say and do the appropriate things – for example, express their gratitude for help or a favor – but who feel nothing, including no gratitude, and thus are not grateful. So too, we could consider people who make restitution for a wrong, but without feeling anything, including remorse or shame. Such lacks can be a moral fault.

Putting the matter this way may be thought to run together three issues: first, whether one can be kind, grateful, or have remorse, say, without affect; second, whether the nature or existence of one's affect bears on the moral quality of one's having or showing the emotion or at least the conventional expression of it; third, as a specification of the second, whether having affect can be needed in order to have or show these in morally correct and required ways. The first was discussed and answered affirmatively in Chapter 1. This answer may, by itself, entail an affirmative answer for the second and third issues. But even if we give a negative answer to that first question, or simply prescind from it, we have reason to give affirmative answers to the other two.

So for example, I hold that not *feeling* gratitude for benefits received or remorse for harms caused can be moral defects. I say "can be" since here, as so often, there is room for justification, exculpation, and excuse. I should feel grateful for the great benefit you bestowed on me, but I am so overwhelmed, even stunned by it, so overcome by feelings of unworthiness, that I do not. Similarly, I can be so taken aback by what I did, so ashamed of myself, that I am unable to feel remorse. In these cases, my not having the right feelings may not show any defect.

Ultimately, we want a fine-grained account of when such considerations do, and when they do not, show a moral failing. Perhaps my being too ashamed of myself to have remorse shows improper self-absorption and narcissism. But for present concerns, what is important is that there are serious ethical and moral psychological issues about how these factors provide good or bad defenses. These could not be serious issues, unless having or lacking emotions and affects can be a matter of moral importance. The only conclusion, then, is that having or not having the right emotions and other affects can be a matter of moral importance.

But simply *having* them is not enough. They must be had in the right way. People who have the right emotions can remain with them for too short or too long a time. Here we could consider people who claim to feel serious remorse at a misdeed, or deep grief at the death of a relative or friend, but are almost immediately back to their old concerns and ways of life. This too can be a moral fault. It might show insincerity. Or it might indicate that the emotion did not go deep enough. Or, of course, it might show no fault, but at most a problem: the matter may be too painful for this person – perhaps for all people of any sensitivity – for reasons that in no way show or depend on defects.

Similarly, it is possible for someone to remain too long – and certainly too lovingly, too sentimentally – with an emotion. These, too, can be morally significant, even moral faults.

There are other ways for people to be emotionally engaged in the wrong ways. One of these other ways is letting one's emotional engagement wander from how and where it should be. This can be unintentional, perhaps showing only a lack of focus and concentration. It can also be intentional, for example, as an attempt to turn away from a disturbing emotion, perhaps through an attempt to distract oneself with what is less confronting. Here we could consider people who, to avoid being remorseful about a wrongdoing – to avoid focusing on it and taking it up with remorse – turn their attention and concern to other issues about the wrongdoing. They might focus on the "forensic" question of exactly how bad their wrong was, or they might let themselves get caught up in amazement, whether wondering or amused, that they could do such a wrong.[10]

Here we could consider what Helen Block Lewis writes in *Shame and Guilt in Neurosis:*

When guilt is evoked, it can merge into a "problem" in the rational assignment of motivation, responsibility and consequences. As the guilty person becomes involved in these problems, it can happen that guilt affect subsides, while ideation about the events continues. Guilt thus has an affinity for "isolation of affect."[11]

We could also consider what she calls "by-passing":

Another kind of defense against shame appears to operate before any affective state is evoked. This defense, which is best described as "by-passing" shame feeling, does not obliterate the recognition of shame events, but appears to prevent the development of shame feeling. This by-passing of shame is accomplished by a "distancing" maneuver. The self views itself from the standpoint of the "other," but without much affect. The person wonders what he would think of himself if he were in the position of the "other." The content of the ideation in question concerns shame events, but without shame affect. Shame affect is by-passed and replaced by watching the self from a variety of viewpoints. (p. 38)

For an example of a different sort of lack of focus or misfocus, consider someone seemingly lost in a passionate embrace, who sneaks a look at the clock to see how much time is left, or whose mind drifts off to think of an upcoming meeting. If this lack of emotional engagement with the other person is not a moral fault, it is at least important in characterizing and evaluating the person and the person's feelings and actions. We could also consider people who listen only vacantly and are really "somewhere else": for example, one's children when being reproved or told what to do. Or we could consider those attending a lecture who, instead of paying attention to

---

10 This is suggested by Richard Moran in "Impersonality, Character, and Moral Expressivism," *Journal of Philosophy,* 90 (1993) 578–595. My thanks are owed to Moran for discussion of this and other issues in this work.
11 New York: International Universities Press, 1971, p. 42.

it, are off in their fantasies and let themselves continue in these fantasies. Such emotional wandering, misattention, and inattention are matters of moral importance and can be moral faults.

For a final group of cases, contrast the following sorts of conversations: between a child and parent discussing arrangements for schoolwork or work around the house; between a surgeon and a nurse during a crucial stage of an operation; among acquaintances at a cocktail party; between parents having dinner, whose sick baby is fretfully asleep in another room. What in one case would be inappropriate or unacceptable emotional wandering or inattention, or preparedness to change emotional attention would be morally acceptable, even necessary, in another.

These cases and the earlier ones show clearly that the nature and extent of affective engagement is morally important. They also show clearly that there is not just one particular amount or degree of emotional engagement and attention that should be had by a person, much less all people, in all situations. This is obvious. What should also be obvious is that this is also personally, socially, and morally important.

Before leaving this issue, I want to mention another important point: lack of focus, in any of its varying degrees and sorts, need not be a defect. It can be exactly what is called for – for example, in order to avoid getting emotionally caught up in pain and intrusions. We should often be glad if people are able to dissociate from horrendous goings-on: goings-on it would be devastating to engage fully with, or even to attend to with full sensitivity.

There has been little direct discussion of such issues in contemporary ethics and moral psychology. But they have come up in discussions of certain "puzzles." Here we could think of the discussion surrounding "one thought too many" – for example, whether a ship's captain who rescues his wife, rather than some other drowning passenger, thinking "she is my wife and I have special obligations to my wife" has not had *one thought too many*.[12] Some think it clear that, and perhaps how, any false or inaccurate thought could be one thought too many, while denying, or finding it hard to explain, how this could hold for any true or accurate thought. Others cast the issue in terms of relevance and hold that if the thought is relevant, it cannot be any too many.

But I think the issue is also – and sometimes is only – a question of appropriateness, especially affective appropriateness. Here, to have one

---

12 See Bernard Williams, "Persons, Character, and Morality," in Amélie O. Rorty, ed., *The Identities of Persons* (Berkeley: University of California Press, 1976), p. 214.

thought too many involves being affectively engaged with what then and there one should not be engaged with, or in ways that one should not.

If this suggestion and my earlier suggestions are correct, we see that the issue of one thought too many is in no way a strange or uncommon issue. It is just an instance of the usual issue of how one should feel and think – for example, where one's attention should be directed, with what intensity, to what proportion, for how long. Indeed, holding that it is a philosophical or moral puzzle how any thought – or any true or accurate thought – can be one thought too many is to suggest that thoughts and affects, thinking and feeling, are outside of the purview of morality. On such a view, all of what one thinks about, how one thinks about it, and one's forms and objects of affective engagement would be outside the ambit of moral concern and scrutiny. I think that this view, rather than the view that there can be one thought too many, is the one that is strange and unacceptable.

Even in these limited areas concerning focus, there is no end to the ways we can go wrong with emotions. But having said what I hope is enough to show at least the existence of these ways, I want to examine yet another way to go wrong with emotions and other affective states: by feeling and acting with various of these. I will focus on spite.

I think it could be morally wrong of me – I would do what is wrong and show myself to be morally lacking – to do something to spite you: for example, tell your superiors that you and I had been embezzling from the company, or were members of an unfavored political group. It would be wrong, at least in part, precisely because it is done out of spite. It would be wrong whether or not your superiors cared – perhaps, unbeknownst to me, they too were embezzling, or were members of that group, or you and they had laid a successful trap for me, to see if I was corrupt or trustworthy. So too, my spiteful telling would be wrong, even if it would not be wrong to tell out of some other motive and with some other emotion, such as contrition.

To be sure, my telling out of spite need not be overall wrong. But even if not overall wrong, it need not be merely prima facie wrong – at least not in the sense that what is merely prima facie no longer counts once overridden, and no longer counts along with the overall judgment. The wrongness of telling out of spite can be a remainder.[13] My telling out of spite could be,

---

13 On remainders, see Bernard Williams, "Ethical Consistency" in his *Problems of the Self* (Cambridge: Cambridge University Press, 1973), p. 179. The topic of remainders and such mixed evaluations – how an act can be overall right but still in part wrong – is a central topic of *Plural and Conflicting Values,* chs. 1–4.

and could remain, prima facie wrong even if telling is overall right; even if the only way I could tell would be out of spite; and even if it is overall right for others, such as the police, to get me to tell, even though they know I would do so out of spite.

At this point, some will claim that morality is action-guiding, and is concerned mainly if not only with guiding action. By this they mean to remind us that all we ought to do in these and other cases is *act,* do some act, and do this well. After all, they say, morality is concerned only with telling us to do, and why to do, some act: that is, an act that can be characterized without recourse to emotions; or at most an act of the sort that would, typically, be done with a certain emotion, but which in this case need not be done with it. Thus, it would not be required to act with kindness, but only to do an act of a sort that would be done with kindness: this is the act that would be "left over" when the kindness is "subtracted" from the act that is done with kindness.

I reject this claim. First, what we often want is to have kindness shown us, to be treated with kindness, not simply treated in a way typically expressive of kindness. As Strawson puts it,

> We should consider also in how much of our behaviour the benefit or injury resides mainly or entirely in the manifestation of attitude itself. So it is with good manners, and much of what we call kindness, on the one hand; and with deliberate rudeness, studied indifference, or insult on the other. (p. 63)

This might be thought unimportant since it is concerned only with what is good or wanted, not duty. But the case against the moral importance of affectivity is that what has affectivity is, as such, morally unimportant all over and quite generally, not just in regard to duty. Indeed, were the argument restricted to duty, it would require an argument showing the extent to which duty is important for morality, value, and evaluation and the extent to which other concerns than duty are important for morality, value, and evaluation.

Strawson's comments help show that the argument that we can have a duty to act with kindness – not simply to do the sort of act typically expressive of kindness – turns on cases. In some cases I must, and in others I need not, perhaps even must not, act with kindness. In some cases, if you have acted with kindness toward me, I might therefore have an obligation to act that way to you – that is, to act with kindness or a similar emotion. Or if I cannot do that, then I must have and perhaps must show regret or remorse. And if I cannot do that, then I may well have failed in multiple ways. As Richard Moran put it, in many interpersonal situations we desire or even *demand* a certain specific emotional response from the other person, and this demand often takes a moral form. That is, it may be of the greatest *moral* importance to us that the other person, for example, feel grateful or sorry, etc.[14]

Second, even the objection that what we have a duty to do is only to do an act typically expressive of emotions recognizes an important role for emotions in regard to duty. The role is to help specify the sort of act we may have a duty to do. To deny this role, more would have to be shown than that we never have a duty to act with an emotion, but only to do the sort of act that would be done with it. It would also have to be shown that none of the acts we have a duty to do, including those typically expressive of an emotion, are our duty for reasons having to do with emotions.

Those making that objection must find a difference in such acts that does not rest on the one being done out of spite and the other done out of contrition. I do not think they will be able to do this. To be sure, there may be many differences between typical acts done from spite and from contrition. But in particular cases, such as the one at hand, there may be no differences – other than the different emotions with which they are done.

I will conclude this section with two related remarks about the evaluative and moral issues just mentioned. First, the values and evaluations of one's having or not having certain emotions, and of the ways one has or does not have them, are rarely, if ever, central to our important ethical works, and they are often enough not even mentioned, much less discussed, in those works.[15] However, I do not think that their absence from our works on ethics shows that these issues lack importance. I think, rather, that it shows an important lack, and indeed something of a lack of importance, in our work in ethics.

However, there is a closely related issue, mentioned briefly in the Introduction, that does figure in recent ethical theory. This concerns what is relevant for evaluating acts and, on some accounts, for individuating them. For our purposes, there are two main views in contention here. One holds that only those features of the world that are constitutively or causally effected by an act – perhaps along with, or, even alternatively, features that

---

14 In a letter to me, with those emphases.
15 They are discussed by Iris Murdoch in *The Sovereignty of Good* (London: Routledge and Kegan Paul, 1970); by me in "Intentions and Act Evaluations," "Act and Agent Evaluations," and *Plural and Conflicting Values,* for example ch. 4, section 3; by Lawrence Blum in *Friendship, Altruism, and Morality* (London: Routledge and Kegan Paul, 1980), "Compassion," in Rorty, *Explaining Emotions,* and "Iris Murdoch and the Domain of the Moral," *Philosophical Studies,* 50 (1986) 343–368; and by Richard Moran in "Impersonality, Character, and Moral Expressivism."

are aimed at – are relevant for evaluating the act, and perhaps for determining what the act is. The other holds that what is relevant includes – whether or not it is restricted to – the agent's intentions, desires, values, and character. These last are not among the "features of the world" constitutively or causally effected by the act, nor are they part of its goal, as understood by the first view.

Returning to the earlier example, the first view denies and the second holds that precisely in virtue of the different values, desires, intentions, and other characterological elements in play, an act done out of spite can be an evaluatively different act than an act done out of contrition, whether or not what they achieve in the world are exactly the same. Further, again precisely because of the different values and other characterological elements in play, what these acts are as acts can be different whether or not what they achieve in the world are exactly the same.[16]

When conjoined with my account of emotions, the second view gives about all the materials needed to show that emotions can be constitutively relevant for act evaluations and values of acts, and perhaps also for the individuation of acts. Correlatively, the first view gives about all the materials needed to hold – mistakenly, I have argued and will continue to argue – that emotions can have only external evaluative importance for acts: for example, by being causes, motives, and added flourishes.

5 Many ordinary goods, especially interpersonal ones, are emotional

Let us now turn to some other ways to see at once the evaluative importance of emotions and other affective states, and also the interpersonal nature of some of these. This will be to move away from a concern with, or just with, duty. The many goods (and bads) that depend on affectivity range from unimportant ones to the most important ones, such as the goods of family and friends, in addition to the goods of play and many forms of work. These various goods depend on affectivity in various ways. To make

---

[16] A recent study of this is found in Garver, *Aristotle's Rhetoric: The Art of Character.* It is a major theme in various of my writings mentioned in note 9, "Intentions and Act Evaluations," "'Ought' and 'Can'," "Act and Agent Evaluations," "The Schizophrenia of Modern Ethical Theories," "Values and Purposes: The Limits of Teleology and the Ends of Friendship," and also in my *Plural and Conflicting Values*, "Self–Other Asymmetries and Virtue Theory," *Philosophy and Phenomenological Research,* 54 (1994) 689–694, and "Abstract and Concrete Value: Plurality, Conflict, and Maximization," in Ruth Chang, ed., *Incommensurability, Comparability, and Practical Reasoning* (Cambridge, Mass.: Harvard University Press, 1997).

clearer what I am claiming, we should remember a question raised in Chapter 1, section 6: how can mere feelings have evaluative and moral importance? Part of the answer was given in that chapter: feelings are rarely, if ever, merely feelings. Another part of the answer is given by filling out what was just claimed: that many goods depend on affectivity. It would be given, for example, by showing how emotions are important, and how part of this importance depends on their affectivity, not just on their nonaffective parts.

It is to this that I now turn -- or, really, return. We often hear complaints from those who live in our very large and difficult cities. (This does not seem a function just of size. I include New York City, but exclude Sydney and Melbourne – the three large cities I have lived in for long periods of time. But I am sure that New York is not the only city that fits this account.) Just living in such a city, but especially after being out and about, shopping, walking, traveling by public transportation, many people are on edge and feel abraded, worn down. They find themselves unable to look at strangers on the street, or be looked at by them, with equanimity and calm, friendly civility. They find themselves suffused with some combination of wariness and weariness, apprehension, and a distressing form of impersonal and general alertness. We might call this syndrome, *metropolis anxiety*.

I do not think I will attract much argument if I say it is not good, not a part of a good life, to have metropolis anxiety. Nor is it good to live so that metropolis anxiety is a normal and natural way of living and experiencing one's background, everyday condition. Indeed, it is clearly bad, and it helps make life bad.

When I – and, I am sure, many others – think about this anxiety, I fantasize about, sometimes even remember, other places and ways of living. To mention only one feature of these places and ways, I think of neighborhoods, with neighbors: people who looked out for us, not to rob us or beg some money, but to chat, ask how things are, make plans to meet for a drink or a game. This fantasy, it should be stressed, has as one of its organizing grounds and themes what earlier was mentioned dismissively as only an evaluative frill: expressed emotions, moods, attitudes, and interests, especially pleasant, supportive, civil, friendly, decent ones.

Again, I am not concerned to discuss the comparative importance of these affective states and what is generally treated in ethics courses, such as duties of justice, nonmaleficence, and the like. So, I am not concerned to question or argue which of these we should favor when they are in conflict – as they often are, at least in our major cities that give rise to metropolis anxiety. I am, however, concerned to point out that many of our desires and goods involve solidarity, community, ways of being with others. Emotions, attitudes, moods, and their attunements with those of other people, are among the principal ways we achieve this.

In what remains of this chapter, I want to illustrate some other ways emotions contribute to important aspects of our lives that are interpersonal and social. I will do this by starting with an entirely familiar context: doing philosophy, as practiced in contemporary, academic departments in the English-speaking world. I will also expand on these comments, with many returns to philosophy.

Philosophy as a discipline, practice, and profession is a complex amalgam of what is individual and what is interpersonal. For the most part, we philosophers write on our own, although some of us do joint papers or books and many give courses with colleagues. As well, many of us take part in reading groups and, of course, give or attend classes. But compared with various other disciplines in the pure and social sciences, and in many other professions and jobs, far fewer philosophers engage in joint research and work. We are mainly organized in departments with each of us more or less on our own, rather than in research groups and teams.

Yet – or is it "Therefore"? – there is much that is emotional, including interpersonally emotional, in doing philosophy. To start with, there is the emotionality of the skeptical, questioning, adversarial method and stance we use in classes, with our texts, and with our colleagues. This is a difficult and many-faceted issue, but some of what I have in mind can be brought out by looking at our use of "I don't understand . . ." as one of the main conversational gambits in philosophical discussion.

This can be used simply to ask for an amplification or clarification; or just to suggest in a standard and polite enough way that an error has been made. But those possibilities are often belied by a lack of interest in replies to these challenges and requests for information – except as material for further challenges. Often, these challenges seem aimed not so much at finding the truth of the matter as establishing the questioner's truth, or even the questioner's right to be recognized as a, if not the, bearer of wisdom and truth on these matters. For many philosophers, these concerns and attendant emotions constitute reasons in favor of being in philosophy. For many other philosophers, however, they are costs that must be borne to do and to be in philosophy. For both sorts of people, our ways of doing philosophy are emotional, either in themselves or by having more external emotional precursors, concomitants, and sequels.

This can be put in a related way that has received some attention recently:

at least as it is now practiced, philosophy is adversarial.[17] Its adversarial and competitive nature interacts in complex ways with our desires for sociality and acceptance. Part of the complexity comes from our wanting acceptance from those we struggle with.

Another comes from not acknowledging to others, or even recognizing, just how adversarial and competitive philosophy is. While we do recognize that sports and business are inherently competitive, gaining much of their allure and power from this, and perhaps also that legal and political processes require competition, I do not know how many of us strongly and openly hold either view about philosophy. Mill's admonitions to the contrary notwithstanding, I do not know how many really welcome different schools of philosophy, say "Continental" and "analytic."

Another part of this complexity comes from the way "I don't understand . . ." can cut off the person whose view is said not to be understood from those who say that they do not understand. It can be felt and suffered as a blow and wound by the person said not to be understood. So taken, "I don't understand your claim that ———" often seems meant and heard as "I don't understand how you could say such a thing" or even "I don't understand *you.*" It can suggest that there is something wrong with you, not just that I do not understand you, and certainly not just that you and I disagree.

Not to understand another or not to be understood by another, especially when that person is important to you, is to be, or to be on the way toward being, cut off from that person. Understanding involves sharing a common world, and agreeing on what it is like. Not being understood is to be treated as an outsider, an alien. It shows a lack of belonging and lack of unity, and often a disturbing or even a dangerous separation. We want to be understood, not simply so that we can accomplish various independently specifiable goals. We want to be understood also so that we can be joined with others.

Theorists such as Heinz Kohut and other *self-psychologists* talk with good reason of our being validated and sustained as a person by being understood by others, and as being invalidated, undermined, and ultimately destroyed by not being understood.[18] Indeed, one way to picture various psychoses is

---

17 Thanks are owed to Terry Winant for discussion here. See Janice Moulton, "A Paradigm of Philosophy: The Adversary Method," in Sandra Harding and Merrill B. Hintikka, eds., *Discovering Reality* (Dordrecht: Reidel, 1983).
18 See also Charles Taylor, "The Politics of Recognition," in *Multiculturalism and "The Politics of Recognition"* (Princeton: Princeton University Press, 1992), reprinted in David Theo Goldberg, ed., *Multiculturalism* (Oxford: Blackwell, 1994), especially pp. 79ff. in the latter.

in terms of the constitutive and more causal ways they involve pervasive, systematic, and uncontrollable failures to understand and be understood.

The interpersonal nature of various activities can also be shown more benignly. Here we can look to the joys we create and share in by working and playing together, the pleasures of a communal life, the interests that are sustained in family life, the special times we appreciate with friends and those we love. Moving to a higher level of theory, we can say with Aristotle that people are political beings. But to get him right, we must extend this, as he did, to the social and interpersonal, not just to what nowadays we call the political. After all, Aristotle also held that to be able to live alone, one must be a beast or a god, not a person. Hobbes, too, was surely right at least about many people when he held that solitariness is a serious defect that one should take the greatest of pains and efforts to avoid. This is not just because we are far more efficient in achieving our own goals when we join together, but rather, as Aristotle and Rousseau emphasized, only when we are joined with others are we truly human, and only when we are joined with others can we live good lives.

We can easily see that many of these and other interpersonal goods involve emotions, indeed are emotional, and that interpersonal emotions help constitute some of these important goods. From the negative side, we could note the difficulties had and caused by people who lack emotional knowledge and sensitivity about their own and others' emotions. Good examples are provided by the sorts of activities and relations open or closed to children whose main reaction to being ignored, jostled, or teased is anger.[19]

These last claims that emotions are needed for interpersonal activities and relations might seem mainly about instrumental preconditions for those activities and relations. I do not think this is right, as can be shown by another brief look at philosophy. For many of us our life in our department and university is, itself, important. This is a life of relationships, of friends and acquaintances, of shared talks, meals, and interests, continued conversations. When these add up well, they add up to a familiar place, a place in which we feel at home and safe, where we feel we are with like-minded people who care for us and like us, even if only coolly. Those members of our department we count as friends may not be character friends, to use Aristotle's term. But neither are they simply pleasure friends or useful friends. They are more like family or family friends (*NE* VIII).

---

19 See, for example, Daniel Goleman, *Emotional Intelligence* (New York: Bantam Books, 1995).

As should be clear, I am here concerned only with the good side of departmental life. Departments, like families, can be unsafe, lonely, bitter places. Hate found in departments can rival the hate we also find in families, in politics, or wherever. As well, nowadays there are moves to think of and evaluate philosophy departments in terms of efficiency and productivity. This has been likened to thinking of them on the model of factories: not dark Satanic mills, but in ways more suited to contemporary life – as quiet, efficient places, business offices, places with no essential provision made for the emotional lives of the workers. What room is made for this is made because of, and is seen and justified in terms of, increased productivity, and not because of or in terms of the intrinsic value, the truly human value, of having emotional lives.[20]

Our workplace must, of course, be thought of in terms of instrumental structures that allow for the work of teaching and doing philosophy. But in addition, it must be thought of in terms of emotional structures that it helps or hinders, embodies or excludes. That the work place – the factory, office, department, store – must be thought of in these two ways, and still others, is a commonplace to sociologists and social psychologists. It is largely ignored by philosophers. Insofar as we notice emotional structures at all, these are largely restricted to structures of intimacy, which unite or separate family, friends, and those in love or sexual relationships. But, our everyday, workaday, life, too, must be understood in terms of the presence and absence of emotional structures.[21]

Here I am thinking not only of philosophy departments in which it is good to work, but also, perhaps too nostalgically, of neighborhood life, the local coffee shops, the brief chats. I am thinking, also, of the life we enjoy in our clubs, sport groups, and in various of our pastimes. Most every boater knows the pleasures of helping and being helped by other boaters, kibitzing and yarning, predicting the weather, discussing the merits and demerits of different boats, different forms of repair and maintenance. Here too, we have important emotional structures. At the least, these are importantly emotional, even if some would not say that they are important.

These emotional structures are part and parcel of our everyday life. Whether they are doing their emotional work well helps determine whether our life is going well. They give the background, the tone, the taste

---

20 On a closely related matter, see Michael Dummett, *Frege: Philosophy of Mathematics*, 2nd impression (London: Duckworth, 1995), pp. viii ff. My thanks are owed Brian Leiter for this reference.
21 Here, too, see Charles Taylor, "The Politics of Recognition" – as reprinted in Goldberg, *Multiculturalism*, especially pp. 79ff.

to our life. And without a background, tone, and taste that are generally good, it is extremely difficult to have a good, or even a decent, life.

Many of these points about the interpersonal and social nature of emotions and their essential connections with value can be put by focusing on the virtues discussed by Aristotle.[22] The virtues are, of course, essential to *eudaimonia;* and emotions are, of course, essential to the virtues. It is common to place the virtues on a scale that starts at the personal and moves to the social – a scale that, not incidentally, also tracks the movement from the arational and irrational to the rational.

Temperance, *sōphrosunē,* has to do with how one stands – internally, in oneself – to one's body and the pleasures and pains that involve its being touched in various ways. It is an *intra*personal virtue. At the other extreme, justice has to do with fairness, where fairness is always *inter*personal (cf. NE V, especially ch. 11). It always involves other people and may not involve the agent personally or directly. It will involve the agent in the way that he or she divides goods with someone else, but justice can also arise in the way the just arbitrator, who has no stake in the matter, divides goods among other people.

Liberality is somewhere between these. It has to do with how – the extent, manner, to whom, and so on – one dispenses wealth and also how one acquires it. Turning to the former, it has to do with how one funds and takes part in enterprises with one's fellows. These enterprises range from the more instrumental, such as repairing municipal buildings, to the more expressive and celebratory, such as a religious rite.

One central point of the celebration is solidarity, being with one's fellows, and to help foster conditions that allow for such fellowship. It is a joining together and an enabling of joining together. The action that is involved – performing the rites, watching the play, hymning the gods – is importantly group action. It is interpersonal. The agent here is the group. And individuals join the group by their own doings.

They also join the group by their feelings. They are with their fellows in feeling and spirit. They attune themselves to each other in communal, joint, interpersonal feeling. I am not here invoking anything mysterious – a group mind, a strange sort of feeling. I am, rather, talking of what we all know and sometimes get: being attuned to and joined with others in our emotions. At an ideal, this involves joint awareness and response, a sharing

---

22 In ch. 4 of *Aristotle's Rhetoric: The Art of Character,* Eugene Garver shows how the emotions discussed in the *Rhetoric* that are properly part of rhetoric are civic emotions. These are emotions of people who are citizens, and that help make them citizens.

of feelings. This is what goes on in many forms of interpersonal play, especially when one is intensely caught up in the play. One forgets oneself, and is taken up, and even "out of oneself" – perhaps even ecstatic – in and by one's own and others' actions and feelings.

In this way, the feelings are social. They concern a social enterprise: an enterprise of a group, perhaps of one's entire society. They are social also by being feelings of the group, or by having one's own feelings attuned to the group. This is part of what it is to be a member of a group. And this is what is wanted in a person Aristotle would recognize as liberal, and to that extent good.

Although my point about social, interpersonal feelings is made well enough by means of liberality, it might be useful to show how even fear can be interpersonal and social. I say "even fear," since courage is the main Aristotelian virtue in which fear figures, and courage, like temperance, is said to be a virtue of the irrational part of the soul, the part we share with animals.

Fear might seem to involve only how the agent is, how the agent can stand danger or pain. But fear as handled by courage may be somewhat different – at least the courage Aristotle is primarily concerned with, courage in military engagements. These engagements are, paradigmatically, group enterprises. True, there may be one-man scouting forays, or fights between two soldiers, or only one soldier may be left to fight against many. Nonetheless, the main concern with fear in courage is what sort of comrade in arms, what sort of member of a fighting group, one will be. Here, it is useful to remember that in some of the fighting formations, one's very life depended directly on the steadfastness of one's fellows. The person on your right held the shield protecting you, you held the shield protecting, not that soldier, but the one on your left, and so on down the line.

To this extent, fear is social. It concerns the social good and the good of a group. But it can also be social in another, related way. In battle, as elsewhere, feelings are contagious and often shared. Despair is said to spread from one soldier to the whole group; it is not merely that one person despairs and then another person despairs, and then another and another – although this is what happens. One person or several people despair and then the whole group, as a group, is demoralized, their joint purpose impeded, if not destroyed, by a group failure. In such cases, the group is the most significant "subject" who is despairing, demoralized, and defeated.

To the extent this is right, what is wanted in a courageous soldier is not simply that within himself, so to speak, he remain steadfast. It is, rather, that he be courageous with his fellows. By this, I mean something along these lines. He should be, if not a tower of strength, then at least not a sinkhole of weakness, sapping the courage of others, weakening them, making them feel weak, tired, vulnerable, and afraid. This, I think, is part of what Aristotle suggests in his discussion of fear in courage. And thus, such fear is interpersonal in yet another way.

Courage, according to Aristotle, also requires spirited confidence, *tharsos*. In many of the ways fear is interpersonal, so is *tharsos*, and thus, once again, so is courage.[23]

There is a somewhat different, but related, way that fear and *tharsos* in courage are interpersonal. One of the central ways that a soldier judges and adjusts his own fear, and his own *tharsos*, is by emotional attunement with his comrades. This can be more or less deliberate. On the more deliberate end of the continuum, from the fact that his most steadfast and experienced comrades are quite fearful, a soldier can conclude that the matter at hand is very dangerous and that a considerable amount of fear is appropriate. On the less deliberate end, one can "give oneself over" to the fear or lack of *tharsos* of the group. Or one may simply find oneself given over to them. Indeed, one may be so caught up in the group's fear or lack of *tharsos* that one does not find oneself at all – not even to be this or that way. One is simply and emotionally part of the group.

In the next chapter, I will amplify and clarify some of these ways that emotions are directly and internally evaluatively important. For present concerns, it is enough that we have seen how common and also how important emotions are for our lives. To take up a point noted at the outset of this work, we have seen that there is far more to our affective life than affective mountains and canyons that overwhelm us. There is also the affective background, the tone, the color, the taste, the feel of an activity. And there are also the myriads of affective activities and structures that are so important for our lives. All this, then, helps us see just how directly and deeply important affectivity is for value and evaluation.

23 *Tharsos* is discussed in *Plural and Conflicting Values,* ch. 5, "Courage . . . and Emotional Coherence," especially appendix 2, "The Object of *Tharsos.*"

6

Emotions as constituents and as added perfections

In this chapter, I sketch two interconnected ways emotions are internally related to value. My sketch is based on Aristotle's two accounts of pleasure in the *Nicomachean Ethics,* as those accounts are usually understood. On this view, in VII.13, he identifies pleasure with *energeia,* that is, value made actual or unimpeded activity; and in X.4, he rejects the identification, holding rather that pleasure perfects or completes *energeia,* "pleasure completes the activity . . . as an end which supervenes [on the activity] as the bloom of youth does on those in the flower of their age" (1174b32 ff.).

There is considerable controversy over how to interpret these claims; whether they are compatible; whether the one is about pleasures, as in pastimes, and the other about the nature of pleasure; whether one is a more mature, reconsidered view that implicitly rejects the other. My discussion of emotions and their value does not depend on accepting one or the other of these interpretations, and I have thus relegated my comments on the issue to section 4 of this chapter. I will argue that emotions are what is valuable in some activities and relations, and that emotions perfect some other activities and relations.

1   Emotions as added perfections

For our concerns, what is important about Aristotle's account or accounts of pleasure is the view of pleasure that it is, or is the perfection of, the actualization of value. Put far too simply, it is pleasant to have what one thinks good come to be, especially if one makes it come to be and achieves it. Again far too simply, this is what pleasure is or what has pleasure or is pleasurable.

According to Aristotle, the connections between emotions and pleasure are also quite direct. As he says, "Further, pleasure is the consciousness through the senses of a certain kind of emotion" (*Rht* I.11, 1370a27 ff.) and "By passions I mean appetite, anger, fear, confidence, envy, joy, hatred, longing, emulation, pity, and in general the feelings that are accompanied by pleasure or pain" (*NE* II.5, 1105b21 ff.). This helps show why emotions reveal value, at least according to Aristotle. The way emotions involve pleasure and pain goes beyond mere accompaniment: that, as it happens, they are found together. Emotions, rather, are ways of experiencing pleasure and pain. Further, such pleasure and pain are to be understood in terms of activity, and thus value and its actualization. I thus take him as holding that one naturally feels pleasure, and has pleasant emotions, if, and to the extent that, as one takes things, things are going well; and pain and painful emotions, if, as one takes things, they are going poorly.

An example might help here. For me to take pride in an achievement of mine is for me to take pleasure in and from the achievement. This is a pleasure that, as we could say, binds together the achievement, me for doing it, for how I did it, and so on. My taking such bound-together pleasure is my taking pride in my achievement. This, I think, is what Aristotle has in mind by explaining emotions in terms of pleasure and pain, and pleasure and pain in ways that put them, or make them suitable to be put, within emotions.

Pleasure, then, reveals values, and it does this in much the same ways and for much the same reasons that emotions also reveal value. Nonetheless, I find analogs to the information claim about emotions – that emotions are valuable just because they reveal value – are not tempting. No matter how important the evaluative information supplied by pleasure – that we value such and such – there should be no temptation to hold that pleasure is evaluatively important only for such information.[1]

My claim, then, is that values and our pleasure – for example, the pleasure we take in ourselves for and in realizing values – are just too bound up together to single out either one as the one that has real importance. As Aristotle writes,

---

1 My thanks are owed to Joseph Waligore for emphasizing this issue, especially in regard to pain, in his doctoral dissertation, "The Joy of Torture: The Happiness of Stoic Sages" (Syracuse University, 1995). Among the works he refers to on this issue are Ronald Melzack and Patrick Wall, "Pain Mechanism: A New Theory," in K. H. Pribram, ed., *Brain and Behavior 2: Perception and Action* (Baltimore: Penguin Books, 1969); Howard Leventhal and Deborah Everhart, "Emotion, Pain, and Physical Illness," in Carol Izard, ed., *Emotions in Personality and Psychopathology* (New York: Academic Press, 1970); George Pitcher, "The Awfulness of Pain," *Journal of Philosophy,* 67 (1970) 481–491; Ronald Melzack and Patrick Wall, *The Challenge of Pain* (New York: Basic Books, 1983); and Nikola Grahek, "Objective and Subjective Aspects of Pain," *Philosophical Psychology,* 4 (1991) 249–266. For a contrary view in regard to pleasure – that its evaluative importance lies at least mainly in the evaluative information it provides – see Elijah Millgram, "Pleasure in Practical Reasoning," *Monist,* 76 (1993) 394–415.

But whether we choose life for the sake of pleasure or pleasure for the sake of life is a question we may dismiss for the present. For they seem to be bound up together and not to admit of separation, since without activity pleasure does not arise, and every activity is completed by pleasure. (NE X.4, 1175a18 ff.)

I want to say something along similar lines for at least some emotions. They are themselves of value, or they and the values they embody "seem bound up together and not to admit of separation."

I am not claiming this of all emotions. As noted earlier, excitement at a roller coaster ride may well not show any value or any valuing. But such inseparability does hold for some, and, I think, many, emotions.

Let us return to my example of pride. I find it hard to take seriously the claim that pride cannot be, in itself, good or bad, but can be good or bad only for what it shows. Bad pride is easy: it can involve an overestimation of what one did, oneself for doing it, the value, even the moral value, of doing it. It is as easy to see why bad pride is, in itself, bad, as it is to see why lying to oneself or perhaps others is bad. Indeed, part of what makes bad pride bad is the deceptions and lies it involves.

Good pride is also easy, especially if we take care that such pride does not move over into bad pride, such as being too full of oneself. I mean, who can doubt the goodness of young children's pride in mastering their bodies and minds: in walking, in running, in climbing, in learning to read and write. Or the goodness of an author's quiet satisfaction, even rather loud exultation, perhaps up to and including a wild glorying, in finally completing after all these many years a very fine piece of writing; or such pride had by a sculptor upon completing a wonderful statue; or by a woodworker on completing a wonderful bedroom suite.

Again, we must take some care. This pride might well be objectionable if these proud people give inadequate recognition to others. And it would be objectionable if they seriously overrate their work or themselves for accomplishing it. But unless one thinks that whatever a human achieves is really due to someone else, or is really very poor, these are simply matters over which to take care. They limit good pride, rather than showing it impossible. So too, we must take care that the pride not be "prideful." It must, rather, be understood mainly in terms of the person's accurate pleasure in the doing and what is done. (Differences between such takings of pleasure and pride are discussed in Chapter 9, section 2.)

The question may remain, Why is such pride good? Or, if the answer to that is clear enough, the question may be, How is such pride good? In many cases, the answer can be given in the form suggested by the X.4 account of pleasure: "pleasure completes the activity . . . as an end which supervenes [on the activity] as the bloom of youth does on those in the flower of their age." Pride completes the activity this way, too.

When we consider activities in terms of what is done or produced, they can seem perfect, and from that standpoint may well be perfect, even if the agents take no pride in the activities or in their doing them. A philosophy paper is not made or shown to be a less good philosophy paper because the philosopher does not take pride in it or in doing it; nor, correlatively, does a perfect paper (if there is such) require the author to take pride in it or in doing it. Rather, the pride is taken in something already good, already complete and, in this sense, "perfect." Thus, such pride – which, as just said, can well be good and help make a life good – is pride in an activity that is *not* made perfect by the pride. It is already perfect. Indeed, its perfection is the ground for the pride.

Thus, to find what is good about such emotions, we must look beyond products – that is, products that can be good, even perfect, without emotions. One place to look is at the agents. So, for example, we can recognize that even though the complex of pride in what is good does not make the product better, it does make the making of the product better. It perfects – makes better – the doing of the activity and the life of the person who does it.

If products are the focus of evaluative attention, emotions are all too likely to seem evaluatively unimportant. But when we focus more on the agents and their activity, we can see how proper pride makes the activity even better, at least in the sense of an added bloom. There is now the agents' recognition of what they did and how they acted, and this recognition is accurate, appreciative, and pleasurable. Even if these do not make the product any better, they do make the producing better. That part of the agent's life is, thereby, made better.

Not to see that such pleasure and engagement make production better can, of course, be a philosophical failure. It is also a morally pernicious failure. For it suggests that what is important is only the product and not also how producing the product is for the agent. Correlatively, it suggests the unimportance of agents as producers. This last view is deeply interconnected with the denial of importance to human and productive activity, as apart from what is produced.

The full strength of these arguments is easily missed if they are cast in terms of pleasure and pain, especially if pain and pleasure are understood as sensations and states. We need also to understand the arguments, and pleasure and pain, in terms of emotions. And we need to understand the importance of emotions, such as pride. This involves seeing the value of pride, say, not just in terms of a pleasurable episode, perhaps supplemented by its instrumental usefulness – "Managers, make sure your workers take pride in their work, and they will be more productive." Rather, its value also, and importantly, has to do with the value of leading an evaluatively charged and evaluatively directed life, of self-approval, and the like. This, in short, is the value of a truly human life filled with truly human activity and emotions.

Many of these arguments for the importance of emotions will, thus, be out-and-out moral arguments, arguing for certain values, and exposing and countering moral mistakes, including the serious mistake of seeing value only in products. Many of these arguments can be traditional, philosophical ones. But – to invoke one of the central themes of this work – other disciplines, such as psychology, sociology, and anthropology, are useful, and often needed here. All of these are useful in presenting, exposing, and diagnosing emotional mistreatments and mistreatments of emotions.

So, for example, to criticize the "ideal" of reason – that is, the ideal of a life of emotionless reason – we can show how such a life allows for, and may allow only for, a life that is both psychologically or evaluatively impossible: psychologically impossible, because it is not among those psychologies people can have; evaluatively impossible, because it is intolerable or is seriously defective, a life of severe incapacitation, even insanity.

Similarly, we will need both philosophy and many of these other disciplines to understand and evaluate many current forms of success, such as being a successful manager, which depend far more on a concern with products than with people. To be sure, successful managers will have a concern – often simply an instrumental concern – with the feelings of others and themselves, so that one and all will be more efficient producers of products. This is how the psychoanalyst and social theorist and critic Michael Maccoby describes what he calls the *gamesman,* who is sensitive to other people's feelings, and perhaps also his own, but mainly to make everyone better players in his game.[2] Both to understand and also to evaluate these forms or deformations of life, we must take into account the writings of such theorists as Chodorow and McDougall. Chodorow writes,

Men, moreover, do not define themselves in relationship and have come to suppress relational capacities and repress relational needs. This prepares them to participate in the affect-denying world of alienated work.[3]

McDougall writes,

2 New York: Bantam, 1978.
3 *The Reproduction of Mothering* (Berkeley: University of California Press, 1978), p. 207.

Individuals who use such escape devices [i.e., suppression of affect] to an exaggerated degree tend to give an appearance of normality in that they are symptom-free and often, because of the stifling of affect, appear able to cope with adversity in all circumstances.[4]

2 Emotions as constituents

In this section, I examine some relations between emotions and value that fit more with the model of pleasure given in VII.13 of the *Nicomachean Ethics:* pleasure is identified with perfect activity, that is, with value made actual. To begin with, there are activities whose very nature and value are connected to emotional involvement. On the positive side, we could consider love and loving activities, friendship and friendly activities; on the negative, hate and hate-informed activities. What is central to such activities is that they are ways, indeed particularly good ways, of expressing those emotions. The thought behind the activity, the feeling expressed by it, is a major part of what is important and valuable about the activity.[5]

Play and playfulness, in their various forms, give us another set of activities having deep and constitutive relations with emotions. (Such activities are, of course, often loving or friendly activities, too.) Here we might start with the more interpersonal emotions, or groups of emotions, that inform play: for example, the emotions that inform loving play between a child and parent, or the engaged play of children, or the playful and amusing conversations of good friends. We should note how difficult, if not impossible, it would be to take part in these activities – to know what to do, to understand what the others are doing – without the relevant emotions.

Another way to see how such emotions are, in themselves, good is to see why those engaged in these forms of play might care whether they or their partners in play have the emotions. We can see this, I think, from the other side, by imagining cases where the affect and emotional engagement are missing. To this end, we should imagine an emotionally engaged child playing with a depressed, affectless parent, or children playing affectlessly with other children or with their own toys, or your friend talking with you about playful and amusing matters, but affectlessly, not engaging emotionally with you.

---
4 *Theaters of the Mind: Illusion and Truth on the Psychoanalytic Stage* (New York: Brunner Mazel, 1991), p. 112.
5 This is discussed in Stocker, "The Schizophrenia of Modern Ethical Theories," *Journal of Philosophy,* 73 (1976) 453–466, and "Values and Purposes: The Limits of Teleology and the Ends of Friendship," *Journal of Philosophy,* 78 (1981) 747–765.

One can want and value emotional engagement, not just for what it allows or produces, but for itself. For example, one wants emotional engagement with those one plays with. Indeed, one of the important reasons for playing is to be emotionally engaged with the play, with oneself, and with others. Often, we play as a way of expressing our feelings and we value playfulness and play for the feelings they express.

Put more generally, we often want engagement with others. We want them to share our joy and grief and we want to share their joy and grief. We want all the people involved to want such a shared life. We want to live with others, in a social, interpersonal life. And, to a greater or lesser extent, depending on the details of the engagement, we want the engagement to be emotional and to be constituted by emotional, interpersonal relations. (I recognize that there are some people who, perhaps for spiritual reasons, want isolation. I am not talking about them.)

To emphasize the point about what is wanted in wanting emotional engagement, we can want others to be emotionally engaged with us in part because such emotional engagement is naturally connected with desires and motives. And we can want to be the objects of others' desires and motives. But we also can want emotional engagement simply for the emotional engagement, even where it involves no motives or desires that involve us, and even where it does not involve action, and is nothing but the emotional ways we are seen and felt.

Much the same holds from the perspective of agents. Here, too, people care enough about the emotions with which they do or produce something, so that they are not indifferent between their doing or producing something and its simply existing or being done. They are, in short, concerned that they do the act or produce the effect. This does not say only that people can be concerned that they, as opposed to someone else, do the act or produce the effect. It also says that people can be concerned that they do or produce it: that they be agents. So too, people can be concerned that their understanding and ways of seeing are emotionally involved and engaged.

This distinction between how emotions are important for action – as an added perfection or as a constitutive part – helps us understand what it is for a process, relationship, or whatever to be *emotional,* and thus what it is for its virtues to involve emotions and perhaps even be virtues of emotions. We can put this in terms that help explain a claim of Chodorow's considered in Chapter 3, section 3. She talked of relational capacities and deficiencies in a dual way: as interpersonal and also as emotional. As she presents matters, these are not simply two characterizing features of those capacities and deficiencies. Rather, they are emotional because and insofar as they are interpersonal. But how, then, are we to understand 'are emotional' here? For it is also central to Chodorow's claims that men's interpersonal relations are deficient in, perhaps devoid of, emotions, and in that sense are not emotional. My suggestion is that Chodorow can be understood as making at least one, if not both, of the following claims. First, emotions are constitutive of those relations and of the capacity to be good at them. Second, such relations are emotional in the sense that this is what healthy or good forms of those relations are like: interpersonal relations are not made good by the addition of emotions, these relations are emotional unless they are deformed.

Something like this is suggested by Strawson in "Freedom and Resentment":

We should think of the many different kinds of relationship which we can have with other people – as sharers of a common interest; as members of the same family; as colleagues; as friends; as lovers; as chance parties to an enormous range of transactions and encounters. Then we should think in each of these connections in turn, and in others, of the kind of importance we attach to the attitudes and intentions toward us of those who stand in these relations to us, and of the kinds of reactive attitudes and feelings to which we ourselves are prone.[6]

Returning to an issue raised in Chapter 4, section 3, we can now say in what sense mathematics is not emotional, even if emotions affect how people do it and even if they are emotional about it – in contrast to family relations, which are emotional. This sense is, at least largely, to be understood in terms of what is internal to the relation, process, or whatever that is in question. So understood, certain family relations are emotional even if for certain people their family relations of those sorts are not emotional. So too, mathematics is not emotional even if some people are emotional about it. The point here is not about lacks in people: that people are doing poorly and should seek help if their family relations are emotionless. People, especially schoolchildren and mathematicians, may also be doing poorly and in need of help if they are anguished or bored by, or simply uninterested in, doing mathematics. Nor is the point about what is necessary for successful work. Mathematics is not emotional. But at least many people are better at doing it by being emotionally engaged with it.

Emotions do not just provide added perfections to family relations, simply making them better. Rather, the emotions are constitutive of the

---

6 As reprinted in Gary Watson, ed., *Free Will* (Oxford: Oxford University Press, 1982), pp. 63–64.

relations. Although the relations can exist without the emotions, when they do they are defective. Such relations are, themselves, complete and perfect only with the relevant emotions. Indeed, without those emotions, those relations may be bad, even destructive. This suggests that the Aristotelian distinction between added perfections and constituents gives us a better way to understand in what way Chodorow's interpersonal relations are emotional – better, that is, than we would have were we to focus simply on their being interpersonal, and were we to understand what it is for relations to be interpersonal just in terms of their being between people.

3 Further issues

I trust that enough has been said to show that – and, in two related ways, how – emotions make acts and relations good. I want now to make some brief comments on some other, related issues: (1) emotions and action, (2) how emotionally infused agency blurs the distinction between emotions as constituents and added perfections, (3) how emotions are important for institutions, (4) emotions and moodlike character structures, (5) how emotionally infused agency fits best in Aristotelian ethics, rather than Kantian or utilitarian ethics.

Emotions and action

I have been concerned to show how emotions are valuable for action, sometimes as constituents and sometimes as added perfections. This connection with action, especially when amplified by the following comments, should help block the charge that in urging the value of emotions – perhaps by focusing on emotions as forms of attention, rather than as, also, involving desire – I have scanted the value of action, activity, and their products.[7]

Activity without emotions can be lacking in value. But, so too, emotions without activity can be lacking in value. Love in a family is a good example. Without emotions, such love is greatly lacking in value, if even possible. But without activity, it is also greatly lacking in value, if even possible. Imagine a child, parent, or spouse who only had "feelings of love," or who only made protestations of love – "But you know I love you" – but never did anything for the supposed object of that supposed love. For love to be valuable, we need to be able to count on both its emotions and also its activities – to

---

7 My thanks are owed to Sidney Morgenbesser and Graeme Marshall for discussion here.

count on both of them continuing and being there when needed or wanted.

Any adequate theory of people or emotions will require action along with emotion, recognizing that we are both active and also emotional beings, that emotions help constitute motives for action and are typically expressed in action, and that acts are done from or with emotions. To be sure, sometimes no action is possible and sometimes doing nothing is what should be done. But emotion without activity can also show personal or moral "problems," such as neurotic or psychotic withdrawal from the world, an "onlooker's" view of life, Oblomov-like inertia, sentimentalism, aestheticism, or the view that one's feelings and how one feels are all that is important. (This is discussed in Chapter 9, especially section 1.)

How emotionally infused agency blurs the distinction between emotions as constituents and added perfections

The concern we have to be agents, especially emotionally engaged agents, goes some way toward crossing, if not blurring, the line between those activities which are constitutively emotional and those which are only perfected by emotions. I welcome this blurring. In putting forward these two ways emotions can be important for value, I never intended that where one of them holds, the other does not.

One example showing the need for such blurring is found in our concern to do what is emotional or what engages us emotionally. In terms of our discussion, we might think that the difference here between those activities that have emotions as constituents and those activities that are perfected by them can be put in terms of whether the emotion is a feature of the activity or a feature of how the agent does the activity. However, this difference may make little, if any, difference to the agent, especially if all the agent wants is to do something so long as it is emotional in the requisite way. Here we might consider someone who says, "I don't really care what I do this afternoon, so long as it engages me, makes me feel alive and connected with the world, or at least is simply fun."

We might, of course, hold that in this case, even though the person may seem to decide just to go swimming, say, what is really chosen is to feel alive, be emotionally engaged, or have fun, or to do one or all of these by swimming. But this last simply makes my point about the ease with which the distinction is crossed and blurred, and the importance of crossing and blurring it. This is also shown by the fact that "aspects" or "subacts" of this act – leaving home, getting the bus, . . . , jumping in the water – can each stand to emotions in either of these two ways. The same holds for other acts or conditions that stand in *in order to* or *by* relations with the act – for example, swimming by doing the sidestroke, going swimming in order to do something fun, or doing something fun just to be doing something that makes one feel really alive.

As this shows, emotions can be connected with the value of the "same thing" in both of these ways. As this also shows, these two ways are conceptually interconnected. They can be seen as differing primarily in regard to where they make things fall on the continuum ranging from defective, through good, to perfect. Put briefly, where emotions are constituents of an item that is good, as in the case of certain forms of play, whatever lacks those emotions will either not be an instance of play at all or will be only a defective instance of it. But if emotions are merely added perfections, as in cases of certain forms of writing, what lacks those emotions can still be a perfectly good instance of such writing.

How emotions are important for institutions

The constitutive arguments for the evaluative importance of emotions were restricted to values constituted by emotions. However, to appreciate the full importance of emotions for value, the argument must be extended to include the institutions, settings, practices, and so on which at once depend on emotions and also give rise to values. These values may, themselves, not be perfected or constituted by emotions.

The dependence here can be "merely causal." It might be that without certain emotions, such as intellectual interest, no one would have bothered to develop mathematics or the intellectual values peculiar to mathematics. The causality may also work via institutions. It may well be that if, in prehistoric times, people had not been organized in families, with their complex emotional relations, nations would not eventually have arisen; and thus without a prehistory that includes those emotions, there would now not be the nonemotional values and concerns characteristic of moral life in nations.

Turning from institutional to personal history and development, it may be that to be a good citizen of a contemporary state, a person must have been raised in a family or familylike institution -- perhaps even a family or familylike institution particularly appropriate to contemporary life. This might be because only such people have the needed stability, or because the loyalty one needs to be a good citizen develops from loyalty engendered by and initially directed to the family and its members. If the claim about either world history or personal history holds, the values and evaluative concerns of nations and citizens may not depend directly and internally on emotions. But they, and what they do depend on, even if at a great remove of time and structure, do depend on families. And thus, these structures and what they directly depend on, do depend on emotions, even if the remove is great and the original emotions are largely, even completely, absent from the later values and concerns.

The dependence can also be more formative, even constitutive. Emotions are constitutively essential for our having the sorts of play and family life we have. Our play and family life can, themselves, give rise to certain values and evaluative concerns that are not, themselves, constituted by those or other emotions. These include fairness to other players, a fair division of labor within the family, justice between generations. These values and evaluative concerns may also involve nonemotional ways of regulating and enhancing what is deeply emotional. These various values and concerns are not, themselves, constituted by emotions in the ways described above. But in different ways, emotions are important for them, too.

Emotions and moodlike character structures

We have just noted an area where emotions constitute or perfect values. Earlier, we noted an area where emotions are important for values because they are important for the generality of life, activity, and thought. There is also an area somewhere between these two. In it we find such concerns as the connections between such general moodlike structures as optimism and pessimism, on the one hand, and values and evaluations, on the other: for example, whether there are evaluative orientations or particularities connected with optimism and pessimism. Similar questions would arise in regard to harshness and gentleness, or differentiated and affiliative personalities. Here we would ask about the emotional structures, values, and evaluations of different sorts of personalities, including those just mentioned and the authoritarian and the liberal personality. We would also ask about the different evaluative and emotional styles of those caught up in pre-Oedipal versus Oedipal conflicts.[8] We would also ask whether there are

---

8 On some distinctions between Oedipal and pre-Oedipal conflicts, see Michael Balint, *The Basic Fault: Therapeutic Aspects of Regression* (New York: Brunner Mazel, 1979).

evaluative and emotional connections turning on such global features of personality as feeling secure in and about oneself versus feeling under threat or of no worth.

How emotionally infused agency fits best in Aristotelian, rather than Kantian or utilitarian, ethics

The importance of emotionally infused agency fits easily into, indeed is an essential part of, Aristotle's ethics. His ethics are famous – or notorious – for requiring correct emotions, along with correct action, for virtue and happiness. Here we might note that if, as said earlier, love requires having and acting on certain reasons and emotions, we have a way to put Aristotle's claim that moral virtue, unlike technical virtue, requires having and acting on the right reasons and emotions, in particular valuing and acting for the sake of the activity and the virtue. For on his view, morally virtuous people are lovers of virtue, and moral virtue involves a love of virtue (*NE* I.8, 1099a5 ff.). This, of course, is part of Aristotle's argument that a morally virtuous life is pleasant for those who are morally virtuous.

This deep and direct involvement of emotions in moral virtue fits less easily into both Kantian and also utilitarian thought. We must, however, recognize that many moral facts are better described by those theories than by those parts of Aristotle's ethics which focus on emotions and virtues. This is to put in another way the point noted earlier that many important products, activities, and other goods are not perfected by emotions, even if their production, or agents considered as producers, are perfected by emotions. In ways already explained, these goods do not depend on emotions. Among these, we find many of the main constituents of welfare, such as peace, health, sufficient food, security, and also many of the main constituents of just and effective commercial and legal systems.

Insofar as utilitarian and Kantian ethics are concerned with these values, these views will naturally be less concerned with emotions than is Aristotelian ethics. But only parts of Aristotle's ethics are deeply and directly concerned with emotions. He, too, recognizes many values that do not require, and often may not even involve, emotions. Here we could look at his discussions of external goods and of the need for laws and obedience to laws. Put briefly, what is often presented as Aristotelian ethics, and what most lends itself to virtue ethics, concerns the virtues of his men. But these men depend, both constitutively and developmentally, on what is not so directly emotional, if emotional at all: they have been raised well, have sufficient external goods, they are law abiding and live in largely law abiding societies.[9]

4 A suggestion about pleasure in books VII and X of the *Nicomachean Ethics*

In these last two sections, I will deal more directly with Aristotle's claims about pleasure. The *Nicomachean Ethics* makes seemingly different claims about pleasure. Book VII.13 holds that pleasure is *energeia,* unimpeded activity. Book X.4 holds that pleasure perfects activity, like a bloom on the cheek. Gwilym E. L. Owen takes VII to be identifying pleasures, as in pastimes, with unimpeded activities. He takes X to be giving an account of the nature of pleasure. Justin Gosling and Christopher Taylor do not find such a difference between VII and X. They hold that both VII and X are concerned to argue that pleasure, or certain pleasures, are the good.[10]

Let us start with the claim in VII identifying or accounting for pleasure or pleasures in terms of activity. (Henceforth, unless made explicit, my use of 'pleasure' or 'pleasures' should be taken as referring to both.) This is presented as an objection to the claim that pleasure is process or that pleasures are processes. My suggestion is that we take it in the way the position it attacks is understood.

Those who identify pleasure in terms of process do not claim that all processes are pleasures, but only that all pleasures are processes. My suggestion is that we should take VII's rejection of that claim in this same limited way. We should not take VII as holding that all activities are pleasures, but only that all pleasures are activities – or, more exactly, not that all unimpeded activities are pleasures, but that all pleasures are unimpeded activities. On this view, VII holds that only certain activities, not just activity in general – and only certain unimpeded activities, not just unimpeded ac-

---

9 On some differences between the Aristotelian emotions discussed here and fear, greed, and self-concern, as emphasized by Hobbes or his followers, and respect, as urged by Kant and his followers, see Annette Baier, "Secular Faith," in her *Postures of the Mind* (Minneapolis: University of Minnesota Press, 1985); Laurence Thomas, "Rationality and Affectivity: The Metaphysics of the Moral Self," *Social Philosophy and Policy,* 5 (1988) 154–172, and *Living Morally* (Philadelphia: Temple University Press, 1989); and Eugene Garver, *Aristotle's Rhetoric: An Art of Character* (Chicago: University of Chicago Press, 1994), and "Aristotle's Moral Virtues Are Political Virtues," unpublished manuscript. Thanks are owed to Garver for showing me these works and for discussion of these issues. Thanks are also owed Thomas for discussion.
10 Owen, "Aristotelian Pleasures," *Aristotelian Society Proceedings,* 72 (1972) 135–152; Gosling, "More Aristotelian Pleasures," *Aristotelian Society Proceedings,* 74 (1973) 15–34; and Gosling and Taylor, *The Greeks on Pleasure* (Oxford: Oxford University Press, 1982). My thanks are owed to John Robertson for discussion of these views and of mine.

tivities in general – can be identified with pleasure. So taken, VII cannot be seen as holding that being an activity or an unimpeded activity – being just any of these – is what it is for a pleasure to be a pleasure.

I take X as agreeing with VII in rejecting an identification of pleasure with process. X holds, with VII, that not all activities are pleasures. But X denies what many think VII holds: that any pleasure just is – that is, is identical with – the activity we take pleasure in. X explicitly makes a further claim that is made only implicitly, if made at all, in VII: that pleasure *perfects* activity. I take this last claim of X as saying that a special sort of pleasure is the final or formal cause of a special sort of activity.

These are special not only in that they are good, but also because what is good in this or these ways plays a primary role in Aristotelian understanding and explanation. The special sort of pleasure is good or noble pleasure, as discussed in both VII and X. The special sort of activity is the sort "identified" in VII with pleasure or pleasures or at least with good pleasure or pleasures. In much the same ways and for much the same reasons, the good activities in question in VII and also in X are said to be good activities. X claims that the final or formal cause of good activities is precisely that they are good pleasures or pleasurable in a good way.

As we might put it: good pleasure is the class characteristic of good activities; or good pleasure is the class characteristic of perfect instances of activities. Put schematically, VII holds that Ps form a proper subclass of As, which, it is essential to note, are good As. X says that being a P is what makes those As that are Ps perfect instances of As: that is, good or perfect instances of good As.

The general arguments of this work and the particular ones of this chapter – including the suggestion that some emotions constitute and some others accompany action and relations – do not depend on accepting my interpretation of books VII and X. Whether or not VII contradicts what is said in X – with VII asserting and X denying an identity claim – is irrelevant to these arguments. Thus, rather than pursue this issue, I want to conclude by noting that the relation between VII and X is a familiar Aristotelian one. For example, throughout the *Nicomachean Ethics*, it is argued that a good person, a *phronimos*, is a person, not, say, a god, and also that this person's being a good person is the final or formal cause of being a good or a perfect instance of a person: that is, of a good person. It is also argued that health or being healthy is a state of the body and that it is also the final or formal cause of a perfect state of a body: that is, of a good body (cf. *NE* X.4, 1174b25).

My reason for showing how we might reconcile the VII and X accounts of pleasure was to show how we *might* do so, while also suggesting a model for *some* emotions. It was not to show that *all* emotions play the same structural roles in regard to what is good that pleasure does for good or complete action. To argue for that, it would have to be shown, first, that those goods that seem to be independent of emotions are really not independent of them, or are somehow not real goods or not really good. So too, it would have to be shown that what makes all goods good has to do with emotions. I do not think that this could be done. Too many understandings of value, too many values, and too many goods seem too far removed from emotions and even the human.

5 How we are also Aristotelians about pleasure

I have said that it does not matter how we decide the issue about books VII and X. But this much should be said: no matter which interpretation we ultimately accept, they can all easily strike us as just too implausible. We might agree that pleasure typically or often shows that the body is working well. Here we might consider the overall pleasurable feelings a person in good physical condition has after moderate exercise. Or we might consider how we feel after a good meal. But pleasure seems irrelevant to the success or perfection of at least many doings and acts. My kidneys can be working perfectly well even though this (as differentiated from my knowledge of this) yields no pleasure. Writing a poem need not be the writing of a better poem – nor need it be a better writing of a poem – by being pleasurable. So too, when depressed, say, one might take no pleasure in doing very good work. So too for emotions.

However, I think we do accept something like Aristotle's view. As already noted, I certainly agree that there is no reason to think that the writing of a poem – especially considered in terms of the poem that is written – is better if the poet takes pleasure in it. But, if we consider this activity as part of the poet's life, and to be evaluated in regard to this, then it is clear how its being pleasurable is relevant. I offer this to suggest that we do join Aristotle in holding that pleasurable, emotionally charged activity helps make a life good and helps make up a good life.

I now want to suggest that we also do join him in thinking that pleasure is a natural feature of good activities done well. To see this, suppose you heard someone say, perhaps complain, that giving a lecture an hour ago was not pleasurable. How might this lack of pleasure be accounted for? Perhaps the lecture was given pretty much simply as a means to something else, perhaps simply to fulfill job commitments. In such a case, its not being pleasurable is easily explained, especially if the job is felt to be degrading, lackluster, or boring. Or perhaps the lecture was given in hard or trying circumstances, with many impediments: the lecture room was too poorly insulated to exclude the noise of construction next door, or music from a concert being given on the floor below (cf. *NE* X.5, 1175b3 ff.). Or perhaps the lecturer was suffering an allergic reaction to the wine served at lunch, or had drunk too much and was very sleepy or addled during the lecture. Or perhaps the lecturer no longer believes that it is worth discussing the topic lectured on. Or perhaps the person suffers from shyness, or feelings of unworthiness, of shame, and thinks that whatever he or she says is really pretty foolish or at best third-rate.

There is no need to go on. My point should be clear enough: there is a strong presumption that barring certain conditions, certain sorts of acts and activities will be pleasurable. Perhaps we hold the still stronger view that normal activities of certain sorts are pleasurable, that other things being equal, these activities will be pleasurable. When they are not, we think of this as needing explanation – an explanation typically given by other elements in the same explanatory and theoretical field.

We might view it as part of our natural, biological makeup that certain sorts of acts are pleasurable – barring certain conditions. This would be to see "Why was the act not pleasurable?" as having a similar standing and force as "Why was that cat born with only three legs?" or "Why didn't I sweat while exercising vigorously on a hot day?" Or we might consider the first as involving more of a conceptual relation, among acts, desires, values, and pleasure. Here we might note that various spiritual maladies, such as depression, that can account for good work not being pleasurable are themselves part of the explanatory and theoretical field containing both activity and pleasure. These maladies can readily answer the question why activity is not pleasurable. They weaken or destroy the presumed link between pleasure and activity. They are among those conditions which make things not equal and which should or even must be absent for there to be pleasure. It is not merely a matter of happenstance, then, that people suffering from these spiritual maladies all too commonly do not find what they do pleasurable. So too, again, for emotions.

Exactly what our view is does not matter. What does matter is whether, as I think, we do hold some such view. For then, along with Aristotle, we also recognize some sort of strong presumption that links activity and pleasure, and, thus, with emotions.

Despite what remains to be investigated, I think we have reached some worthwhile conclusions about some relations between emotions and value and evaluation. We have seen that we want many of our important activities and relations to be infused with pleasure and, more to the point, with emotions. Once again, if an explanatory, justifying account for this is needed, it is readily given: such emotionally infused activities and relations are essential constituents of a good human life. We want to live in emotionally infused ways with ourselves and with others, and it is positively good to live this way, and bad not to. And this is not simply because of the information we get about values, beliefs, and desires by means of the emotions. It is partly that. But it is also the sheer importance, the sheer vital human importance, of living with others and oneself in emotionally engaged ways. We might, thus, supplement Socrates' dictum that the unexamined life is not worth living with our own dictum that the unfelt life is not worth living.

We can put these points in terms of two issues that arose early in this work: first, the information claim; and second, the question of how mere feelings, affectivity, and feeling qualities of emotions can be morally important.

The information claim

It may be a fine and wonderful thing that I learn from people's emotions that, for example, they have particular moral concerns around which they are people of integrity. But what is also important, perhaps far more important, is that they have those concerns and are people of integrity. So too, it may be a fine and wonderful thing that I learn from the affection of those who love me that they care for me, and that I know that they care for me. But what is also important, perhaps far more important, is that they care for me, that they hold me warmly, in their hearts, in their minds, and perhaps, in their arms.

Mere feelings

As seen throughout this work, and as just summarized in regard to the information claim, affectivity including the affective elements and feeling qualities of emotions cannot be understood in terms of mere feelings. Perhaps there is no reason to deny that they are feelings – except to avoid the danger of error and confusion. But in recognizing that they are and involve feelings, we must also recognize that these feelings, perhaps like most feelings, are hardly mere feelings. There is hardly anything they merely are.

In brief, then, to ask why we should care about, and attach any moral importance to, such "mere feelings" is, in effect, to ask why we should care about being cared about, why we should care about being held warmly, in the hearts, minds, and arms of those we care about. It is, more broadly, to ask why we should care about a vital, engaged, life, with and within ourselves, and with others. Once that question is seen as asking these questions, its answer will also be seen.

7

Some further ways emotions help with evaluative knowledge

This chapter returns to more epistemological issues. The focus here will be on how emotions – especially those that help constitute acts and relations, as discussed in the previous chapter – can allow for and help constitute evaluative knowledge. This will complement what has been done elsewhere in this work, primarily in Chapter 3, "Emotional problems suggest epistemological problems."

1 Emotions as epistemologically useful for justifications and for countertransference

In this section, we call attention to three ways emotions help us gain knowledge and understanding, especially of emotion-involving acts and relations. First, we can learn the nature, meaning, and value of emotions and emotional states, such as love, by experiencing those emotions and states. We do not mean only that by experiencing love, by feeling its full force, we know what it means and why we care about it. We mean also that to love is to have a particular way or ways of organizing and understanding the world, to be focused on and interested in particular issues, to be concerned with certain possibilities, and to know and experience the world in certain, particular ways.

Second, quite generally, by engaging emotionally with others, we learn emotions: how and when to have them, how to recognize our own and those of others, and the significance of each. In much the same ways that we learn and understand language – what we and others mean by what we and they say – we learn and understand emotions, what we and others mean by our and their emotions and emotional expressions. This allows for and, we think, requires being able to do this on one's own, by imagination – both linguistic imagination, often called thought, and emotional imagination, rarely called thought.

Emotions can be epistemically useful in a somewhat different, third way, too. We can learn what someone else is feeling by our emotional reaction to him or her. For example, we can learn that someone we are playing with is bored by means of our own emotional engagement – perhaps boredom or frustration and disappointment – in that play. This, in fact, is similar to a current view in psychoanalysis about countertransference: that a full understanding of an analysand requires emotional engagement, including countertransference, by the analyst, and that the understanding gained through these emotions can be more accurate than knowledge gained in other ways. As McDougall writes,

> The latent significance of the patient communications depends to a considerable degree, above and beyond its meaning, on the tone, mood, and emotion conveyed by the analysand's voice, manner of speaking, gestures, and body posture. The psychoanalyst also needs to be keenly aware of his or her own emotional and bodily messages, while introjecting those of the patient. This interchange then provides the analyst with floating hypotheses about the analysand's inner world.[1]

Much the same holds in other fields and professions, such as philosophy, law, as well as psychoanalysis, and also in "mere" conversation. We are given clues and evidence about, indeed find out, what others are thinking, and also what they are really saying, by how they speak, how they hold themselves, whether they are relaxed or stiff, and the like. So too, we find this out by our responses in thought, feeling, and action: by what we think, feel, or say as they are speaking, and afterward. In all these cases, sensitivity to and attunement with the other are needed. Here we would emphasize that having and attending to emotions is not just useful for these activities but, rather, is part and parcel of being actively engaged in them.

We would also emphasize that the need for sufficient emotional engagement complements the need for sufficient emotional distance, which is needed to avoid enmeshment or other forms of excessive identification. Just as there are problems and dangers for psychoanalysts in understanding their patients, there are similar problems and dangers elsewhere, even in regard to more propositional understandings. I can misunderstand what you say by being too self-absorbed and thus too distant from your world of understanding, not going beyond what I would have meant had I uttered your words. And I can also misunderstand what you say by lack of distance, occasioned, for example, by idealization: by being too caught up in your

---

[1] Joyce McDougall, *Theaters of the Mind: Illusion and Truth on the Psychoanalytic Stage* (New York: Brunner Mazel, 1991), p. 150. For discussion of issues both raised by McDougall and also in the previous several paragraphs, see Daniel Goleman, *Emotional Intelligence* (New York: Bantam Books, 1995).

way of seeing things, taking you as too much of an authority about the truth or reasonableness of what you say, rather than using my own judgment. I may thus, perhaps along with you, not understand that what you say is mistaken, implausible, or nonsense.

2 Some other claims about the epistemological usefulness of emotions

We can use these various ways emotions are epistemically useful for evaluative knowledge to justify and show the importance of the claims made by Iris Murdoch, Lawrence Blum, and Martha Nussbaum that loving attention and other forms of emotional knowledge are essential for ethical knowledge.[2] As we see matters, their claims develop naturally from, and are grounded in, the situations they discuss: for Murdoch, the mother-in-law coming to understand and appreciate her daughter-in-law; for Blum, person-to-person relations, including friendship and intimacy; for Nussbaum, family relations as depicted in Henry James's novels. What is evaluatively important about these situations is importantly, and often largely, the emotions and the relations that are based on and express emotions that make them up, and that make them the very interesting and evaluatively important situations they are. We think that this focus on what is emotional helps motivate and sustain these philosophers' rejection of "rule-based" moralities: moralities cast in terms of discursively stable rules, and contrasted with moralities emphasizing judgment.

Before examining their views on this distinction, we want to offer an observation. It often seems that these philosophers are concerned with emphasizing either the ways our morality is a shame morality, not just, as often thought, a guilt morality; or that we would be better off if our morality were more of a shame morality than a guilt morality. At the least, many of their positive views about judgment and particularity, and many of their negative ones about rules, fit well with aspects of shame moralities, rather than guilt moralities. For example, insofar as shame moralities are concerned with ideals, we can see why here at least articulations may be impossible and why judgment is so important. Further, shame morality is

2 Murdoch, *The Sovereignty of Good* (London: Routledge and Kegan Paul, 1970); Blum, *Friendship, Altruism, and Morality* (London: Routledge and Kegan Paul, 1980), "Iris Murdoch and the Domain of the Moral," *Philosophical Studies,* 50 (1986) 343–368, and "Particularity and Responsiveness," in Jerome Kagan and Sharon Lamb, eds., *The Emergence of Morality in Young Children* (Chicago: University of Chicago Press, 1987); and Nussbaum, *Love's Knowledge* (Oxford: Oxford University Press, 1990), and "Equity and Mercy," *Philosophy and Public Affairs,* 22 (1993) 83–125.

deeply concerned with emotions and emotional relations, and thus to be concerned with shame morality is to be concerned with emotions and emotional relations.[3]

There is also an advantage in thinking of these philosophers' claims this way: it lessens the need to deal with such problematic historical, interpretive issues as exactly which philosophers or schools propound a rule-based morality that excludes judgment about particulars. Here we might note the meagerness of the fare Nussbaum, in particular, offers us. In "Equity and Mercy," she offers us a saying of Anaximander (DK, fragment B1) and early preclassical Greek legal practice as exemplifying such a rule-based legal system. She also mentions some modern legal theorists who *may* be committed to, and *may* also argue in favor of, such a legal system. In addition some modern, academic ethical systems may be rule-based in this way. But most, if not all, classical moralities emphasize the need for judgment. One of the few examples of rule-based morality found in our philosophical tradition is that of Aristotelian practical syllogisms. But Aristotle's ethics is correctly celebrated for not being rule-based. And finally, largely because of Wittgenstein, rule following, itself, is often understood in terms of judgment, rather than in terms of fully articulated rules applied in fully articulated ways.

We do agree with Murdoch, Blum, and Nussbaum about the importance of emotions for evaluative knowledge. Nonetheless, our arguments for our common position may go against some of theirs, most clearly Nussbaum's where she is concerned to contrast the moral roles of emotions and rules. She argues that emotions are necessary for morality because morality is concerned with particulars, as stressed by Aristotle, whereas rules can handle only what is general.

We do not agree. As Eugene Garver notes, that position suggests that

the role of emotion . . . is [only] interstitial, that only on those occasions when argument and rules are incomplete do we have to turn to the emotions to make judgment determinate. . . . The *Rhetoric* shows, instead, that the emotions are continually at work in good decisions.[4]

Further, moral emotions can also be about and important for what is general, such as a general social policy implementing capital punishment. Many find the general policy, the very idea, of capital punishment repellent

---

3 Thanks are owed to Daniel Haggerty and Sean McAleer for discussion here, especially in regard to Bernard Williams, *Shame and Necessity* (Berkeley: University of California Press, 1993), and Nussbaum.
4 *Aristotle's Rhetoric: An Art of Character* (Chicago: University of Chicago Press, 1994), p. 108.

and barbaric. And many also take the fact that they and others are repelled to be morally significant. It shows, they think, much about the moral character of those who do and those who do not have the feeling, and also much about the policy, itself.

Third, we might wonder where, if anyplace, rules – that is, rules without judgment, as portrayed by Nussbaum – are important. After all, particulars, and judgment about particulars, are found and needed, not just in ethics, but in medicine, art, civil engineering, philosophy, to list only a very few of the disciplines we could have listed.

Now, we do think that emotions are needed in these areas. As argued in Chapter 4, especially section 3, they are needed in these areas just as they are generally needed for human knowledge and activity. And as argued in "Intellectual Desire, Emotion, and Action,"[5] many areas of knowledge and activity, such as the study and practice of history or philosophy, require their own particular emotions. And clearly, a good feel for the relevant particulars is needed if one is to be good in these areas.

But there are important dissimilarities between the ways emotions are important for those parts of ethics Nussbaum, Murdoch, Blum, and we are concerned with and the ways they are important in these other areas. The relation is constitutive in those moral cases. But, it must be emphasized, not all moral cases do have constitutive emotions. Nor do all nonmoral cases that require judgment about particulars have constitutive emotions. Thus, we cannot explain why certain moral cases and certain sorts of moral judgment require emotions just in terms of their being moral cases and cases of moral judgment. Nor can we explain this just in terms of their being about particulars or being about moral particulars.

3   Some general points about emotions and practical, often unarticulated, evaluative knowledge

To return to our more positive theme, understanding and evaluating many situations that are constituted by emotions can be done best by emotional engagement. This is to say that "You had to be there, doing that to appreciate it correctly" can be right. The claim that many situations constituted by emotions are best understood by emotional engagement can also be taken as making the far more difficult claim that the emotions and emotional engagement provide or constitute the evaluative knowledge and that they

---

5 Michael Stocker, in Amélie O. Rorty, ed., *Explaining Emotions* (Berkeley: University of California Press, 1980).

do this because they embody, express, and really are that knowledge. Put in another way, emotions are necessary for evaluative knowledge of such situations precisely because emotionally engaged people, in their emotional engagement, embody, express, and thus really have evaluative knowledge. The evaluative knowledge we are here concerned with is deeply practical, often involving intelligent and knowing practice that is importantly unarticulated. (Our account of such practicality also helps show how, in Aristotelian ethics, virtues are practical.) We have a particular reason for focusing on how what is unarticulated can be useful for and can even help constitute evaluative knowledge. This reason is directly tied to our understanding of emotions as developed in the first chapter, "The irreducibility of affectivity." Content theorists can allow for the full articulability of emotions – if, that is, they can allow this for content. But affectivity does not allow for such articulability. And this, we think, leads many philosophers to think that emotions as affective cannot help constitute evaluative knowledge.

We start by making some general comments on how we learn through practice. We will then apply this to our concerns with emotions and value. It may seem natural that we learn *how* to do various things, engage in various activities and practices, by means of practice: by trying to do or even doing what we will eventually learn to do. But how, it may be asked, can we learn what is true, right, correct, good, or bad from practices? How, that is, can we learn "*that's*" – "that ———" – without articulation?

This last question can be taken as asking how can we learn except from articulations. It can also be taken as asking how can we be said to have learned if we have not achieved articulations. What we mean can be brought out by considering a claim Broadie makes about Aristotle:

> The ungeneralizability of the *orthos logos* into a rule does not entail that it cannot be articulated by means of statements employing general terms. It is a *logos* after all. What cannot be relied upon to hold good beyond the present case is its *orthotēs*, its correctness.[6]

Whether or not intended this way by Broadie, these words can allow that until the articulation in regard to this particular case is made, we lack knowledge. We lack it in that we do not know the articulated *orthos logos*. Perhaps we also lack it in that we are not yet being guided by it.

These words can, thus, be taken as making the following conjoint claim: what we learn from need not be articulations; but we have not learned until we have articulations. They can also be taken as making a somewhat

---

6 *Ethics with Aristotle* (New York: Oxford University Press, 1991), p. 76.

different conjoint claim: what we learn from need not be articulations; and we can have knowledge even if we do not have the articulation, provided that it is possible for someone, perhaps the person in question, to make the articulation, or perhaps provided only that there is a possible articulation. There is a still stronger position. It also holds that what we learn from need not be articulated. It goes on to hold that we can have knowledge even if we do not have the articulation and even if the articulation is not possible, in the ways just indicated.

In what follows, we will show the possibility of unarticulated knowledge and unarticulated sources of knowledge of these various sorts. Let us start by asking, once again, how it is possible to learn without articulation. We do not take this as asking for a general account of the workings of practices in helping us acquire "that's." That would pose a set of problems, encompassing almost the whole range of human learning in all its varieties, and far too large and complicated for any useful, brief answers.

Rather, we take this question as suggesting that we can learn "that's" only from what is articulated. We reject this suggestion. It might well be possible to argue discursively against it, perhaps by pointing out the logical problems in requiring articulations and commentaries to learn and understand all "that's" – including, presumably, those "contained" in those articulations and commentaries, and also including the backgrounds we need in order to understand them. But we think it also useful to take note of the extent to which various human activities use and depend on articulations and on unarticulated practices.

At one extreme we have almost, if not entirely, complete articulations. Here we might consider telling people the steps they must follow to use a computer program. Here "nearly everything" they must do, must be told to them: "At the prompt, type your user number, then press Return, then type in your work area, then . . ." But even this presupposes a lot – for example, that they know how to type. Thus, the use of 'nearly'.

So too, we have commentaries on sacred texts, including not only a lecture that one is listening to or a text one is reading, but also the entire corpus of lectures and writings. We also have cases where someone who is very suspicious – someone threatening to jump from a ledge, say – must be told exactly what you are doing and why: "I am coming somewhat closer to you so that we can talk more easily, I am moving my arm because it is developing a cramp." And we also have conversations of those so concerned with their love relationship that all they talk about with each other is the relationship: how it is going, what this or that shows about it, what their talking about it shows.

As some of the following examples suggest, there may be cases at the other extreme: where we learn "that's" from what is completely or almost completely unarticulated. But, for our purposes, this is less important than is the fact that many of the "that's" that we learn, we learn from what is at least in part unarticulated. It is to this fact we now turn, focusing on unarticulated practices and the knowledge they embody and teach. The practicality in question may be relatively mild. It might be important only in the way that leading someone to your house embodies and expresses your knowledge of how to get there. But this can be knowledge you are unable to express verbally or by using a map. Here we think it obvious that there is a way to articulate the knowledge – that is, a way that is or can be possessed by others – that you can only show. (To some extent this changes our concern from knowing that to knowing how. It also changes our question about the possibility of learning "that's" without articulation to questions about the evaluative–epistemic role of unarticulated knowledge how.)

Much the same point can be made where it is unclear whether there is, or even could be, an articulation of the knowledge. Here we might think of knowledge of a particular dance performance – a particular dancing, by a particular dancer, on a particular occasion. It might be thought that there is no notational system that could accurately get all the important details: that is, not just where the feet should be in a given temporally ordered sequence, but also where the arms should be, their suppleness or rigidity, the forwardness or the modesty of the torso. In this case, a movie, or a group of movies from many angles showing all aspects of the dancer, might be thought necessary – at least for many of us.[7]

Let us change our focus from knowledge of a particular episode to that of a skill. There seems no way to give a general and fully detailed account of how a parent can play well with a child. Similarly, these seems no way to give a general and fully detailed account of how to keep up an amusing conversation with a friend. Nor, for that matter, does it seem possible to give a general account of how to do good philosophy, psychology, and so on. For much the same reasons that we cannot give these general accounts, we may not be able to give an articulated "recipe" adequate for producing even a single episode. We might, however, be able to give an articulated account of how a particular episode is good or bad.

---

7 We say "at least for many of us" because *Labanotation* is such a form of notation. Thanks are owed to Beth Genné, professor of dance history, for discussion.

Is there much of a place, then, for articulations in practices? Speaking about himself, Barnett Newman, an abstract expressionist of the New York School, seemed to say no, when he said that "aesthetics is to me as ornithology is to birds."[8] But whatever his intent, his words do allow that aesthetics might be a source of knowledge for *other* people. After all, in many areas there are multiple routes to knowledge. We think this is clearly how it is for aesthetics, as is shown by the different ways artists and critics can come to have knowledge about the same thing. (We leave it open to what extent the knowledge is the same knowledge and to what extent the knowledge of and in aesthetics is also practical knowledge.)

If this is the way it is for ethics and emotions, we can straightforwardly allow that emotions can serve as a means to ethical understandings that can also be reached in nonemotional ways. Correlatively, we can summarily reject the argument holding that since ethical understanding can be reached in nonemotional ways, emotions are thus shown irrelevant for ethical understanding.

Of course, in allowing for multiple routes to knowledge, we need not accord them equal weight or priority. There are many cases where one must accord priority to the artist's knowledge over the critic's; the knowledge shown by the person playing well with the child over that of the "play expert"; the knowledge shown by a good philosopher over that of accounts of what makes for good philosophy. And here we might remember the moral advice Aristotle gives only as "second-best" advice: if you, yourself, lack proper ethical understanding, perhaps because you lack proper emotions, you can nonetheless do what you should by following the example of a good person, who has correct emotions.

We can also take Newman's claim as raising the issue whether theory and theoretical knowledge can help or harm practice. Perhaps the knowledge – or perhaps one's focus on it or taking it as one's model, not just simply having it – can interfere with the engagement or spontaneity that good practice requires. Pursuing this would involve examining the arguments that artistry can require active, attentive engagement in the practice of the art, and that it can be impeded by focus on aesthetics. We do not mean simply that when one should be fully engaged with the work, one's central focus of attention is on the aesthetic theory, or even that one has it in mind as a background concern. Any of these forms of attention might or might not be distracting in much the way that thinking about how stylishly you

---

8 Thanks are owed to the art historian Elizabeth Cross for this quotation and discussion.

are driving might involve taking your mind off the road, thus leading you to take a curve poorly.

We do recognize those dangers. But we think there is another, often more serious, danger: taking artistry to be the implementation of the theory, taking it that art is good to the extent that it fulfills the criteria of the theory. Here we might think of artists who look to rules and critics, rather than themselves, for guidance and direction – and who, even if not inevitably, then at least not surprisingly, produce modish, routinized, or merely academic art.

Much the same holds for play, conversation, and other emotional interchanges. Here we might think of those who look to rules and "experts" to find out how play, conversations, and other emotional engagements "should be," rather than to attending to and engaging with the activity, themselves, and others involved in the activity – and who, not surprisingly, are not attuned to the activity, themselves, or those others.

So far, then, we have presented illustrations of learning from what is unarticulated. We turn now to some other cases illustrating how this can involve emotional engagement with others.

Let us start with a person's beginning. We doubt that many will disagree that the worlds of children – the worlds they experience, as they experience them – are presented to them in largely unarticulated ways. This is clearest, perhaps, for infants. But it should be clear that at all stages of life, from the time we are infants, we learn from what is unarticulated. We learn a good part of what the world is like, what is expected of us, what to expect of the world, how to get on with other people by and through experiences and practices that to some large extent are unarticulated.

Here we could use again an example mentioned earlier: young children of depressed parents may, as it were, conclude from the ways their parents treat them "I have been bad" or "I am bad and inadequate." We say "as it were" because the children almost certainly do not articulate any of this. And depressed parents may well not say to their children, "You are bad" or "If you were a good child, you would cheer me up" or even "I want to be left alone" or "Nothing pleases me." They may "only" enact or give expression to such thoughts. The depressed parents' unarticulated ways of being or not being with their children are then, we may theorize, interpreted by the children as expressing and giving rise to the thoughts and feelings, "I am bad," "I am inadequate." For, as we may also theorize, those unarticulated experiences require the children to choose between seeing their parents as bad or seeing themselves as bad; and as painful as the latter is, the former would be devastating. (As this example shows, we can acquire many false beliefs from what is unarticulated, just as we can from what is articulated.)

For other illustrations of the importance of unarticulated practices, we can look to the ways children and adults are socialized into various groups, roles, and activities. Anthropologists note with some puzzlement that rules concerning avoidance – that is, who can be with whom under what conditions – and rules concerning incest are learned very early by children, often without explicit instruction. Turning to lighter matters, introductions and inductions may involve some articulation of what is to be done: "we catch the ball after it bounces once and before it bounces three times." But it also includes much that is shown, not articulated, by example, shouts of encouragement and criticism. It also includes what may be of greatest importance: simply joining in the activity and trying to fit in.

Here we should note that, very early in such inductions, children and adults have many views – know or at least believe many "that's" – about these activities. School-age children might protest the unacceptability of the clothes their parents offer them: "None of the other kids wear that any more." The children learned and know these rules without their having been articulated. So too, they know these rules even without articulating them – and certainly before they do articulate them, perhaps in an effort to stop their parents from causing them embarrassment by making them wear the wrong clothes.[9]

Double binds[10] provide us with another significant area to look at to see the importance and power of learning through unarticulated practice, especially those that involve emotions. For our purposes, we can characterize a double bind in terms of a person's being given contradictory messages, perhaps by being "shown" one thing and told something contrary. A good example is found in the case of an institutionalized boy, who upon getting somewhat better is visited by his mother. Pleased to see her, he runs to embrace her. Perhaps still thinking of him as troubled or dangerous, she

---

9 Thanks are owed to Sarah Larsen for this example and discussion.
10 On double binds, see, for example, Gregory Bateson, Don Jackson, Jay Haley, and John Weakland, "Toward a Theory of Schizophrenia," *Behavioral Science*, 1 (1956) 251–264, reprinted in M. Berger, ed., *Beyond the Double Bind* (New York: Brunner Mazel, 1978); Frantz Fanon, *The Wretched of the Earth* (New York: Grove Press, 1965), and *Black Skins, White Masks* (New York: Grove Press, 1968); and Sandra Lee Bartky, *Femininity and Domination* (New York: Routledge, 1990). Thanks are owed to Robert Daly for discussion here and for the example, given just below, of the institutionalized boy, drawn from John Weakland, "The 'Double Bind' Hypothesis of Schizophrenia and Three-Party Interaction" in Don Jackson, ed., *The Etiology of Schizophrenia* (New York: Basic Books, 1960). In using this example, we do not mean to imply agreement with the view that schizophrenia is caused by this kind of mothering or these kinds of communications.

recoils. This bewilders, hurts, and annoys him. Seeing this, she says, "What's the matter with you, don't you love me anymore?" Here, the boy's views – that is, various of the "that's" he knows or believes – are an unstable amalgam of what the mother showed and what she said. It requires considerable judgment to know how he or we should compare the truth and evidentiary power of what she shows with what she says, and how these tell against each other.

So too, we could consider similar difficulties faced by members of groups – for example, women, Jews, Blacks – who are told, as part of official policy and ideology, "Of course you are equal and will be treated equally with everyone else," but then are treated less than equally. What are these people to believe? Are they to believe what is shown or what is articulated, or some unstable amalgam of the two?

In all of these cases, there are other very difficult features that must also be factored in. The boy has to come to a view that somehow combines both what his mother says and what she shows. But in addition, his view must also take account of what, as he feels matters, it means for him to have a mother who endangers him, and who cannot or will not protect him. A parallel to this for women, Jews, and Blacks is the need to take account of what it means to live in a self-deceived or hypocritical society – for example, one that is unfriendly, even hostile, but which proclaims itself to be friendly.

These issues and problems are important for showing how we learn from what is, itself, unarticulated – both what, when learned, is articulated and also what we may be unable to articulate. They also sustain a claim made in section 1 of this chapter that quite generally by engaging emotionally with others, we learn emotions: how and when to have them, how to recognize our own and those of others, their significance.

We conclude this section with some points about how what is unarticulated can bear on emotions and value and then with a point about knowledge. First, many of the practices and activities we have discussed in this chapter are interpersonal. They have to do not just with many people working, playing, and living together, but also with their doing this in ways that involve interpersonal emotions in the various ways discussed earlier in this work.

Second, many of the ways practices are taught, whether the teaching is explicit or not, depend on emotions. Here we could consider, for example, frustration and annoyance at the new kid on the block who plays the local game incorrectly; coos of pleasure at one's infant who responds "correctly"; the dismay and fear the mother showed her schizophrenic son. Aristotle notes early in book II of the *Nicomachean Ethics* that socialization, in particular the training that results in virtues and vices, proceeds by the twin applications of pleasure and pain. We can easily read this as saying that it proceeds by means of the emotions of the children, such as their pride in pleasing their tutors, and the emotions of those raising them, such as their pride in how quickly their charges learn.

Third, many of the practices in question involve emotions and emotionality. Many, indeed, are emotional practices. Here we could consider ways of being with, "relating to," our parents or children. So too, we could think of the virtues, as discussed by Aristotle. As shown in Chapter 5, section 5, in regard to liberality and courage, many of these are in part constituted by having the right interpersonal emotions.

It should be emphasized that in urging the importance of what is unarticulated for knowledge, including evaluative knowledge, we do not reject the importance of articulation for knowledge – especially if it is gained through reflection on the unarticulated doings and practices. We acknowledge that reflection and articulation may change, or show the need for a change in the practices. All that we claim is that the practice, now modified to take account of the articulated knowledge, can nonetheless still retain epistemological priority over both the reflective knowledge that led to the change and reflective knowledge about the now-changed practice.

For anyone who might still doubt that this qualifies as knowledge – and for those who would appreciate yet another way of putting the point – we offer some comments by Stuart Hampshire:

Why has it often been thought that concentrating on abstract argument, remote from ordinary perception, is the highest activity of a person, the nearest to the divine? Because Aristotle and the Christian theologians have told us so, and their fiction has passed into the language we use when we distinguish reason from emotion, or intellect from imagination, or science from art. Fully within the rationalist tradition, Kant in the *Critique of Judgment* categorized the visual arts as free works of imagination, and thus inaccessible to reasoning and to explanation, as well as the domain of unaccountable genius. This has become the conventional wisdom.

Partly as a consequence of meeting and talking with Giacometti not long before he died, I came to doubt this traditional picture of the mind. It began to seem a convenient academic myth, and a mere invention. "In the beginning was the logos" or rational principle ("The Word" in the Authorized Version), makes articulate reason the source of all things and the sole clue to reality. But is it not obvious within our experience that there are in fact many different kinds of thought associated with the making of things and that some kinds of thought, typically human, are remote from rational discourse and are no less interesting?

Talking with Giacometti, I felt him to be the equal of anyone that I had ever met in the intensity, the concentration, and the continuity of his thinking. From his earliest beginnings as an artist he had made his art into a series of thoughtful experiments attached to a series of linked inquiries, each arising from past failures, and, less often, from past successes. It would not have been easy for him at any stage to give an explicit account in words of his inquiries, and of their outcomes. His intentions went into his carving and modeling and drawing and painting as he "gazed" (his chosen word) at what he was doing, and as he continually corrected it. Looking at any object that he had made, he thought of alternatives that he felt impelled to follow up, not knowing whether they would prove to be better, but believing that perhaps they might be. In retrospect we can see that in his replies to many questions, he was able to recapture in words some of his earlier thinking and some of his past and present intentions, but hardly ever completely and hardly ever with certainty.[11]

4 How emotional-evaluative knowledge can be practical

So far we have sketched some general points about practices and practical knowledge, especially insofar as these are unarticulated and involve emotions. We want to focus on some ways we can understand emotions and the moral knowledge they involve in terms of practices and practical knowledge, again especially insofar as these are unarticulated.

We will start by using what we have shown in order to put a claim – a claim many think Aristotle makes – that emotions are necessary for evaluative knowledge. The claim would be that the general knowledge, or what it is knowledge of, is too complex and difficult to articulate and can only be shown, and that emotions are part of such showing. It could, nonetheless, hold that there are knowledge-giving, discursive, articulate commentaries about some, or even all, particular cases. And it could also hold that what is known in ethics, in contrast with how we know it, has no essential connection with emotions.

Now, we do think emotions would be shown important for evaluative knowledge by being shown to play these roles. However, there is a far stronger position, which correspondingly accords far more epistemological importance to emotions. This stronger position holds that emotional engagement, especially engagement that is at once knowing and emotional, is a primary or a typical way – whether or not the only way – to have and express the knowledge. A related way to put this is that we have knowledge in and of practice: the knowing practice embodies, expresses, and really is

---

11 "A Way of Seeing," review of *Looking at Giacometti* by David Sylvester, *New York Review of Books*, 42, no. 12 (July 13, 1995) 46–49, p. 46. A contrary view, asserting the need for articulation and linguistic formulation, is found in R. Jay Wallace, *Responsibility and the Moral Sentiments* (Cambridge, Mass.: Harvard University Press, 1994), for example, p. 22.

the knowledge. Even more strongly, it could be held that the emotional practical knowledge has epistemological priority over other knowledge, including articulated and reflective knowledge. Such practice has precedence over theory. This need not go so far as holding that the heart has its reasons which reason cannot know. It need hold only that if reason does know them, it gets them from the heart.

To put our position, we start with some comments on Aristotle. He held that each good person requires correct emotions to know how to act and how to be. Thus, it might seem that he would agree with Newman's claim – that aesthetics is to him as ornithology is to birds – transposed to ethics. This may be right about the usefulness, the practicability, of an articulable ethics. But even a Newman-like claim is not strong enough to capture Aristotle's claim that ethics does not admit of a complete, detailed account. For his claim is also that there is no account of ethics that is as complete, even if as useless, as ornithology is for birds.

We thus offer a stronger reading of Aristotle's claim that emotional engagement – and more generally, virtue – is necessary for evaluative knowledge. It is that, in part because of their correct emotional engagement, good and wise people, those who are *phronimos*, embody, express, and determine what is morally correct. It can be useful, and it may be necessary, to reflect on their practice in order to know how to act well and be good. But the way reflection on their practice achieves this is not, or not only, because such reflection allows us to find the underlying principles of the practice: principles which we can then use to know, but now reflectively and articulately, what to do and how to be. Rather, or in addition, the reflection can directly enable us to act and engage emotionally in evaluatively informed and informing ways. It can help us to learn to practice their practice, so that we too can know what to do and how to be. So too, for them and their reflection on their own practice.

Our conclusion, then, is that emotions and emotional practices can be vital for value and evaluation. We can apply this general point to an issue that will be discussed in Chapter 8, section 2: the relations between equity and mercy, as raised in Nussbaum's "Equity and Mercy." As will be argued, there is nothing in the facts, nor in a judge's knowing all the facts, that would require the judge to act with equity instead of mercy or mercy instead of equity. What determines this is the judge's character and personality, whether, for example, the judge is or is not gentle.

Further, knowledge of whether a given decision is merciful, as opposed to equitable, might also involve, even require, emotions. Knowledge here might involve demonstrations, rather than articulations. And emotional reactions could help us recognize whether a decision is merciful, without our being able to say in what its mercifulness consists. We might be able to articulate this in regard to particular cases, even each particular case. Nonetheless, we could still be unable to articulate what mercy is in a way that, by these articulations, would allow future cases to be decided mercifully. We might, rather, have to content ourselves with claims about what – that is, whatever – a gentle, affiliative, merciful person would decide when expressing and acting with those traits.

It must be emphasized that to hold this view – about mercy or more generally – is not to hold that criticism of the decision is impossible. Nor is it to hold that only those who are gentle can criticize it. As in the case of art, even those who cannot produce epistemologically primary works may, for all that, be able to make sound judgments.

5 Emotions as important, but perhaps not necessary, for evaluative knowledge

We have argued that there are many different ways emotions can be important for evaluative knowledge. We have not argued, as McDowell seems to, that one can have such knowledge only if one has those emotions.[12] Our arguments have been aimed, rather, at showing that emotions provide important access to such knowledge.

We see little reason to think that incorrect emotion, or lack of correct emotion, must preclude evaluative knowledge. As suggested in Chapter 3, section 3, successful scam artists and interrogators can have evaluative knowledge without having the relevant emotions. In a similar vein, David Charles notes that one might be good at and, indeed,

> enjoy spotting what is just in order to predict what just people will do, perhaps even in order to frustrate them (or as an agreeable sociological study). So it does not follow from this requirement that only the just, with the right motivations, will unerringly spot what is just. They might achieve their success for different reasons.[13]

Further, as will be suggested in the Chapter 9, section 1, discussion of spiritual maladies, various affective lacks and disorders are compatible with evaluative knowledge. For example, when depressed I can still know what

---

12 In "Virtue and Reason," *Monist*, 62 (1979) 331–350, and "Values and Secondary Qualities," in Ted Honderich, ed., *Morality and Objectivity* (London: Routledge and Kegan Paul, 1985), reprinted in Geoffrey Sayre-McCord, ed., *Essays on Moral Realism* (Ithaca, N.Y.: Cornell University Press, 1988).
13 "Aristotle and Modern Realism," in Robert Heinaman, ed., *Aristotle and Moral Realism* (London: University College of London Press, 1995), p. 152, n. 15.

is good, even though I am "unable" to pursue it. This split between evaluative knowledge and emotions is, of course, part of what makes depression so distressing. To be sure, one may become evaluatively less accurate when depression sets in or gets deeper. As Freud writes in "Mourning and Melancholia," "In mourning, it is the world which has been become poor and empty; in melancholia it is the ego itself. The patient represents his ego to us as worthless, incapable of any achievement and morally despicable . . ."[14] Nonetheless, the relations here are not, or not always, strong enough to sustain the claim that only with emotions can one have evaluative knowledge.

It might be countered that depression may well rob people of evaluative knowledge and that, as the use of 'rob' suggests, they must have acquired the knowledge while they were still in good emotional shape. In turn, this would suggest that to have ethical knowledge, one must either have or have had the relevant emotions. We agree that in many cases this is the way it is for many people. But we also think that this is not the way it is for many people in many cases.

We do, however, think a social analog to this might well be right. At the least, it seems monumentally improbable that a group of people joined in a society would have the requisite patterns of thought, attention, and desire unless the relevant emotions were part of the social fabric. But if those patterns are part of that social fabric, individuals who generally or at particular times lack the emotions may still be able to have access to the relevant knowledge – precisely by having access to the social fabric, the way it is enforced, lived, and so on.

Just as there are social forms of the roles emotions may have to play for evaluative knowledge, there are social forms of how lack of emotions is consistent with having the knowledge. For example, those who are alienated from the emotions of their "masters and betters" can make at least many, if not all, of the same judgments as would these latter. Here it may be helpful to think of a deeply divided society, with a class of people, perhaps even slaves, serving their masters and betters. To be sure, some of the servants may truly have those emotions and some may have them in alienated, inauthentic ways. This latter may be enough to make our point. But in any case, some of the servants may lack all those emotions, but still know what their masters know.

We need not pursue these issues. They may well show that a person need

---

14 In volume 14 of *The Standard Edition of the Complete Psychological Works of Sigmund Freud*, ed. James Strachey (London: Hogarth Press, 1986), p. 246.

not have correct emotions to have evaluative knowledge. They also allow and perhaps even show that emotions of a society or part of a society, and also some people at some time, are important and perhaps even necessary for such knowledge.

A correlate of this for doing ethics is that emotional engagement is very useful, whether or not necessary, for doing ethics well. (We mean, of course, engagement generally, not at each and every time we are doing ethics.) Without such engagement, we may well introduce into our theories theoretical versions of those serious evaluative errors that, we have claimed, are naturally connected with not having the right emotions and not having emotional knowledge.

PART III

Case studies: Philosophical and other complexities of emotions

8

The interdependence of emotions and psychology

The third part of *Valuing Emotions* is concerned with showing what must be understood to understand emotions and what, in order to be understood, requires an understanding of emotions. In this chapter, we focus on some ways psychology and emotions play these complementary roles. In Chapter 9, some aspects of Aristotle's assumed psychology are examined: those having to do with affectivity and self-concern. Chapter 10 is a broad study of *orgē,* anger, as depicted by Aristotle. Its primary concern is to show how an understanding of just that one emotion requires an understanding of, near enough, the entire character and also many social arrangements of Aristotle's men.

This chapter is divided into four sections. The first concerns a worry we have about the common use in philosophy of killing another person as just an example or as *the* example of action. The second is about some relations between empathy and sympathy. The third concerns shame. The fourth is about the value of painful emotions.

1   Killing another person – just by way of example

Killing and letting die are among the more common examples of acts found in action theory and ethics. In this section, we want to discuss what the use of this example may show.[1] We also want to show how emotions do or do not enter into this example and what that shows. And finally, we want to urge an end to using this example as just an example of just any act. For reasons to be discussed, it will help our presentation to expand 'killing' to 'killing another person' or 'killing other people'.

Our reason for urging an end to using killing another person as a general and neutral example of an act is not that we think philosophers should avoid discussing killing another person. The killing of other people is a vitally

---

1   Thanks are owed to Elsa First for discussion.

important issue, an issue that bestrides the world, and that certainly must be discussed. Nor is our point that because killing another person is different from other acts, we think that philosophers should stop using it as the chosen example of acts. We do agree about the difference. But, by itself, that would show that just as philosophers cannot depend solely on examples of killing another person to illuminate many other acts, so too they cannot depend solely on those acts to illuminate acts of killing another person.

Our point is that philosophers, like so many in our society, have serious difficulties in thinking and feeling clearly about killing other people. For many sorts of reasons, we think and feel strangely and inaccurately about killing other people. And we also, perhaps therefore, think and feel strangely and inaccurately when we use killing other people as just an example to do ethics.

To see this, let us consider why philosophers use killing another person as our example. We find it hard to accept the usual answer that philosophers simply want an example: as might be said, a general and neutral example of acts, of doings and nondoings. In order to question whether this is all that killing another person is – namely, just an example of action – we might consider what would happen in and to philosophical discussion in ethics or action theory, if rape was used as the general and neutral example: for example, the rape by a relative, perhaps a parent, of a three-year-old child, or, to paraphrase from a recent newspaper account, the rape of a woman "who asked for it by wearing sexy clothes." Here, the terrible particularities of the act would almost certainly obtrude and obstruct general and neutral discussion.

What is at issue here is not the gravity of rape. For no matter how or why we might compare the gravity of rape and that of killing another person, killing another person is surely a very grave matter. Nonetheless, we philosophers use it as a general and neutral example. And we do so frequently. How is this possible? What are we thinking or feeling, or not thinking and not feeling, that would be impossible in the case of rape?

The frequency of using killing another person as a common philosophical example could easily suggest that philosophers are a bloodthirsty lot, or perhaps extremely hostile and angry, perhaps interested in doing away with other people, or simply in being alone. There might be something to this, as is suggested by philosophers' very strong demands for shared understandings, for others to accept our views, the strength of our disagreements, the heat and duration of our fights, and the like.

What concerns us at least as much as the frequency with which killing another person is used as an example is the way it is treated. Almost invariably, the examples of killing other people are presented in affectless, denatured, flat ways. This is so common that it might well be asked what emotional state philosophers are in: what emotional states are encouraged in and by, and are proper or endemic to, the discipline. This can raise the same worries and suggestions as about the frequency of the example. It might also raise the question of whether we are suffering from one or more of the combined emotional, evaluative, epistemic defects discussed in this work, such as dissociation or intellectualization.

It may well be unfair and improper to single out philosophers here. For the real answer, or at least a considerable part of it, might be that philosophers (like so many others) have gotten caught up in or by our society's general tolerance of, even liking of, mayhem, violence, and killing people. We are here not concerned with whether in fact as a society we do tolerate this, although the amount of violence in the contemporary United States, the wars and violent political and social disputes throughout the world, and the general inaction, and even indifference, to these can suggest tolerance. Nor are we concerned with whether the seeming tolerance here is born of acceptance or alternatively of resignation. Rather, we are concerned with the toleration, reaching even positive embracing, of depictions of killing other people in our films and writings. Violence, especially killing other people, sells – so those in the media suggest they know.

Here, it is essential to note how the killings of other people are portrayed. They are not presented as common and everyday – which they are. Nor are they presented as terrible, the end of a person's life, and the end of many other people's hopes and possibilities of a decent life – which they are. Rather, they are presented as somehow exciting, as unusual, uncommon, or as something that happens to special, unusual people, or people in unusual circumstances. Killing another person is, at least often, romanticized and stylized and aestheticized – even presented as a pleasing, aesthetic spectacle, as in the lyrical, slow motion, final death scene in the film *Butch Cassidy and The Sundance Kid,* and in the film *Bonnie and Clyde* where the final death scene is done in slow motion. Or it is turned into a macabre joke, as in the film *Harold and Maude;* or into some other sort of joke.

To be sure, we philosophers rarely, if ever, depict or use killing another person in any of these exciting, aestheticized, or joking ways. But this difference is, in our view, far less important than what is common to the way we and popular thought and entertainment depict killing another person. What is common is precisely that both depictions are so inaccurate and so common.

Perhaps killing other people is treated in these inaccurate ways because it is at once such a pressing problem and one we lack the emotional, political, and social resources to deal with realistically and usefully. Adults in our society seem to have no way to do this, either in fantasy or in actual life. Children at least have fairy tales and games to allow them to deal with such matters, and gain mastery and resolution.

We might add that it has been suggested that, as shown by their games of "bang, bang, you're dead," children can play at killing where killing is devoid of the emotional freight we claim it carries. But we think that this shows a serious misunderstanding both of why such games are so popular and also of children. If death were just "child's play," children would not play at it.

To the extent that we philosophers join in our society's views about killing other people – and it would be difficult for us to avoid this entirely – this raises serious questions about our combined emotional, evaluative, epistemic states. We should surely wonder what the internal costs are of denaturing the example of killing another person, making it a matter of amusement or fascination, or flat and nonemotional; and how directing attention in these ways stops us from thinking clearly and deeply about killing, itself, or what it is supposed to be just an example for.

This is to say also that it is unclear to us how much better, if better at all, it would be if philosophers did give "full emotional weight" to examples of killing other people. As is shown by the use and misuse of photographs and films of war atrocities to stir public opinion, there are many difficulties in making proper assessments when we are emotionally fully engaged with such terrible goings-on. Many people lack the combined intellectual, emotional, and evaluative skills to be able to deal with these issues, giving them their full emotional weight, without either getting carried away or engaging in or falling into dissociation, or both.

Our worries about the use of killing another person as a philosophical example are not just speculative or theoretical. In various of Stocker's classes – advanced ones, with students well on their way to becoming professional philosophers – students have used the example of killing another person: or to use their words, the example of killing. A student, having had his argument shown inadequate by a fellow student, changed his example to that of his stabbing the other to death. When queried, these students, including the one who offered the stabbing example, denied any particular feeling about killing another person. They said, "But killing is only an example." When queried, they replied that no hostility or anger was involved, indeed that no feeling at all was involved. Many seemed not to understood why it was even thought that feelings might be involved. However, they almost always used 'killing', rarely 'killing another person'. And when they were asked to use the latter, again just as an example, they found this difficult. They could use the killing of another person as an example, so long as they did not have to mention that it was of another person. Then it was just a killing, and just an example.

Some might conclude that these students showed that they are not to be relied on to judge whether something does or does not involve emotionality. And those who agree with us that emotions can be relevant to moral judgments might conclude that these students showed that they are not to be relied on to make certain moral judgments, especially those that are about emotional matters. Thus, only if we know that a given issue does not turn on emotions could we rely on their ethical judgment and argument.

We think this is mistaken. Dissociation and intellectualization need not be global. Most people who suffer from these defects suffer from them in only certain areas, not in all areas. Similarly, the fact that our society has such trouble understanding and dealing with killing other people does not show that it has similar trouble in understanding and dealing with every other "problem." Put another way, the problems and conflicts of thinking about killing other people – and especially in making this nonemotional – may well involve distortions about killing other people and what that is used as an example for. But problems that are less conflicting may involve far less, perhaps even no, distortion. Thus, these students and other philosophers might be generally quite reliable in their evaluations.

More generally, it is possible that for some philosophers, 'killing' really is just a placeholder for just any action. This might explain why these students had no trouble using killing as an example, but had trouble with using killing another person as an example. This might also be to say that in using killing, or perhaps even killing another person, as an example, there need be no dissociation or the like going on here; nor need there be any partaking in our society's falsified ways of thinking about and picturing killing another person. For our part, we would like to think this. But we find it implausible and far too hopeful about philosophers' powers of insulating themselves from the world around them. Our view is that when we do use killing of other people as just an example, we run the very real and serious risk not only of trying to clarify what is obscure by what is even more obscure, but also of trying to clarify what is obscure by what is, itself, not only obscure but also misleading, distorting, and obscuring.

2 Empathy and sympathy

In this section we examine an important, frequently made, and fundamentally hopeful and ameliorative claim. This is the claim that with full empathic understanding of others, we will almost necessarily come to like and accept them, or in any case soften our negative views about them. Put colloquially, this is the view that to know people is to like them. This is also Seneca's "bet" as Nussbaum puts it in "Equity and Mercy":[2]

> The narrative-medical [full empathic] attitude asks the judge to imagine what it was like to have been that particular offender, facing those particular obstacles with the resources of that history. Seneca's bet is that after this imaginative exercise one will cease to have the strict retributive attitude to the punishment of the offender. One will be inclined, in fact, to gentleness and the waiving of the strict punishment mandated in the law. (p. 103)

The bet, put briefly, is that full empathy will lead to sympathy. Whatever the odds of Seneca's winning his bet, we must recognize that it depends on highly contingent and variable matters: such as why one is interested in the other, how one views and treats oneself, whether the facts allow one to identify with the offender and whether, in personality, one is more affiliating or more differentiating.

We will give brief sketches of how these are important both for philosophical understanding in general and for understanding particular issues about empathy. What we say about these issues is intended also to show the need to pay attention to concrete details, not just their abstract form, and also to the great variability of personalities, character sorts, cultures, and societies. If such attention is paid, it is difficult not to be uneasy about claims in philosophy, psychology, popular thought, or wherever that all people always and universally or quite generally or even typically do, think, or feel in certain ways.[3]

Whether full empathy engenders sympathy clearly depends on *why one is interested in the other person*. Here we could think of those, like psychoanalysts and teachers, whose everyday work can depend on having full empathic understanding of another person while, at the same time, maintaining necessary distance. To achieve their important goals, they may need to avoid sympathy – while also maintaining full empathic understanding.

---

[2] *Philosophy and Public Affairs*, 22 (1993) 83–125. On this issue, see also Max Scheler, *The Nature of Sympathy* (Hamden, Conn.: Archon Books, 1970); and John Deigh, "Empathy and Universalizability," *Ethics*, 105 (1995) 743–763.
[3] See also Elizabeth V. Spelman, *Inessential Woman* (Boston: Beacon Press, 1988), especially ch. 6, "Woman: The One and the Many."

It also clearly depends on *how one views oneself.* Some people who dislike themselves are, for that reason, harsh on themselves and on anyone who seems like them.

Let us now turn to *the facts:* Some people come to be seen as worse, and less deserving of mercy, the more you know about them. To know these people is to hate them, and to know them better is to hate them more. Often, this is due to its becoming more and more difficult for you to see how ever they could have done what they did. Instead of sympathy there may be at best bafflement and a sense of confronting an alien being, and at worst a stronger and stronger view that here we are confronted by evil. As described in his *The Killing of Bonnie Garland,*[4] this is what happened to the psychoanalyst Willard Gaylin as he came to know the convicted murderer Richard Herrin more and more.

But suppose that the facts do allow for identification. In such a case, Seneca may well win his bet provided that the judges have an affiliative personality: that is, a basic stance to others of identifying with them, of being like them. Here, upon learning of the difficulties and temptations the defendant faced, and remembering that they also faced difficulties and temptations, perhaps similar ones, judges might feelingly conclude that they and the defendant are really quite similar, both in the same boat, and that there but for the grace of God go they; and they might then naturally be merciful in their sentencing.

But if judges tend to differentiate themselves from others – if, in Nussbaum's terms, they have a "we/them mentality" (p. 103) – full empathic understanding of others will provide a multitude of ways for them to distinguish themselves from those other people, with the effect or goal of continuing to dislike them or treat them harshly. For judges of this sort, upon learning of the difficulties and temptations the defendant faced and remembering that they also faced perhaps similar difficulties and temptations, they might feelingly conclude that they and the defendant are really quite different since they struggled and overcame where the defendant succumbed. It would, thus, be expected and even natural for them to be harsh in their sentencing.

As well, some people *identify with the aggressor.* In classical psychoanalytic terms, such identification is a neurotic defense that can be characterized in terms of its genesis. Infants or young children "conclude" or "assume" that certain people – typically adult care-givers – who treat them harshly and aggress against them are right to do so and that they should be treated in

---

4 New York: Penguin Books, 1983.

those ways. Later in life, they may continue to identify with the aggressor – not just those aggressors, but quite generally – by thinking and feeling it morally necessary and natural to treat others, perhaps their own children, in similarly harsh and aggressive ways. Perhaps extending the proper use of 'identification with the aggressor', we think it usefully describes many people, no matter how they came to this view, who think it entirely natural and proper to treat others harshly and aggressively. We would also extend it to cover those who, with perhaps more benign effects, simply identify with and want to "get with the strength" and who, so often, seem to be among or about to join "the big battalions," whichever and wherever they are.[5]

In addition, there are people who quite generally have contempt or hatred for the weak. And there are also people who are harsh on others in order not to face up to their really being similar. Describing how this last can work, Vladimir Jankélévitch writes,

> You are almost like me. The similarity between us is so plain that in the eyes of the world you are my brother. But, to speak honestly, you are not my brother. My identity, in relation to you, consists precisely of the ways in which I am different from you. Yet the more you resemble me the harder it is for anyone to see these crucial differences. Our resemblance threatens to obliterate everything that is special about me. So you are my false brother. I have no alternative but to hate you, because by working up a rage against you I am defending everything that is unique about me.[6]

Before continuing, we would note that this last helps explain the strangely virulent animosity between people and groups who share almost the same positions and ideologies, leading some to spend more time fighting with their closest neighbors, rather than their common, and real, enemies.

Our overall conclusion, then, is that it is quite often false that knowledge of others will produce sympathy and liking. In many people, for many different reasons, knowledge produces dislike and hatred, and more knowledge produces even more dislike and hatred.

It thus looks as if empathy will lead to sympathy only for those who are already sympathetic. It may also be that sympathetic people are really the sort of people Seneca was concerned with, since these were people like him, and they were also good people. So understood, Seneca's claim, and Nussbaum's, would be a claim about how it is, not for people in general, but

---

5 See, for example, Anna Freud, *The Ego and the Mechanisms of Defense* (London: Hogarth Press, 1937); Alice Miller, *The Drama of the Gifted Child* (New York: Basic Books, 1981), *For Your Own Good* (New York: Farrar, Straus, Giroux, 1983), and *Banished Knowledge* (New York: Doubleday, 1990).
6 As presented by Paul Berman in his instructively entitled "The Other and the Almost the Same," *New Yorker*, 70, no. 2 (February 28, 1994) 61–71, p. 62.

for good people. That Nussbaum sees this is shown by her pointing out that Aristotle's demand for knowledge of all particulars leads him only to justice as equity, whereas Seneca's particularism comes with – both as cause and effect of – his gentler, nonretributive, and sympathetic form of justice (pp. 97ff.). Once again, it thus looks as if empathy may lead to sympathy only for those who are already sympathetic.

3 Shame

We now turn to shame, to show in another way how understanding an emotion requires understanding much else about a person, where this understanding requires the help of many disciplines other than philosophy. Our main concerns here are structural and psychological, with correspondingly less attention paid to the moral and moral psychological issues.

In Chapter 2, section 2, there was a sketch of Helen Block Lewis's account of shame given in her *Shame and Guilt in Neurosis*.[7] She holds that shame is of the self; and that it is a painful awareness of the self, aroused by the fear that one has not lived up to one's ego ideals or imagos. (As noted there, imagos are internalized idealizations, primarily of one's parents.) Our present concern is not to defend the adequacy of this, even as a start of an account of shame. To mention two problems, it seems to include some forms of anger and guilt, such as anger at oneself and guilt for having not lived up to one's ego ideals or imagos. Second, as noted by Daniel Haggerty, 'fear' can be cognitively too weak or too strong: too weak in cases where there is no uncertainty, but knowledge, that one has failed; too strong in cases such as one where

> a small child who is deeply and profoundly ashamed "all at once," as it were, by the mocking contempt (or some other attitude, such as bemusement) of a parent who "catches" the child masturbating. The parent, invested with the power of the child's lost primary narcissism, may arouse secondary narcissism and momentous shame without the child fearing or believing anything in particular about its relation to the (internalized) ego ideal.[8]

---

7 New York: International Universities Press, 1971.
8 In an unpublished paper on shame that comments on an earlier version of this section. He refers us to Sigmund Freud, "On Narcissism, An Introduction," and Janine Chasseguet-Smirgel, *The Ego Ideal: A Psychoanalytic Essay on the Malady of the Ideal* (New York: Norton, 1984). For other reasons to think that fear – not to say knowledge, beliefs, and thoughts – may be too demanding, see Chapter 2, section 3, and, as mentioned there, Stocker, "Emotional Thoughts," *American Philosophical Quarterly*, 24 (1987) 59–69; John Deigh, "Cognitivism in the Theory of Emotions," *Ethics*, 104 (1994) 824–854; and Jenefer Robinson, "Startle," *Journal of Philosophy*, 92 (1995) 53–74.

Despite these problems, however, Lewis's account seems correct and important in areas and ways that raise serious problems for other views about shame.

Among these views are two held by Gabriele Taylor in her *Pride, Shame, and Guilt: Emotions of Self-Assessment,*[9] along with many philosophers, psychoanalysts, and others. The first is that shame is to be understand in terms of an audience: "in feeling shame the actor thinks of himself as having become an object of detached observation, and at the core to feel shame is to feel distress at being seen at all" (p. 60), and "It is because the agent thinks of herself in a certain relation to the audience that she now thinks herself degraded" (p. 68). In *Shame and Necessity,*[10] Bernard Williams makes a very similar claim:

> The basic experience connected with shame is that of being seen, inappropriately, by the wrong people, in the wrong condition. It is straightforwardly connected with nakedness, particularly in sexual connections. The word *aidoia,* a derivative of *aidōs,* "shame," is a standard Greek word for genitals and similar terms are found in other languages. (p. 78)

Taylor's second claim is that, especially for those in a shame culture, this audience is to be understood in terms of, even as constituted by, a real or imagined "honour group" (pp. 54–57). She writes:

> We distinguish between the "externals" of honour, the reputation and distinction accorded to him [the man of honor in a shame culture], and the actual possession of such virtuous qualities. A man may have either one without the other. But such distinctions do not make sense in a shame-culture. . . . if a man has lost his reputation then he has lost his value in the eyes of all the members of the group, and this includes himself. . . . Self-respect and public respect stand and fall together. . . . The "public" in this case constitutes an honour-group. (p. 55)

To the extent that Lewis is right about the role of ego ideals and imagos in shame, we will have to reject Taylor's two claims and Williams's claim, or at least recognize that they do not hold universally or perhaps even generally. As Lewis's discussion makes clear, the ashamed person's ego ideals and imagos, and that person's fear of not living up to them, need not function in an audience-like way, nor need the person who feels shame feel like an object of detached observation. Even when giving rise to shame, these ego ideals and imagos can be felt to be as deeply internal as any other internal or internalized part. People feeling shame can view and feel themselves as

---

9 Oxford: Oxford University Press, 1985. Our views about shame, including our criticisms of Taylor, are similar to those presented by Sandra Bartky in *Femininity and Domination* (New York: Routledge, 1990), especially ch. 6, "Shame and Gender."
10 Berkeley: University of California Press, 1993.

subjectively, as identifyingly, even if not as approvingly, as they ever do. So too, these ego ideals and imagos need not be or be felt as aspects or derivatives of an honor group, whether internal or external.

Some comments by Andrew Morrison are useful in putting these matters and also in urging caution when contrasting the interpersonal and the intrapersonal:

> From the vantage point of Kohut's (1971) formulation regarding "overwhelming grandiosity," or the demands or goals of a strict ego ideal (the ideal self), shame can be appreciated as an essentially intrapsychic, internal experience. Of course, internalization of objects and their representations in the formation of the ego ideal and ideal self, along with the need for the selfobject function in self-development, ultimately puts these intrapsychic structures into an interpersonal, or intersubjective, framework. But this is true as well for all human development, including the identifications that generate the superego and lead ultimately to guilt as well as to shame, with inevitable reflections of an object-filled environment.[11]

Two final points should be made. The first is that Taylor and Williams recognize, or at least come very close to recognizing, that shame is not to be *understood,* even if it is sometimes usefully *pictured,* in terms of being seen. Our reason for thinking this of Taylor is that the omitted part of her "It is because the agent thinks of herself in a certain relation to the audience that she now thinks herself degraded . . ." is "but she does not think of this degradation as depending on an audience. Her final judgment concerns herself only: she is degraded not relatively to this audience, she is degraded absolutely" (p. 68).

Our reason for thinking this of Williams is that his first sentence, quoted earlier – "The basic experience connected with shame is that of being seen, inappropriately, by the wrong people, in the wrong condition" – ends with a reference to "Endnote One, Mechanisms of Shame and Guilt." In that note, he says that his earlier claim about shame and being seen, especially when naked, was too simple and misleading; that the more accurate view is that nakedness and being seen naked are signs of being at a disadvantage and suffering a loss of power; and that recognition of disadvantage and suffering is what is central to shame (p. 220).

The second point is that on Taylor's criteria about honor groups, we may well be forced to understand, or misunderstand, the *Nicomachean Ethics* as not urging a shame-based ethics. For it devotes considerable pains to distinguish between the awards and honors, considered as the externals of

---

11 *Shame: The Underside of Narcissism* (Hillsdale, N.J.: Analytic Press, 1989) pp. 15–16. He is referring to Heinz Kohut's *The Analysis of Self* (New York: International Universities Press, 1971).

honor, and honor proper. (See, for example, I.5, 1095b24 ff., and VIII.8, 1159a13 ff. Honor and honors, especially as treated in Aristotle's ethics, are discussed in Chapter 10, especially section 3, "Slights, flattery, and recognition by others.")

To return to the main themes of this section: Lewis and Morrison are important, also, in furthering our claims that an understanding of emotions requires an understanding of people's psychologies, much else about them, and also much that lies outside them in, say, their social settings. We will show this, first, by taking up some of what Lewis said about the painfulness of shame.

We agree that it is entirely natural for it to be painful to believe or even simply to fear that one is not living up to one's ideals – here, one's ego ideals and imagos – and for this to result in shame. However, as natural as this is, there are other possibilities. We mean humanly attainable alternatives, not just logical possibilities. (In saying this, we leave open the question of whether they are also desirable.)

It is certainly possible that, upon fearing that one might not be living up to one's ego ideals, one does not take this with shame, but instead take it in a neutral or accepting way, perhaps even a loving way. Here we might think of the attitudes of good parents, good care-givers, good nursery school teachers, and other good teachers of, especially, young children; and how they view and deal with normal, everyday "failures" and "errors" of their charges.[12]

These loving, accepting, or neutral attitudes will not be harsh, punitive, or judgmental; nor will they focus on, much less emphasize, the defectiveness of their charges or of what they have done. Perhaps they will not even see their charges and their acts as defective, as failures. These attitudes need not involve blindness to what was done, nor to the character of the person who did it, nor to how the acts and characters can, and perhaps must, be improved. Nor need they involve complacency, but can instead involve the firmest of resolves to make corrections. Nonetheless, these attitudes will not include scorn and contempt; nor need pain, whether felt or to be inflicted, play much, if any, role in them.

In the previous section, it was argued that "seeing all the facts" must be augmented by various attitudes and types of personality and character to have any hope of guaranteeing empathy. Our present argument about

---

12 We owe this figure of a nursery school teacher to Marilyn McCord Adams, "Theodicy without Blame," *Philosophical Topics*, 16 (1988) 215–245, where she asks us to consider how the problem of evil looks if we think of God as a nursery school teacher, rather than lawgiver and judge.

shame makes a parallel claim: shame requires more, or other, than fearing that one is not living up to one's own ideals. To have any hope of guaranteeing shame, the fear must be augmented by various other attitudes and types of personality and character.

This can be put in terms aimed directly against the content claim, discussed in Chapter 1. Suppose that I have contempt for Jack, and that this is due to – a content theorist might say, is nothing but – my belief that he failed to live up to his ideals, my valuing those ideals and his living up to them, my desire that he live up to them, and the like. Even though my contempt is due to those factors, it is certainly possible for you to have all those beliefs, values, and desires, but nonetheless not hold Jack in contempt. To explain this difference, we might note that I am judgmental, punitive, and harsh, whereas you are gentler, less judgmental, less punitive.

As this strongly suggests, to have any chance of succeeding, the content claim must make claims or assumptions about character. But since character is itself importantly affective and must be understood in terms of affect, the content claim cannot make use of it. If, as we think, character must be understood as being, itself, affective and emotional, we now can see why, not just that, the content claim fails: character mediates between the judgments figuring in the content claim and emotions. Those judgments yield and constitute particular emotions only for those with the requisite character. Again, because I am harsh and judgmental, but you are gentler and more understanding, the judgment that Jack did not live up to his ideals generates and constitutes contempt in me, but not you.

We now want to show another way that general psychological facts are important for shame and the ways it is experienced. Our particular concern here is whether the shame is *contained* or *localized* or instead is *globalized and spread through the entire self.* Many writing about shame hold that shame is always globalized, meaning that shame is always of the *entire* or the *whole* self. This is found in Lewis's work, where she talks of shame in terms of a "failure of the whole self" (p. 40). We read Taylor as holding this, when in her chapter 3, "Shame," she holds that precisely because they are localized, what are thought of as instances of localized shame are really instances of guilt, not shame (see, for example, p. 53). It is also found in any number of psychology texts, such as Merle A. Fossum and Marilyn J. Mason's *Facing Shame: Families in Recovery:* "Shame is an inner sense of being *completely* diminished or insufficient as a person."[13]

In what follows, we are more concerned to sort out various possibilities

---

13 New York: Norton, 1986, p. 5; emphasis added.

than to discuss which author held exactly what. So we will talk primarily of what, correctly or not, we take their claims to mean. To start with, we take them as focusing on feelings of shame that can be expressed by 'I am ashamed of *myself* for ———'. The blank could be filled in by (a description of) a feature or state, such as my *meanspiritedness,* whether at a moment or more generally. It could also be filled in by an action, such as *how I treated you,* whether one time or more generally. Correlatively, we take the claim that shame is of the entire person as *not* focusing on feelings of shame that can be expressed by 'I am ashamed of *my* ———', where the blank can be filled in by some feature, state, or doing.

There are, clearly, close connections between these two sorts of expressions and the feelings of shame they express. So too, there are important evaluative issues about when we can or cannot "conclude" one from the other. But just as it is conceptually possible, and just as it can be morally proper, to hate the sin without hating the sinner, it is also conceptually possible, and at times morally proper, for sinners to be ashamed of their sins without also being ashamed of themselves for sinning – at least as shame is understood by those we are criticizing.

This had better be right. Otherwise, there will have to be perhaps surprising differences between shame and pride, and among 'I am ashamed of my ———', 'I am not ashamed of my ———', and 'I am proud of my ———'. For there will often enough be simultaneous fill-ins for all these schemata. Thus, if all these schemata are about the entire self in the same way, the self will often enough be found as and at the same time entirely shameful, entirely not shameful, and entirely worthy of pride. (This may be problematic only to the extent that the emotions and their constituent evaluations are unmixed and unambivalent. But, as will be seen, these are just the ones in question.[14])

Our conclusion, then, is that 'I am ashamed of my ———' *need not* express shame of the person's entire self in the sense of holding it entirely, overall, and unambivalently shameful. First, shame at some feature of mine might not have spread to shame of *myself* or my *self* at all, much less shame of *all* of myself. Here we could think of a man who is ashamed of being bald without being ashamed of himself, or of himself for being bald. Second, when I am ashamed of my ———, what I might be ashamed of might not be *me* at all. I might be ashamed of my dog or the wreck it made of your yard, but not ashamed of myself at all.

Another way to take the claim that shame is of the entire self is to

---

14 Thanks are owed to Daniel Haggerty here.

understand 'the entire self' as the self as a whole. So understood, the claim is that the self, when such an object of shame, is *nonpartitionable*. That is, shame takes the *whole* person as its object. This seems right, but only as a conceptual, not a moral, point; and it is the moral, not the conceptual point, that is in question.

To put our position, we will start by noting that just as shame can take a *whole* person as its object, so can many other emotions. When I am angry at John for wrecking the car, I am angry at John, the whole person. There is no part or aspect of John that I am angry at. We mean, of course, that there is no part or aspect of John that I am angry at *instead of* being angry at him. After all, I could be angry at his reckless driving, as well as at him, taken as a whole. Indeed, his recklessness could be my ground for being angry at him. Nonetheless, there is only a difference of specificity, not object, between 'I am angry at John' and 'I am angry at John on account of his recklessness'; but there is an important difference of object between either of them and 'I am angry at or about John's recklessness'.

Not all emotions have whole, nonpartitionable objects. If you are *annoyed* about the clothes John is wearing to an important meeting, you might be annoyed only about the color of his socks, and not about all his clothes, taken as an ensemble, and not even about everything concerning his socks. You might find their length and pattern, as well as the rest of what he is wearing, entirely acceptable. Similarly, you might *admire* or be *frightened* of some parts of a city without admiring or being frightened of the whole city.

As just seen, some emotions do and some others do not have objects that can be partitioned. But at least some emotions seem to take either a partitionable object or a nonpartitionable one. If you are *annoyed at John's clothes,* the object may well allow for partition. But if you are *annoyed at him* for wearing those clothes, you are annoyed at him, the whole person, John. Similarly, you could admire him or be frightened of him – again, of all of him, and you might admire or be frightened by only some aspects of the city, not all of it.

Whether objects of emotions – or these objects of these emotions – are partitionable thus does not seem due to the emotions. Put almost tautologically – only locating, not accounting for, the facts about partition – whether an object is or is not partitionable seems due to the nature of the object: whether that object allows for partition or instead must be understand globally and as a whole.

Let us now apply this to the claim that shame is always globalized. We take that claim to be intended as an important, substantive evaluative and moral psychological claim about a person suffering shame. This is to take it as holding more than that when the self is the object of shame, the self is nonpartitionable: as going beyond holding that 'myself' in 'I am ashamed of myself' functions like 'John' in 'I am angry at John' and unlike 'city' in 'I admire the city – not all of it, but some parts of it'. If simple inspection of these cases does not show why we take that claim as making more than this conceptual point, the following might do: absolutely nothing of an important and substantive nature about John is shown by the fact that my anger at him is directed at the entire person, him. Nor need there be any important and substantive difference between my anger at his socks and my anger at his entire ensemble of clothes.

The more that we think is intended is that the self, considered as a whole, is felt to be through-and-through defective or unworthy. Putting this in various, related ways: the whole self is exactly what one is ashamed of; the object of shame is the self, the whole self, and nothing but the self; 'self' and 'myself' are the whole and the full and fully correct names or even descriptions of what one is ashamed of.

To be sure, this allows that shame can be aroused by particular or localized grounds, such as one's own meanspiritedness. But it goes on to hold that what one is ashamed of is one's whole self. So understood, when I am ashamed of myself for my meanspiritedness, I am not, or not just, ashamed of my meanspiritedness, or of being meanspirited, or of myself as meanspirited. My recognition of my meanspiritedness may well have occasioned or grounded my shame. Nonetheless, the shame takes my whole self as its object, "spreading" itself throughout the whole of my self.

The problem we have with the claim that shame is always globalized is that it seems simply false. Shame need not be globalized. I can be ashamed of just my meanspiritedness, or of my being meanspirited, or even of just my meanspiritedness to Jones during yesterday's meeting. My shame need not spread through the rest of me – not even palely or wanly. While ashamed of my meanspiritedness to Jones or even of my streak of meanspiritedness, I need not be ashamed of other "parts" or "aspects" of me or of my self, nor need I be ashamed of my whole self even in part or to some extent, again not even palely and wanly. I need not "conclude" from my recognition of being meanspirited to Jones, or people like Jones, or even in general, that I am a failure as a person. Even while ashamed of my meanspiritedness, I can still see and feel myself to be at least a moderately good person, a good friend to Smith, a decent teacher; I can still take some pleasure and some pride in these last; and I can be overall at peace with myself, and even proud, on the whole and overall, of myself and my life.

Shame, then, might well involve the painful fear that one has not lived up completely to one's standards or ideals, that one has failed "to approximate the shape of the ideal self."[15] But one can fear this without fearing that one has completely not lived up to one's standards or has failed to approximate the shape of one's ideal self.

Our argument might be taken as making a point about logical form: as arguing that it is invalid to conclude "I am ashamed of myself for *totally not* living up to my standards" from "I am ashamed of myself for *not totally* living up to my standards." It might thus be thought to turn on the point that it is a fallacy to argue from 'not totally ———' to 'totally not ———'. But this representation of our argument is mistaken. It suggests that we have a diagnosis of why those three theorists and others held that shame is always globalized: namely, that they argued fallaciously. But we have no diagnosis to offer. We do not know why these authors and others held that shame is always globalized.

Further, even though that argument form is fallacious, not every instance of that form fails. In some cases, success can be due to the concepts filling in the blank. One can infer '2 + 2 = 5 is totally not correct' from '2 + 2 = 5 is not totally correct'; and that 'the number 3 is totally not even' from 'the number three is not totally even'. So too, it can be a matter of empirical necessity, or some weaker form of nonetheless strong generality that an argument of that form works. Suppose certain sorts of parrots are either totally red or totally green. From the fact that one of these parrots is not totally green, it follows that it is totally not green. Similarly, from the fact that helium does not form molecules with other elements, we can conclude of a molecule that is not totally helium, that it is totally not helium.[16]

Applying this to shame, there could be reasons of sufficiently strong psychological necessity to guarantee that all people or all people of a certain sort who are *not totally* satisfied with how they have lived up to their standards are *totally not* satisfied with how they have lived up to their standards. To see whether all or even some people are like this, we must examine people – not the concept of shame.

Perhaps some people are like this. But not all are. Shame does not always, in all people, spread throughout the entire self. Putting our view positively, it is possible to be *partially* ashamed, to be ashamed of only part of oneself. Again, I might be ashamed of myself for how I treat Jones, but not be totally ashamed of myself. This could be for better or worse. It could be due to my having an accurate understanding and evaluation of myself, which helps me

---

15 Morrison, *Shame: The Underside of Narcissism*, p. 35.
16 Thanks are owed to Daniel Haggerty for this example.

see my flaws for what they are – merely flaws rather than typical of my whole being. Or it could be due to my being unable or unwilling to see how typical that flaw is, and how it resounds through me or has flawed counterparts through all of me.

Our claim, then, is that partial shame is both conceptually and psychologically possible. But, of course, shame need not be partial. All too obviously and all too easily, it can be global. One psychoanalytic explanation of this is that shame all too easily evokes younger self-states; and as contrasted with adults', infants' and children's thoughts and feelings are less differentiated and less modulated, and more black and white. Their shame is thus typically intense and global.

In any case, global shame is the most florid and most disturbing sort of shame. This, on its own, may account for its being taken as the paradigm and purest example of shame.

Moreover, it is all too possible and all too easy for people to move, perhaps even unstoppably, from localized shame to globalized shame: from, for example, shame at my meanspiritedness toward Jones, to shame at all of myself. Such intrapersonal ease has an interpersonal analog. This is the ease with which one person shaming another person so easily escalates and globalizes, moving easily, sometimes unstoppably, from particular defects to more and more general ones, and finally to the global, to the whole other person.

Here we might consider what parents, infuriated by a child, say to or yell at the child: "You should be ashamed of how you treated your sister this afternoon." They might easily move, with perhaps a pause after the chastised child looks at them with sullenly glazed eyes, to "You should be ashamed of how you always treat her." And then, with or without further "provocation," to "You should be ashamed of how you treat all of us and all your friends," and then easily and with devastating finality to "You should be ashamed of yourself," and even "You should be ashamed of yourself; you are just no good at all."

Such ease is among the major reasons why shame, whether interpersonal or intrapersonal, is so often an enemy of good relations, good management, sensitive control, and education. To be more accurate, such ease is a problem, especially when conjoined with the very painful way so many people experience globalized shame. Let us explain.

You might think that accurate self-assessments are so important for living well and doing well, they should still be important for living and doing well even when they result in shame. You might also think that since shame is painful, experiencing or fearing it would provide a strong incentive to change. You might, thus, think that it would be useful to tell your children or students why they should have localized shame – or even induce it in them – in regard to some *limited* aspect of their character, abilities, work, or whatever. For, putting all these thoughts together, you think that they will take what you say to heart and will change their ways.

Things might turn out as you thought and hoped. But often they do not. All too often, almost as soon as people have been told that they should have limited shame, many are overcome by globalized shame, which entirely defeats your hopes.

Globalized shame can do this in any number of different ways and through any number of different routes. It may be difficult for those suffering the shame to think of what they could do to improve. They might think the task too large, requiring redoing all of themselves. Or they might be caught up in such a globalized way of viewing the self that they lose the ability to think with enough specificity to see how or where to start.

Second, globalized shame can be devastatingly painful and overwhelming. In saying this, we are allowing that not all globalized shame is like this. It certainly seems possible to have a weak but pervasive shamed distaste for oneself. But strong globalized shame is common.[17] Some people who are strongly and globally ashamed fall apart or spend all their energy in attempts to prevent falling apart. Others become angry, even enraged – and often not toward those who have engendered the shame.

These comments are intended to help illuminate shame. They are also intended to illustrate once again one of our main theoretical points: why we need to pay attention to individual differences, including those of personality and character, to understand emotions – perhaps even what they are, and certainly how they may be experienced and expressed.

We should further note that shaming is dangerous not only when it is one person doing this to another person, or a person doing it to him or herself, but also when it is a people or a nation doing it to another people or nation. It is dangerous and certainly misguided to think that we can settle our problems with others by shaming or humiliating them. We can put this in a way that reverses the order of explanation, but that may get the order of wishing right: it might be regretted that shaming is so ineffective, even dangerous, since it is so much easier to shame others than to solve our problems with them.

As a counterpoint to these dangers, some points on the other side should also be made. First, there are ways to appeal to ideals and failures to live up

---

17 Thanks are owed to David Kim here.

to them that are not shaming at all, but perhaps simply encouraging. Second, there are also ways to limit shaming to the matter at hand.

Third, turning now to ethical theory, we want to offer the following speculation linking the issues discussed under the heading of internalism and externalism and those aspects of our ethical theories and practices in virtue of which they are thought of as guilt-based rather than shame-based.[18] What we mean is this. Some contemporary philosophers think it impossible or at least highly improbable that people can be motivated by duty, especially where this is connected with guilt and feelings of guilt. Others think this is possible, but only after moral education that somehow manages to get people interested in duty. But from the outset and quite naturally, shame is obviously motivating. There just is no problem in seeing how shame is motivating. As just noted, it can be all too motivating. (This invites us to take the problems of moral motivation that occupied Socrates, Plato, and Aristotle not as problems over how it is possible for moral beliefs to motivate, but rather over how to get people to have the correct moral beliefs.)

These last three points and many of the previous ones raise various questions. One is whether in these different cases the same emotion of shame is experienced. One way to ask this is by asking why we say that these people have the same emotion of shame, and that their differences in experience and expression are due to different personalities or characters. Why not say, perhaps far more simply, that their emotions of shame are different sorts of shame? Our answer would be in terms of the usefulness of allowing that both emotions and also personality and character have independent, even though interrelated, status and importance.

Various other questions also arise quite naturally. How are we to distinguish between rage as a defense against feeling such shame and rage as an attack on the person who provoked it? What determines whether the outcome of shame is rage, or a collapse, or a far more controlled and even reasonable reaction? What determines whether the shamed person remains in one of these states, or varies or cycles through them? What determines how severe and how globalized any collapse is? What determines how "the entire self" is felt in globalized shame, and why shamed people remain with one or the other of these, or alternate between them? If shame is so dangerous, how did or do shame cultures manage to be successful, rather

---

18 This is suggested by Bernard Williams in *Shame and Necessity*, especially under the heading of "necessary identities." Thanks are owed Daniel Haggerty and Sean McAleer for discussion here.

than simply, quickly, and disastrously destroying themselves or succumbing to external dangers?

To indicate how we would answer these questions, we return to an earlier theme. As should be clear, we agree that it is all too easy to move from localized shame to globalized shame. However, we do not see this move, or the ease with which it is made, as conceptual of shame. Put simply, this move is not necessary: it is not conceptual of shame that it always ends up as shame of one's entire self. Whether it does – and if it does, how easily it does – depends on many contingent and variable facts and states.

We will simply list some of these. Among the most important is one's ego strength: whether one is then and there strong, resilient, basically hopeful; or instead weak, depleted, fragile, pessimistic. In addition, these facts and states include one's recent history and experience, such as one's state of physical health; whether one has recently had various ego-strengthening experiences, such as feeling well loved, feeling part of a strong family or community, having a book or article accepted, receiving a promotion or award or the reciprocation of one's amorous attempts; or whether one feels poorly loved, alone, lonely, and on one's own, and abandoned; whether one has recently experienced such ego-weakening experiences as the death of a loved one or of a love relation, a rejection of one's work or of one's attempts at intimacy and love.

Another important element determining how shame is experienced is narcissism. In ways discussed in Chapter 10, section 1, whether shame is more localized and contained or more globalized, spreading over or into the whole self, depends on the character and strength of one's self-love and one's narcissism: for example, how "touchy" or "exposed" one feels, how easily one feels one's whole self threatened or called into question, the sorts of defenses one has of one's narcissism, whether they are in good or poor repair.[19]

This, of course, is to acknowledge that globalization of shame can be natural for certain sorts of people, such as those with a weakened, fragile ego, with serious issues of narcissism, without much internal resilience or external support. Indeed, we would say that the fact that they naturally experience shame as of their entire self is diagnostic of their being such people. So too, it may be natural for and diagnostic of such people to experience shame or more shame where other, stronger, or less depleted people would feel no shame or less shame.

---

19 On love of self, see Pauline Chazan, "Self-Esteem, Self-Respect, and Love of Self: Ways of Valuing the Self," forthcoming in *Philosophia*.

Perhaps we would even be willing to say that it is conceptual of being such people that they experience shame these ways. We see little danger in saying this – provided that it does not encourage us to think that globalized shame is conceptual of shame, or of shame as experienced by all people.

We want to conclude this section by putting one of its points in a general and abstract way. We have seen in regard to empathy, scorn, contempt, and shame that in order to understand both why people have those emotions and also what those emotions show about those people, we must understand the beliefs, desires, and evaluative views of those people. But this is not all. We have also seen that in order to understand these issues, we must, also, understand character, psychology, and emotional makeup. We would extend this to hold for many, if not most or even all, other emotions and affective states.

4 Painful emotions

Much of this work is concerned with showing the value of emotions, both in general and, at times, in particular. There is, however, a group of emotions that some philosophers think cannot ever be shown good, and which they think we would always be better off without. These include the painful emotions. The boundaries of this group may be unclear, but it clearly includes shame, regret, and grief. According to these theorists, the problem with these emotions can be put as follows: to feel shame, regret, or grief, especially over what is past will do no good; all it does is add insult to injury.[20] Somewhat more mildly, Sigmund Freud comments in "Mourning and Melancholia" that why mourning "should be so extraordinarily painful is not at all easy to explain."[21]

Valuing Emotions does claim that emotions are evaluatively important and have tremendous value. But it is in no way concerned to deny that obvious fact that many instances, as well as many sorts, of emotions are bad. It might thus seem a matter of indifference to this work whether or not painful emotions as a class are bad. We do not see it this way, however. Our disagreement is not with the claim that all or some painful emotions are bad. It is with how reasons offered for this claim deny evaluative importance to emotions, misunderstand the psychological elements and structure of emotions, and misunderstand the ways emotions fit into our lives.

20 Thanks are owed to Karen Neander and Georges Rey for discussion here.
21 In volume 14 of *The Standard Edition of the Complete Psychological Works of Sigmund Freud*, ed. James Strachey (London: Hogarth Press, 1986), p. 245.

It might seem paradoxical for us to hold that claims asserting the badness of certain emotions deny their evaluative importance. Being bad is, after all, one way of having evaluative importance. Our objection, however, is to these claims' denying emotions the sorts of evaluative importance argued for at length in *Valuing Emotions.* They deny emotions their own particular forms of evaluative importance. We are thinking here of the claims that painful emotions are bad that are compounds of mistaken evaluative and ontological views about emotions. The mistaken evaluative views are hedonistic accounts of value. The ontological views are that emotions are simple, often bodily, sensations and mere feelings, lacking complexity and meaning. Put together, these views see emotions as evaluable without regard to their complex meaning structures.

Although these views are conceptually independent of each other, they are often enough put forward together and rightly attacked together. We can recognize this compound view in the crude and simple hedonisms roundly attacked by Plato in the *Philebus,* Aristotle in the *Nicomachean Ethics,* and by many contemporary antihedonists. As we have seen, emotions are not sensations or mere feelings, whether or not they involve the body. Nor, as we have also seen, does their value lie in simple amounts of anything, including pleasure and pain. Rather, as urged throughout this work, their value lies importantly in how they enter into and help constitute our personal, interpersonal, social, and civic lives.

That compound view of hedonism does not recognize organic wholes both in general and, in particular, those that are obvious candidates for painful emotions that are, nonetheless, good – obvious candidates, that is, for those of us who accept such evaluative categories. Many people think that sadness over what is bad can form a good organic whole: for example, sadness over the loss of an important work of art in a war, or the loss of an important scholarly institution, such as the burning of the library at Alexandria. For retributive reasons, as well as for more general considerations of organic wholes, many hold that remorse over evil can be good: holding, for example, that if you have acted maliciously or contemptuously, giving expression to racism, say, it can be, as such, good that you feel regret or remorse.

Many objections to these claims about organic wholes come from those advancing resolute, straightforward and, we think, relatively simple hedonisms, perhaps incorporated into similarly resolute and relatively simple utilitarianisms. These are views that "simply" see such elements as pain as bad on their own, and cannot see how they could cease being bad when in combination. So, they hold that punishment quite generally – including such self-punishment as feeling regret or remorse – is good only if it helps reform or deter, say. On their view, it is never good as such. And they also hold that no whole that contains it would be made worse just by its absence, as differentiated from the hedonic consequences its absence entrains.

We do not see how to continue with the arguments about painful emotions cast in terms of organic wholes, except by markedly changing the focus of this work. For on our view, the dispute really turns on general issues about organic wholes, and not on issues particular to painful emotions and any organic wholes they help constitute. And, in fact, we think that many of the arguments that all painful emotions are bad (and, of course, many arguments that some are good) seem to be nothing more than instances of arguments about larger structures of value and evaluation.

We also think that, too often, these larger views are so deeply held, and so resistant to piecemeal testing, that it seems impossible to examine painful emotions on their own, much less use these emotions to examine those claims. Instead of being available for open examination, those emotions are already understood just as instances of, even just as stand-ins for, those views. Thus, what often really separates philosophers who seem to disagree about the value of painful emotions may have little to do with those emotions, considered on their own, but only with those far larger evaluative views. As we would put the matter, somewhat tendentiously, many of these disagreements reveal a failure to pay attention to emotions themselves and their particular nature and importance for life and value.

This said, we continue with our arguments that some painful emotions can be justified. We start by restating what is obvious: many painful emotions are not good. In many cases, these emotions are bad, and we would be better off without them, because of the pain they involve. (So too, of course, for many pleasurable emotions, as argued by the *Philebus*.)

But some can be justified, for example in the way the pain of the traveler in the parable of the Good Samaritan can be justified, and also in the way that the bad parts of Leibniz's best of all possible worlds can be justified. In the Good Samaritan case, there was something good for the Samaritan to do, because of the traveler's pain and suffering caused by his beating. The traveler's suffering was necessary for the Samaritan's good deed and, given that the traveler was injured, what the Samaritan did was good. In saying this, it is acknowledged that it would have been better had the beating not occurred, even though this would also have made the Samaritan's good deed impossible. This, of course, is the lesson of the "paradox" of the Good Samaritan: we cannot infer that something is good from the fact that it is necessary for what is good.

In Leibniz's case, it is better that the bad occur along with the rest of the best of all possible worlds. But the bad is only necessary for that world and its goodness: it is not a necessary part of what is good about that world.

Similar considerations, with as much or as little justificatory power, are readily found for painful emotions. One general theme here is that it is not possible for people in general or for people like us to avoid painful emotions, at least not without giving up too much else. So, it has been urged that at least for people like us, the capacity to love requires the susceptibility to grief over the loss of a love: we get attached to those we love in ways that occasion pain on detaching from them. The real, imagined, or feared loss of a love is not met just with, say, gratitude over what we had while it lasted. For we do not see the person we love just as a wonderful loan. Nor do we see those we love the way many feel about good weather: when we have it, we can delight in it, but when it goes, this can be regretted but should not be suffered as a loss, much less as a loss of a possession.

In certain ways, such justifications of painful emotions may be like those of both the traveler's pain and of the bad part of Leibniz's best of all possible worlds. But we may be told that in one particular way, they seem like only the former. In Leibniz's case, the bad part is necessary for the best of all possible worlds. But in the Good Samaritan case, the beating is necessary only for the world that includes this beating being as good as it can be. This is to say that it would have been better had the traveler not been beaten, even though this would have deprived the Samaritan of an occasion to do a good deed. Maintaining this analogy, we may be told that painful emotions are justified only because we are not so good as we might be, or only because we are bad people: better people, such as Stoic sages, will not need painful emotions in order to have good emotions, such as love.[22]

For example, we will be told that such people do not feel grief over the loss of a loved one, but rather only some such emotion as gratitude that they benefited from and enjoyed that relation as long as they did. Turning now to another emotion, we will be told that these people will not be angered by the loss of their possessions or even by someone's stealing their possessions. They may, instead, understand and pity the thief, and, again, be thankful that they had the use of those possessions as long as they did. (On a far smaller matter, one of us was urged not to regret losing a prized sweater in a train station, but instead to be pleased that a homeless person would now have a good sweater.)

---

22 Thanks are owed to Joseph Waligore for discussion and his "The Joy of Torture: The Happiness of Stoic Sages" (Ph.D. dissertation, Syracuse University, 1995).

We have various worries about these people. We do not know whether they are possible, or whether, instead, they may only be thought possible. Further, we do not have a full enough picture of what their lives would be like. To mention only one point, we do not know whether those people would be able to maintain human, adult relations with each other – for example, of the sorts Strawson described and praised – or would instead have only other sorts of relations with each other. Nor do we know what those other relations would be like. Until we know what is involved here, we do not know either if these people are possible or, if they are possible, how to evaluate their lives.

We have another reason for not continuing our discussion of these people: *Valuing Emotions* is, for better or worse, about us. And we are not Stoics, much less Stoic sages. We love in attached ways. It is central to our love that it involves attachment, not just liking; and this attachment must be recognized as a form of possession of the deepest sort. At the least, I possess the one I love by having made that person part of my very self; I possess that person by that person's being part of me.

Now, this might be thought a feature only of narcissistic love. Perhaps it is. But we do not think that this helps sustain the analogy between the goodness of what the Samaritan did and the goodness of our grief over lost love. The Samaritan's deed required something bad – the suffering of the traveler – with which it dealt well. The analogy requires that the narcissism needed for, and handled well by, grief is itself bad. But we do not think that the narcissism of good grief must be bad.

One way to put this is that we find the claim that such possessiveness is a feature *only* of narcissistic love strange, if not misleading. It is, first, unclear whether wholly nonnarcissistic love is possible for beings like us. Second, such possessiveness and narcissism are features of healthy and normal narcissism, not only of excessive narcissism, much less of only pathological narcissism. These different forms of narcissism are discussed in Chapter 10. Here it may be sufficient to take note of what Freud suggests in "Mourning and Melancholia." Talking about both nonnarcissistic (as he calls it, anaclitic) and also narcissistic love, he suggests that it is simply a fact, albeit a very deep fact, about us that "giving up" a lost love requires detaching from "innumerable . . . impressions" and that this "is not a process that can be accomplished in a moment, but must certainly . . . be one in which progress is long-drawn-out and gradual" (p. 256).

We take this as saying that the change from being pained by a loss to feeling only gratitude over what good we had when we had it would require, at the least, an extremely thoroughgoing and serious change to the very nature of our love and to some of the deepest and most pervasive parts of our character. We have no idea whether such changes are possible; nor how they might be effected; nor what we and our love would be like were they effected. Thus, we do not have any idea how to evaluate these claims about feeling no grief, but only gratitude.

As shown throughout this work, however, we do have some thoughts about those claims. We feel about them the way we feel about the use of Spock of *Star Trek* (as discussed in Stocker's Preface): we see no way to tell whether and to what extent this is fantasy. Without being able to give realistic and at least somewhat detailed answers about these issues, we find it pointless even to speculate about even the conceivability of these rather limited matters.[23]

With this we end the present line of argumentation. We are reasonably confident in those arguments so far as they went. But we do not think they went far enough. For no matter how accurate and how well taken, these arguments show painful emotions only necessary for what is good, leaving untouched the worry that in themselves they are bad. We want now to turn to some other and more powerful justifications of painful emotions – justifications that go beyond showing those emotions merely necessary for what is good. These arguments will make essential use of psychological facts, models, and ideals – and it is by turning to psychology that we will be able to show how we can do more to justify painful emotions than simply show them necessary for what is good, in either the Good Samaritan or the Leibnizian way.

As we see matters, many doubts and questions about the justifiability of painful emotions depend on an ideal – or, far more accurately, a *fantasy* – of wholly positive emotions. This is a fantasy or fantasy-ideal of a life and of emotions without tension, conflict, and ambivalence. This fantasy-ideal is found in our tradition, at least from the time of Plato. But, we want to emphasize, many of the most positive and valuable emotions, such as those of love and friendship, are complexes of ambivalences, composed of intertwined positive and negative, pleasurable and painful emotions, affects, and other elements. For example, most, if not all, forms of love are amalgams of approach and avoidance, merging and distancing, breaking and keeping

---

23 We therefore wonder what R. Jay Wallace has in mind when, without any detail or discussion – without any showing how it is conceivable – he claims about much more extensive areas that "it is at least conceivable that cultures might exist in which people are subject to natural emotions without being subject to the [Strawsonian] reactive attitudes." *Responsibility and the Moral Sentiments* (Cambridge, Mass.: Harvard University Press, 1994), p. 32.

boundaries, possessing and letting go, and other forms of conflict, tension, and ambivalence. The exception – and it is important that it is the exception – may be various "oceanic" states of complete merging with the other or others, if not also the universe.

According to this fantasy-ideal of complete harmony, painful emotions will not be part of an ideal life. It also holds that a life is always better for the absence of painful emotions. But if we are right about emotions so very often involving conflicts and tensions, and so very often being complex compounds of elements of different valences, a life without painful emotions would be a life without whole ranges of emotions. It might well not be a life at all and most certainly it would not be an ideal life or anything even approaching a good life.

We are not suggesting the clearly false and ridiculous view that once this ideal of harmony is given up, all painful emotions will be seen as good. What we are suggesting is that having given up that ideal of complete harmony, we will be in a good, or at least a better, position to assess painful emotions. We will be able to see how they are expressions, or causes, or effects of what is truly human; and we will also be able to see what is good or bad about that. We will, for example, be able to see whether they are parts of normal and healthy self-concern and an accurate appreciation of the world; or whether, instead, they are parts of various distortions, excesses, and deficits in understanding and self-concern. To take an example from Aristotle, we will be able to see whether a given soldier's fear is an expression of cowardice perhaps conjoined with an overestimation of the danger; or whether it is an expression of a Celt-like love of danger; or whether it shows a proper appreciation of both himself and the danger he faces (cf. *NE* III, especially 7). All that we will have given up by giving up that fantasy-ideal is the ready-made criticism of painful emotions that they are bad simply because they do not satisfy that ideal.

As we trust is clear, our claim is not that painful emotions are good in themselves in the sense of being good on their own.[24] We have argued only that they are good in themselves when they are part of a good whole. We would note that, as argued by Plato in the *Philebus* and by Aristotle in the *Nicomachean Ethics*, this way of something's being good in itself is one of the more usual ways whatever is good in itself is good in itself. It is not a way that is reserved – and certainly not a way that is reserved as a last-ditch way – to show how what seems bad really is good and good in itself.

We would also note that this claim is not a repeat of the earlier claim that

---

24 Thanks are owed Terry Winant for discussion.

painful emotions are necessary for a good life, in the manner of the Good Samaritan or in a Leibnizian way. It is rather that, when these painful emotions are good, they are in fact good because they are necessary ways of experiencing, dealing with, and resolving necessary tensions, conflicts, ambivalences. Put in terms of love, the nature and the value of love, and of particular emotions of love and of particular love relations, involve experiencing and dealing well or poorly with tensions, conflicts, jealousies, hurts, and fights. If an explanation of this were needed, we might look to theories that show how adult forms of love combine, reformulate, and recapitulate various conflicting aspects and elements, often of earlier states that give rise to adults' forms of love; and how, also, mature love between people involves tensions, struggles, and even fights over boundaries and responsibilities.

By calling these ways necessary, we mean that they are the only good ways we have for dealing with these problems. By calling these problems necessary, we mean that having them is part of what it is to be people like us. By this last, we mean far more than that *as it happens* we have these problems and that we see no way not to have them. We mean also that not to have these problems is not to be a person like us. We further mean that attempts not to have or not to deal with these problems are deeply implicated in various of the serious neuroses, borderline conditions, and psychoses mentioned throughout this work. And finally, we mean more than that these problems must be put behind you – must *have been* solved, gotten around, or otherwise accommodated – in order to have love relations. They are not a hurdle that is to be jumped or evaded. Rather, *continuing* to deal with these problems is part of what love is and part of why it is so important to us.

Our claim here is similar to Mill's on inquiry and thought. Struggle and contention are not merely instrumental means for ongoing good intellectual life and thought, they are essential and continuing aspects of it. Similar points can be put in Hegelian or Marxist terms about thought and history. These claims and our claims reject the ideal of harmony and lack of all tension in favor of an ideal that involves at least some struggle and tension. On our view, then, we have no reason to think that this fantasy-ideal is humanly attainable. We also have no reason to think that it is attractive. And we have some considerable reason to think of it as an ideal that, fortunately for us, we cannot achieve.

We want to put our claim in two other, related ways. We do not think that painful emotions are understood correctly if they are seen as defects – or even as defects that can, somehow, be made good.[25] Taking them this

---

25 The following paragraphs summarize arguments given in Stocker, *Plural and Conflicting*

way would be like taking the resistance of marble to being sculpted as a defect or constraint, the absence of which would make sculpting better; or like taking our having bodies affected and "limited" by gravity, as a constraint engendering defects in ballet. In both cases, such resistance and difficulties help inform the possibilities and excellences of those activities.

There is a second way we go seriously wrong if we think of painful emotions as defects, and if our evaluations are based on fantasy-ideals requiring the absence of defects. A few illustrations should help make the point. Error has at least as good a claim as pain always to be counted as a defect. Thus, if evaluations are based on an ideal requiring the absence of defects, we will have to downgrade teaching and learning: for these require errors, if only to be overcome. Such an ideal will also block the celebration of overcoming ignorance, or of thinking really think well of a person, a people, or a theory that has been shaped by its triumph over error. These could be seen as at most second best, not really good, but perhaps an occasion for rejoicing that things were not worse.

Similarly, an ideal life without defect will presumably be a life without scarcity. But then, liberality and charity will have to be downgraded. An ideal life without defect will also involve no human or natural dangers. Thus, courage will have to be downgraded. If disease is seen as a defect and thus absent from an ideal life, medical and healing skills will have to be downgraded. So too for effort, or at least painful effort. Thus, wishing rather than hard work will be sufficient, and, correlatively, endurance and perseverance will have to be downgraded.

We think this is sufficient to reject the claim that an ideal life will exclude all defects or "defects," and that a life will always be made better by their absence. If this is not enough, perhaps this will make it so: we doubt if anyone has any idea what such a life would be like or whether it is good or even possible – even for a god, much less for a person. We say this even though we are also sure that defects in general, including the ones just mentioned, are to be fought against and minimized, perhaps even with the realistic goal of eliminating them, or at least as many as we can. But we are also sure that they are, nonetheless, essential features of human life, at least as we know and can imagine human life.

It might seem that, in one of two ways, our argument commits a fallacy not unlike the fallacy of composition. The first, and not very serious charge, is that we have argued that an ideal life would have painful emotions from

---

Values (Oxford: Oxford University Press, 1990), especially ch. 3, "Dirty Hands and Conflicts of Values and of Desires in Aristotle's Ethics," in particular pp. 63–64.

the fact that an ideal life has painful *aspects* of emotions. We mention this charge, less because it must be taken seriously, and more just to have a place to make some related points.

Our argument cannot be seen as committing that fallacy where those painful aspects are, themselves, painful emotions. And often at least, the painful aspects of emotions are also emotions in their own right. So, for example, my anger at you for stealing my car can be composed of such "subemotions" as anticipated and already felt frustration at having to deal with the police and insurance company, and feeling betrayed by someone I thought was a friend. To be sure, emotions are not individuated that clearly or that well. We typically cannot make much sense of "how many emotions is he now experiencing?" (We except from this the somewhat special sense of asking about the constituents and purity of an emotion: for example, whether my anger at you is or is not also composed of frustrated sexual desire or jealousy.) Nonetheless, it is clear enough that some emotions can contain other emotions, not just aspects of emotions.

Thus, those who agree that good or ideal lives can contain painful aspects of emotions, while also holding that good or ideal lives cannot contain painful emotions, will have to tell us the size of the emotions they have in mind. They will also have to tell us why they are concerned only with emotions of that size, but not with emotions of other sizes, and why they are not concerned with painful aspects of emotions unless these aspects are, themselves, emotions.

Let us now turn to the second and more serious charge that we have committed a fallacy of composition. The "area" of this charge can be seen as a correlate of the one just discussed: if emotions contain subemotions, those subemotions are part of larger emotions. This invites the second charge: that we have illicitly argued from the claim that a good life will have painful emotions because it is made good by the way it handles problems, to the conclusion that those painful emotions are not bad.

This charge is right about one point. We do take a whole life or a large portion of a life as having evaluative primacy over its smaller parts, including its particular acts. Putting the issue in the other direction, we hold that smaller parts of a life, including acts, are often to be evaluated in terms of the larger parts or the whole life they help constitute, rather than evaluating those larger parts in terms of the value, or the sum of the values, of the acts they contain.[26]

---

26 Aristotle comes to mind here. See also Bernard Williams in many of his writings, including (with J. J. C. Smart) *Utilitarianism, For and Against* (Cambridge: Cambridge University

Further, we do want to allow that large portions of a life – such as adolescence, time spent in graduate school, being a parent of young children – or even an entire life could have only a few dominant emotional themes and tones. What we mean by this can be seen by looking again at Angell's claim about those who find "a *humdrum, twilight quality* to all our doings in middle life, however successful they may prove to be. There is a loss of *light and ease and early joy.*"[27] The emphasized phrases characterize a whole life or a large part of a life as having a pervasive, overarching emotional tone or state.

This way of thinking of the "size" of emotions sees them not, or not just, as eventlike, but rather having a whole life or a large portion of a life as their location and perhaps also their object. For those of us who want to emphasize the evaluative importance of emotions, this fits well with seeing a life, or large portions of a life, as what is evaluatively important, and perhaps even as evaluatively prior to its smaller parts, including its acts. It gives us a way to see the values of emotions as values of a large part of a life or even a whole life, suffusing through or spread throughout the whole life or part of a life. This contrasts with seeing them as, somehow, scattered here and there, in small bits and pieces, and then evaluated in terms of an additive sum of the values of these various items.

It must be emphasized that we do not hold that, since painful emotions in general are necessary parts of what is good, each and every painful emotion is good. Nor do we hold even that each and every painful emotion that we do want to justify is good. Nor do we hold that wherever a large-scale emotional state or portion of a life depends on painful emotions for its value, the absence of any of its painful emotions would result in an overall loss of value. So, in regard to a good love relation that is in part constituted by the way it confronts some particular struggles and fights, our claim is not that since the love relation is overall good, it would be made worse by the absence of just any one of those fights.

We, of course, do hold that various struggles could enter so deeply into

Press, 1973), and "Persons, Character, and Morality," in Amélie O. Rorty, ed., *The Identities of Persons* (Berkeley: University of California Press, 1976); Alasdair MacIntyre, *After Virtue* (Notre Dame, Ind.: University of Notre Dame Press, 1981); Margaret Walker, "Moral Particularity," *Metaphilosophy*, 18 (1987) 171–185; Russell Hardin, *Morality within the Limits of Reason* (Chicago: University of Chicago Press, 1988), especially ch. 5. Stocker's discussions of this are found in *Plural and Conflicting Values,* especially ch. 10, section 2, and in "Abstract and Concrete Value: Plurality, Conflict, and Maximization," in Ruth Chang, ed., *Incommensurability, Comparability, and Practical Reasoning* (Cambridge, Mass.: Harvard University Press, 1997).

27 "The Sporting Scene – Distance," *New Yorker,* 56 (September 22, 1980) 83–127, p. 127, emphases added.

the constitution of a particular love relationship that it would not be the same relation without those struggles. All we hold here is that the lack of those struggles would make for a different relation. We do not also hold that such a lack must make for a worse relation.

Our central claim is that the elimination of *all* fights and pains might well not make things better. The issue here is not just about pain, fights, and emotions and their value and evaluation. It is also about a far wider philosophical issue. What we have here is at least very similar to what Mackie's INUS relation was intended to help us understand about causation. (C stands in an INUS relation to *e* just in case *c* is an insufficient but necessary part of a condition which is unnecessary but sufficient for bringing about *e*.) The problem in regard to causation is that considerations like those just canvassed would also stop us from holding of a cause of something that it is a cause. For it is often possible that an effect could have come about without the cause that, in fact, did cause it.

Our problem is, further, very similar to, if not simply an instance of, the "paradox of the lottery": even if you know of each lottery ticket that it is unlikely to win, you also know that it is unlikely, if not impossible, that none will win. Put schematically, even where we see that we cannot conclude that "*all* x's are ———" from "*each* x is ———," it can be difficult to see how to justify any such claim as "*a particular* x, x_j, is *not* ———." We think this is, or is very close to, the issue we face here about negative and painful emotions. We may be unable to show that any particular painful emotion is justified by arguing that its absence would make matters worse. Nonetheless, we can see that without enough of such emotions, matters would be worse. And we can further see that there is no nonarbitrary way to distinguish that painful emotion from those that would be enough.

To sum up this discussion of painful emotions and their value, we have argued that taken generally and as a whole painful emotions can be good: perhaps not good on their own, but good in themselves as parts of larger wholes. Even though painful, this need not make those wholes even in part bad; nor need it be that those wholes would be better without those emotions. These emotions are justified in ways other than that of the traveler's pain. For in that case, even though the pain was necessary for what was good, it would have been better had that good not been possible. They are justified in ways other than the bad that is necessary for Leibniz's best of all possible worlds. For in that case, the bad element does not enter into the goodness of that world, other than being necessary for it. We have also suggested that a proof of this would involve us in various very difficult and very general philosophical and psychological problems.

We have also, we think, *proved* that to understand and evaluate painful emotions, we must also understand and evaluate much else. This "much else" includes character, personality, many other psychological states and entities, interpersonal and social relations, and individual and group particularities and similarities – and now, we also see, large and difficult, very general evaluative issues.

9

Affectivity and self-concern

This chapter and the next one have several intertwined goals. One is to continue presenting case studies of many of the links between emotions and value discussed in the earlier chapters. Another is to examine some of Aristotle's views on these links. I will do each while and by doing the other. I have several reasons for this conjoint focus. It allows me to advance the study of how emotions are essential to value and evaluation. It also allows me to present some of the ways Aristotle thinks emotions important for thought, action, and life, as well as for value and evaluation. And it allows me to do this without relying on his view, which many find controversial, that emotions are necessary for and partly constitutive of virtue and *eudaimonia*.

It further allows me to show how an understanding of emotions, even one sort or instance of emotions of one person or sort of person, requires the resources and techniques of philosophy, psychoanalysis, sociology, anthropology, and history, to name only some of the needed disciplines. This will help us see some significant differences between our emotions and those of Aristotle's people. It will also help us see how these differences are due to and also help constitute different values, different social and interpersonal structures and relations, different psychic and characterological features and formations, or some combination of these and perhaps still other factors.

The detail and complexity of what will be discussed here is so great that these two chapters will at best be only a sketch of only some features of Aristotle's people, and of only some relations between value and emotion.

The bulk of this chapter is an abbreviated and revised version of "Affectivity and Self-Concern: The Assumed Psychology in Aristotle's Ethics," *Pacific Philosophical Quarterly*, 64 (1983) 211–229. For help with that paper, my thanks are owed especially to John Campbell, K. R. Jackson, Brian Loar, and Graeme Marshall. For help with this chapter, my thanks are owed to Norman Dahl, Aryeh Kosman, and Charles Young.

In this chapter and the following one, extensive use is made of the *Rhetoric*. Some might wonder whether we can find Aristotle's psychology in the *Rhetoric*, since, they think, it does not present his general views and considered opinions, but only what he thinks is useful for rhetoricians. To be sure, the *Rhetoric* may offer only rough characterizations of what is treated at length and with subtlety elsewhere. Nonetheless, it does have deep interconnections with the rest of Aristotle's ethical and political writings.[1] And in any case, it is hard to see how Aristotle could think the *Rhetoric* useful for rhetoricians, if he thought it presented or relied on an inaccurate psychology.

The plan of the chapter is as follows. Section 1 gives a very brief account of spiritual maladies we know all too well, but are absent from the psychology Aristotle attributes to his men. Section 2 considers Aristotle's discussions of anger and pride, and sections 3–5 examine his account of fear and pity, to show how the psychology he attributes to his people explains why he ignored or rejected these spiritual maladies. These sections are largely independent of each other. When taken together, they help fill in the details of the psychology and psyche of Aristotle's man.

1 Spiritual maladies

Put briefly, the psychology Aristotle attributed to the people – generally, the men – he discusses takes them to be proud, striving, spirited, and active, who like themselves quite well and take themselves seriously, immediately, and personally. This is not a universal and philosophically neutral psychology, but rather a particular and highly determinate one. We know full well, from novels, from the psychological literature, and from our own lives, that care, concern, and interest can suffer vicissitudes, even to the point of going into partial or total eclipse. One can "fall" into depression, or *accidie* (sloth or spiritual tiredness), or despair, or hopelessness, or so many other spiritual maladies. When "seized" by these spiritual maladies, we lose care, interest, and concern quite generally.[2] For a graphic description of what melancholia, depression, is like, we could hardly do better than this passage from Sigmund Freud's "Mourning and Melancholia":

---

1 This is shown powerfully in Eugene Garver, *Aristotle's Rhetoric: An Art of Character* (Chicago: University of Chicago Press, 1994).
2 The following discussion of absence of care and other spiritual maladies is based on "Desiring the Bad," *Journal of Philosophy*, 76 (1979) 738–753, and on "Psychic Feelings: Their Importance and Irreducibility," *Australasian Journal of Philosophy*, 61 (1983) 5–26, which, in revised form, appears as "The Irreducibility of Affectivity," Chapter 1 of this book.

The distinguishing mental features of melancholia are a profoundly painful dejection, cessation of interest in the outside world, loss of the capacity to love, inhibition of all activity, and a lowering of the self-regarding feelings to a degree that finds utterance in self-reproaches and self-revilings, and culminates in a delusional expectation of punishment.[3]

To be sure, without care, concern, and interest, we may continue to plan and seek, and certainly to wish and to have longings, and, in at least these ways, still have desires. Further, we may continue to act, perhaps out of a now lifeless habit. Thus, it is possible to act without care. But without sufficient care, we may well "give up," find things "too difficult," "not worth it," and not act. When we "care about nothing" or even have too little care, we do not seize opportunities nor do we heed demands. Our hearts are simply not in them.

It must here be emphasized that even if we fail to act because of insufficient care, we may continue to know what is best. Indeed, one of the features that can make loss of care so distressing is the continuing knowledge of what is good. Thus, we cannot take the phrases used to depict lack of care – such as, "too difficult," "not worth it" – as indicating a change in values, much less a loss of value and values, at least not of value and values in the world.

(I say "at least not of value and values in *the world*" to acknowledge that people suffering those spiritual maladies may feel a loss of value in themselves. They may feel themselves as being of less value. As Freud also says in "Mourning and Melancholia," "In mourning, it is the world which has become poor and empty; in melancholia it is the ego itself. The patient represents his ego to us as worthless, incapable of any achievement and morally despicable" [p. 246].)

If I am right, a number of points must be kept in mind. One can cease caring even though one retains one's moral and other evaluative views, including beliefs and knowledge. One can lose one's active engagement with the world without losing one's moral and evaluative views of it. Correlatively, the absence of care makes intelligible not doing what one believes best. Thus, to explain a person's doing what is best, we need to posit sufficient care.

By 'sufficient' I mean sufficient for active engagement. This covers a lot of ground and excludes many different sorts of lack of activity. To mention some of the latter that have already been noted, there is the neurotic or psychotic withdrawal from the world, exhibited by the man described by

---

3 From volume 14 of *The Standard Edition of the Complete Psychological Works of Sigmund Freud*, ed. James Strachey (London: Hogarth Press, 1986), p. 244.

Clara M. Thompson as having a "markedly detached personality," who is "unaware of any personal emotional contact with other human beings. He is an onlooker at life."[4] Lack of active engagement can also come in such other forms as Oblomov-like inertia, sentimentalism, aestheticism, or the view that one's feelings and how one feels are all that is important. (These were mentioned in Chapter 6, section 3.) It can also come in the form of one's desires being only wishes or longings.

Aristotle's people are, on the contrary, active and actively engaged with the world. Indeed, Aristotle does not appear even to recognize, much less discuss, these forms of lack of care and lack of active engagement in the world. His holding that having a virtue involves emotions and commitment, love of that virtue and of virtue, pretty clearly precludes such lack of care in good people. So too, he does not discuss such lacks in people who are not good. Nonetheless, he spends considerable time discussing emotions, character, and the development of both, and he does so with subtlety, according them a central role in his ethics.

Why did he not discuss them or even not recognize them? I think we should take seriously the possibility that the explanation for this is to be traced to his having a different view of psychology and moral psychology, especially of emotions and affectivity, than we have. For as just noted, it cannot be traced to a lack of interest in emotional issues or a lack of subtlety about them.

What should also be explained is spiritual maladies' total or near total absence in classical Greek literature. We would be hard pressed to find anyone characterized in these works as, say, depressive. However, these larger, cultural issues go beyond the scope of this book, even though exploring them might well help us understand Aristotle's psychological assumptions. It might also help us determine whether his not dealing with spiritual maladies show his views mistaken or whether they were accurate about the people he discussed.

2 Anger and pride

In *Rhetoric* II.2, Aristotle writes, "Anger [*orgē*] may be defined as a desire accompanied by pain, for a conspicuous revenge for a conspicuous slight at

---

[4] From "Development of Awareness of Transference in a Markedly Detached Personality," ch. 13 of *Interpersonal Psychoanalysis: The Selected Papers of Clara M. Thompson*, ed. Maurice R. Green (New York: Basic Books, 1964), p. 111. Originally published with the same title in *International Journal of Psycho-Analysis*, 19 (1938) 299–309. This is also mentioned in Chapter 3, section 2.

the hands of men who have no call to slight oneself or one's friends" (*Rht* II.2, 1378a31 ff., tr. Roberts). Such *orgē* is central to Aristotle's man as depicted in the *Nicomachean Ethics* and the *Rhetoric*, and it is the central topic of the next chapter. For the purposes of this chapter, we should note three points about the *Rhetoric* characterization of anger. First, anger concerns only a very limited group of people: the agent or a person close to him, such as a friend. Second, it is a reaction to an undeserved slight: to an act of undeserved contempt, spite, or malice (*Rht* II.2, 1378b13 ff.). Third, the response to such a slight is to desire revenge or redress. We must ask what sort of person is it who takes note of slights, to just such a group of people, and who responds to such slights with such desires.

We can start our answer with two passages from the *Nicomachean Ethics* – passages that come as close as any I know in that work to recognizing people with the spiritual maladies mentioned earlier. Of those who have the defect of having too little anger, Aristotle says in IV.5: "It is thought that they do not feel [*aisthanesthai*] or resent [*lupeisthai*] an injury, and that if a man is never angry he will not stand up for himself; and it is considered servile to put up with an insult to oneself or suffer one's friends to be insulted" (1126a6 ff., tr. Rackham). And in IV.3, we read:

The small-souled [*mikropsuchos*] man deprives himself of the good things that he deserves; and his failure to claim good things makes it seem that he has something bad about him . . . for (people argue), if he deserved any good, he would try to obtain it . . . men's ambitions show what they are worth, and if they hold aloof from noble enterprises and pursuits, and forgo the good things of life, presumably they think they are not worthy of them. (1125a19 ff.)

Even though Aristotle does allow that there are small-souled men, we should note the sort of thing he says about them and, he says, is thought about them. Typically they are not aware of slights, nor do they feel them. If they are aware of them, they do not resent or are not pained by them. It is supposed that were people to be pained by or to resent the slights, they would react angrily. So even here we do not have a person who is pained by slights but, because of a spiritual malady, does not resent them, or resents slights but, because of a spiritual malady, does not seek redress. (For our purposes, there is no need to adjudicate between taking '*lupeisthai*' as 'resenting' with Rackham and as 'being pained by' with Ross.)

Perhaps the small-souled man fails to notice slights as he should or fails to be pained by or resent them as he should *because* he cares too little for himself. This possibility is suggested by the passage from IV.3. Nonetheless, it is presumed that if people do feel the pain of a slight, they will resent it; and if they resent it, they will seek redress.

Consider the man said by Aristotle to be capable of anger. This man is not a small-souled man. He does pursue those goods he thinks he deserves. He is not servile. He holds dear his own, and his friends', honor, *timē*. He takes himself to be good and to be important. He cares about and for himself – and this to the point of demanding redress if he is slighted. He is, in short, a proud man – but he need not be a great-souled, *megalapsuchos*, man. Further, he is a man who will act to defend his honor, because he is proud.

To understand this more fully, let us examine pride: first, the pride given by 'He is proud of himself for his achievements', then the pride given by 'His strong sense of pride explains why he so jealously guards his honor'. My concern is to show how pride in oneself for one's qualities differs from simply holding that one has admirable qualities. I will begin with some ways pride involves identification.[5]

I can be proud of myself for my achievements; and I can be proud of my sister for hers. She is, after all, my sister. I can also be proud of the American revolutionaries for their achievements. After all, I am an American and identify myself as such. But, even though I recognize and am thankful for the great achievements of various French people in both the American Revolution and in their own revolution, I am not, and do not think I can be, proud of the French for those achievements. For I in no way identify myself as French. Nonetheless, I may be proud to be a philosopher because of the roles various French philosophers played in French politics and society. So too, I can be proud of various French philosophers for having resisted temptations to which many other intellectuals succumbed. I do identify with philosophers.

It might, then, be thought that to understand pride we have to understand identification. For my part, I think we have to understand them together: a discussion of pride will illuminate and be illuminated by a discussion of identification. (This section continues with the former; the latter is the topic of Chapter 10, section 6.)

Let us start with some cases of pride in other people. Suppose that I am proud of my nephew because, as I think, he got the best grade on an exam in his class. Upon finding out that I had misheard and that it was his sister who did this, I might or might not "shift" my pride to her and become proud of her. I might think so unfavorably of her, perhaps finding her so conceited, that nothing she does moves me favorably. Or I might not care about or for her. I might "just" not warm to her, or identify with her. Or I

---

5 My thanks are owed to Brian Loar for discussion here.

might think that being first was – that is, would have been – an accomplishment for my nephew who was never a good student, but that doing well is very easy for her.

For a somewhat different case, suppose that all you think you know about your father's grandmother is that she did something very admirable in saving her home, and, on account of her doing that, you are proud to be a descendant of hers. Perhaps you are even somewhat proud of her. Since this is all you know about her, we might think that your pride is really of just whoever was a close paternal ancestor of yours who did ————. When talking with your father, you find out that the woman who admirably saved her family was his, not your, great grandmother. To complete the story, let us suppose that this is the first time you remember having heard anything about, or even having thought about, your father's great grandmother. So now, all you know about her is all you "knew," all you believed, about your great grandmother.

To be sure, there is a sense in which all along you were proud of your father's great grandmother. And clearly, upon learning the correct family history, you might become proud of her, or at least proud of being descended from her. But you might not. Again, there are any number of possible reasons or explanations. Your pride might have been based on your thought that your great grandmother had saved her home during a war, by convincing enemy soldiers to leave it alone. You find out that your father's great grandmother saved it well before the war, and did so by walking several blocks to the bank to make a mortgage payment, when the mailman failed to call at the house. (This raises questions about why such a story has been passed down through the generations. Perhaps it testifies to the wonderfully comforting ordinary everydayness of your family.)

The explanation of your not shifting your pride might instead lie in you. Perhaps you were embarrassed by misremembering what someone, most likely your father, must have told you or for having misremembered it in a way that could suggest that you have put yourself in his position in the family. Or perhaps you were able to develop such pride in an ancestor only when you were younger and more open. You now may welcome the opportunity to rethink the whole matter and give up all pride in your family, especially your distant relatives. Or perhaps you just find that your great-great-grandmother is just too distant from you for you to identify with her.

These various factors can also play a role in pride in oneself. Suppose that I hear colleagues discussing someone in ways that lead me to admire that person and to think that that person should be proud, perhaps even must be proud, if he or she agrees with my colleagues' assessments. Only later do I find out that I was the person being talked about. I might thereupon come to be proud of myself, perhaps even admire myself, on account of those very same qualities. But, I might not. To be sure, both my colleagues and I can say truly of me that the person I admired was me – and in that sense I did think I should be proud. Nonetheless, it is entirely possible that I do not become proud of myself.

For any number of reasons, I might be unwilling or even unable to be proud of myself or admire myself even for reasons that I found and still find entirely adequate for being proud of or admiring someone else. To mention some of these reasons: I might have much higher standards for myself. Perhaps as a variation on that, perhaps for other reasons, I might think that whatever I could do well was really of no worth, and certainly not good enough for pride or admiration. Or I might dislike myself enough so that I could not bring or even allow myself to feel admiration or pride in regard to whatever I did, much less of myself or myself for doing something even if I recognized that it was of considerable worth and was done well. Or I might be given to asceticism of the spirit, a form of self-abnegation. Or I might suffer from general affective flatness, anhedonia, or dysphoria.

Proud people do not merely think they have good qualities. Nor do they merely think that they are good because, as they believe, they have those good qualities. Even where such beliefs are essentially self-referential, and the people in question know that *they* are the people involved, these beliefs need not add up to pride. Nor need they even yield pride. Using a term that figured in the argument against the content claim – an argument made here by these comments about pride – those beliefs might be "affectless mere cognitions." People with such beliefs might be profoundly uninterested in their good qualities. They would not be proud, nor would they be *taking* themselves in a proud way.

Pride, typically, involves *taking pleasure* in oneself or one's qualities. But that is still not enough for pride. People who are *glad* or *grateful* that they have the qualities they do, and are the people they are, also take pleasure in themselves or their qualities. But, for all that, they need not be proud of themselves or proud people.

Nor is pride guaranteed if, in addition to such pleasure, we add responsibility. People may be glad, and grateful, in regard to their qualities and themselves even if they think they are morally responsible for making themselves good in that way. They still might not be proud, but only pleased that their work – which is or includes themselves – turned out well. Thus, to take up a "puzzle" discussed by some medieval philosophers, one can take pleasure in being humble without – contradictorily – "falling into" pride. More generally, one can recognize that and how one is good without being proud. To be humble and have humility, one need not *missee* or *not* see one's own good qualities.[6]

On the other hand, people can be proud of themselves in regard to what they do not believe they had a hand in bringing about. Some people are proud of their lineage and family history. So, we must ask what pride consists in, since it clearly does not consist in only the conditions just mentioned.

Proud people may be *puffed up* with pride or *strut* and *vaunt* themselves. This would distinguish them from those merely glad or grateful. But those notions seem more explained by, than explanatory of, pride.

It might seem natural to say that the proud person, including Aristotle's proud man, is concerned with honor. This may well be true. But our glad or grateful people can also be concerned with honor and indeed with their own honor: for example, to protect it. They might think that their qualities, not they, themselves, deserve recognition and protection, as Socrates spoke of his wisdom and himself in the *Apology* (30c ff.).

So again, we must ask how do proud people take themselves and their honor differently from grateful people? The following answer should prove useful, even though it is incomplete. Both proud and grateful people are concerned with the complex constituted by themselves and their good qualities. But only the proud people focus on – or better, *take* – these qualities *personally*.

This brings to the fore what is central to the pride of Aristotle's men who are capable of anger. They take slights personally. (Perhaps the use of 'taking something personally' most familiar to us is that in regard to insults.) They take their honor personally. But this answer, though helpful, raises two questions similar to the original one: what is such differential focusing, and what is it to take something personally? As we will see, answering the second also helps answer the first.

It is not enough for taking something personally that one holds "This is mine" or "This affects me." You can recognize that something good is your own but not care about it or about yourself because of it. Nor is it enough to say that taking something personally is taking it from your own point of view. As noted earlier, your own point of view comes in different varieties:

---

6 But see Julia Driver, "The Virtues of Ignorance," *Journal of Philosophy,* 86 (1989) 373–384. My thanks are owed her for discussion of this and much else in this work. I remember with pleasure the discussions Norman Kretzmann and I had in the 1960s about this puzzle.

for example, proud or thankful ones. This goes some way toward showing that the notion of taking things personally cannot be explained in terms of a purely cognitive understanding of a structural relation: for example, seeing this to be your own. Rather, that notion must be understood in terms of at least partially affective ways of taking those things. (This is a continuation of the argument of Chapter 1 against the content claim. It is also similar to the argument of Chapter 8, sections 2 and 3, about moving to empathy from "seeing all the facts," and about moving to shame from seeing that one is not living up to one's ego ideals.)

We can support these various points by noting that people can take a personal affront dispassionately, but take with terrible passion a slight to their religion. It might be suggested that they do not *feel* the personal affront as striking home. But this suggestion involves us directly with affectivity, not simply the cognitive and structural. The latter involves people seeing that they stand in a certain structural relation to the affront: it is aimed at them and it hits them. The former, affectivity, involves their feeling this. (As shown throughout this work, and as discussed explicitly at the end of Chapter 1, affectivity involves far more than simply feeling, simple feelings. It also involves whole ways people *take* themselves.)

Consider these people's felt slight to their religion. We might say that they take this slight personally, or that they *identify* with the religion.

These, however, seem to mean something like this. These people take the slight to their religion the way we naturally expect people to take a slight directed against themselves. This, in turn, seems to mean something like: the normal sort of person, definitive of what we would naturally expect, has precisely the psychology we are concerned with explicating — that of a proud person.

To help highlight the features discussed in this section, let us consider the sort of detachment had, as some think of them, by Zen masters. Such people may take nothing personally, neither themselves nor anything else. Nonetheless, they need not have an objective, God's-eye point of view. They may take what does concern them as concerning them, not simply someone or other. They may take pleasure in their good qualities and perhaps even in themselves for having them. They may find many things worth preserving or attacking. They need not acquiesce in personal slights or other wrongs. These, however, do not add up to taking things personally. And there is no reason to think of the Zen master's detachment as a spiritual malady. If this is right, there are importantly different sorts of detachment.

Here we would do well to consider, also, the possibility of understanding good people who, perhaps like the Zen master, do not easily feel their honor called into question, but who, perhaps unlike the Zen master, are like this because they are kind, nonjudgmental, nonpunitive, and are at least somewhat like a loving nursery school teacher (discussed at the end of section 3 of Chapter 8). We should note that if a person with such nonpassionate and nonangry reactions to slights can be a good person, then Aristotle and many modern Aristotelians are mistaken in holding that anger is essential to a good human life. At best, anger is essential to various forms of good human life. This may not be so dismissive as it might seem. For anger may be essential to a good human life as we know it.

To bring our discussion of anger and pride to a close, the following, though still incomplete, may be useful: proud people take things and themselves personally, where we understand that notion in light of our presumed psychology. (This will be discussed further in Chapter 10.) Despite its promissory status, this claim allows us to distinguish the proud person and thus the person capable of anger from the person with a God's-eye point of view, from the grateful person, from the Zen master, and, most importantly for us, from those with various of the spiritual maladies.

For it was central to those maladies that people suffering them do not care, especially not about themselves. Perhaps they do not think well of themselves. Or thinking well of themselves, they may not think that they can or perhaps that they deserve to be protected and defended. Or even if they think they can and should be protected, they lack the energy, the care, to do anything about it.

3 Harm, fear, and pity

In his discussion of fear in the *Rhetoric* II.5, Aristotle writes that, "Speaking generally, anything causes us to feel fear that when it happens to, or threatens, others causes us to feel pity" (1382b26 ff., tr. Roberts). He repeats the same view in his discussion of pity (*Rht* II.8, 1385b27 ff.). But, for at least three reasons, he does not hold that fear and pity differ only in regard to whether the endangered person is oneself or another.

First, although fear for oneself receives almost all his attention, he allows that one can fear also for those *close enough* to one. A parent can fear for a child (*NE* III.6, 1115a22 ff., and *Rht* II.8, 1386a19 ff.). Pity, too, requires closeness. The pitier must feel close enough to the pitied person (*Rht* II.8, 1386a27 ff.) – but far enough away not to fall within the range of fear.

The grounds, then, on which we feel pity are these or like these. The people we pity are: those whom we know, if only they are not very closely related to us – in that case we feel about them as if we were in danger ourselves. For this reason,

Amasis did not weep, they say, at the sight of his son being led to death, but did weep when he saw his friend begging; the latter sight was pitiful, the former terrible, and the terrible is different from the pitiful; it tends to cast out pity and often helps to produce the opposite of pity. For we no longer feel pity when the danger is near ourselves. (*Rht.* II.8, 1386a17 ff.)

The closeness that fear and pity require involves emotional closeness. Thus, care is essential for *engaging* the values and actions of these emotions and the emotions, themselves. I can be afraid of something only for those I care very much for: myself or those very close to me. So too, I am angry only on behalf of such people. I pity others who are not felt too far away. The operative notions here are affective and emotional – engagement, feeling, care – not purely cognitive. For even if you are too distant from me for me to pity you, I can still see you are endangered.

Second, pity can be for something that one knows to have happened. But fear can be only for something believed still to come. Third, pity can be only for what, on the pitier's view, is not deserved: one cannot pity criminals their just punishment. But criminals can fear their punishment whether or not they believe it deserved. Our notions of fear and pity come at least close to satisfying the second and third requirements.

4 Fear

Aristotle takes fear, *phobos,* to be *active.* Here we might note that '*phobos*', and its verbal forms '*phobeo*', '*phobeomai*', still had in Aristotle's time as one of their central meanings the meaning they had in Homeric times: *being put to flight,* rather than the inner state that might lead to flight.[7]

The activity of fear is brought out in claims in the *Rhetoric* and the *Nicomachean Ethics.* In *Rhetoric* II.5, we read that "those who think that they have already suffered all possible ills and are coldly indifferent to the future, like those who are being beaten to death" will not be afraid of what is about to happen to them, for in order to fear, it is necessary "that there should remain some hope [*elpida*] of being saved from the cause of their distress. A sign of this is that fear makes men deliberate, whereas no one deliberates about things that are hopeless [*anelpiston*]" (1383a3 ff., tr. Freese). In *Nicomachean Ethics* III.6, we read that "Yet at sea also the brave man is fearless [*adeēs*], but not in the same way as the seamen; for he has given up hope [*apegnōkasi*] of safety while they are hopeful [*euelpides*] because of their experience" (1115a35 ff., tr. Ross).

[7] See Georg Autenrieth, *A Homeric Dictionary* (Norman: University of Oklahoma Press, 1958).

One might also, or instead, suggest that those people are all played out, lacking enough energy to muster up fear or even a mere wish for escape. (On wishing, see *NE* III.2, 1111b20.) But that there is this other, perhaps better, explanation is relevant for understanding Aristotle only because he does *not* present it – perhaps because he does not recognize such a lack of care and energy, or the associated spiritual maladies. It is important to note that what is not discussed is only the *total* or *near total* loss of care and energy. Both in the *Poetics*' treatment of catharsis and also in the typology of anger given in *Nicomachean Ethics* IV.5, sharp changes and reversals of emotional energy are discussed.

For a long time, the claim that fear requires hope – say, of escape – struck me as mistaken. To be sure, whether or not it is mistaken, to understand Aristotle we must see why he offered it and whether, by his own lights, he had good reasons for doing so. A further reason for investigating this claim is that I am now not so certain that it is even mistaken.

My reason for thinking it mistaken was that even if people *know* that something terrible is about to happen, they may be afraid. But how could they, then, have hope? One difficulty with my reason lies in saying what it is to have hope. I may sincerely believe or even know that there is no possibility of escape. But I may still be hopeful about escape. I may *hope against hope* for escape. (For our purposes, there is no need to distinguish between being hopeful and hoping for.) Even a person being beaten to death may hope for a last-minute reprieve. And clearly, this person can be afraid.

If this counts as having hope, we cannot require that the agent *believe* that the danger will be escaped. At most, escape must be seen as a possibility. But such *seeing it as possible* cannot be explained or even constrained by requirements of believed probability. People can be hopeful about an outcome which they believe strongly or even know to be monumentally less likely than its contrary – winning a national lottery, say. And people can lose hope about something they know is very likely to come about – that their child will get into a good college, say.

How, then, can we characterize the differences between the person with hope and the person without hope? I think that to do this we will have to abandon the clear, but inadequate, probabilistic account of the belieflike component of hope in favor of the following unclear, but more adequate, account: The difference between these two sorts of people is a *cast of mind*.

People who can be afraid see the world in terms of possibilities, in terms of things getting better. Thus they are hopeful. They see the world from the standpoint of an active person, rather than, say, a passive, or disinterested, or played-out spectator. They see the world in terms of what they can do –

including what they can do to make it better. Moreover, they take the possibility of effecting such change *seriously*. Taking the possibility of their effecting change seriously is what the active nature of fear comes to.

Is this requirement of hope and activity for fear plausible? I am not sure. But Virgil Aldrich convinced me that a very good case can be made for the claim that fear requires hope. Briefly put, hope is necessary to distinguish between someone who is *stupefied* by impending danger and someone who is *afraid* of that danger. Again briefly put, stupefied people, but not people who are afraid, have been frozen into immobility. Stupefied people see themselves simply as about to be subjected to what is to come. Similar considerations bear on the distinction we make between resignation and fear.

One worry about this claim is that we may think it is true but simply far too much of an understatement to say that people feel fear when they feel terror, whether stupefied or not. It might be like saying that rape is rude.[8]

Another worry is that the following may describe a case of fear. A person racked with periodic pain knows that it will recur. The person no longer even hopes – has any hope – that it will not. But still, the pain in general and the next bout of it is – I think we can allow – feared. But even without hoping that the pain will not recur the patient can hope that the next bout will be delayed or made a bit less severe by some medicine just administered by the doctor. And it is unclear whether, failing all such hopes, the emotion is fear, not resignation or stupefaction.

But even if considerations like these show that fear requires hope, they do not show that fear must be active. Indeed, they show the contrary. That person can hope that the pain will be less this time because of medicine just administered. There is no requirement at all that the hoped for lessening of the pain be attributable, or believed attributable, to an action of the patient. So, even if our fear does require hope, it does not require activity. But Aristotle required both hope and activity for *phobos,* or more exactly hope because of activity for *phobos.*

How can this difference between Aristotle and us be explained? Some obvious explanations are that I am mistaken in my interpretation of our views or Aristotle's, or that our views or his are mistaken, or that 'fear' as used by us poorly translates '*phobos*'. But I want to offer another explanation which strengthens my general claim that Aristotle assumes that his men have an active character.

My explanation is this: given certain psychologies, including certain

---

8 This is discussed in Chapter 2, section 4. Thanks are owed to Lynne McFall here.

values, it is all too natural for people who do not think that they can make a difference to think that there is, therefore, no hope for them. The psychologies would include such views as, "The world is largely indifferent to the fate of people" and "Other people are all too often indifferent to the fate of others." To this, conjoin such evaluative views as, "It is a person's – or a man's – role to take care of himself" or "A good man is one who can and does take care of himself." These inform the view that people are, or had better be, active. They can also form the basis of an outlook which has it that one's only or one's main hope is oneself.[9]

Here I want only to suggest that these views about the "friendliness" of the world and the requirements of self-sufficiency can be found in Aristotle.[10] Further, even we find it intelligible and common enough that people who have no faith in their own powers should feel bereft, alone, and hopeless.

My claim, then, is that Aristotle's treatment of fear shows that he takes his people to be active. But, it might be wondered whether – if I have made out this claim – I have not proved too much and made my claim self-refuting. The objection would be that Aristotle does see that those who are afraid are active *but only insofar as they are to count as being afraid*. Thus, the supposed metapsychological point about those who are afraid would be only a conceptual point about the use of 'fear'.

Were my claim based only on Aristotle's saying of those who are afraid that they are, or see themselves as, then and there active, this objection would be telling. But my claim is also based on Aristotle's holding that *the* reaction to danger to oneself is fear. Thus, he takes people *in general* – not simply those who do, or when they do, experience fear – to be active.

This, I suggest, is borne out by various of Aristotle's discussions of fear. So in *Nicomachean Ethics* III.7, courage is said to involve a mean in the continuum of reactions to certain sorts of dangers. (See also *Rhetoric* II.5, 1382b30 ff.) At one end of the continuum, there are those who rush fearlessly into battle, having too little fear, like the Celts; at the other end, there are cowards, who feel too much fear and run away. Nowhere do we find stupefaction, resignation, or inactivity in the face of danger.

---

9 Originally I had qualified this with 'at least if one is a man', thinking of the historical period Aristotle was concerned with. Lynne McFall noted that this is how it is for many women now, especially those who cannot count on a man – "their man" – not to abuse them, much less to take care of them.
10 See Arthur W. H. Adkins, *Merit and Responsibility* (Oxford: Oxford University Press, 1960), and "'Friendship' and 'Self-Sufficiency' in Homer and Aristotle," *Classical Quarterly,* n.s. 13 (1963) 30–45.

Here we might note that various spiritual maladies can explain lack of bravery and thus a sort of reaction to fear that is discussed by Aristotle. However, he does not account for it this way, but rather in terms of a lack of confidence or boldness, *tharsos* (*NE* III.7, 1116a1) and perhaps also in terms of softness and lack of endurance (*NE* VII.5, 1149a5 ff., and VII.7). Lack of confidence or boldness and softness and lack of endurance can also be explained in terms of various spiritual maladies. But this explanation, too, is not given.

It may be that Aristotle recognizes a spiritual malady that can explain cowardice and also what he offers as explanations of that. For at *Nicomachean Ethics* III.7, 1116a3, he says that a coward is *duselpis,* despairing (following Ross) or despondent (following Rackham). But being *duselpis* is not taken up and used as a direct explanation of cowardice or of its explanations. And, second, even the *duselpis* person is not said to be stupefied, resigned, or inactive in the face of danger. Instead, being *duselpis* leads, we may assume, to the feeling and action of cowards: excess fear and flight. So, even if the spiritual malady of despair or despondency is recognized, it plays no, or no important, role.

It is important in two ways for my claim that Aristotle does not offer explanations in terms of spiritual maladies. First, it bears out my general claim that he does not recognize spiritual maladies. Second, it bears out my specific claim that he sees only active responses to dangers and fear.

In conclusion, then, Aristotle holds that fear – the reaction to felt danger – is active. Further, as suggested earlier, care is necessary for fear: care for oneself in order to have fear for oneself, and care for others in order to have fear for others. Thus, Aristotle takes his people to have an active cast of mind and to care for and about themselves. They do not have those spiritual maladies centering on lack of self-care and lack of a sense of oneself as an agent, or those centering on a feeling of hopelessness, of being caught up in a world that offers no escape.[11]

5 Pity and self-pity

In the discussion of anger and fear, I was concerned to develop several aspects of the agent's *active cast of mind,* especially the agent's active and

---

11 For a related discussion of seeing oneself as an agent, and also taking oneself personally, see David Sachs, "Self-Respect and Respect for Others: Are They Independent?" in O. H. Green, ed., *Respect for Persons, Tulane Studies in Philosophy,* 31 (1982), 109–128, especially pp. 122–123, and also "How to Distinguish Self-Respect from Self-Esteem," *Philosophy and Public Affairs,* 10 (1981) 346–360.

caring involvement with the self and with matters concerning the self. In this section, I discuss self-pity. Self-pity is a nonactive way of taking oneself, which we know well, but which is not discussed in Aristotle.

In the *Rhetoric* Aristotle says, with some qualifications, that fear is self-regarding and pity, *eleos,* is other-regarding. This characterization of pity precludes self-pity. Further, the account of fear in *Nicomachean Ethics* III has only cowardly, brave, and Celt-like reactions to fear, again leaving no room for self-pity. (Also precluded are various other, detached modes of taking or not taking the danger.) The question for us is why does Aristotle allow only for other-regarding pity, while we allow for both such pity and self-pity.

In order to make the question clearer, it should be noted that '*eleos*' can mean pity, and also compassion or mercy. Both pitying a person on account of some feature and feeling compassion or mercy for a person on account of some feature involve focusing on the complex of that person and feature. As with various other emotions considered here, differential focusing is important. Compassion or mercy involves focusing on the bad feature, especially as it is seen and felt by the person – one feels *with* the person in the sense that to some extent one understands and feels the feature in the way the person does. One is saddened by the feature, so taken, and thus saddened for or about the person. When distinguished from compassion or mercy, pity involves focusing on the person and feeling sad about the person on account of the feature. Such pity may, thus, involve looking down on, even despising, the pitied.[12] This comes out in epithets constructed around 'pity': "I pity you, you pitiful, no good ———." No comparable epithets using 'compassion' or 'mercy' come readily to my mind.

Clearly, this understanding of pity does not answer to Aristotle's understanding of '*eleos*'. After all, he holds that we can feel *eleos* only for those felt close enough to us. But there are other ways of taking 'pity', which have it closer to compassion or mercy and which have the pitier feel far more at one with the pitied. This might suggest that we translate '*eleos*' by 'compassion' or 'mercy'. My reasons for not doing this are partly to avoid special overtones of 'compassion' or 'mercy', but mainly to allow for an easy comparison of pity and self-pity. For, even where the pity of self-pity involves degrading ways of looking at oneself, it need not involve looking down on oneself.

However, my argument does not depend on translating '*eleos*' as 'pity' rather than 'compassion' or 'mercy'. For I am concerned with two issues.

12 For these accounts, see Lawrence Blum, "Compassion," in Amélie O. Rorty, ed., *Explaining Emotions* (Berkeley: University of California Press, 1980).

The first is the absence of a self-regarding form of this emotion in Aristotle. And in his work I know of no discussion of self-regarding *eleos* – whether it be self-pity or self-regarding compassion or self-regarding mercy. The second is the distinction between what I will call pity and self-pity. This distinction can be made in terms of compassion or mercy – by taking self-pity as the self-regarding correlate of other-regarding compassion or other-regarding mercy.

Having made clear enough what is meant by '*eleos*' and the term I will use to translate it, 'pity', let us investigate how pity and self-pity bear on our concerns. To avoid issues concerning the role of time and desert in regard to pity and fear, let us suppose that tomorrow I am to have a cavity filled – a rather painful process for me. There are any number of emotional reactions I can have to this. One would be fear. Another would be self-pity. What are the salient differences for us between such fear and self-pity?

One natural place to look is at the object of the emotion. But both fear and self-pity here seem to focus on the same object – my having a tooth drilled. And both seem to have the same thoughts about it – it will be painful; and the same feelings about it – I look forward with pain toward it. If this is right, we must look elsewhere for a distinction between fear and pity.

It might be said, however, that different aspects of that complex are focused on: fear focuses on the pain, self-pity on the self. This is true enough, but we need an account of such differential focusing. As seen in regard to anger, it may be difficult to provide such an account.

To bring out what is salient for both the distinction between fear and self-pity and also for an account of such differential focusing, let us look at three descriptions of self-pity from David Milrod's "Self-Pity, Self-Comforting, and the Superego":[13]

[1] . . . cases of pervasive self-pity and self-comforting are characterized by withdrawal and isolation which severely interfere with object relations, often to the point of a major decathexis of object representations. (pp. 505–506)
[2] In self-pity, the individual treats the self as the suffering object and turns the comforting activity toward the self. (p. 509)
[3] The wound or injury, which is so important in the genesis of self-pity, will under ordinary conditions evoke quite a different response. The usual response would be an active move toward self-protection or a retaliatory attack of some kind. The absence of this expected response, in self-pity, suggests that the expression of aggression has been curbed. (pp. 515–516)

---

13 *Psychoanalytic Study of the Child*, 27 (1972) 505–528. This work also presents a useful bibliography on psychoanalytic studies of self-pity.

In [3] Milrod presents to us as the *usual* responses those responses found in Aristotle's discussions of fear and anger: self-protection and retaliation. But as the two earlier quotations point out, self-pitiers turn away from active involvement in the world and away from the danger, and turn toward themselves. Not acting on the world, self-pitiers act on themselves by comforting themselves.

To be sure, some self-pitiers do try to get back at their tormenters. Thus, they are active. However, my claim about self-pitiers not having an active cast of mind does not depend on their doing nothing in the external world. Rather it depends on their particular, inwardly directed forms of activity. Put another way, it shows that their activity is in some way really a form of passivity and that their passivity is in some way a form of activity.

It also shows complexities in the notions of activity and passivity and in their interrelations – complexities we must take account of to understand the previous sentence, and similar seeming paradoxes or seeming contradictions about, say, passive aggressiveness.[14] Such aggression is hardly passive in a metaphysical sense. Its passivity lies "only" in its being covert, hidden even from the aggressor. Its superficial manifestations are not aggressive nor are they typical expressions of aggression. They are disguised as something else, often something that is the very reverse of aggression and at times something that is, again superficially, mere absence.

We can apply these last claims and findings about self-pity to our understanding of Aristotle: the importance of understanding just which psychological sorts are and which are not discussed by him is shown again by this resentful self-pitier. For the resentment born of self-pity is importantly different from the resentment found in the angry indignation of Aristotle's man. And the resentful self-pitier's character has important connections with the possibility of weakness of will and of taking pleasure in action. But this sort of person was not discussed by Aristotle.

My goal so far has been to show that the sort of self-concern in regard to danger that self-pity involves is very different from the sort that fear or anger involves. Yet another way to highlight the particular sort of self-involvement of self-pity is to contrast it with other-regarding pity.

If I pity someone, there may be a strong presumption that I will try to

---

14 For a very useful discussion of these complexities, see David Rapaport, "Some Metapsychological Considerations concerning Activity and Passivity," published originally (in English) in *Archivos de Criminología, Neuropisquitaria Disciplinas Conexas* (Equador), 9 (1961) 391–449, and reprinted in *The Collected Papers of David Rapaport*, ed. Merton M. Gill (New York: Basic Books, 1967). My thanks are owed to Elizabeth Hegeman and to the psychiatrist Howard L. Berkowitz for discussion of what is passive in passive aggression.

help that person. But I can pity someone I cannot even comfort or otherwise help – for example, someone who is dead. Second, the presumption of help is only a presumption. For my emotion toward someone I can help to count as pity, I need not help that person. But I do not pity myself, unless I do comfort myself – perhaps in the ways suggested by Milrod. Just consider the important and obvious difference between people who, without self-pity, look back with sorrow on the way they were treated as children and people who feel self-pity on account of how they were treated as children.

Thus in its own way, by involving self-comforting, self-pity is active. But other-regarding pity need not be active at all, much less in ways similar to those of self-pity. That self-pity is active does not mean that I cannot have toward myself what I have toward another when I have inactive other-regarding pity toward that person. Rather, it means only that this inactive self-regard is not self-pity. It might be merely a registering with sorrow that I have been harmed.

These, then, are sketches of some of the important differences between self-pity and other-pity. Here we might note a point about us revealed by this discussion. Self-pity and other-pity, as we understand and experience them, differ in whether the endangered person is oneself or another. They also differ in many ways that flow from these differences of, as might be said, mere identity. But of course, there is nothing *mere* about the difference between self and other. This is shown by the fact that our concerns with self are of markedly different sorts than our concerns with others. It is also shown in myriads of psychological structures that take up the self or others or both.

We might even hold that the differences between self and other are so great, especially as they bear on other-regarding pity and self-pity, that it is a mistake to think that there is a common element – pity – in both of these. However, we need not take up this suggestion to see that other-pity and self-pity are importantly dissimilar. One way to see this is to note the different ways each is or is not unattractive or even repellent.

As characterized by Milrod, self-pity is clearly unattractive and repellent. I do not think this is due to its concerning the self. After all, self-directed compassion need not be unattractive or repellent. But this last is, really, I suggest, to say also that self-directed compassion – at least when not unattractive and not repellent – is not self-pity. Other-directed pity and even other-directed compassion can be unattractive or repellent, too: for example, by involving unattractive or repellent condescension.

But – and this helps make my main point – condescension is not the typical other-regarding correlate of what is centrally unattractive and repellent in self-pity. What I think is central to the disagreeableness of self-pity is in part that self-pity involves an abandonment of active concern for and with oneself. More significantly, the disagreeableness has to do with the nature of such abandonment, and in particular how it is expressed and enacted. It has to do with what self-pitiers do instead of engaging in activity. It is the way they comfort themselves and what they are like when they are engaged in such self-comforting.

In focusing on this last as what differentiates the pity of self-pity and that of other-pity, I am not denying that there can be very similar, very disagreeable, ways of engaging in other-pity. Here we could think of people who simply "comfort" others: who, say, instead of helping them, as they could, rock them in their arms and coo to them. But this is an atypical way other-pity is disagreeable. Similarly, even if one can treat oneself in ways close to condescension, this is not what is typically disagreeable about self-pity.

I do not think there should be much disagreement with my claim that the background concerns and character structures of those who engage in disagreeable other-pity are typically quite different from those of people who engage in self-pity. I mean both that these two sorts of people have different forms of concern and engagement with people quite generally, and also that the forms of engagement self-pitiers have toward themselves are different from those such other-pitiers have toward those others they pity in those ways.

This brings us back to an earlier concern: we need to understand such expression and enactment, along with such background structures, in order to understand what self-pity is, and what its particular combination of abandonment and self-comforting are. We need, that is, to go beyond a structural-cognitive account – a version of the content account – of abandonment and self-comforting. It is, clearly, not just simply not taking care of oneself in usual, effective ways, holding oneself and rocking back and forth. Here, as in so many other places discussed in this work, understanding the nature and value of these human phenomena requires recourse to affectivity and affective structures.

We can bring this out from the "other side." I may see you as another person, but take personally what concerns and happens to you. Thus, I might not pity you, but feel with you. Nonetheless, I need be under no illusion that I am you. It might be claimed that I, therefore, do not *really* see you as another person. But for this not to indicate madness, it must be understood as saying something like: I see and care for you the way normal people see and care for themselves. Correlatively, to engage in self-pity often involves *taking* oneself in a way normal people take others – as objects to be comforted – without, however, really believing that one is an other person. It, thus, involves a peculiar sort of self-distancing.

6 Concluding remarks

In this chapter, I have shown some of the ways Aristotle's ethical views are shaped by his views about the psychology and moral psychology of his people, and their emotions. This, in addition to the interest they have on their own, led me to discuss some implications of Aristotle's not seeing, ignoring, or quickly dismissing many important features of our psyches – in particular, many spiritual maladies we suffer.

In whatever ways we ultimately explain Aristotle's "omissions," we must acknowledge that the sorts of people he described in his ethical and psychological writings differ from us so far as both their emotions and their values and evaluations are concerned. Thus, if we wish to make use of his works in ethics and moral psychology, we must take great care. Many of his ethical and moral psychological descriptions and prescriptions are meant for those who have the psychology Aristotle took his people to have. Whether and to what extent we must modify or reject his ethics and moral psychology for our ethics and moral psychology are questions that are as difficult as they are important.

10

The complex evaluative world of Aristotle's angry man

The focus of this chapter is *orgē*, anger, especially as discussed in the *Rhetoric*. This chapter has several intertwined goals: to present a case study of many of the claims of the earlier chapters; to examine what Aristotle says or shows about emotions and their connections with value; and to do each by doing the other.

This chapter will also allow for further illustration of the claim that an understanding of emotions – even one emotion of one sort of person – requires the resources and techniques of philosophy, psychoanalysis, sociology, anthropology, and history, to name only some of the needed disciplines. They are needed to present an account of *orgē*; to show how it differs from our anger; and also to see whether these differences show only that 'anger' is not a perfect translation of '*orgē*', or whether they also show differences between Aristotle's men and us. (We say "men," not "people," because, as will be discussed, Aristotle's treatment of anger is restricted to men.)

The plan of this chapter is as follows. Section 1 makes some general comments about *orgē*, and 2 discusses ways *orgē* shows Aristotle's men to be narcissistic. Section 3 examines the nature of slights and flattery, and what they show about people's concern for recognition by others. Section 4 examines some ways the categories of the personal and impersonal are important for emotions and value. Sections 5 and 6 explore two additional interpersonal issues important for emotions and value: who gets angry on behalf of whom, and closeness and attachment. The general format of these sections will be to present some claims made by Aristotle, and then to discuss these claims and more general issues raised by them about emotions and values.

1   *Orgē* and value

Many of us do not think highly of anger or of people when they are angry, much less of angry people. We may thus differ from Aristotle who held that a good person, a *phronimos*, must be capable of getting angry. As he says in the *Nicomachean Ethics,* not to get angry, and simply "to endure being insulted and to put up with insults to one's friends is slavish" (IV.5, 1126a8, tr. Ross and Urmson). And also, it is praiseworthy and virtuous to be "angry at the right things and with the right people, and, further, as he ought, when he ought, and as long as he ought" (IV.5, 1125b32 ff.).

Just as he holds that it is possible for someone to be angry correctly, he also holds that it is possible – and in fact easier for most people – to be angry incorrectly, and thus for one's anger to show that one is not a wholly good person. And indeed, we think that much of what he says about anger in the *Rhetoric* has to do with how people can – and can, by rhetoric, be led to – go wrong about and with anger. In any case, we think that the *Rhetoric* account will show us a lot about anger that we – whether or not joined by Aristotle – think questionable, if not disreputable.

In the *Rhetoric* Aristotle writes, "Anger [*orgē*] may be defined as a desire accompanied by pain, for a conspicuous revenge for a conspicuous slight at the hands of men who have no call to slight oneself or one's friends" (II.2, 1378a31 ff., tr. Roberts). *Orgē* must be understood in evaluative, even moral, terms. To mention three points. First, this account of *orgē* concerns men, not women. We might account for this by noting that *orgē* involves what Aristotle sees as the concerns of men, not women. This focus on men, not women, shows that an understanding of *orgē* requires an understanding of gender differences, and thus the use of philosophy, psychology, psychoanalysis, anthropology, sociology, history, and literature.

The second point is that the slight giving rise to anger is said to be without call, undeserved. *Orgē* is thus, itself, a moral notion. Third, to be slighted is to be denied due importance, honor, and respect.[1] It is to be treated with contempt, spite, or insolence (*Rht* II.2, 1378b14). It is to be treated as bad or worthless: "slighting is the actively entertained opinion of something as obviously of no importance" (II.2, 1378b10 ff.). *Denied importance* is the key here: ". . . for it is the unimportant, for good or evil, that has no honor paid to it" (II.2, 1378b31).

Anger and slights, then, do not have to do with mere harm or deprivation of benefit, such as a fair loss to a just competitor, or a nonnegligent, unintended, accidental damaging of something one values by someone else, or an act of retaliation, or an act that is done because it is profitable (II.2, 1378a31). Any of these, when recognized as such, might well arouse

---

[1] For a study of honor and slights, and of other notions important for *orgē*, see Douglas L. Cairns, *Aidōs: The Psychology and Ethics of Honour and Shame in Ancient Greek Literature* (Oxford: Oxford University Press, 1993).

enmity, *echthra,* the topic of *Rhetoric* II.4. But if the nature of these enmity-arousing harms, including the intentions and rights of the person doing the harming, is recognized, they could not arouse anger, *orgē*. None of these, we should also note, need be a denial of importance.

We can put this in a way that helps us see the interrelations of those two points about the moral nature of anger: Aristotle's depiction of anger and those who get angry shows us men who are concerned with their importance, dignity, and with the honor and respect all or some others owe them. According to this depiction, precisely by striking at these men's sense of importance, their dignity, respect, and honor, an anger-arousing slight strikes at, and may well harm, their moral core. It is shaming.

These claims about importance, dignity, respect, honor, and shame are not just about how Aristotle's man feels. They also show and are about social relations. So, Aristotle writes, one can be slighted by one's equals and one's superiors: "Thus again a man looks for respect from those who he thinks owe him good treatment, and these are people he has treated well or is treating well, or means or meant to treat well, either himself, or through his friends, or through others at his request" (II.2, 1379a7 ff.). And also, "A man expects to be specially respected by his inferiors" (II.2, 1378b35). Inferiority here can be either in regard to the issue at hand, such as the oratorical ability of someone criticizing a person's speech, or it can be more general, such as one's birth or wealth (II.2, 1379a1 ff.). Inferiors must, however, have enough standing to be taken seriously. The undeserved contempt of young and uneducated children for one's public speaking, say, may thus not be able to arouse *orgē* in a good adult.

Importance, status, and standing must, thus, be investigated to show the social ordering – the sociology – of Aristotle's society, and also to understand *orgē*. Among the issues here are issues of standing: who is more important than whom, who owes what to whom, who can anger whom, who are those on whose account his men should be angry and "as honorable men [are] bound to champion – our parents, children, wives, or subjects" (II.2, 1379b28 ff.). These must be investigated to show the sociological and social circumstances of Aristotle's men. So too, we must investigate the combined historical and sociological question of whether there are special features of Athenian society that brought issues of standing to the fore – for example, whether changes from more traditional to more democratic forms of power made these relations, including their limits and requirements, more uncertain and more dangerous.[2]

---

2 Thanks are owed to the psychiatrist Ronald Filippi for raising this issue.

On our view, these investigations, especially the sociological and the psychological ones, differ mainly in emphasis, not kind. To mention only two points: first, whether something is a slight, uncalled for, and is felt as hurtful, depends heavily on social expectations and social relations. Second, as Bernard Williams said about some related emotions, "these are shared sentiments . . . and they serve to bind people together in a community of feeling."[3] Thus, even though in what follows we emphasize how the anger of Aristotle's men shows their character, we are also, sometimes explicitly and more often implicitly, interested in how it shows their society. Much of what we say about the one also bears on the other.

2   Narcissism and Aristotle's angry man

If one of Aristotle's men is not accorded the rank and respect he thinks due – in ways proper to him, to what he is doing, to the other person, and so on – he suffers. He experiences the lack of respect as a deep wound to himself, that is, to his self. To understand this wound, we must understand this self. One key to understanding these wounds of anger, and thus Aristotle's men, is to see the wounds as narcissistic wounds, to see these men as narcissistic, and their society and social arrangements as allowing, perhaps fostering, narcissism.

In saying this, we follow Freud and psychoanalysis generally, and understand narcissism as involving a deep lack, an emptiness, in the self, a profound feeling of unalterably not being good, of not being adequate, and certainly not being lovable.[4] We do not understand narcissism as involving excess self-love. In fact, we understand the activities and attitudes often taken as showing excessive self-love as really being attempts to hide this lack

---

[3] *Shame and Necessity* (Berkeley: University of California Press, 1993), p. 80.
[4] Narcissism is one of the main theoretical and therapeutic concerns of psychoanalysis, and any adequate bibliography on it would include a large proportion of all works in psychoanalysis. Among the classical works, we have found the following especially useful: "Mourning and Melancholia," in volume 14 of *The Standard Edition of the Complete Psychological Works of Sigmund Freud*, ed. James Strachey (London: Hogarth Press, 1986); Otto Kernberg, *Borderline Conditions and Pathological Narcissism* (New York: Jason Aronson, 1975); and Heinz Kohut, *The Analysis of Self* (New York: International Universities Press, 1971). Useful collections are found in Andrew P. Morrison, ed., *Essential Papers on Narcissism* (New York: New York University Press, 1986); and Joseph Sandler, Ethel Spector Person, and Peter Fonagy, eds., *Freud's "On Narcissism: An Introduction"* (New Haven: Yale University Press, 1991). Good bibliographies and discussions are found in Sheldon Bach, *Narcissistic States and the Therapeutic Process* (New York: Jason Aronson, 1985); and in Andrew P. Morrison, *Shame: The Underside of Narcissism* (Hillsdale, N.J.: Analytic Press, 1986). On narcissism in classical Greece, see Philip Slater, *The Glory of Hera* (Boston: Beacon Press, 1968).

from oneself and to fill it up. Narcissists are unable to sustain self-respect and self-regard. They need others to reassure them of their goodness, that they are the way they would like to be. They are like a sieve, always needing new reassurance of their goodness, because they cannot sustain this "belief" in themselves. Thus, quite naturally, narcissists find flattery flattering.

Unless others are reassuring them, narcissists give the appearance of being unable to believe, or unable to sustain the belief, that they are good. But narcissism is poorly characterized as a problem of belief. It is not the beliefs but narcissists, themselves, who are in trouble. Narcissists need support, not evidence. They need support so that they can hold the belief, not evidence that would justify or lead them to hold it. In this, they are like those who need encouragement and support – again, not evidence – to be able to espouse, or even just hold, unpopular views. Narcissists need help in being able to accept and hold onto the belief – to take it in, to accept evidence for it as evidence, to make and keep it a live and effective belief.

There is a further reason for philosophers not to see narcissism as a problem of belief – especially not a problem over the belief that one is good, honored, or respected. What narcissists want along these lines is not what philosophers discuss under these headings, but what, at best, are their developmentally primitive, undifferentiated precursors.

We want to continue this discussion of narcissism by making three caveats. First, even in psychoanalysis, narcissism is not fully and finally articulated. There is widespread agreement about its core, leading features. But much else, including its variations, is a matter of active research and controversy. Thus, it is not entirely clear what would follow about Aristotle's men if they and their anger are narcissistic. Further, even were narcissism fully articulated, what we will present is, at best, only some evidence, rather than proof, that Aristotle's men and their anger are narcissistic.

Second, narcissism comes in different varieties or strengths. It may be severe and pathological, serving as the central organizing structure of a personality. It may also be far less severe, serving to differentiate and characterize other central organizing structures – in, say, a narcissistic form of obsessiveness or of hysteria. So too, it can be far more healthy, perhaps entirely healthy.[5]

It must be emphasized that we have no interest in claiming what we see no evidence for and lots of evidence against: that Aristotle's angry men are

---

5 For a useful, brief discussion of these issues, see Kernberg, "Factors in the Treatment of Narcissistic Personalities," reprinted in Morrison, *Essential Papers on Narcissism*.

pathologically narcissistic. For example, there is no reason to think of them in all the ways Otto Kernberg describes pathological narcissists:

> Their emotional life is shallow. They experience little empathy for the feelings of others, they obtain very little enjoyment from life other than from the tributes they receive from others or from their own grandiose fantasies, and they feel restless and bored when external glitter wears off and no new sources feed their self-regard. (p. 213)

Nonetheless, in important ways, Aristotle's men do seem narcissistic in character – in ways to be urged.

Third, there is considerable difficulty in understanding other people and their emotions. If the people are from our culture, we can make use of shared meanings and background assumptions, given by and helping constitute similar social and psychological settings. The difficulties are multiplied manyfold if those we are trying to understand are from other cultures; more so if we are trying to understand them by means of techniques and categories developed in and for our culture; and still more so if those techniques and categories are not fully defined. There is the real danger that we will simply misunderstand these people or be led to think of them as far too much or far too little, like us – because the ways we think about them are designed to work for us.

So, for example, it might be thought that instead of seeing Aristotle's men as narcissistic, we should see them as living in a society constituted by various structures – structures that, if "lived out" by us, would show *us* narcissistic, but which, when lived out by Aristotle's men, do not show *them* narcissistic. So for example, their being slighted might not be seen as engendering *feelings* of narcissistic wounds, feelings of being treated as an inferior. Rather, their being slighted actually shows them inferior or shows that they are treated as inferior – inferior, that is, by the standards of their society, as these standards are constituted by and help constitute their society. Here we should remember Gabriele Taylor's claim that "if a man [of honour in a shame culture] has lost his reputation then he has lost his value in the eyes of all the members of the group, and this includes himself. . . . Self-respect and public respect stand and fall together."[6]

This objection of anachronism would be easily replied to if it holds only that we have unjustifiably assumed that Aristotle's men and our present-day

---

6 *Pride, Shame, and Guilt: Emotions of Self-Assessment* (Oxford: Oxford University Press, 1985), p. 55. Thanks are owed to Joel Garver for arguing that our use of narcissism is anachronistic in exactly this way – a way that treats the self ahistorically. He urges, instead, Michel Foucault's historicized account, especially as found in *The Use of Pleasure* (New York: Vintage Press, 1985).

narcissists have the *same feelings* – where 'same feelings' is understood as 'same *mere* feelings' in the sense of the same tingles and pangs, or where 'same feelings' has to do only with how the feelings feel to and *in* the person in question. This latter has feelings as, if not private, then at least almost wholly interior to the person. The easy reply to that objection, taken these ways, is found in the various arguments given against taking feelings as either panglike or as lacking significant interpersonal and social features.

But this objection can be taken as making a far more serious claim. It is that the most we have shown is that feelings are *seriously interrelated* with interpersonal, social, political, and other structures. The objection might point to the fact that almost all remains to be said about these serious interrelations. But the main criticism raised by this objection is that we have yet to give any reason to believe, one way or the other, whether people living in different societies can have the same feelings. In particular, we have not given any reason to believe, one way or the other, whether feelings with a given structure – as a structure would be described and offered by psychoanalysis, say – are really the same feelings irrespective of the societies of the people who have those structured feelings. So, for example, we have given no reason to believe that it does or does not matter whether those feelings are or are not adequate representations of value as found in the society in question.

This goes beyond saying that more than moderate narcissism would be called a pathology for us, but perhaps not for Aristotle's men. It also says that this difference shows up in the very nature of these feelings, provided that they are properly described: even if from various perspectives it looks as if our narcissists and Aristotle's men have the same structure of feelings, they do not (again, as a structure is described and understood by psychoanalysis). If they seem to have the same feelings and the same structure, that is simply an artifact of an inadequate theory. The inadequate theory here might be psychoanalysis, or the theory that would apply the very same psychoanalysis to both us and Aristotle's men.

This issue is important. We might finally conclude that any adequately fine-grained and sensitive psychoanalytic account will show that Aristotle's men and our narcissists cannot have the same structure of feelings – perhaps because such structures of feeling must be understood in terms of social structures that make Aristotle's men's structure of feelings socially appropriate and encouraged, whereas our narcissists live with other and less friendly social structures. We might, on the other hand, conclude that such "external" facts do not show up in structures of feeling in general, or those of narcissism in particular: that even if Aristotle's men's emotional structure is favored by their society, and even if that structure accurately reflects and reproduces the values of their society, it can still be a structure of narcissism, and indeed the very same structure of the very same narcissism as had by our narcissists. The only difference – as it might be put, somewhat tongue in cheek – is that our narcissists suffer that structure, whereas Aristotle's men enjoy it.

But since our concerns in this work are mainly with people like us, we will not pursue these questions about the interrelations of philosophy, psychoanalysis, psychology, history, sociology, and anthropology.[7] We will simply acknowledge the possibility that what we will show in this chapter is not what Aristotle's angry men are like, but what we would be like if (though still living here and now) we were like them. We do not think of this as much of a concession or retreat. For we would take our arguments to have been quite successful if they show only what we would be like or what we are like, whether or not they are mistaken about Aristotle's men. They would show us a lot about ourselves. And they would also show us a lot about how to read or not read Aristotle, and how to apply or not apply to ourselves what he says about his men.

This said, let us consider some reasons for thinking that Aristotle's angry men are narcissistic. These will include seeing how they are caught up in uncertainty, comparison, ranking and how they are vulnerable to and dependent on others to establish and confirm their status and thus, as they feel things, their value. We start with Aristotle's observation that in these areas where people are uncertain about, perhaps even doubt, their quality, slights are wounding, or especially wounding:

We feel particularly angry on this account [contempt] if we suspect that we are in fact, or that people think we are, lacking completely or to any effective extent in the qualities in question. For when we are convinced that we excel in the qualities for which we are jeered at, we can ignore the jeering. (II.2, 1379a36 ff.)

Now, it is hardly noteworthy that these people are angered by being jeered at. Indeed, it would be noteworthy – suggesting something special about their character, such as great humility or contemptuous disregard of those others – if they did not mind that. What we find noteworthy about

---

7 These issues are discussed by many authors, including Arthur Kleinman, *Patients and Healers in the Context of Culture: An Exploration of the Borderland between Anthropology, Medicine, and Psychiatry* (Berkeley: University of California Press, 1980); Alan Roland, *In Search of Self in India and Japan: Toward a Cross-Cultural Psychology* (Princeton: Princeton University Press, 1988); and Richard A. Shweder, *Thinking through Cultures: Expeditions in Cultural Psychology* (Cambridge, Mass.: Harvard University Press, 1991).

these people is that being jeered at arouses more anger, is more painful, when they think that the criticism it contains is justified.

One way to take this passage is as laying out the way *orgē* is aroused by shame or by something very similar to shame. So understood, the claim is that the pain aroused by being jeered at is, potentially, composed of two elements, each of which on its own, as well as in various combinations, can help constitute a form of shame. The first element is "simply" that of being jeered at by others – certain specific others or just anyone of some moment. The second is the pain of one's realization that one really has the defect that is jeered at. The first readily lends itself to a more other-directed sort of shame – that one looks bad in the eyes of others. The second readily lends itself to a more inner-directed sort of shame – that one fails to measure up to one's own standards.[8]

But, in addition, we might think that there is something excessive or not quite right here. Aristotle's angry men seem pained by seeing themselves as they are and they seem to require others to help them, or at least not hinder them, in *not* looking at and *not* seeing themselves as they are. Further, and as something of an explanation of what was just said, for these people to note or be reminded of a defect is especially painful. It is remarkably shaming.

Other sorts of people – including, we think, Aristotle's best people, those who are *phronimos* – may well not be so angered by jeers that correctly identify their deficiencies. They may, instead, look at themselves with candor and honesty; and they may accept criticism, especially justified criticism, without anger.[9] In contrast with the angry people depicted in the *Rhetoric,* those who are *phronimos* are self-sufficient and self-assured – and assured by themselves and their own judgment – or at least more so than these angry people as we have depicted them. We will return to this.

Let us now turn to insolence, one of the grounds of anger. People are insolent, Aristotle says, because of the pleasure they take in thinking themselves better than others (II.2, 1378b27). Being, as they think, better than others helps constitute or ground their feeling themselves good. More substantially, it helps constitute their goodness as they feel this. They are pleased not just by what may be revealed by their being better than others. They are pleased also that they are better than others.

Many people are like this. Some think all people are. We disagree. However, those who are like this can present us with interesting, even

---

[8] We are indebted here to Bernard Williams's discussion in *Shame and Necessity,* ch. 5, "Shame and Autonomy," especially pp. 95–98.
[9] Thanks are owed to José Benardete for discussion here.

though nonuniversal, connections between value and forms of thought and feeling. Narcissism involves powerful psychic mechanisms that make it completely natural to move from "I am more important than others" to "I am important" and from "I am not more important than others" to "I am not important," and perhaps more generally from "I am better than others" to "I am good" and from "I am not better than others" to "I am not good." To spell this out: narcissism involves its being natural to treat comparatively what we will call self-referential values, roughly those values agents see and feel as bearing on themselves.[10]

But as natural as it is for many people to treat values this way, there is no conceptual need, nor any general psychological need, to do so. It is both conceptually and humanly possible to treat some values, even some self-referential values, noncomparatively. Grammar reflects this in its distinction between *relative* and *absolute* values, especially as these are found in grammatical comparatives and superlatives. *Relatively:* there can be only one *wisest* person, who must be wiser than all others. *Absolutely:* many can be among the *wisest of* people, some of whom may be less wise than others. Similarly, as well as having a *best* friend, you can be the *best of* friends with several people, some of whom are less good friends of yours than others; so too you can be a *most excellent* friend without being the most excellent friend.

How good or bad you are and feel yourself to be *can* be independent of how good or bad others are. You may be better than others, but all of you, including the best, can be bad. You may be worse than others, but all of you, even the worst, can be good. And that someone is better than you need not take value away from you; nor need it show a standard you fail to meet.

We are not suggesting that it is always narcissistic to treat value, or simply self-referring value, comparatively. In some cases, if one person achieves a value, acquires a good, others will not: if I win a race or that person's hand, you will not. Some standards are set by how well or poorly certain exemplars do, and some standards are inherently competitive. Perhaps whether you are a good runner depends on how you would do in a race with good runners. And quite generally, competition and enjoyment of competition need not be narcissistic. It can express a fullness of being, and a desire to

---

10 For a discussion of how comparative and noncomparative evaluations, especially of the self, are important in Rousseau's *The Social Contract, Considerations on the Government in Poland,* and *Letter to D'Alembert,* see Charles Taylor, "The Politics of Recognition," especially section 3, in his *Multiculturalism and "The Politics of Recognition"* (Princeton: Princeton University Press, 1992), reprinted in David Theo Goldberg, ed., *Multiculturalism* (Oxford: Blackwell, 1994).

glory in that, to play freely and openly – rather than a lack in one's being. (In saying this, we also want to call attention to the remarkable, but little-discussed, fact that philosophers in our tradition have not had much good to say about competition, if they have had anything at all to say about it.)

Further, in their various forms, utilitarianism and game theory encourage a sort of comparative evaluation, rather than absolute evaluation, whether or not the value is self-referring. They do this by holding, in their different ways, that to choose what is lesser over what is better is to act immorally or irrationally. Thus, they require comparative, rather than absolute, evaluation in regard to the right, even if not in regard to the good – that is, in regard to which good to pursue, even if not in regard to what is good.[11]

So, our claim is not that one need be narcissistic to treat values comparatively. Nor need narcissists treat even all self-referring values comparatively. They can think a meal they are having is good, and can enjoy it fully, even if they also think that others are having better meals.

We could say that it is constitutive of narcissists to treat those values comparatively which strike at the self. However, this rules out few, if any, values. For the absence of most any value can strike at a narcissist's self in some circumstances. This could be taken as a problem for our characterization. Or it could be taken as showing the very tight connections among a person's values, how that person treats those values, and that person's sense of self. This, we think it clear, is Aristotle's general position. And, inspired by him, we might offer the following as a characterization of a narcissistic treatment of value: it is to treat the wrong values as self-referring and comparative, to treat values this way too often, at the wrong time, in the wrong circumstances, and so on.

A related way to put this is to acknowledge that *importance*, which is so central to *orgē*, is easily and naturally seen as comparative, as involving rankings of importance, of who is more important than whom. At the least, so many of our practices, institutions, and relationships that pay attention to importance are concerned with comparative importance. It is possible to see everyone as having, not just importance, but equal impor-

---

11 Arguments from within traditional moral theory against such comparative evaluations and in favor of absolute evaluations are given in Stocker, "The Schizophrenia of Modern Ethical Theories," *Journal of Philosophy*, 73 (1976) 453–466; *Plural and Conflicting Values* (Oxford: Oxford University Press, 1990), especially under 'comparative value'; and "Abstract and Concrete Value: Plurality, Conflict, and Maximization," in Ruth Chang, ed., *Incommensurability, Comparability, and Practical Reasoning* (Cambridge, Mass.: Harvard University Press, 1997).

tance, or to see everyone as just having importance where there is no concern with how much importance. But this often requires a special effort or way of thinking – for example, seeing us all as God's children, or as citizens, or as a member of the kingdom of ends, or as just one person among others. If importance is so easily and naturally involved in ranking and a concern to rank, we can see why importance is such a central evaluative notion for narcissists: why the concern that one be more important, not just important, is so central to narcissism.

Aristotle's insolent men – joined by many of us – are also interesting for the ways such comparative value gets enacted in comparative advantage and treatment. They mistreat those they think inferior, if only by not showing them due respect, or by lording over them their felt superiority. They act as if being better than others is to have power over them and also to be entitled to treat them poorly.

Various psychic mechanisms can effect such a union. For our purposes, one of the most important is narcissism, and its involving a move from feeling good about oneself to no longer feeling a need for others, and to its thus being all right to treat these others as one wishes. To this, there can be the added fillip that it was painful, even humiliating, that earlier one had to rely on them to feel oneself good; and now one can get recompense for that. This is especially important for Aristotle's men. Being self-sufficient is an important part of their understanding of what it is to be a good man (see, for example, *NE* I.7). Thus, being vulnerable to others and dependent on them must surely be a source of considerable tension – and thus an important part of the psychic mechanism connecting felt superiority and insolent treatment.

Another well-known mechanism – which may, itself, be connected with narcissism – is that of "manic entitlement." Here we could think of graduation-day antics, riotous celebrations over one's team winning the championship; or of the "innocent" depredations of Nietzsche's joyful blond beasts. So too, we could think of the mania that can replace, or alternate with, depression. For this last, and also for some general connections between mania and manic entitlement, we should consider Sigmund Freud's suggestive claim in the final paragraph of "Mourning and Melancholia" that "The accumulation of cathexis which is first bound and then, after the work of melancholia is finished, becomes free and makes mania possible must be linked with regression of the libido to narcissism" (p. 258). So too, we should consider his claim about mania in "Group Psychology and the Analysis of the Ego": "the ego and the ego ideal [having been] fused together, so that the person, in a mood of triumph and self-satisfaction, disturbed by no self-criticism, can enjoy the abolition of his inhibitions, his feelings of consideration for others, and his self-reproaches."[12]

Those caught up in such joyful mania can feel good, powerful, and full of themselves. They also, or therefore, can feel free and indeed freed from all restraints, and entitled to do whatever they want. They and their interests become their whole world – other people and their interests do not count, and may not even be noticed. This helps explain some of the harm wrought by those caught up in mania. To this we can add grievances and hatreds, many based on imagined or real slights, that can now be settled. Once again, feeling oneself better than others can lead to feeling able and entitled to get even.

It may well be difficult to see how these connections are made. But it is also difficult to understand the deep connections between power and value throughout our moral, political, and theological thought. We do, however, think it noteworthy that in various early childhood ways of being, there are deep, seemingly natural, connections between felt power and freedom to do what one wants. One conclusion we might, thus, reach is that these connections between power and value seem basic and primitive both developmentally and morally. With this, we end our discussion of mania.

The psyche of Aristotle's angry man is, further, constituted by a desire, rising to the level of a demand, that he be a center, if not the center, of attention, concern, and understanding – much as, as psychoanalytic students of infants tell us, the very young and narcissistic infant "requires" being a, if not the, center of a parent's attention, concern, and understanding. So, friends are required to pay very great attention to friends: "Again, we feel angry with friends . . . if they do not perceive our needs . . . for this want of perception shows that they are slighting us – we do not fail to perceive the needs of those for whom we care" (*Rht* II.2, 1379b13 ff.).

Once again, this suggests that there must be considerable tension between the demands for self-sufficiency and vulnerability to and dependence on others – in this case, friends. Thus, there is serious and real tension, not just conceptual tension, in Aristotle's understanding of a good life, a life of *eudaimonia*. For it must be at once a self-sufficient life and also a life with friends.[13]

---

12 Volume 18 of Strachey, *The Standard Edition of the Complete Psychological Works of Sigmund Freud*, p. 132. Morrison's *Shame: The Underside of Narcissism,* from which we drew this quotation, p. 27, has a good discussion of this.
13 See, for example, *NE* I.7, 1097b10. On the general issue of friendship and self-sufficiency, see Arthur W. H. Adkins, "'Friendship' and 'Self-Sufficiency' in Homer and Aristotle," *Classical Quarterly,* n.s., 13 (1963) 30–45.

Consider the clash generated from the following claims about anger:[14] anger involves "a desire . . . for a conspicuous revenge"; it "must always be attended by a certain pleasure – which arises from the expectation of revenge" (II.2, 1378b2 ff.); it "is also attended by a certain pleasure because the thoughts dwell upon the act of vengeance, and the images then called up cause pleasure" (II.2, 1378b8 ff.); and, "we feel angry with friends . . . if they do not perceive our needs." Thus, unless our friends are attentive to our needs, we will desire a conspicuous and pleasing revenge against them. Here we should compare what Kernberg says of pathological narcissists, "When abandoned or disappointed by other people they may show what on the surface looks like depression, but which on further examination emerges as anger and resentment, loaded with revengeful wishes, rather than real sadness for the loss of a person whom they appreciated."[15]

We might well wonder how Aristotle – and, insofar as he is an accurate reporter, how Greek society – could allow for such unfriendly treatment of friends by friends, while also holding friendship in such high regard, indeed thinking it necessary for a good life. We can now suggest that one reason why friendship is so important and so valued is also a reason why failures of friendship are so serious, so painful, calling for a conspicuous and pleasing revenge. A man depends on his friends to be able to see and feel himself as good. He depends on them to meet his needs to see and feel himself good, especially the need that he not feel himself dependent on them. If his friends fail to meet his needs, they strike a serious and deep blow: they show he is not self-sufficient and thus not good. They also show, or at least suggest, that he is too weak and unimportant to command respect and respectful, attentive consideration. Put somewhat too strongly – to express the deep fear this involves – he is not simply let down or abandoned by friends who fail to meet his needs, he is diminished and threatened, and his whole being and well-being are called into question.

Thus, only if the friends of one of Aristotle's men perceive his needs and act to satisfy them before he has to ask them for help will he be able to avoid suffering from his needs not being met. For these needs include his need not to have to ask for help to satisfy other needs, not just those other needs. So, whether his friends meet his needs or he suffers from unmet needs, a clear-sighted understanding of friendship will show him that friendship is dangerous and, indeed, is something of a setup for disappointment and

---

14 Thanks are owed to Barbara Stock for calling attention to this clash.
15 "Factors in the Treatment of Narcissistic Personalities," as reprinted in Morrison, *Essential Papers on Narcissism*, p. 213.

disillusionment. It calls, or runs the risk of calling, self-sufficiency into question.

Friends and friendships do this while being, at the very same time, necessary for the mistaken belief – the illusion – that one is self-sufficient. Friendship, then, is both necessary and highly problematic for such belief. Attentive friends, by their friendly attention, are needed to preserve the illusion of self-sufficiency. They do this in much the same way that high status does – by ensuring that needs will be attended to very quickly, if not anticipated and met before they even call for attention. By providing a highly attentive and unobtrusive "support service," both friendship and high status thus help sustain narcissistic illusions of self-sufficiency. They thus also give us reason to think that an Aristotelian good life, a life of *eudaimonia,* is available only to the very few.

The relations of friendship revealed by *orgē* are, thus, not all friendly relations. Nor perhaps are they the sorts of relations we have with our friends. But they are hardly foreign to us. We need only consider typical reactions we have to losing someone we love to a rival or by betrayal, especially as these contrast with typical reactions to losing someone we love through illness and death. As we know through bitter or sad experience – and by studying Sigmund Freud's profound "Mourning and Melancholia" – loss of a love to a rival or by betrayal, or even the fear of such a loss, can result in melancholia, depression, as well as rage and desires for revenge. It can easily and naturally involve having and dwelling on pleasing fantasies of revenge, not to say doing pleasing acts of revenge. And both melancholia and such rage can often be explained by narcissism and the narcissistic wound of such a feared or actual loss. This is to say little more than that Hell hath no greater fury than a lover scorned. As with love, so with loyalty and trust. They, too, can easily turn into hate in those who feel or fear they have been or will be abandoned or betrayed by political or religious movements. In these ways, then, we are like Aristotle's men and our friendships and loves are like theirs.

Let us continue with anger, focusing on how it involves pain. Aristotle recognizes that different people are angered, slighted, by different things.

Thus a sick man is angered by disregard of his illness, a poor man by disregard of his poverty, a man waging war by disregard of the war he is waging, a lover by disregard of his love, and so on in other cases too. Each man is predisposed, by the emotion now controlling him, to his own particular anger. (II.2, 1379a19 ff.)

What angers us can differ, according to what causes us pain: the pain is the frame of mind in which a person, not yet angry, is most disposed to become angry (II.2, 1379a10 ff.). This is to say that when one of Aristotle's men is hurting, he is more likely to become angry than he would be if he were not already hurting. Perhaps when he is hurting, he is more likely to notice a slight and take it as a slight, or take it as more of a slight than it is. Or perhaps, his hurting makes him touchy enough so that he mistakes what are not slights for slights. So, he might take others' concern with their own projects as indicating, if not motivated by, a lack of concern for him; or as indicating, if not motivated by, an "actively entertained opinion" of him "as obviously of no importance." His anger embodies and enacts the thought – whether or not he explicitly thinks it – "I am hurting and if those other people did not have an 'actively entertained opinion of' me 'as obviously of no importance' they would notice this, and, having noticed it, would attend to me and my needs."

This might be seen as expressing, once again, these men's excessive expectations or demands for attention, especially from their friends. It might also be seen as expressing their expectation or demand that their friends "see into them," know what they want and need, even, or especially, without being told this. As such, it comes at least close to expressing an expectation or even a demand for a mystical union of care and understanding. The narcissism of these expectations and demands is obvious.

Perhaps this is right. But it should not be passed off as unusual, or merely as a pathology, especially not just a pathology peculiar to Aristotle's angry men. Not wanting to be understood would be unusual and pathological. To see this, let us start with a concern correlative to wanting to be understood, wanting to understand. Where we do not understand, we can feel lost, bewildered, excluded, and even despairing and outraged. Here we might consider all that is meant when a philosopher says, "I don't understand your claim" (discussed in Chapter 5, section 5). In particular, we should examine why this is a way – for many, the favored way – of announcing a disagreement and launching an attack, a demand for justification. So too, we should examine why disagreements, when understood as a lack of shared understandings, are so unsettling. After all, they could instead be seen as a way to avoid stultifying sameness, and a way of showing a wonderfully enticing plurality of ways to live and to view and understand the world.[16]

It is possible to want to understand without wanting to be understood. And in a limited compass, there is nothing unusual about this. There is, after all, the sometimes acceptable pleasure in making ironical comments that only you understand. But when the limited compass is exceeded, matters

---

16 Thanks are owed to Lleni Pach for this observation.

change. The solitariness, the solipsism or assumed self-sufficiency, of a person who quite generally wanted to understand but not be understood, would be remarkable. Here we could think of someone who thought that living as a spy was the way to live: not just here and now to achieve certain, limited purposes, but quite generally. Or, we could consider someone who thought that using Gyges' ring at all times was the way to live. Perhaps even more remarkable and disturbing would be a person who neither wanted to understand nor wanted to be understood.

So, the question is not just why Aristotle's angry men expect and demand to be understood. It is also why so many people, including many philosophers, care so very much to understand and also to have their understandings accepted as the correct understandings; and why so many people, including many philosophers, care so very much to be understood.

Some particular points can be made about why we want to be understood. Let us start by noting what children may do when thwarted and stymied by an everyday travail of growing up, such as being ignored or insulted by the popular children in their class. With despair and rage, totally beyond the reach of being comforted, they scream, "You don't understand me" or "If you understood me, you would help me."

Our point here is not about the appropriateness of their rage and despair. It has to do with the complete appropriateness of expressing the rage and despair in terms of not being understood. To help illuminate the demand to be understood and the considerable pain in feeling misunderstood, we want to ask why the children's pain leads to their feeling misunderstood, or at least not understood. The question for us is why their pain does this: what is the route between their feeling pain and their feeling not understood? We cannot answer this, but we can make some suggestions that may also help us understand the need to be understood.

Perhaps the pain raises the question of how others stand to them, much as suggested by Aristotle: if I really were joined in a common world with those others, they would take care of me; thus, if they are not taking care of me, then either we are not in such a world or they do not care for me. Or perhaps not being cared for feels just like not being understood. And indeed it may be this in one's memories of one's life as an infant, where one was both helpless and not understood, and one because of the other. As a third possibility, which can stand on its own and can also mediate these two possibilities, it may be that those in pain think that the others have a responsibility to understand them because they have a responsibility to take care of them, especially if they are in pain and need care. The thought here might be put: were you really my friend, my parent, someone who loves me, you would have paid sufficient attention to me to notice my pain, and having noticed it you would have taken care of me.

The connection between pain and understanding might also be seen as expressing a deep conceptual feature of human life: showing what it is to live in a caring or loving way, or even in simply an accepting way, with others; and showing also, why we want such a life. We have in mind claims that we are social beings, and that our society is made possible by understanding, not just habit and reflex. We are beings who, on our own and with others, try to understand – not so much anything in particular but rather anything and everything. We want both to join in shared meanings and impose our own meanings. These lead inevitably and naturally, despite the great unclarity of the route, to the thoughts that if you do not understand me, we cannot live together or share a social life, and that if I am sufficiently misunderstood by enough people, I cannot live a human life and cannot even be a human being.

Many of these reasons are reasons for wanting to understand. They also tell strongly against the philosophical temptation of solipsism.

Let us now turn to how Aristotle's angry men react to slights. We should first note that the slight's having caused pain is not sufficient for anger: to be angry at a time requires pain at that time. Aristotle does not say that anger is just caused by pain, but rather that "Anger may be defined as a desire accompanied by pain." He also says that "anger can be cured by time" (*Rht* II.4, 1382a6–7). What is cured is, we might say, the accompaniment of pain, not pain's just having certain effects. Put another way, time can erase the effects of pain: not by changing history and erasing the fact that pain had those effects, but by stopping pain from continuing to have those effects and stopping what was painful from continuing to be painful.

Aristotle's men do not just suffer such pain. They want and try to get their own back, to reestablish their position: with themselves, with the person who insulted them, and with "their public." They do this by hurting those who slighted them and making them suffer pain, not just suffer harm, not even the "ultimate" harm of death (II.4, 1382a8 ff.).

We could see this last form of getting back at the person as indicating that the reestablished position is to be known and felt, and thus public. And we could see it as indicating a childish desire of angry men to repay in kind the pain they suffered.

For the latter, we should remember the opening words of the *Nicomachean Ethics*: "every act and pursuit is thought to aim at some good."

The good aimed at in anger is the suffering of the other. This raises the question of what must a person be like to have another's suffering as a good. Narcissism gives us one powerful answer: the narcissistic psyche is fragile and primitive, narcissism is not a very successful defense of such a psyche, narcissistic rages are powerful and primitive, and such rages are occasioned by narcissistic wounds.

We should also remember that anger is occasioned by the pain of slights. One is not slighted by mere harm or deprivation of benefit, as by an act that is seen and felt as a fair loss to a just competitor, or a nonnegligent, unintended, accidental damaging of something one values by someone else, or an act of retaliation, or an act that is done because it is profitable. Rather, a slight involves contempt, spite, or insolence, which all involve a disregard for the pain of the slighted person, and often pleasure in such pain. Thus, anger and its cause both involve pain – of the angered person. And anger always, and its cause sometimes, involve pleasure in anticipated, if not intended, pain – now of the other person.

Aristotle's men do not suffer the pain of slights in a self-pitying way. They do not turn in on themselves or toward some third party for solace and comfort. That is a typical reaction of those who take slights with shame, not anger. Here, of course, we are talking of the shame that is more allied with self-pity than the shame that arouses and may help constitute *orgē*. As this, and much else discussed here, shows, there are close connections and large overlaps between shame and guilt, especially if guilt is understood as correlative with anger.[17]

Those caught up in the shame of self-pity take the discrepancy between how they evaluate themselves and the lower way they are treated by another as showing they are defective, in the wrong, perhaps even deserving the slight. Aristotle's men, on the contrary, get angry at such a discrepancy between how they evaluate themselves and the lower way those who slight them seem to evaluate them. His men get angry at such a discrepancy and take themselves to be wronged, the slight undeserved, and the slighting other to be wrong and to be attacked.

We have here, then, differences in the direction and object of blame: Aristotle's angry men blame their tormentors, hold them responsible, and seek to punish them. But other sorts of people who are more given to shame, blame themselves, hold themselves responsible, and punish themselves, or accept their suffering as deserved punishment.

---

17 See Williams, *Shame and Necessity*, ch. 5, "Shame and Autonomy."

These differences can be illustrated and illuminated by views of three psychoanalysts, Helen Block Lewis, Melanie Klein, and Harry Stack Sullivan. Lewis writes,

Shame is the vicarious experience of the significant other's scorn. A "righting tendency" often evoked by shame is the "turning of the tables." Evoked hostility presses toward triumph or humiliation of the "other," i.e., to the vicarious experience of the other's shame.[18]

This hostile reaction might seem to be very similar to what happens in *orgē*. To some extent it is, and this helps answer the earlier question of why Aristotle's angry men want to retaliate in open and public ways. But to some extent, shame and *orgē* differ, in two important, related ways – ways that bear out our claim about the difference between Aristotle's men and people given to shame. In many cases, the *other* that Lewis is talking about is, in her terms, the superego, and more particularly the ego ideal or imago of the person who feels shame. And when the *other* really is another person, Lewis says, "the retaliatory impulses . . . were quickly short-circuited by guilt, back upon the self" (p. 54).

Following Melanie Klein, differences between *orgē* and shame are shown in the differences between the schizoid/paranoid stance of blaming others for one's pain and suffering and the depressive stance of blaming oneself for this.[19] These differences between *orgē* and shame can also be seen as showing the malleability and indeterminacy suggested by Harry Stack Sullivan when he held

that transfer of blame, or attribution of causality, could rescue the self from having to own painful or shameful attributes. Blame could be transferred either (1) away from the self, onto fate and impersonal forces, or (2) onto a personified Other in a paranoid way, or (3) onto the self – as when it is easier for people to blame themselves for illness or misfortune than it is for them to face an anxiety-provoking sense of helplessness.[20]

These different stances are of signal importance for many issues about emotions, moral psychology, ethical and political theory, and various practical issues. Some brief comments should be enough to show this.

First, *emotions:* as we have seen, issues of blame and attributions of responsibility are central to many emotions. In this regard, these stances may show us both the nature and also the location of some differences between

18 *Shame and Guilt in Neurosis* (New York: International Universities Press, 1971), p. 42.
19 See *Love, Guilt and Reparation, and Other Works, 1921–1945* (New York: Delta Books, 1977), and *Envy and Gratitude and Other Works, 1946–1963* (New York: Delta Books, 1977).
20 The quotation is from Elizabeth Hegeman, "World View As Cultural Parataxis," *Contemporary Psychoanalysis*, 30 (1994) 424–441, 426. Sullivan discusses this in *Personal Psychopathology: Early Formulations* (New York: Norton, 1965), pp. 66–71.

shame and guilt. For one of the more striking differences between guilt and shame is how guilt, unlike shame, involves blame and attributions of responsibility. We are talking about structures, not instances, of guilt and shame. After all, I can feel guilty about and also be ashamed of the very same failures or features of them. Here we might also note that failures and other acts and states that ground guilt, shame, or both can be, and can be seen by the agent and others to be either within or outside the control of the agent.

Second, *moral psychology:* these different stances help show that Aristotle's men did not suffer from spiritual maladies, such as depression. And to some extent, they help explain that.

Third, *ethical and political theory:* these stances help show, once again, problems emotivists and expressivists have in giving reductive accounts of ethical notions in terms of anger. For they help show just how ethicized anger is and always was. They do this by helping show the centrality of responsibility and blame for anger, of different forms or locations of responsibility for different sorts of blame.

Taking note of these stances also helps us understand and construct accounts of rights, responsibility, and punishment by helping us see the sorts of dangers that law and morality should guard against, what our "natural" entitlements are, who is presumptively innocent and who is presumptively to blame in fights and collisions. So, to the extent that I see myself to blame for my own misfortunes, I will be unlikely to have the same understanding of my rights vis-à-vis others as I would if I "naturally" and generally see others as being to blame for my misfortunes. To take a very minor, if indicative, case: we can learn a lot by studying the differences between people who expect others to make room for them as they walk down the street, expecting an apology if they are impeded or bumped into, and another sort of person, those who think they should give way and apologize. (Perhaps these people will also differ in their very understanding or concept of justice.)

Fourth, *practical issues:* these stances – these directions of blame and attributions of causality – are also of signal importance for various very practical issues. At a high level of generality, affecting our whole culture, there are the very difficult and very troubling ways we are so concerned with blame – with "playing the blame game" and with litigiousness, to mention only two very disturbing aspects, if not forms, of contemporary life.[21] At a somewhat more personal level, there are the difficulties experienced by people who themselves are, or who live with others who are,

---

21 Thanks are owed to Bonny Kent for discussion here.

unable to accept responsibility for what they do and what happens to them. Here we find, on one side, those who so often manage to find others to blame for problems of their own making; and, on another side, those who can never take, much less seek, credit for what good they have done.

On a combined personal and political level, one of the serious effects of oppression is that many who are oppressed do not think that they are oppressed, but rather that their misfortunes are due to nature – "that's just the way things are" – or due to some fault of their own. In addition to being an effect of oppression, these ways of seeing things also sustain and enable the oppression to continue.[22] Thus, Aristotelian-like anger is an important part of liberation from oppression – whether psychological, economic, or political. For what is needed is to cease seeing the oppressive, bad treatment as natural or deserved, and to see it, instead, as a wrong done without justification, and thus to be angered by it.

3 Slights, flattery, and recognition by others

Aristotle's men can be slighted by their inferiors, equals, or superiors. In these different cases, the ground of the slight is different in ways that make the sort of the slight different. Being slighted is, in this way, parallel to being flattered, to which we now want to turn briefly.

Aristotle says in his discussion of friendship in the *Nicomachean Ethics* that we take pleasure in being flattered by our inferiors, not because we take their flattery as showing how we are – and thus not as showing we deserve honor – but because it indicates their love for us (VIII.8, 1159a13 ff.). He here must be thinking of a certain sort of flattery, not the flattery that simply acknowledges our power over them and their dependence on us.

In contrast, people like being flattered by "those in positions of authority because of their hopes (for they think that if they want anything they will get it from them; and therefore delight in honor as a token of favor to come)" (VIII.8, 1159a19 ff.). And finally, "those who desire honor from good men, and men who know, are aiming at confirming their own opinion of themselves; they delight in honor, therefore, because they believe in their own goodness on the strength of the judgment of those who speak about them" (VIII.8, 1159a22 ff.).

Here we should note the prominence this gives to evaluative views of a person: we want and value flattery because we want and value being

---

[22] See Frantz Fanon, *The Wretched of the Earth* (New York: Grove Press, 1965), and *Black Skins, White Masks* (New York: Grove Press, 1968), and Sandra Bartky, *Femininity and Domination* (New York: Routledge, 1990), especially ch. 2, "On Psychological Oppression."

thought well of both by others and by ourselves. We want and value flattery by good people, not because this portends favors to come, but because it allows us to think well of ourselves. And we want and value flattery by our inferiors because it shows that they think well of us, perhaps love us.

Slights are natural contraries of acts of flattery. Whether slighted by an inferior, an equal, or a superior, slights show that one is not loved and not respected and that one is not thought important, perhaps that one is thought unimportant. This is painful in itself. It also gives a special character to the distress and pain, the shock and chagrin, of the attack on oneself one can feel by being slighted. Further, slights tell against one's hopes, not just of being well cared for by others, but simply of being safe with and from others. Having been slighted, one can now see and feel oneself – directly or indirectly in the eyes and hearts of others – to be threatened or at least open to attack, undefended by strength, love, or respect.

In addition, just as with the benefits of flattery, there are harms of slights that are more tied to the statuses of those slighting and those slighted. Slights by your inferiors are a wounding and hurtful denial of their inferiority. Among other things, this calls into question your being able to rely on them to do your bidding, to keep their place, and mind their own business, rather than interfering with yours. Slights by your equals are a wounding and hurtful denial of your equality with them. Among other things, this calls into question your being one of them, able to count on their good wishes and on their willingness to enter into reciprocal relations based on mutual respect. You may now fear that they will treat you as an inferior, having no importance, liable to have your favors and goodwill not seen by your fellows as requiring return, but seen instead as their due, as owed them by an inferior. If you are slighted by those you acknowledge as your superiors, the authority of their bad opinion of you forces you to think poorly of yourself.

For its own sake and also for what it shows us about slights, let us now return to flattery, in particular to what people like about it. Aristotle notes that one reason we want to be flattered is that we want to be thought well of both by others and by ourselves. But, as Aristotle recognizes, this is not just one desire. Many different desires – some mutually exclusive, some not – are correctly described as "wanting to be well thought of by oneself and others." Here are some possibilities. What one wants in wanting to be well thought of by oneself and others can be evidence for a view: that they flatter me is evidence that I am good. It can be a desire for the truth of a claim: that I, the flattered person, am good. It can be a desire for the existence of a certain belief or attitude: that I am loved by those who flatter me. It can be a desire for something to be done: that those who flatter me show me respect and give me honors, or pay certain sorts of attention to me.

These different desires typify and express different sorts of character and personality. They also allow us to put some of the main differences between those people Aristotle considers good and those he considers bad, and between those who are good on account of their contemplative activity, as discussed at the end of book X of the *Nicomachean Ethics,* and those who are good on account of their more practical activity, as discussed earlier in that work.

To see this, let us consider a claim about honor made early in the *Nicomachean Ethics:*

Further, men seem to pursue honor in order that they may be assured of their merit; at least it is by men of practical wisdom that they seek to be honored, and among those who know them, and the ground of their excellence; clearly, then, according to them, at any rate excellence is better [than honor]. And perhaps one might even suppose this [that is, excellence] to be, rather than honor, the end of the political life. (I.5, 1095b27 ff.)

If we focus on its first and last clauses – "men seem to pursue honor in order that they may be assured of their merit" and "one might even suppose this [that is, excellence] to be, rather than honor, the end of the political life" – we can construct a dialectical argument about the value of honor and being honored. Its point would be to show that in wanting honors, we really want to be virtuous. The dialectical structure of the argument would be similar to the ascent argument of Plato's *Symposium:* having achieved a higher level, we see what we could not see at the lower level that what we really wanted at the lower level can be achieved by, and indeed only by, something at the higher level; and that, not only do we now not want what we wanted at the lower level, but, even at the lower level, we only thought we wanted it.

Many people in our culture, too – making a connection between being a good person and being modest and humble – hold that this dialectical argument is right about why a good person wants honors. The thought here is that the very best people will not care, at least not very much, whether they are honored and receive honors on account of their virtue. There are two qualifications that should be made here. These people may well want to receive them, if they do receive them, on account of their virtue for one important reason: precisely because they are concerned to be good and also because they want to be, and perhaps are, modest and humble, they will be unsure whether they are, in fact, good. Thus, they can want honors "to assure themselves of their own merit." But it is the epistemological role of the honors, the evidence and assurance, not the honors as such, that interests them. On this view, the very best people want honors only for epistemological reasons – to give them evidence for the truth that they are good people.

Perhaps, then, virtue is its own reward – at least for the very best people. But as we and Aristotle know, this is not how virtue is for many people. They want recognition for virtue in the form of honors and praise. "They seek to be honored... on the ground of their excellence." This is different from wanting assurance that you are good so that you can think – think the thought – that you are good.

Wanting such recognition can be morally questionable and unattractive. Improper pride is a serious danger here. But there are other dangers, too, as the following sketches show.

Many who want recognition for virtue are far too much like children who run to their parents saying "See how good I am. Aren't I really good?" expecting in reply, "You are so good; you are Mommy's and Daddy's good little darling." Further, we all know people who "never" are able or concerned just to do what is good; and who, when they are concerned to do what is good, are also concerned that their good acts be acknowledged, if not celebrated. As is said, perhaps more out of annoyance than a concern for literal truth, some people seem as concerned that their good deeds be recognized as they are to do them. Here we might think of the public figure who seems "always" to have the media on hand to record good works, or someone, perhaps a friend who seems "always" to want grateful acknowledgment of every gift.

These tag line descriptions of the public figure and the friend can be fleshed out in many different ways, giving many different sorts of people. Perhaps the commonest way to imagine these people is to see their desire for acknowledgment as rather crass: they do their good deeds in order – largely in order, perhaps only in order – to get something of benefit to themselves. So, the public figure wants publicity to help in a future campaign. Such crass desires are all too common. And where one of these crass desires lies behind good deeds, we have ready ways to characterize and criticize the person for having that desire and trying to satisfy it that way.

For the sake of accuracy – and to help us further appreciate the complexities of the relations between emotion and value – we must recognize that there are other ways to flesh out those descriptions and to understand the desire for acknowledgment of good deeds. For example, those with such a desire may be suffering from a narcissistic, primitive deficit in mirroring. It is as if those parts of themselves that are not witnessed or validated are not really there, but are missing and not real to them. For such people, it is thus natural that not being paid attention – such as not being given what they think of as due thanks – is felt as a grave threat.

These people are different from those who suffer from what might be called superego narcissism. These people feel a moral demand – a demand of moral entitlement coupled with a demand of moral requiredness – that their contributions be accurately acknowledged. They feel slighted if their good deeds are not acknowledged, especially if the good deeds of others are acknowledged. Their demands for recognition, and complaints about not getting recognition, are often moralistic and self-righteous. So, while they do feel slighted if their good deeds are not recognized, they do not feel this slight just as something they suffer. They feel it is as an affront to propriety or morality, itself: "It's not for me that I want what I did acknowledged, it's to keep the record straight." Moreover, they are aggrieved not just by a lack of recognition, but also by those people who should, but do not, give them recognition. It is not just that the improper distribution of recognition must be corrected. Those others who failed to distribute recognition appropriately must be rebuked and made to correct both that distribution and themselves.

Let us now turn to *spectatorism* – living just as a spectator, even a voyeur, and not also as an agent; or living like Clara Thompson's patient who has a "markedly detached personality" and is "unaware of any personal emotional contact with other human beings. He is an onlooker at life."[23] Spectatorism in its various forms, joined with exhibitionism in various of its forms, also provides us with another set of ways that the desire for recognition can be unattractive.

In such cases, instead of my attending to what I am doing or experiencing, I focus on others seeing what I am doing or experiencing, or on my own seeing what I am doing or experiencing. Such a desire may be thought to involve activity, not for the sake of doing something, but rather for the sake of being seen to do it. Another, and perhaps a better, way to put the matter is that the activity and goal here is making a display and being seen, and in this sense gaining recognition.[24] Even when such display is not a

---

23 From "Development of Awareness of Transference in a Markedly Detached Personality," ch. 13 of *Interpersonal Psychoanalysis: The Selected Papers of Clara M. Thompson,* ed. Maurice R. Green (New York: Basic Books, 1964), p. 111. Originally published with the same title in *International Journal of Psycho-Analysis,* 19 (1938) 299–309.

24 The issue here is similar to one discussed about activity and passivity in regard to self-pity in Chapter 9, section 5. As also cited there, see David Rapaport, "Some Metapsychological Considerations concerning Activity and Passivity," published originally (in English) in *Archivos de Criminología, Neuropisquitaria Disciplinas Conexas* (Equador), 9 (1961) 391–449, and

goal, it can inform a worry: instead of having a goal of making a good display or showing myself off well, I can worry about what sort of display I am making of myself – and the display can be for myself, for others, or for both. Whether a goal or a worry, we are here concerned with structures of being self-conscious, of shame, and, once again, of narcissism.

We could continue to sketch other unattractive ways to be too concerned with the self. But there is no need to do this. Even if, as we doubt, exhaustive lists could be produced, our purpose was not to show all the unattractive ways we can be too concerned with the self, or even all the unattractive ways this can involve desiring recognition for virtue. It was to show that there is a multiplicity of such unattractive ways, with the subsidiary goal of showing that not all of these involve pride or crass self-interest.

Seeing this is important. It is also important to see that wanting recognition for virtue need not be unattractive. Let us start by noting that we want and think it good, or even necessary, to be accepted by and admitted into a shared life with those we think well of. It is hard to exaggerate how devastating such exclusion can be. In addition, we want those we may not think well of to treat us in certain ways – on account of their thinking well of us. Similarly, the importance of thinking well of oneself goes well beyond simply believing – having the view or even knowledge – that one is good. It also involves accepting oneself, having self-esteem, self-regard, feelings of entitlement, being at home and at peace with oneself. And these, even if they involve belief, go well beyond it.[25]

This helps us see that wanting recognition for virtue can be part and parcel of the desire to live a responsible and responsive life with others. It can be a desire to live within a community of people who recognize "the virtues of common pursuit,"[26] who are alive to and appreciate each other,

---

reprinted in *The Collected Papers of David Rapaport,* ed. Merton M. Gill (New York: Basic Books, 1967).

25 On this distinction between self-regard and believing that one is good, see Pauline Chazan, "Self-Esteem, Self-Respect, and Love of Self: Ways of Valuing the Self," forthcoming in *Philosophia.* See also her "Pride, Virtue, and Selfhood: A Reconstruction of Hume," *Canadian Journal of Philosophy,* 22 (1992) 45–65, and her doctoral dissertation, "Moral Theory, Moral Understanding and the Moral Self" (University of Melbourne, Victoria, Australia, 1992), which Michael Stocker takes great pleasure in having helped supervise in its early stages. On the general distinction between emotionally having a belief and holding it true, see Stocker, "Affectivity and Self-Concern: The Assumed Psychology in Aristotle's Ethics," *Pacific Philosophical Quarterly,* 64 (1983) 211–229, now Chapter 9, and "Emotional Thoughts," *American Philosophical Quarterly,* 24 (1987) 59–69.

26 To use the title of Nancy Sherman's "The Virtues of Common Pursuit," *Philosophy and Phenomenological Research,* 53 (1993) 277–299. Thanks are also owed Sherman for discussion. See also Charles Taylor, "The Politics of Recognition," in *Multiculturalism and "The Politics of Recognition"* (Princeton: Princeton University Press, 1992), reprinted in David Theo Gold-

including what each contributes; and who, as a part of living within such a community, give thanks and recognition, assurance and mutual support. These last can be everyday and low key – little, if anything more than a smile or a "thank you" for a favor or for cooperative work. They can also involve larger-scale celebrations – some form of thanksgiving. There need be nothing unattractive about this or about wanting it. Indeed, not having or not wanting this can, itself, be questionable and unattractive (see, for example, *NE* IV.3 1125a19 ff.).

We take this to be what Aristotle argues. It cannot be overemphasized that he spends most of the *Nicomachean Ethics* – nearly all but the last half of the last book, X – showing how one can achieve *eudaimonia,* be a good person and lead a good life, in combined practical, social, and political ways. Using our terms, these ways involve living in and taking part in a responsible and responsive society, where this involves recognizing and acknowledging others for their virtue, and wanting recognition and acknowledgment for one's own virtue. These ways of living with others involve having various emotional relations and interrelations with others, being able to have certain emotional stances to others and oneself, and having these sustained and validated by others. These forms of emotions and emotionality are possible only in a social setting – and indeed in one that is in part constituted by these very relations.

It is not only for the truth, or only to secure the truth, that these good people want to be recognized on account of virtue. The assurance and recognition they want involve something done in regard *to* them, and often *for* them. They want assurance in the form of praise and honors. They want public recognition. They want spoken or enacted, acknowledged, recognition.[27]

In short, then, these people want to be treated in certain ways by others. They want to live in emotionally engaged ways, with others and with themselves. They do not want just to have evidence for certain beliefs, nor just to have those beliefs.

Much the same holds for flattery. To see this, we should ask why we like being flattered. Do we like the flattery by our inferiors because it shows that they love us – that is, because what they do gives us reason, perhaps good and sufficient reason, to think that they love us? Or do we, perhaps also, like having done to and with us what they do in showing their love of us? So too, do we like flattery by our equals because of what this allows us to think

berg, ed., *Multiculturalism* (Oxford: Blackwell, 1994).
27 See, for example, *NE* IV.3, especially 1123b17–24 and 1124a5–9. Thanks are owed to Margaret Walker for discussion here.

of ourselves? Or do we, perhaps also, like having done to and with us what they do in treating us as equals, such as including us in their activities as equal participants? We think that in all these cases, what is done to and with us – seen as expressing these views – is an important source of liking the flattery.

We find it difficult to come to such a view about why, according to Aristotle, we like flattery by good people: "those who desire honor from good men, and men who know, are aiming at confirming their own opinion of themselves; they delight in honor, therefore, because they believe in their own goodness on the strength of the judgment of those who speak about them" (*NE* VIII.8, 1159a22 ff.). Here, it seems, others are important but only for fostering and sustaining beliefs. We say "only" here to locate what is important, not to denigrate what is located. Belief in one's own goodness is vital to much that is important and good.

Virtue, then, is not just its own reward for at least one of Aristotle's two sorts of good people – those whose *eudaimonia* is practical, not contemplative. But for both sorts of good people, virtue regulates their desire for honors in two ways and in this sense is greater than honors. They want honors only on account of their virtue. And they want honors only to the extent, and in the ways, in the circumstances, and the like that it is virtuous to want it. So, they do not want honors earned by someone else, nor do they want more honors than called for, or honors given in divisive and unseemly ways.

Further, both sorts of good people have a concern for the self. They do not want simply that there be virtuous people. They want that they, themselves, be virtuous. Nonetheless, because of the ways virtue informs their lives, including their desire for honors, their sorts of self-concern are virtuous. In particular, they do not involve a selfish, overconcern with the self. That would involve wanting and pursuing what is not good, or forms of wanting and pursuing that are not good (see *NE* IX.8). Thus, neither sort of good person wants or pursues a life of honors as that is popularly understood: honors even without virtue, and a desire for honors whether or not they lie in a mean or are too many, for the wrong reasons, at the wrong times, and the like.

More should be said about the desire for public recognition – especially if we are concerned with the dangers of narcissism. As we have seen, this desire is common among many good people, whether or not among the very best. Further, this desire when had by good people might seem, almost as a matter of necessity, morally innocuous. For if they are good, they will not do just anything to get recognition. They can still have the very highest standards – wanting praise for and only for being good. It was for such reasons that Bernard Williams held that there is nothing epistemologically dangerous or suspect about a scientist wanting fame, at least not if what is wanted is fame for important discoveries: such a scientist will be just as guided by science, by truth and evidence, as will a scientist who, selflessly, pursues science.[28]

This parallels claims made about Aristotle on pleasure. From his view that good people will get pleasure only from good activities – since pleasure is intrinsic to, and individuated according to, its activity – it has been concluded that, on his view, good people cannot go wrong by pursuing pleasure since, for them, to pursue pleasure is to pursue and do good activities. For these reasons, Julia Annas holds that "the good man should not avoid pleasure but should positively pursue it, if it is of the right kind."[29]

But we do not think matters are so clear as this, about either truth or pleasure. There is still room to go wrong, both in regard to what is desired and also the ways it is desired. Let us start with a danger that arises if we take Williams's claim about *the desire for the fame of discovery* in a way he clearly did not intend. This way allows that one can have such a desire without caring whether or not one has made the discovery and whether or not what is discovered merits fame. Moved by such a desire for the fame of discovery, a person can steal or otherwise misappropriate such fame. One can want to be "known" or "recognized" as the discoverer of something even though one knows that one did not discover it. Turning to what is discovered, people with this desire might allow or even encourage a false and inflated view about what is discovered – even about what *they* discovered. The epistemological dangers of such a desire are obvious.

There are also epistemological dangers if we take *the desire for the fame of discovery* in another way that Williams did not intend: as the desire for merited fame for discovering what merits fame for being discovered *by that person*. After all, discoverers might suffer from a handicap that makes their "discovery" of some paltry or already well known truth remarkable or deserving of fame. Here we could think of an *idiot savant* or of untalented thinkers. *What* they discover may not, in itself, be remarkable even where the fact that *they* discover it is. Or we could think of the fame a four-year-

---

28 In his 1993 Woodbridge Lectures at Columbia University. Thanks are owed to Max Deutscher for discussion about this and much else in this work, and to Linda Alcoff for discussion of this issue.
29 "Aristotle on Pleasure and Goodness," in Amélie O. Rorty, ed., *Essays on Aristotle's Ethics* (Berkeley: University of California Press, 1980), p. 291.

old has and even merits, at least within the family, for discovering that churned cream turns into butter. Or we might consider a somewhat similar situation where a work, not the person, gets fame by being done by a famous person – for example, just any drawing or doodling by Picasso, or just any letter or other piece of writing, even just a signature, of Napoleon.

One serious epistemological danger of this sort of desire is that people, and not only people who seek fame, may come to see the field of inquiry as a place for personal aggrandizement or display. So, for example, the field may be thought interesting, indeed graced, by that person "working" in it. It may have value "projected" onto it by that person being in it, much as we project value onto what is liked, worn, or touched by those we are in love with. Less endearingly, that field can have value projected onto it in the way narcissists project value onto what is theirs – their work, their possessions, their . . . – just because it is *theirs*.

Another epistemological danger of such a desire is thinking of the field of inquiry as one that should develop, sustain, or even glorify the people doing it rather than the field of inquiry itself. What we have in mind can be brought about by the following contrast. In elementary schools the teaching and doing of mathematics is quite properly focused on the pupils, on developing them and their capacities, helping them become able to do mathematics and certainly preventing them from shying away from it. But at mathematics research institutions, there is a far greater, if not exclusive, focus on mathematics as inquiry. We might well have doubts about a research institution that is less concerned to encourage work in the field than to glorify its benefactor or members.

There is a somewhat related danger where the untalented or famous people also have institutional or political power. Here we might think of Lysenko and what he did to the study of biology in the Soviet Union.

As said, Williams was not concerned with either of these sorts of desire for the fame of discovery. His concern was with the desire for *properly earned and deserved* fame of discovery. For you to have such a desire, you must want to merit fame for discovering something that merits fame for being discovered. Such "truth-respecting" desire might seem at worst harmless and probably very useful. It might seem that a scientist could not go wrong from such a desire, and indeed that scientists with such a desire will naturally try to do the best science and will thus advance science.

We do agree that such a desire can be good – good for science. And this may generally or often enough be how it is. But such a desire can be, and undoubtedly sometimes is, dangerous. The scientist with such a desire might be too concerned with showy and easily publicizable science, with work that, if it succeeds, will attract fame, even merited fame. Another danger is being too unwilling to undertake hard work or take chances, lest one fail and be known as a failure or simply not be known as a success. Both of these can lead to poor and uneven development of science – to mention only one issue.

There are also the dangers – the social, personal, and interpersonal dangers – of being too concerned with even properly merited recognition and fame. We all know how difficult it is to work when overly concerned with recognition, and how difficult it is to work with others who are overly concerned with their own recognition. Such concern – "I discovered this," "I said this first," "It is mine," "You got it from me" – can be ridiculous or ugly, not to mention divisive. And it can easily pose dangers for science and other forms of inquiry – when they are considered as bodies of claims and also when they are considered as disciplines and enterprises undertaken by people.

Such concerns often put great, even destructive, strains on joint, cooperative enterprises, such as science and on other interpersonal, cooperative, group enterprises. And since so very much of human life is made up of such enterprises – and correlatively, since so very little of life is made up of entirely single person enterprises – these concerns put great and often destructive strains on, near enough, all of life.[30]

In pointing out these last, social and interpersonal dangers, we are not praising self-abnegation. That, too, has many dangers. Nor are we ignoring the dangers of not giving recognition to others, perhaps even stealing from them. This can force people to be wary, rather than open, with colleagues, and to be zealously insistent in demanding recognition for themselves, if they are to get even some of the recognition they deserve. Nor are we rejecting the value of paying attention to questions of who is due what recognition. On all sides, and in all directions, there are very real difficulties in evaluating, modulating, and directing concern for attention and recognition.

Science is just an example of what we have already seen. In all areas of life, there are serious issues about recognition and attention: who should get

---

30 A concern to distinguish and isolate one's own doings from those of the group is central to many issues discussed as problems of moral luck. These issues are discussed by Maurice Merleau-Ponty in *Humanism and Terror* (Boston: Beacon Press, 1971); Sherman in "The Virtues of Common Pursuit"; Margaret Walker, "Moral Luck and the Virtues of Impure Agency," *Metaphilosophy*, 22 (1991) 14–27, reprinted in Daniel Statman, ed., *Moral Luck*, (Albany: State University of New York Press, 1993); Claudia Card in "Responsibility for Moral Luck," forthcoming in her *Character and Moral Luck* (Philadelphia: Temple University Press); Susan Wolf in "The Moral of Moral Luck," unpublished manuscript.

or give them, on what occasions, what are the inducements to give them or the sanctions for not giving them, . . . Narcissists magnify these problems, with their demanding need for others to assure and reassure them of their worth, showing by way of acts and attitudes of respect, love, obeisance, that they are good. We cannot know in general how – for example, by what social arrangements and distributions of power and care – all this will get played out. But we can know that the ways it gets played out will have serious implications for those caught up in them.

Much the same, but perhaps more intrapersonally, holds for pleasure. Suppose we agree with Aristotle about the extremely tight connections between pleasure and activity – pleasure is, or is an added perfection to, activity; pleasures are individuated *qua* pleasures according to their activity; and good people will do only good activities and pursue only good pleasures. Nonetheless, there are dangers even for good people who pursue those pleasures. Even these people can become too interested in the pleasures. Perhaps they restrict their activities to those that are pleasing. Instead of working on frustrating problems in philosophy, say, they work on what they know can be handled with pleasure. Or instead of working with unrewarding students, they spend their time on students it is a pleasure to teach. Or instead of laborious research, they spend their time in pleasing discussions.

Even if they do not restrict their activities, they can change the focus, the point, of the activities. For example, feeling somewhat low, I might undertake an activity that I know I can do well and that, when I do it well, is pleasing. Suppose that this becomes a way of life for me, that I quite generally engage in those activities in order to escape from my otherwise unhappy life – and to escape into pleasure. Or perhaps in a more self-glorying way, out for self-congratulation, I engage in those good activities that, if I do them well, will give me pleasure. I do them so that I can feel, like Jack Horner, "what a good boy am I." Here there is a sort of self-regarding exhibitionism – similar to other-regarding exhibitionism, where we do good activities in order to get the very pleasing admiration of those we want to impress so that they will admire us.

We, thus, see how pleasure can be dangerous. We also see how, contra Annas (p. 290), we can accept both Aristotle's warning about pleasure given early in the *Nicomachean Ethics* – that we ought to feel toward pleasure as the elders felt toward Helen (II.9, 1109b7–12) – and his later views in books VII and X that some pleasures are good, indeed excellent.

Some might object that our argument requires that doing philosophy for the sake of pleasure is or can generally be the same as doing it for its own sake. But we think our argument can be seen as a reductio ad absurdum of the claim that they are or generally can be the same. The problem comes in specifying what it is to do an act for its own sake – especially to help us understand Aristotle's claims about the goodness of so acting. Perhaps we will have to be satisfied with following Aristotle on virtue and give as our general account: good acts must be done as good people good at doing those sorts of acts would do them. This is to say that the acts are done for the reasons good people do them and with their emotions.

In short, Aristotle's good person need not act, and must not generally act, for the sake of pleasure. This is so even if, as Aristotle holds, a good person does good acts for their own sake and is pleased by this, and even if as many hold, 'I do x because x-ing pleases me' says just about what 'I do x for its own sake' does. For, at least when said by good people, 'I do x because x-ing pleases me' does not say the same as, and may be inconsistent with, 'I do x for the sake of pleasure'.[31]

4   The personal and the impersonal in some emotions

At the outset of the discussion of Aristotle's angry men, we said that we can investigate anger and its involvement with status and concern for importance, respect, and honor as showing both the sociology and the character of these people. We also said that these investigations differ mainly in emphasis. This section and the following two sections will comment on some of the complex relations between the psychological and the sociological. The present section discusses the personal and the impersonal in emotions; section 5 discusses who can get angry on behalf of whom, and section 6 discusses emotional closeness.

Aristotle writes that anger "must always be felt toward some particular person, for example, Cleon, and not man in general" (*Rht* II.2, 1378a34 ff.). We will first suggest some reasons to think that, as this may suggest, *orgē* is a far more personal matter for Aristotle's men than anger is for us. We will then suggest some contrary or moderating reasons to think that our anger may not be any less of a personal matter for us than *orgē* was for Aristotle's men. We are interested in whether there is a difference in how personally involving *orgē* and anger are. To mention a minor concern of ours, this will

---

[31] We have been helped here by Amélie O. Rorty's comments on *focus* in "The Place of Pleasure in Aristotle's Ethics," *Mind*, 83 (1974) 481–497, pp. 494–496. Thanks are owed to John Robertson for discussion. On some differences between acting *because of* and *for the sake of*, see Stocker, "Values and Purposes: The Limits of Teleology and the Ends of Friendship," *Journal of Philosophy*, 78 (1981) 747–765, and "Morally Good Intentions," *Monist*, 54 (1970) 124–141.

help us see some further connections between shame and anger. And to mention a major concern of ours, this will also help us see some of the ways the personal and impersonal are important in emotions and value.

Aristotle holds that his men have *orgē* only when they take personally a slight delivered by a particular person. For present purposes, it will be useful to divide this into two separate claims. First, *orgē* involves a slight's being *taken personally*. Second, and perhaps for that reason, the slight giving rise to *orgē* is given by a person. To see whether our anger differs from *orgē*, we will, thus, ask whether our anger at slights involves slights that are taken personally, and whether the slights must be given by a person.[32]

It is vital to keep in mind that the anger of ours we are comparing with *orgē* involves slights. For some of our sorts of anger are very close to, if not identical with, *echthra*, enmity, discussed in the *Rhetoric* at II.4. Among the differences between *echthra* and *orgē* is the fact that *echthra* need not be directed at any particular person. One can have it toward a class of people: "Anger is always concerned with individuals – Callias or Socrates – whereas hatred is directed against classes: we all hate any thief and any informer" (*Rht* II.4, 1382a4 ff.). Similarly, many cases of our anger need not be directed at any particular person. And further, many of our cases of anger do not require any target or provocation. For example, we can see that a person is angry – is an angry person – in much the way we see that the ocean is angry: the person and the ocean are just lashing about.[33] This is not a point about dispositions: that if someone or something gets in the person's or the ocean's way, it will attract destruction and arouse anger, or that the person or ocean is all too prone to anger, too easily aroused. It is a point about how they are now. They are already angry. But, as said, that anger is not the anger that concerns us.

We want, first, to consider arguments that *there is a difference between our anger and orgē*. People in our society know all too well that institutions, such as universities and corporations, can arouse anger by their slights. Here we might think of a university's quotas based on race, sex, or religion, clubs that do not admit people of a particular race, religion, or gender, or a bank's refusing to lend to, or an insurance company's refusing to insure, anyone living in "red-lined" areas.

We must ask whether these slights are, or can be, taken personally. To do this, let us start by asking what it is to take a slight personally – in the way that *orgē* involves taking a slight personally. It cannot be required that the

---

[32] Thanks are owed to Eugene Garver.
[33] Thanks are owed to José Benardete for this figure.

slight be directed at the man it angers. When they are slighted, Aristotle's man can, and according to Aristotle should, get angry on behalf of his friends and others he is bound to protect. Nor can it be required that the slight be directed at him or any of these people, if 'directed at' implies that they were intended as the targets of the slighting or even that the slighting was intentional. Merely failing to show any of these people enough respect — as distinguished from showing them disrespect — can, on Aristotle's view, be a slight that is sufficient for anger.

Nor can 'taking it personally' be understood in terms of whether the grammatical form of the insult is personal or instead impersonal. Here we could compare an insult to a particular person for being a ———, "You dirty, deceitful ———," and an insult to a group to which that person belongs, "All ———s are dirty and deceitful." Focusing on grammatical form, we could say that only the former is personal. The insult can still be impersonal in grammatical form even if it is delivered to someone known to be a member of that group, and perhaps even if it is delivered to someone for being a member of that group: "I should have expected you to be dirty and deceitful, since this is the way all ———s are" or even "All ———s, including you, are dirty and deceitful." In the cases that are personal in form, it is as if the insulted person is directly attacked, and being a ——— is offered as a rationalization, often not even a reason, for that. In the general case, it is as if the insulted person is there only incidentally, "All ———s are dirty and deceitful, and, as it happens, so therefore are you."

Consideration of these various possibilities easily shows that such grammatical form — in particular, being grammatically personal — is neither necessary nor sufficient for an insult's being taken personally. For neither of these is necessary or sufficient for the insult to be felt as striking home, to be hurt by it, to feel wounded and insulted by it. We are quite confident and clear about this — even though we are unclear about the general determinants and conditions for an insult's being taken personally. The general issues are too complex and variable, and too dependent on the particularities of personality and character, to allow for generality and clarity.

To mention only some factors: whether an insult is wounding and how wounding it is depend on interactions among the character of the insulted person, the nature of the insult, and how that person "places" such insults. So, we can easily imagine cases where the grammatically personal insult is more personally wounding, and other cases where the grammatically impersonal one is more personally wounding. How people can take a grammatically personal insult personally is obvious. But, even if less obvious, people can also take a general insult personally. They might find the impersonality of the insult to be an added insult: that their individuality is not recognized, and they are insulted simply as members of a despised group.

They might say of their tormentors, "They didn't even have the decency to look at me, to see and hate me as a person." We can also easily imagine very similar cases where people do not take personally, or take less personally, a grammatically impersonal insult, and indeed take some comfort from the generality of the insult: "They weren't really talking about me, but only against a group of people, my people, whom they stupidly misunderstand because of their bigotry." We can also easily imagine very similar cases where people take an impersonal insult very personally – perhaps because they so much identify themselves with, identify themselves as a member of, the insulted group, or because being treated as just one of a group is, itself, personally wounding.[34] And we can also easily imagine cases where both reactions occur in the same person, simultaneously, intermixed, or sequentially.

So too, a person might take personally an insult that is aimed at someone else. Aristotle notes that his men can feel *orgē* if one of their friends is slighted. And we can feel anger if we, somehow, identify with the target of a slight. We might read an insulting attack – an attack by someone we do not know on someone else we do not know – for holding certain political, social, or philosophical views. If we, too, hold or sympathize with those views, we might take the insult personally – perhaps even feel oneself a target of the insult – especially if we think that the attack was not so much on the person who was attacked, but rather on that person simply as a holder of those views. In taking the insult as an insult to just anyone holding those views, we can, even though we need not, take it personally.[35]

Consideration of these cases and factors shows once again that we cannot understand what it is to take an insult personally in terms of its intended goal, or in terms of its grammatical form. These, we suggest, are cognate points to – or perhaps just illustrations of – the argument in Chapter 1 against the content claim that we cannot accept an account of emotions just in terms of nonaffective content. As just noted, in taking the insult as an insult to just anyone who holds those views, we can take it personally, but we need not. There is no reason to think there must be a difference in nonaffective content between the case where we do take it personally and the other where we do not take it personally. There may only be a difference in affect: in how the content is taken.

---

[34] Our thanks to Laurence Thomas for discussion here.
[35] Thanks are owed to Kirsten Mayer for this case.

Perhaps, then, *taking something personally* is what we might call an ineliminably psychological notion: what is needed for me to take a slight personally is that it be felt as attacking "me or mine." To make it clear that this is not an affectless, content account of taking a slight personally, we should follow Aristotle and say something like: what is needed for me to take a slight personally is that it be felt, with pain, as hurtfully attacking "me or mine." Even if, as we think, this is inadequate as an account, it will allow us to continue with our investigation of differences between conditions for Aristotle's angry man to feel *orgē* and those we need to feel angry.

Suppose now that "to feel, with pain, me or mine hurtfully attacked by the slight" is sufficient for, or even is identical with, feeling the slight personally. What, then, are we to say of those people slighted by being excluded from various clubs or universities on the basis of race, religion, or gender, and those refused loans or insurance because of their race or where they live? Surely, some of them can feel with pain that this treatment is hurtfully directed at "them or theirs." They can take it personally – even though the policy is quite general and may be so far unrelated to them, personally, that it was enacted before they were even conceived.

So, it seems that we can be slighted by an institution, and that we can take this personally. To see whether our anger is or is not like *orgē*, we still have to see whether our anger also requires that the slight be given by a person. Before taking this up, however, we might ask why Aristotle's men could not feel personally slighted by institutions.

Perhaps there are particular reasons, having to do with our different situations, that explain this. Perhaps his men could not be, or feel, personally slighted by institutions because feeling that would make it very difficult for them to think of themselves as self-sufficient, and thus very difficult for them to think of themselves as good men. At the least, it would be difficult for us to think of ourselves as self-sufficient if we are clear-sighted about our need for institutions – especially if we are also clear-sighted about their general indifference to us. Perhaps, then, belief in self-sufficiency requires seeing one's life in person-to-person ways, rather than in ways mediated by institutions.

In any case, we do not think that we can correctly see our present lives in person-to-person ways. Our reason here is that if people are to be able to see their lives in person-to-person ways, they must live in certain sorts of societies or social arrangements, such as at a time of little industrial and technical specialization, when at least most of one's needs are supplied in and by the home, by one's family, its servants, and workers. Alternatively, it requires enough power to make others supply those needs unobtrusively and as if by nature: as if these others were part of an attentive family, owing personal service and favors to those they serve. Or, it requires an illusion that this is how life is – an illusion various people have reason to foster and sustain for themselves and others.

This leads to a second possibility as to why Aristotle's men could not feel slighted by institutions. Or rather, why they were not, or were only rarely, slighted by them. The reason is that they were unlikely to be slighted by them. And the reason for this is that they were the elite, socially and politically at the top of their society, and thus unlikely to be slighted by its institutions.

Putting these two together, we get a third possibility. Perhaps Aristotle's men could not feel slighted by institutions because they saw the functionaries of institutions as individuals and as acting as individuals, rather than seeing them institutionally, merely acting as agents, impersonal agents, of the impersonal institution. So, even were it offered, they would not accept a functionary's claim, "There is nothing personal in what I am doing to you." The connection we are relying on here is that it is natural for members of the elite to get or expect to get special, personal treatment. Certainly, this is true of – indeed, it is a characterizing feature of – narcissists. And one might well wonder whether it is possible for those neither of the elite nor narcissists.

Perhaps also, Aristotle's men could not feel slighted by institutions because generally there was no effective way to gain a conspicuous revenge against them.[36] Alcibiades is a conspicuous exception here.

Now for the argument that *there is little, if any, difference* between our anger and *orgē*: that our anger, too, requires taking slights both personally and also to be delivered by a person. It may be agreed that nowadays people are angered by, feel insulted and slighted by, how institutions treat them; and clearly, they can take this personally. But we should notice how this is done – or at least one of the more usual and more effective ways it is done. Somehow or other, the institution is personified. Sometimes it is treated as if it were a person, not an institution. And sometimes someone in or representing the institution is fixed upon as the "source" of the insult and the target of anger. Here we might consider how important politicians and demagogues find being able to blame some particular person or people.

We might also consider why, in military training, the enemy is represented as particular, despicable people. Perhaps they are real people, or perhaps they are merely stereotypes. It is thought, and probably correctly,

---

36 Thanks are owed to Christopher Conn for this suggestion.

that it is difficult to get our soldiers worked up enough, to feel strongly enough, to kill other people for "justice" or for "free trade." But this is far easier – perhaps all too easy – if they think of the enemy in terms of particular people and actions, such as atrocities that particular people have committed or, unless stopped, are about to commit.

So too, it seems inappropriate or foolish, not merely pointless, to be angry at one's car even for breaking down, much less for letting one down by breaking down. (We are not concerned with the value of "letting off steam.") But perhaps a person can be found to blame: perhaps the mechanic who has worked on the problem; one's friend who was supposed to, but did not, take the car to the mechanic; sloppy workers on the assembly line; company managers concerned only with the bottom line. Then the anger at the breakdown, at being let down, might be at least plausible.

The point here is not that the car is not a human. It can be appropriate and not at all foolish, perhaps not even pointless, to get angry at a neighborhood dog that always barks at you or tries to bite you as you pass. We understand how you can think that the dog dislikes you and "has it in" for you. Dogs are thought of as having "personality" and character – disliking some people and liking others, as having moods and emotions, such as jealousy. Dogs live not only juxtaposed to us, but also with us. They join in our lives and we can take personally what they do to us.

This, we think, is why we are able to get angry at dogs. It is not due to the bother or danger they cause us. For despite the far greater danger snakes pose, it seems far harder, if not impossible, to understand being angry at a snake, even one that frequently menaces you as you walk to your garden. The reason we would offer for this is that we think the snake acts as a matter of natural reflex, without – and thus not expressing – any personality, character, or feelings. So too, to return to the car case, it is important that getting angry at the car often seems to involve thinking of it as out to get us, as animated by a malicious or perverse imp.

These various cases suggest that in order for us to get angry, we have to feel that the object and cause of our anger is at least capable of having corresponding, human feelings toward us, such as anger or lack of respect. This is to say that anger requires seeing the cause of our anger as a person, or as if it were a person; and also as a person we can hurt in return. This is also to say that to be able to experience anger and take it personally, we must see its object as a person and its cause as a person.

To return to the cases of institutions, in these cases, too, there are real or imagined people or beings with peoplelike emotions. There are those officials who enforce, or simply go along with, the offensive practices.

There are also those real or imagined people who continue to uphold those practices for their own bad reasons. Witness the power and naturalness of conspiracy theories. There are also ways of thinking of the institution itself, or those people it is thought of as acting for, in terms of, say, "The rich man," "The white man," or the portentous "They" as in "They – and you know who they are – are to blame for ————." Similarly, people who are objects of hatred and prejudice, such as Jews and Blacks, are often seen and hated as classes and groups, that is in terms of *all* Jews or *all* Blacks. But this often, if not typically, goes along with seeing and hating them in personified ways, such as "The Jew" or "The Black man."

These cases strongly suggest that the personified form is the easiest, if not also the most appropriate, one for anger. They suggest that anger is not just a personal reaction and emotion, but is an interpersonal reaction and emotion. Anger involves being in an interpersonal relation with a real or imagined being like us. That is, a being who, as we imagine, is also capable of being in, and who is already in, a similar interpersonal relation with us, and who can cause us pain out of a lack of regard for us and who can be caused pain in return. This, of course, is what Aristotle requires for *orgē*.

This is to say that our anger, or its clearest and strongest instances, are far more like *orgē*, at least in regard to the issue of the personal, than we might think. It is also to suggest a modification to a claim made earlier: part of the account of why anger involves taking things personally has to do with its being interpersonal. It is taken personally because of the particular interpersonal relations it involves.

Thus, our anger, at least in its strongest forms, seems inappropriate and literally misguided in regard to the institutionally caused harms that we suffer due to the institutions and institutionally mediated parts of our society. It is misguided and inappropriate for the same reasons that anger at one's car or a snake is misguided and inappropriate. There is no person to get angry at and to join with in the interpersonal relation of anger. The same should hold for Aristotle's men. But if we are right, they mis-see their relations to society and others as face to face, rather than mediated by institutions. They mis-see matters in a way that, were it accurate, would make *orgē* appropriate for what in fact are the institutionally mediated harms they suffered.

To end our investigation of whether *orgē* and anger differ in regard to the personal, we would like to repeat and emphasize three points. First, the categories of the personal and impersonal are of central emotional and moral importance. Differences in the personal or impersonal make for important emotional and moral differences – of kind, not just amount.

Second, here, as so often when examining emotions, the personal must be understood as including the interpersonal. Third, we see once again just how rich a source the interpersonal is for what is personally so important in emotions and related values.

5 Who gets angry on behalf of whom

We now turn to a related but somewhat different aspect of anger: who gets angry on behalf of whom. We have already noted on behalf of whom, according to Aristotle, *orgē* is to be felt, whom "honorable men [are] bound to champion," namely "our parents, children, wives, or subjects" (*Rht.* II.2, 1379b28 ff.). Investigating a parallel question for us – whom we feel bound to champion – would, no doubt, repay the labor. But because of the size of this task, we will here make only some very brief comments about the sociology and interpersonal relations of our anger – those on whose behalf we get angry.

Let us start by noting how people might be annoyed, even angered, by others getting angry on their behalf, thinking this presumptuous, not the proper concern of these people; or, if those others are their parents, thinking this shows that their parents are thus failing to treat them as independent.

Here, we must ask about the age of the child. If very young, almost any insult may arouse and merit anger from the parents. An exception will probably have to be made for insults which are part and parcel of "normal" children's play. But if the insult is, say, of the child's schoolwork by a teacher or other authority – perhaps one who said, "Since you are a girl, you cannot be expected to do any better," "All you people are sloppy thinkers" – then parents' lack of anger suggests something wrong, such as forced or craven acceptance of inferiority or an indifference to the child. Matters are different if the child has grown up and is well into professional life and, say, has a book reviewed insultingly by a leading authority in the field. Here the parents' simply commiserating with the child may be an entirely adequate response, and their anger, especially if expressed publicly, inappropriate. It might, however, be completely appropriate for the author's colleagues and others in the field to be angry and to show that.

As just seen, we must also ask who feels the anger. In some families, only one parent gets angry on behalf of children. Perhaps quite generally, only one parent is emotional. Sometimes this is really how it is, and sometimes the nonemotional parent is emotional by means of that other parent, who is emotional for both of them. Or there may be a division of emotional labor that is more related to particular concerns. In regard to many matters, it may be held to be a mother's job to get angry at how the children are treated. The father may be called upon to get angry only for certain, perhaps very grave, wrongs. Some or all of these divisions of emotional labor might be thought pathological. But in different societies, various of them are also the social norm.

In laying out these possibilities, we are, clearly, making significant assumptions, among other things, about what these people and their societies are like. If it is seen that we are doing this, and why we are doing it, one of the central points of this work will have been made: that emotions show – and cannot be understood, unless we understand – much about a person and much about that person's society. Even if we disagree with Aristotle about particular conditions for anger, we agree with him that to understand and evaluate anger and other emotions, we depend on such categories as the personal, the impersonal, the institutional, and the general.

6 Closeness and identification

In this section, we will examine closeness, another of the highly complex, variegated combined psychological and sociological categories illustrated by Aristotelian *orgē*. This will involve us, almost immediately, with identification. Both closeness and identification come in a huge, perhaps an unending, and perhaps even a bewildering number of varieties. To mention only some that have been mentioned, there are the different closenesses and forms of identification of feeling called upon to answer for others, of identifying with the aggressor, and of affiliation; and to mention two sorts of negative closeness and identification, we have those of contempt or hate for the weak, and those of differentiation. This great variety is only to be expected: closeness and identification are or constitute aspects, grounds, and sorts of interpersonal relationships as well as what intrapersonally helps account for and constitute these relationships. To see the great variety of these relationships is, in effect, to see the great variety of forms of closeness and identification; and conversely. Correlatively, to see the moral importance of either the relationships or those forms is to see the moral importance of the other, and indeed of both.

This said, let us investigate some forms of closeness and identification shown by Aristotle's account of *orgē*. He says that for a man to feel *orgē*, he must feel himself or his friends slighted by some particular other person. Among other things, this implies that a person cannot have *orgē* toward himself – for something that he did, whether or not to himself. In this way, we find *orgē* similar to some of our emotions of or connected with anger. We do not think that one can be aggrieved or righteously indignant about what one did – whether or not to oneself. Nor do we think it possible to be insolent to oneself. But we do think it possible to spite, abase, insult, and show contempt or disrespect for oneself. And, of course, for these last reasons, and for many other reasons, one can be annoyed or angry at oneself.

The reasons why some of these and other emotions do and some do not apply to oneself are, themselves, a mixed lot. In this, the issues are like those surrounding the doctrine that *volenti non fit inuria,* that in acting voluntarily one cannot wrong oneself or treat oneself unjustly.[37] Aristotle held a version of this, as do many other philosophers. Some hold it because of the central conceptual role they give to voluntariness in accounts of justice. Others hold it for more empirical reasons, holding that interests are central to justice, and holding further that it is impossible, or just too unlikely, that people would voluntarily and knowingly go against their interests. But we reject that claim, because we think that people all too easily and all too frequently cheat themselves and let themselves be treated unjustly – for example, by not insisting on their due or by being too helpful and too accommodating, or by too frequently putting the interests of others before their own.

But we do agree that *orgē* cannot be felt toward oneself, and we also hold that one cannot be aggrieved or righteously indignant about oneself, and that one cannot be insolent to oneself. We are confident about this, even though we do not have much of an explanation for it. Perhaps insolence is central to such anger. Contempt and spite could also be important, at least in their insolent variations: insolent spite and insolent contempt. Or perhaps the difficulty in allowing for the desire for self-regarding retaliation and revenge is important in explaining why *self*-regarding *orgē*-like anger is not possible. Perhaps that desire is conceptually essential for *orgē*-like anger: if one does not desire revenge and retaliation, then whatever one's emotion, it is not *orgē*-like anger. Or perhaps the relation is somewhat more indirect, showing the essentially interpersonal nature of *orgē,* and also of feeling aggrieved and righteous indignation, to mention only some forms of anger.

In any case, some forms of our anger do seem like *orgē* in regard to one issue of closeness. But we may disagree about whether even these forms of anger require closeness of the injured party. After all, we can and do get angry over the treatment of strangers. But we are unsure whether this shows

---

37 *NE* V.11. Thanks are owed to Bonny Kent for discussion of these issues.

a difference between us and Aristotle's man over causes of anger or alternatively whether it shows that 'anger' sometimes is a poor translation of '*orgē*'.

To support the latter, we should note that at least often, we differentiate between personal and impersonal anger. If we are angered by a slight to a friend, especially a close friend, we may say, "I feel this personally," "I am personally offended, personally angered by this," or "I am aggrieved by this." We do not think these would be said – nor that the feelings they express and report would be felt – where the ground of anger is a stranger's being insulted.

We can feel our friend's slight. Sometimes we are hurt by their hurt. We not only feel for them, we feel with them. We can join them in feeling this personally and being aggrieved. But with strangers, it is unusual, and perhaps difficult, to do more than sympathize with them for their hurt and for being slighted.[38]

Further, if all our forms of anger were indifferent to closeness, then what angers us when a stranger is unjustifiably slighted should be, at least often, the stranger's being unjustifiably slighted. But we think what angers us is, at least generally, if not almost always, the stranger's being unjustifiably *harmed:* harmed *as it happens* by an unjustifiable slight. The anger does not seem to be over the stranger's unjustifiable slight *qua* such a slight. It seems to be the same as anger over unjustifiable harms, whether slights or not.

The only seeming exceptions that we can think of are no exceptions at all. I can be aggrieved by and take it personally if you harm or insult a stranger in my presence. For I can take what you did as showing that you think I do not care about such things or as showing that you do not think me good or important enough so that you have to be on good behavior around me. But in such a case, what I feel personally is your slight to me, not to the stranger. So too, I can be aggrieved by and take personally harm to a stranger if I somehow feel responsibility for the stranger, and feel aggrieved because my responsibility was not properly discharged or respected. But here, I am directly concerned, by way of the responsibility I was unable to discharge.

The closeness of the anger we have just been discussing is somewhat like, but should be distinguished from, anger aroused in me by the misdeeds of

---

[38] In "Expressivism, Morality, and the Emotions," *Ethics,* 104 (1994) 739–763, Justin D'Arms and Daniel Jacobson discuss how anger can vary in ways that vary with varying closeness. We clearly agree with this. And we also agree with their argument that this is a serious, if not insuperable, problem for the expressivist account of wrongness given in Allan Gibbard, *Wise Choices, Apt Feelings* (Cambridge, Mass.: Harvard University Press, 1990).

people I identify with, those who are close to me.[39] I may be righteously indignant about and aggrieved by the misdeeds of my country or its leaders – such as the contemptuous, spiteful, or insolent way they are treating another country or a local minority. Here, the anger is not over the fact that they thought me unimportant: that notwithstanding my opposition to what they were planning to do, they still did it. How, without megalomania, could I think that they should have paid attention to me and taken note of my importance, and that they should have listened to me?

Rather, my anger is grounded on two other features. It is about what they did, their bad action. Here, both that *they* did it, and also *what* they did are important. We typically do not get angry at similarly bad acts done by other countries – or more exactly, countries with which we do not identify, which are harming others with whom we also do not identify. But in the case of my anger at misdeeds by my country, I do identify with the country and its leaders. I feel them to be close enough to me so that what they do arouses my anger.

We have already seen (in Chapter 8, section 2) how closeness is important for anger – by being a cause of it. As noted in the discussion of affiliative versus differentiating character sorts, some people identify negatively and hostilely with those they feel similar to, getting angry at them, precisely to differentiate themselves from these others. As Vladimir Jankélévitch put how these people may think:

My identity, in relation to you, consists precisely of the ways in which I am different from you. . . . the more you resemble me the harder it is for anyone to see these crucial differences. Our resemblance threatens to obliterate everything that is special about me. . . . I have no alternative but to hate you, because by working up a rage against you I am defending everything that is unique about me.[40]

This or a similar sort of identification can be heightened by your feeling, correctly or not, that you are seen and identified as joined with those others; and by your feeling, correctly or not, that you are called upon to answer for those others. So, as discussed in Sartre's *Anti-Semite and Jew,* just as anti-Semites may use the misdeeds of any Jew to downgrade any other Jew, anti-Semites may also think that any Jew can be called on to answer for the misdeeds of any other Jew. But neither a French Jew nor a French Catholic is likely to think that just any French Catholic can be called upon to answer for just any French Catholic. Similarly, many Whites in the

---

39 Thanks are owed to Sidney Morgenbesser for pointing out and discussing this additional sort of identification.
40 As presented by Paul Berman in his "The Other and the Almost the Same," *New Yorker,* 70, no. 2 (February 28, 1994) 61–71, p. 62.

contemporary United States call on Black leaders to answer for, to denounce and disavow, objectionable statements made by other Blacks, especially other Black leaders. This is so even though the Whites know that the Blacks they call upon to answer for those others have no control over those others, and indeed have no connection with them except that they all are Black or Black leaders; and even though, typically, Whites do not see the need for them or their White leaders (often they are, themselves, those leaders) to condemn objectionable statements made by Whites about Blacks.

Just as those who are targets of prejudice may be called upon to answer for the misdeeds of others "like them," they may, in various ways, accept this role. Some accept it explicitly and publicly – defending, explaining, disavowing, attacking their fellows. Some others, while denying any responsibility for those others, and any responsibility to answer for them, nonetheless do at least give the appearance of accepting one or both of these sorts of responsibility – as shown by their embarrassment and shame over the misdeeds of those others.

Sartre suggests that this sort of identification – feeling called upon to answer for others "like you" – is a characteristic of victims, of anti-Semitism and racism, say; and that it is not a characteristic of those who are and feel themselves full and powerful members of society. So, French Jews have this sort of identification with other French Jews, but French Catholics do not have it with other French Catholics.

This is not merely a matter of identification – if, indeed, there are any cases of *mere* identification. Those who are prejudiced are often extremely sensitive to, on the look out for, misdeeds – or what can be portrayed as misdeeds – done by those they are prejudiced against. So, anti-Semites might well focus on misdeeds by a Jew who is a complete stranger to them and who has harmed people who are also complete strangers to them. They may be glad and feel vindicated in having their views "confirmed." They may also be glad to join in, even initiate, anger against this Jew. Here, there is a closeness born, not of caring identification, but of negative identification, born from and filled with hate.

This seems right so far as it goes. But it may be useful to expand on some points. First, let us consider some interpersonal, social, and political assumptions. Sartre claims that French anti-Semitism of his time is intelligible only as an interplay of post-Enlightenment individualism, on the one hand, and on the other, atavistic, essentially magical, noncausal forms of thinking of people as members of communities, races, and the like. He claims that French anti-Semites think of themselves in terms of belonging to a mystical union of the real French, and that they also think of all Jews in terms of belonging to a mystical union of the whole body of Jews. On the other hand, those who embrace post-Enlightenment individualism – according to Sartre, most French Jews and many other French people – think of themselves as individuals, who happen to be French or Jewish or both.

Identification of people, others or oneself, in terms of a group can give expression to prejudice, such as anti-Semitism or racism. And perhaps such prejudice requires thinking of people that way. Nonetheless, such identification need not have anything to do with prejudice. It may bespeak some other sort of group solidarity, having nothing to do, as victim or victimizer, with prejudice. Indeed, if Sartre is right in holding that group identification was typical of pre-Enlightenment thought, we can see that, at least in pre-Enlightenment times, such identification need not show prejudice. It may have "merely" coexisted with prejudice, sharing causes, and providing fertile ground for prejudice.

Identification, as it figures in prejudice, often involves being or feeling called upon to answer for strangers who are "like you." Indeed, being or feeling so called upon is one of the significant features of this sort of identification. It often involves a very particular sort of power relation. Not just anyone can make me, or make me feel, answerable for others, especially for strangers; and if I do or can refuse to be or feel answerable for others, I thereby show my power. So, prejudice – with its demands of being answerable for others, including strangers – involves a very significant power relation of correlative superiority and inferiority.

We certainly agree that group identification coupled with such demands of answering for others can show prejudice. Sartre claims that this is how it was for French anti-Semites and Jews. But there are any number of explanations of why people are or feel themselves called upon to answer for people, including strangers, "like them." Some explanations involve power relations essential to prejudice. But some show power relations that are not connected with prejudice. So, a parent may tell the oldest child, "You will have to answer for any mischief these younger ones do." Similarly, a conqueror may tell leaders of a defeated community, "You will be made to answer for any trouble any of your people cause us."

Further, even where being or feeling oneself called upon to answer for others involves power relations, it need not give expression to superiority or inferiority. It can be freely and willingly assumed by an equal as a pledge or bond, in order to gain position and power: to gain an official position, I could affirm that I will answer for any errors the others make. It can also be part of a project of self-aggrandizement or of arrogating power to oneself:

"I am the representative for these people." Although we easily could, there is no need to continue adding to this list.

Let us consider some other sorts of determinants of being or feeling called upon to answer for strangers who are "like you." Many people think that the Germans, even those born after the end of World War II, should identify with and feel shame over what their country and fellow Germans did in that war. And many Germans did feel such shame. Perhaps what is operative here is the severe gravity of what Germany and the Germans did. We offer this as a psychological account, not a moral account: we can see how the gravity can "force" such identification without thinking that the justifiability of such identification depends on such gravity.

In addition, context can be important for identification. Some people are embarrassed if, while in a foreign country, they see another person from their country acting boorishly, for example by treating a postal clerk with contempt. Others may see the person from their country act boorishly, and simply shrug or simply feel sorry for the clerk. But few of even the first sort of people would feel much, if anything, about the same sort of rudeness to a postal clerk back home. They may experience it simply as a bit of unpleasantness that in no way bears on them at all, much less all people of their country.

There are innumerable other ways context can be important. To pick one at random, some people are embarrassed by, even ashamed over, a family member doing in public what, when done at home, is accepted without any adverse feeling – for example, telling dialect jokes or burping. Other people are "more consistent," accepting the same behavior in both places or finding it embarrassing in both. The embarrassment, whether consistent or not, may suggest enmeshment, a particular sort of excessive identification. (Enmeshment is discussed in Chapter 3, section 4, and Chapter 6, section 2.) But enmeshment is only one sort or explanation of excessive identification, embarrassed or not. Others have to do with shame and concerns about how one is seen in certain public arenas.

As we have seen, then, there is no one sort or account of identification and closeness. We have also seen that there are any number of different social, psychological, and contextual grounds and factors important for them. And we have also seen that different cases or sorts of anger can involve different sorts of identification and closeness, some of which are very similar to, perhaps even the same as, and some of which are significantly different from those found in *orgē*.

One difference worth a further comment is that, as we have seen, in many cases of our anger, unlike that of *orgē,* the closeness is between the angry person and the perpetrator of the misdeed, not between the angry person and someone who suffers from the misdeed. Perhaps Aristotle should have included this sort of closeness as another ground for *orgē*. After all, it does seem to be another ground for at least some of our *orgē*-like sorts of anger, such as being aggrieved or righteously indignant. We say this without in any way denying that there are also some important differences between anger grounded by the misdeeds of those we feel close to, and the clearly *orgē*-like anger grounded in the harms suffered by those close to us.

Let us turn now to closely related, but different aspects of *orgē*. We have already seen how the desire for retaliation and revenge is important for *orgē* and how it is important for various sorts of our *orgē*-like anger. We do not think a desire for retaliation and revenge need be part of our anger at those close to us. We may "only" feel sad, embarrassed, regretful, remorseful, ashamed, or revolted. These combine with the anger to give us, for example, anger tinged with sadness, or anger fueled by revulsion. Similarly, even if I cannot be righteously indignant about or aggrieved by what *I* do to others or myself, I can be angry at myself for this, and in my anger at myself I can be sad, embarrassed, regretful, remorseful, ashamed, or revolted.

Consider the anger of anti-Semites, as discussed by Sartre, and the anger of those who want to differentiate themselves from those they feel too similar to themselves, as discussed by Jankélévitch in Berman's "The Other and the Almost the Same." Such anger often, even typically, includes the desire that the targeted people suffer. Indeed, especially for those Sartre discusses, it is almost as if – if it is not simply that – they want those targets to continue to exist to be hated and made to suffer, rather than just disappear. In this, their desire is like the desire Aristotle says is involved in *orgē*, in contrast with the desire involved in *echthra*, enmity: those with *orgē* "would have offenders suffer for what they have done," whereas those with *echthra* "would have them cease to exist" (*Rht* II.4, 1382a15 ff.).

Nonetheless, we may not want to call such desire for suffering a desire for revenge and retaliation. For the misdeed that is said to be the ground of anger anger may really function as little more than an excuse or a welcomed opportunity for wanting and even enacting what is, for unprincipled reasons, falsely characterized as revenge and retaliation. Both the anger and its attendant desire to cause suffering are moodlike: they are preexisting, freestanding, and ready to hand, just awaiting an opportunity to show themselves.

We have seen enough to recognize that closeness is needed to help us understand how people feel connected enough, close enough, to misdeeds and harms done to or by others to be angered by those misdeeds, harms, or people. This is important both for our general understanding of our forms of anger, and also for helping us see that various forms of our anger, like *orgē*, require closeness.

Much remains be to investigated about closeness. We have not examined, except very cursorily, either the detailed or the general natures and roles of closeness – not even in regard to one form of anger, much less in regard to the varieties of anger and of other emotions and relations. Nor have we discussed the ontological or methodological question of whether closeness explains anger, or rather is shown in and by anger. Nor have we examined whether *orgē* and one or more of our sorts of anger involve the same sort or sorts of closeness. More generally, we have yet to see whether closeness – perhaps of the same sort, perhaps not – figures differently in emotions described by Aristotle and our emotions, and correlatively, whether his people are different from us in regard to closeness.

These are immensely important issues. But they are also immensely large issues. Since we have already said something about anger and closeness – perhaps enough to point the way to these further investigations – we will only make some very brief observations about how various other emotions, some as described by Aristotle and some as experienced by us, are sensitive to closeness and relationship. This, in turn, will help us see how these and other emotions help explain, show, and constitute structures of attachment, closeness, and vulnerability.

Let us start with an issue that has received some attention recently, and that has come up in various ways throughout this work: distinguishing between shame and guilt. Even if it is easy enough to determine which of these is being experienced, it is notoriously difficult to describe the differences between them. These differences will, of course, be between characterizations, not instances, of shame and guilt. After all, in some cases I can feel guilty and ashamed over exactly the same matter for exactly the same reasons.

Certainly, the categories often used – responsibility and control, acts versus states of character, and the identity of the agent – are insufficient, and they are often of little, if any, use. *Responsibility and control:* I can feel regret and also fully fledged guilt over what I know I was inculpably unable to avoid, such as failing to discharge a parental obligation. So too, even though I know that my inability is inculpable, I can still feel ashamed over doings or nondoings, such as not discharging that obligation; over states of character, such as being afraid of heights; and over states of my body, such as a physical deformity.[41]

---

[41] See, for example, Robert Adams, "Involuntary Sins," *Philosophical Review*, 94 (1985), 3–

As to *acts versus states of character,* I can feel both ashamed and guilty about what I did. So too, I can feel both ashamed and guilty that I have a state of character, such as being meanspirited. As to *the identify of the agent,* I can feel guilty over what I did or what I am like, and I can also feel ashamed of both of these. And as just seen, I can also feel guilty or ashamed of others for their acts or states of character.

What may be of use, however, are the particular and differing ways we may identify *with* ourselves or others for shame or guilt to be possible or alternatively impossible. As noted, I can feel guilty or ashamed about the doings or character of my government, or my children, or, when abroad, the rudeness of a fellow American. But special stories apart, I cannot feel guilty or ashamed about the doings of a foreign government, or about a complete stranger. Even if we were able to give a complete account of the differences between shame and guilt, doing so would lead too far afield. But we can make several points and suggestions that might be useful. There are various sorts of grounds for being able or unable to have such guilt and such shame in these different cases, and for what would be in those special stories. These grounds are also grounds for different sorts of identification. Differences in identification are among the important differences between shame and guilt, because of the different ways these identifications involve the self, or different aspects of the self, or even different sorts of selves.

Here we might consider the various ways we identify with others, including the various ways we can be enmeshed with them, to see the ways we are identifying with them when we feel ashamed of them. So too, we might look at the different sorts of identification and self-distancing found in compassion toward oneself and self-pity. For, as it seems to us, self-distancing is a feature of at least many instances of guilt over just having a characteristic. (This guilt is to be differentiated from guilt over doing something that engendered the characteristic or over not doing something that would eliminate it). At least often, when we feel guilty over such a characteristic, we are – or it is as if we are – treating ourselves externally, like someone else, in much the manner of self-exhortation.

Let us now turn to some ways closeness is important in some other, and more everyday, nontheoretical ways. We will start with minor, but common enough, emotions about cars and driving. Those who would query our use of such cases and emotions – thinking perhaps that they are trivial or

---

31; Nathaniel West, *Miss Lonelyhearts* (New York: New Directions, 1969); and Erving Goffman, *Stigma, Notes on the Management of Spoiled Identity* (Englewood Cliffs, N.J.: Prentice-Hall, 1963).

are too involved with day-to-day life – should remember that Oedipus slew his father in a fight over who should give way to whom at a crossroads.

It is hardly noteworthy if I am annoyed by your delaying me by driving too slowly. But, special considerations apart, I will likely not be annoyed by your delaying others by driving too slowly. Some of those special considerations change the case so that once again, you cause me bother. I might be waiting for the other people you delay. Another sort of such considerations is far more important for present purposes. Here, because of the ways I care for those others, even identify with them, I am annoyed by your delaying them.

Or consider another driving case: parking a car well out from the side of the road, rather than pulling close to the curb. We know many people who react with amused contempt to any driver who parks this way delaying others. But, when they, themselves, suffer such delays, they typically react with annoyance, even anger, rarely with contempt. And still more rarely – and then only in somewhat special frames of mind, such as some forms of detachment and ruefulness – do they react with amused contempt.

In these cases, differences in emotional distance engender different emotions – annoyance if I or someone close to me is delayed, and perhaps no feeling at all or amused contempt if a stranger is delayed. As this shows, closeness and distance cannot be seen simply as bearing on the strength of an emotion – as if a change in distance only changes the strength of what is otherwise the same emotional response.

Fear and pity, *phobos* and *eleos,* as understood by Aristotle, are also good examples of how emotional distance and difference of emotions are interrelated. (See Chapter 9, sections 3–5.) He holds that, in general and with an important proviso about closeness, whatever causes me to feel fear when it threatens or happens to me, causes me to feel pity when it threatens or happens to others (*Rht* II.5, 1382b26 ff., and II.8, 1385b27 ff.). Fear and pity, then, are about the same harms and dangers. The difference is that in the case of fear, I am the harmed or threatened person, whereas for pity, someone else is. More exactly, although fear for oneself receives almost all his attention, he allows that one can fear also for those who are very close to one. So, a parent can fear for a child (*NE* III.6, 1115a22 ff., and *Rht* II.8, 1386a19 ff.). Pity, too, requires closeness. The person who pities must feel close enough to the pitied person (*Rht* II.8, 1386a17 ff.) – but far enough away not to fall within the range of fear.

Thus, according to Aristotle, whether danger to a person arouses in me fear, pity, or neither – and perhaps no feeling at all or only sadness and regret – depends on the closeness of the endangered person to me. And this closeness is shown by whether danger arouses fear, pity, or neither. Similarly, whether a slight to someone angers me depends on and shows that person's closeness to me.

For some of us, however, pity can range far more widely.[42] It can extend to those who are quite distant. We may even pity animals, such as a wounded sparrow seen along the roadside. We think that this shows that our experiences of closeness — of feeling close, and thus being close — differs from Aristotle's men's.

This may suggest that our evaluative-emotional world is less concerned with closeness and relations than Aristotle's. Perhaps this is right, or perhaps just as we are indifferent to some areas of closeness Aristotle's people were concerned with, they are indifferent to some areas that are of concern to us. Such comparisons, especially when they go into issues of amount — who cares more about closeness — are difficult and, too often, unrewarding. Rather than pursue them, we want to turn to what might be thought to be a principled reason for rejecting the importance of closeness for emotions. This reason is made up of two parts. The first asserts universality, holding that emotions should be mediated only by value, no matter whose. The second asserts proportionality, holding that emotions should be proportional in strength to the amount of value involved.

(There is a familiar analog to this conjoint view about emotions about acts. This is the claim that only value and its amount, not whose it is or its kind, are relevant for act evaluations. Such a view holds that the distinction between self and other should make no difference to act evaluations, and that the "strength" of act evaluations is proportional to the amount of value involved. Straightforward consequentialist maximization is one such theory.)

We reject that claim of universalistic proportionality. And we reject both its claim of universalism and its claim of proportionality. We think it is quite generally true that, for us as well as for Aristotle's people, emotions that are appropriate and that show one to be a good person need not vary just with the value of what the emotion is about.

This can be put in terms of what we have written. The present claim goes well beyond what one of us argued elsewhere: that the self–other distinction is foundational for thought about ethics and, more generally, about people; and that, frequently enough, what would be anomalous and in need of justification is the lack, not the presence, of moral distinctions between self and other.[43] As much of this book is meant to show, understanding

---

42 Thanks are owed to Jonathan Bennett for discussion here.
43 On that distinction, see Stocker, "Agent and Other: Against Ethical Universalism,"

emotions and evaluations in terms of sorts and degrees of distance and closeness complements, and indeed improves on, understanding them in terms of just the self–other distinction.

This has been argued for in any number of ways. But to put it here, let us start by noting that in terms of value taken generally, atrocities and massacres are hugely worse than the death of a parent, say. The view that emotions should be proportional to value would, thus, hold that the proper emotional reaction to the massacres and atrocities should be hugely greater than the appropriate bereavement and mourning. Perhaps we can imagine what such hugely stronger or hugely greater emotions would be: for example, suffering long periods of intense self-torment followed by a painful suicide or lifelong service or devotion to the memory of the victims. But these are not required.[44] And in many cases, they are inappropriate – an inappropriate giving up on life or a lack of due moral and emotional proportion.

We should add that these last claims are about people who merely know about these happenings, and perhaps have suffered from them. They are not about people who bear responsibility for these losses and terrible events. The emotional demands on those who bear responsibility for the happenings may well be different. For some of these people, it might be that nothing in a human life would be adequate – not even long periods of self-torment followed by a painful suicide or a life of service and devotion to the memory of their victims or to helping survivors or some other appropriate people.

Were our emotional responses, or our proper and appropriate emotional responses, proportional to value, it would be near enough impossible to explain how we could, or should be able to, read in a calm and unbothered way about past atrocities, such as those done by Ghengis Khan. Unless for some special reason, we get caught up in the story, we do not feel fear for his victims. We doubt if we even feel pity for them. It is not that we think they

---

Australasian Journal of Philosophy, 54 (1976) 206–220. See also Michael Slote, "Morality and Self–Other Asymmetry," *Journal of Philosophy,* 81 (1984) 179–192. In *From Morality to Virtue* (New York: Oxford University Press, 1992), Slote holds that this asymmetry is anomalous, and to be explained away or at least shown not basic. See also Stocker's commentary on *From Morality to Virtue,* "Self–Other Asymmetries and Virtue Theory," *Philosophy and Phenomenological Research,* 54 (1994) 689–694, and Slote's reply, "Reply to Commentators," *Philosophy and Phenomenological Research,* 54 (1994) 709–719.

44 Thanks are owed to Frances Kamm for this example. A locus classicus of the general problem of how much regret one should feel is Bernard Williams, "Moral Luck," in his *Philosophical Papers* (Cambridge: Cambridge University Press, 1982). On mourning and its excesses, see Sigmund Freud, "Mourning and Melancholia."

do not deserve our pity. Rather, we feel little more than a small shudder of sadness on their behalf – so little that it is too much to say that we feel even a slight amount of pity for them. They are simply too distant from us to affect us even that much.

Matters are different if one identifies with those victims – as, say, present-day Jews do with the victims of the Holocaust, as present-day Armenians do with those killed in their dispersal and massacres following the First World War, and present-day Afro-Americans do with those who died while being transported to be slaves or while they were slaves. Our point here is not that only those who already identify with these and other victims can feel for them. Rather, it is to suggest that at least part of what it means to identify in these cases is to feel with and for these victims.

To draw several final conclusions about distance and closeness: first, these last cases may not be entirely useful in helping us with the literal understanding of the earlier question, Can we can feel something like *orgē* for strangers, or can they evoke only our less personal anger? Our reason for thinking this is that these victims may not be, in the required sense, strangers to those who now identify with them. But these cases may be very useful in helping us with a different, and we think deeper, understanding of that question: what is it to be a stranger, and who is a stranger to whom?

Second, we see that distance can be both an explanation and also a justification for not being emotionally engaged with certain values at all, or not being engaged with them in proportion to how much general value they involve. (For this to be more than a definitional point, distance and closeness cannot be given simply by amount of engagement.)

Third, various emotions which are absolutely basic and central to our life and to our values are sensitive to self and other, and distance and closeness, not just value and amount of value. This goes a long way toward showing that at least some of our basic values and evaluative structures are to be understood in terms of self and other, and distance and closeness, not just value and amount of value.

7 Size

This section continues our criticism of universalism and proportionality in regard to emotions. Let us start with Aristotle's claim that "On some actions . . . forgiveness is [bestowed], when one does what he ought not under pressure which overstrains human nature and which no one could withstand" (*NE* III.1, 1110a23 ff.). This may be talking only about second-person or third-person evaluations and emotions: those concerning other people and their acts. If so, a close analog also holds for first-person evaluations of acts and agents, and emotions about these. In first-, second-, and third-person cases, even if an act that merits forgiveness involves far more disvalue than an act that merits blame, the act that merits forgiveness can also merit a far "gentler" emotion than the act that involves less disvalue. So too, in regard to the agent: the agent who is overstrained may deserve no blame at all, but only pity or forgiveness, while the other may deserve no pity or forgiveness, but only blame – again, even though the former may have done what involves far more disvalue.

Much the same holds for events that "merely" befall people. Some losses – such as the death of a young child by murder, an accident, or illness – may so overstrain a person that no accurate correlation can be made between the value of what happened and the strength of the "proper" emotion. At least as clearly, no such correlation can be made between the value of what happened and an evaluation of a person for having or not having emotions of the "right" strength.

Consider, for example, a person whose child has just been murdered. We can easily imagine this person in quiet, dissociated shock, or wild with grief, or filled with vengeful rage, or stunned over what society has become, or saddened to the core. We find none of these emotions even questionable, much less untoward or indicative of a poor character. And indeed, we do not have much, if any, sense of what would be the right amount of emotion – right, either in regard to what was suffered or the emotions a good person would have. In contrast, however, it is easy to see how we might think poorly of, or at least have serious questions about, a parent who felt no more concern about a child being in danger of losing an arm to an infection than about the child's suffering a minor burn. This holds both for a parent who "downgrades" the former to the level of the latter, or who magnifies the latter to the level of the former.

We must add that our claims concerning emotions about terrible events are consistent with also holding that some emotions and emotional reactions to these terrible events are, at best, questionable, if not deplorable. Here we might consider parents who – not as a manifestation of shock, but quite sincerely and as an accurate and straightforward expression of their feelings about the death of their infant – say, "Well, you win some, you lose some."

To this, too, we must add something: these comments are about people like us – that is, people with adequate medical care, living in adequately safe environments, and the like. But lacking these, many other people have only a small proportion of their children live to the age of five. For these people, a lack of emotional investment in infants and young children might be precisely what is called for and what even the best people in those situations would feel.[45]

A general point about the cases just considered should be made. Especially in those cases where people are overstrained, the criteria and measure for evaluating acts and agents are not, or not largely, the value or disvalue of what is done or of what happens. Similarly, the criteria and measure for the appropriateness of emotions about such doings and those who do them are not just the value or disvalue of those doings. Rather, at least to some large degree, it has to do with the person and how the person came to be in such a situation, how the person bears it, and so on.

If I am terrified by snakes, I might feel overstrained, driven to distraction and crazed, by the thought of continuing down a path on which I see a snake I know to be relatively harmless. But my being overwhelmed and crazed by the snake tells against me. It shows me weak, or soft, or phobic, or with some other defect. Further, that poor evaluation of me carries over, in complex ways, to evaluations of my terror and other attendant emotions. The matter is quite different for those who are overstrained by what is truly overstraining – such as, on some accounts anyway, Agamemnon by having to choose between Iphigeneia and the progress of the fleet against Troy. Such people may deserve pity and forgiveness, not blame. Correlatively, their terror or madness may deserve acceptance, or, at the least, no adverse word or thought, and perhaps even a compassionate lack of scrutiny and attention.[46]

8 Conclusion

Too much material was covered in this chapter for a substantive summary. But this more methodological one may be of some use. Focusing on *orgē*, this chapter was a case study of many of the claims made earlier in the work. These included claims about the very complex and equally important relations between value and affectivity. They also included claims that an understanding of emotions – even one emotion of one sort of person – requires the resources and techniques of philosophy, psychoanalysis, sociology, anthropology, and history, to name only some of the needed disciplines.

---

45 On this see, for example, Nancy Scheper-Hughes, *Death without Weeping: The Violence of Everyday Life in Brazil* (Berkeley: University of California Press, 1992).
46 In developing these views about what overstrains us, we think we join, and we know we have been helped by, Williams, *Shame And Necessity*, pp. 134–135.

11

Some final conclusions

The issue of "size," discussed in the previous chapter, raises many general issues that must be settled to complete the task of *Valuing Emotions*. It does this by raising the issue of how emotions, especially how appropriate emotions, are related to what we are like and to our human possibilities. To appreciate – to understand and evaluate – the connections between emotions and value and evaluation, this is one of the most important, and most difficult areas needing investigation.

But if, as I believe, that is an area of central concern for ethics, we have no real option but to emphasize and investigate the importance of emotions for value and evaluation – and correlatively no real option but to give up hope, or even an interest, in many other forms of ethics. I mean those that look beyond humans to some feature or possibility of reason, the universe, or whatever. This choice – between the importance of emotions and a "pure" ethics or at least an ethics not based on people – may be central to the long-standing worry about the importance of emotions for ethics. For many theorists, emotions are just too human-centered.

To be sure, even for theorists who are willing to deal with what is human-centered, many issues remain. One very large one that has come up repeatedly in this work – sometimes explicitly and more often implicitly – has to do with what probative force, if any, is to be attached to emotions and the values they help constitute and in this and other ways reveal; and, how is this to be shown, or argued for, even to those sympathetic to such answers?

I think it is important, even necessary, to use and reuse what lies behind Strawson's claim that "The existence of the general framework of attitudes itself is something we are given with the fact of human society."[1] But in doing this, we must also examine that fact of human society. And this, I

---

1 "Freedom and Resentment," reprinted in Gary Watson, ed., *Free Will* (Oxford: Oxford University Press, 1982), p. 78.

think, requires us to raise, and try to answer, a very general worry that Samuel Levey put to me in discussion:

> It may well be both that all the forms of society we can imagine involve reactive attitudes and also that humans can be imagined only as living in such forms of society and as having reactive attitudes. For all that, these forms can also embody incompatible views: that moral responsibility requires reactive attitudes, but that the world allows only for objective attitudes. Thus, we may have to take Strawson as showing that all forms of society we can imagine, because they require reactive attitudes, also require self-deception or some other way of not thinking about the way the world is.

Many will dismiss this worry, thinking it just too metaphysical. Many of these people, and some others too, may also think that it somehow undercuts itself by taking seriously – perhaps even talking from a standpoint that requires – the elimination of what makes it, and our investigation of it, possible. This, of course, is precisely the fact of human society. But many of the same worries about emotions arise from a far less sweeping standpoint. Even from such a standpoint, one can object that more must be done to show the value of acts, relations, and institutions than simply that they are constituted by emotions. Nor, to make a correlative claim, is it enough to show that emotions are necessary for knowledge of what we value. In all cases, we need to evaluate both the emotions and the acts, relations, and institutions.

We can see this at a very low level, one that is safely removed from any hint of metaphysics or of denying or eliminating the fact of human society. Many of us think that *orgē*, as described by Aristotle, is itself deplorable, or that the classical Greek society was in part deplorable because of the many roles of *orgē* in that society. Those who think this are hardly likely to conclude that the values such anger reveals and helps constitute should be accorded much positive weight. Quite generally, where a society is deplorable, we do not say much, if anything, in favor of particular values by saying that they are revealed and constituted by the emotions that also help constitute that society.

This obvious point raises the question of how we are to assess an emotion or emotions, and from what standpoint we are to do so. (This question, clearly, can be limited to one particular emotion, perhaps of one person at one time, or extended to the fact of human, that is emotional, society.) It might be thought that since an emotion is in question, we must find a standpoint that does not involve emotions: that to judge an emotion by emotions would be to let the defendant also be the judge. But, if this is not just a piece of foundationalism, which as such will never be satisfied, it seems just another instance of tendentious treatment of emotions and, implicitly, another instance of tendentious comparisons between emotion and reason. It is, after all, frequently necessary to examine some instances of reasoning, or of principles of reason, perhaps because they have failed us. I doubt it would be held that since instances or principles of reasoning are under investigation, we must go outside of reason.

In any case, many of the most important ways to assess emotions do make use of emotions. In saying this, I recognize how emotions can be criticized for success or failure in serving certain values, for perpetuating certain values and disvalues. The anger described by Aristotle may well give expression to, and also perpetuate, improper hierarchies. However, these criticisms importantly and typically involve emotions, or what can be understood only in terms of emotions.

I have two interrelated sorts of reasons for holding this. The first is found in an augmented version of Strawson's and Taylor's[2] arguments that many of our most important evaluations of emotions, and of social and other structures, are made, and perhaps can be made only, in terms of other emotions or structures constituted by emotions. The augmentation would involve showing that these structures are good, or that enough of them are good enough.

The second – which also plays an important role in this augmentation – is that many criticisms of emotions and, more generally, affectivity, along with structures that depend on them, are made against some conception or other of human life, both intrapersonal life and also interpersonal, social life. And human life is through-and-through affective and in large and important ways constituted or perfected by affectivity. Further, human life, in its various forms, is judged in terms of affectivity – importantly, by whether and how it succeeds or fails in developing, expressing, and satisfying affective needs. And such success or failure is, itself, understood and evaluated in terms of affectivity.

My reply, then, to the worry about the need to evaluate emotions and other affective states is that we can and do evaluate them. We can and we do in fact do this in terms of the lives they foster or hinder. These lives are to a greater or lesser extent constituted or perfected by, and also evaluated in terms of, affective states. Thus, at least one central way to evaluative these lives and their elements is in terms of what affective states they help or

---

2 "Self-Interpreting Animals," in *Human Agency and Language, Philosophical Papers*, volume 1 (Cambridge: Cambridge University Press, 1985).

hinder, engender or preclude. One, but only one, way to do this, then, is in terms of met or unmet emotional needs.

In conclusion, emotions and other affective states are essential to value and are, themselves, valued and valuable. They are forms of lived, engaged, human value. And these include, just to take a very unprincipled selection, the personal, the impersonal, closeness, friend, neighbor, family, stranger, honor and slights. They are central not only to personal life, but also to interpersonal life, and to social and political life. They are also central to what makes these sorts and aspects of lives good, bad, or indifferent. They help show and constitute a considerable part of very large and complex evaluative, psychic, and social worlds. At the same time, they are to be understood within those worlds. In addition, emotional knowledge – including both knowledge and understanding of emotions and also the knowledge shown in emotions – is important, often vital, for knowledge and understanding of value. Indeed, much evaluative knowledge just is such emotional knowledge.

In claiming that emotions help constitute our worlds, I am in no way claiming that they settle all moral issues about those worlds, not even all moral issues about emotions in general, or even all moral issues about the emotions in question. Certain sorts of anger – perhaps even *orgē* – may be expressions of at best dubious, if not immoral, characters and interpersonal or even social relations. And certain emotions, such as those that inform racism, are always dubious, if not immoral.

I think there should be little controversy over this; or even over a claim that naturally goes along with this: that human value and moral wisdom require more than emotions, emotional ability, and emotional knowledge. Both Aristotle and psychoanalysts quite generally, joined by Hegeman and me, and no doubt by most philosophers, insist on this. However, now joined by not so many philosophers – but perhaps several additional ones because of *Valuing Emotions* – we also insist that emotions are of great moral importance, and that human value and moral wisdom require emotions, emotional ability, and emotional knowledge.

References

Adams, Marilyn McCord, "Theodicy without Blame," *Philosophical Topics*, 16 (1988) 215–245.
Adams, Robert, "Involuntary Sins," *Philosophical Review*, 94 (1985), 3–31.
Adkins, Arthur W. H., *Merit and Responsibility* (Oxford: Oxford University Press, 1960).
— "Friendship and 'Self-Sufficiency' in Homer and Aristotle," *Classical Quarterly*, n.s., 13 (1963) 30–45.
Adler, Jonathan, "Testimony, Trust, Knowing," *Journal of Philosophy*, 91 (1994) 264–275.
Alexander, Franz, "Fundamental Concepts of Psychosomatic Research: Psychogenesis, Conversion, Specificity," *Psychosomatic Medicine*, 5 (1943) 205–210.
Alexander, S., "Foundations and Sketch-Plan of a Conational Psychology," *British Journal of Psychology*, (1911).
Alston, William, "Moral Attitudes and Moral Judgments," *Nous*, 2 (1968) 1–23.
— "Feelings," *Philosophical Review*, 78 (1969) 3–34.
Angell, Roger, "The Sporting Scene – Distance," *New Yorker*, 56 (September 22, 1980) 83–127.
Annas, Julia, "Aristotle on Pleasure and Goodness," in Amélie O. Rorty, ed., *Essays on Aristotle's Ethics* (Berkeley: University of California Press, 1980).
Anscombe, Elizabeth, "Modern Moral Philosophy," *Philosophy*, 33 (1958) 1–19.
Aristotle, *Nicomachean Ethics*, translated by W. D. Ross (London: Oxford University Press, 1925).
— *Nicomachean Ethics*, translated by Harris Rackham, Loeb Library (Cambridge, Mass.: Harvard University Press, 1947).
— *Nicomachean Ethics*, translated by W. D. Ross and J. O. Urmson, in Jonathan Barnes, ed., *The Complete Works of Aristotle* (Princeton: Princeton University Press, 1984).
— *Rhetoric*, translated by John Henry Freese, Loeb Library, (London: Heinemann, 1926).
— *Rhetoric*, translated by W. Rhys Roberts, in Jonathan Barnes, ed., *The Complete Works of Aristotle* (Princeton: Princeton University Press, 1984).
Armstrong, David, *A Materialist Theory of the Mind* (New York: Routledge and Kegan Paul, 1968).
Arnold, Magda, *Emotion and Personality* (New York: Columbia University Press, 1960).
Aune, Bruce, *Reason and Action* (Dordrecht: Reidel, 1977).

Autenrieth, Georg, *A Homeric Dictionary* (Norman: University of Oklahoma Press, 1958).
Ayer, Alfred J., *Language, Truth, and Logic* (New York: Dover, 1952).
Bach, Sheldon, *Narcissistic States and the Therapeutic Process* (New York: Jason Aronson, 1985).
Baier, Annette, "Hume's Analysis of Pride," *Journal of Philosophy*, 75 (1978) 27–40.
"Secular Faith," in *Postures of the Mind* (Minneapolis: University of Minnesota Press, 1985).
Balint, Michael, *The Basic Fault, Therapeutic Aspects of Regression* (New York: Brunner Mazel, 1979).
Thrills and Regressions (Madison, Conn.: International Universities Press, 1987).
Bartky, Sandra Lee, *Femininity and Domination* (New York: Routledge, 1990).
Bateson, Gregory, Don Jackson, Jay Haley, and John Weakland, "Toward a Theory of Schizophrenia," *Behavioral Science*, 1 (1956) 251–264, reprinted in M. Berger, ed., *Beyond the Double Bind* (New York: Brunner Mazel, 1978).
Bedford, Errol, "Emotions," *Aristotelian Society Proceedings*, 57 (1956–1957) 281–304.
Benson, John, "Varieties of Desire," *Aristotelian Society Proceedings*, supplementary volume 50 (1976) 177–192.
Berman, Paul, "The Other and the Almost the Same," *New Yorker*, 70, no. 2 (February 28, 1994) 61–71.
Bibring, E., "The Mechanism of Depression," in P. Greenacre, ed., *Affective Disorders* (New York: International Universities Press, 1953).
Block, Ned, "Troubles with Functionalism," in Wade Savage, ed., *Minnesota Studies in the Philosophy of Science*, volume 9 (Minneapolis: University of Minnesota, 1979).
Blum, Lawrence, *Friendship, Altruism, and Morality* (London: Routledge and Kegan Paul, 1980).
"Compassion," in Amélie O. Rorty, ed., *Explaining Emotions* (Berkeley: University of California Press, 1980).
"Iris Murdoch and the Domain of the Moral," *Philosophical Studies*, 50 (1986) 343–368.
"Particularity and Responsiveness," in Jerome Kagan and Sharon Lamb, eds., *The Emergence of Morality in Young Children* (Chicago: University of Chicago Press, 1987).
"Emotion and Moral Reality," unpublished manuscript.
Brenman, M., "On Teasing and Being Teased: And the Problem of 'Moral Masochism'," *Psychoanalytic Study of the Child*, 7 (1952) 264–285.
Brennan, William, "Reason, Passion, and 'The Progress of the Law'," *Cardozo Law Review*, 10 (1988) 3–23.
Brentano, Franz, *The Origin of Our Knowledge of Right and Wrong* (New York: Humanities Press, 1969).
The Psychology of Aristotle (Berkeley: University of California Press, 1977).
Breuer, Josef, and Sigmund Freud, *Studies on Hysteria* (New York: Basic Books, 1957).
Brierley, M., "Affects in Theory and Practice," *International Journal of Psycho-Analysis*, 18 (1937) 256–268.
Broadie, Sarah, *Ethics with Aristotle* (New York: Oxford University Press, 1991).

Bromberg, Philip, "'Speak! That I May See You': Some Reflections on Dissociation, Reality, and Psychoanalytic Listening," *Psychoanalytic Dialogues,* 4 (1994) 517–547.

Buechler, Sandra, "Emotions," in Donnel Stern, John Fiscalini, Carola Mann, and Mary Lou Lionells, eds., *The Handbook of Interpersonal Psychoanalysis* (Hillsdale, N.J.: Analytic Press, 1995).

Bürger-Prinz, H., and M. Kaila, "On the Structure of the Amnesic Syndrome," in David Rapaport, ed., *Organization and Pathology of Thought* (New York: Columbia University Press, 1951).

Burnyeat, Myles, "Aristotle on Learning to be Good," in Amélie O. Rorty, ed., *Essays on Aristotle's Ethics* (Berkeley: University of California Press, 1980).

Cairns, Douglas L., *Aidōs: The Psychology and Ethics of Honour and Shame in Ancient Greek Literature* (Oxford: Oxford University Press, 1993).

Card, Claudia, "Responsibility for Moral Luck," forthcoming in *Character and Moral Luck* (Philadelphia: Temple University Press).

Charles, David, "Aristotle and Modern Realism," in Robert Heinaman, ed., *Aristotle and Moral Realism* (London: University College of London Press, 1995).

Charlton, William, "Force, Form, and Content in Linguistic Expression," *Aristotelian Society Proceedings,* 84 (1983–1984) 123–143.

Weakness of Will (Oxford: Blackwell, 1988).

Chasseguet-Smirgel, Janine, *The Ego Ideal: A Psychoanalytic Essay on the Malady of the Ideal* (New York: Norton, 1984).

Chazan, Pauline, "Moral Theory, Moral Understanding and the Moral Self" (Ph.D. dissertation, University of Melbourne, Victoria, Australia, 1992).

"Pride, Virtue, and Selfhood: A Reconstruction of Hume," *Canadian Journal of Philosophy,* 22 (1992) 45–65.

"Self-Esteem, Self-Respect, and Love of Self: Ways of Valuing the Self," forthcoming in *Philosophia.*

Chodorow, Nancy, *The Reproduction of Mothering* (Berkeley: University of California Press, 1978).

Femininities, Masculinities, Sexualities (Lexington: University of Kentucky Press, 1994).

Cicero, *Tusculan Disputations.*

Daly, Robert W., "Schizoid Rule-Following," *Psychoanalytic Review,* 55 (1968) 400–414.

"The Specters of Technicism," *Psychiatry,* 33 (1970) 417–432.

Damasio, Antonio R., *Descartes' Error: Emotion, Reason, and the Human Brain* (New York: G. P. Putnam's Sons, 1994).

D'Arms, Justin, and Daniel Jacobson, "Expressivism, Morality, and the Emotions," *Ethics,* 104 (1994) 739–763.

Davidson, Donald, "Belief and the Basis of Meaning," *Synthèse,* 27 (1974) 309–323.

"Hume's Cognitive Theory of Pride," *Journal of Philosophy,* 73 (1976) 733–757, reprinted in *Essays on Action and Events* (Oxford: Oxford University Press, 1980).

Deigh, John, "Cognitivism in the Theory of Emotions," *Ethics,* 104 (1994) 824–854.

"Empathy and Universalizability," *Ethics,* 105 (1995) 743–763.

Review of Douglas Walton, *The Place of Emotion in Argument, Informal Logic,* forthcoming.

Dent, Nicholas J. H., "Varieties of Desire," *Aristotelian Society Proceedings,* supplementary volume 50 (1976) 152–176.

Descartes, Rene, *The Passions of the Soul,* in *The Philosophical Works of Descartes* translated by Elizabeth S. Haldane and G. R. T. Ross (New York: Dover, 1931).

DeSousa, Ronald, "The Rationality of Emotions," *Dialogue,* 18 (1979) 41–63, reprinted in Amélie O. Rorty, ed., *Explaining Emotions* (Berkeley: University of California Press, 1980).

The Rationality of Emotion (Cambridge, Mass.: MIT Press, 1987).

Deutsch, Helene, "Some Forms of Emotional Disturbance and Their Relationship to Schizophrenia," *Yearbook of Psychoanalysis,* 1 (1942) 121–136 (New York: International Universities Press, 1945).

Devereux, George, *Basic Problems of Ethnopsychiatry* (Chicago: University of Chicago Press, 1980).

Dewey, John, "The Theory of Emotion," in *The Early Works, 1882–98,* volume 4 (Carbondale: Southern Illinois University Press, 1971), originally in *Psychological Review,* 1 (1894) and II (1895).

Dinerstein, Dorothy, *The Mermaid and the Minotaur: Sexual Arrangements and Human Malaise* (New York: Harper and Row, 1976).

Driver, Julia, "The Virtues of Ignorance," *Journal of Philosophy,* 86 (1989) 373–384.

Dummett, Michael, *Frege: Philosophy of Mathematics,* 2nd impression (London: Duckworth 1995).

Duncker, Karl, "On Pleasure, Emotion, and Striving," *Philosophy and Phenomenological Research,* 1 (1941) 391–430.

Epictetus, *Discourses.*

Erikson, Erik, *Insight and Responsibility* (New York: Norton, 1964).

Falk, W. David, "Fact, Value and Non-natural Predication," in *Ought, Reasons, and Morality* (Ithaca, N.Y.: Cornell University Press, 1986).

Fanon, Frantz, *The Wretched of the Earth* (New York: Grove Press, 1965).

Black Skins, White Masks (New York: Grove Press, 1968).

Federn, P., "On the Distinction between Healthy and Pathological Narcissism," 1929, in *Ego Psychology and the Psychoses* (New York: Basic Books, 1952).

Fenichel, Otto, *The Psychoanalytic Theory of Neurosis* (New York: Norton, 1954).

Ferenczi, Sandor, "Notes and Fragments II," 1930, translated and reprinted in Michael Balint, ed., *Final Contributions to the Problems and Methods of Psychoanalysis* (New York: Brunner Mazel, 1980).

Finnis, John, "Intention and Side-Effects," in R. G. Frey and Christopher W. Morris, eds., *Liability and Responsibility* (Cambridge: Cambridge University Press, 1991).

"*Bland:* Crossing the Rubicon?" *Law Quarterly Review,* 109 (1993) 329–337.

Foot, Philippa, "Moral Arguments," *Mind,* 67 (1958) 502–513, reprinted in *Virtues and Vices* (Oxford: Blackwell, 1978).

"Moral Beliefs," *Aristotelian Society Proceedings,* 59 (1958–1959) 83–104, reprinted in *Virtues and Vices* (Oxford: Blackwell, 1978).

Virtues and Vices (Oxford: Blackwell, 1978).

Fossum, Merle A., and Marilyn J. Mason, *Shame: Families in Recovery* (New York: Norton, 1986).
Foucault, Michel, *The Use of Pleasure* (New York: Vintage Press, 1985).
Frankfurt, Harry, "The Faintest Passion," Presidential Address to the Eastern Division of the American Philosophical Association, 1991, *Proceedings and Addresses of the American Philosophical Association,* 66 (1992) 5–16.
Freud, Anna, *The Ego and the Mechanisms of Defense* (London: Hogarth Press, 1937).
Freud, Sigmund, *The Standard Edition of the Complete Psychological Works of Sigmund Freud,* edited by James Strachey (London: Hogarth Press, 1986).
Freud, Sigmund, and Josef Breuer, *Studies on Hysteria* (New York: Basic Books, 1957).
Fridja, N. H., *The Emotions* (Cambridge: Cambridge University Press, 1986).
Gartner, Richard, Dodi Goldman, et al., Letter in *New York Review of Books,* 42, no. 1 (1995) 42–43.
Garver, Eugene, *Aristotle's Rhetoric: An Art of Character* (Chicago: University of Chicago Press, 1994).
"Aristotle's Moral Virtues Are Political Virtues," unpublished manuscript.
"Aristotle's *Nemesis:* Practical Rationality and the Emotions," unpublished manuscript.
Gaus, Gerald F., *Value and Justification* (Cambridge: Cambridge University Press, 1990).
Gaylin, Willard, *The Killing of Bonnie Garland* (New York: Penguin Books, 1983).
Gean, William, "Emotion, Emotional Feeling and Passive Bodily Change," *Journal for the Theory of Social Behavior,* 9 (1979) 39–51.
Gibbard, Allan, *Wise Choices, Apt Feelings* (Cambridge, Mass.: Harvard University Press, 1990).
Gilligan, Carol, *In a Different Voice* (Cambridge, Mass.: Harvard University Press, 1982).
Goffman, Erving, *Stigma: Notes on the Management of Spoiled Identity* (Englewood Cliffs, N.J.: Prentice-Hall, 1963).
Goleman, Daniel, *Emotional Intelligence* (New York: Bantam Books, 1995).
Gorkin, Michael, *The Uses of Countertransference* (Northvale, N.J.: Jason Aronson, 1987).
Gosling, Justin, *Pleasure and Desire* (Oxford: Oxford University Press, 1969).
"More Aristotelian Pleasures," *Aristotelian Society Proceedings,* 74 (1973) 15–34.
Gosling, Justin, and Christopher C. W. Taylor, *The Greeks on Pleasure* (Oxford: Oxford University Press, 1982).
Grahek, Nikola, "Objective and Subjective Aspects of Pain," *Philosophical Psychology,* 4 (1991) 249–266.
Greenberg, Jay, and Stephen Mitchell, eds., *Object Relations in Psychoanalytic Theory* (Cambridge, Mass.: Harvard University Press, 1983).
Greenspan, Patricia, "A Case of Mixed Feelings: Ambivalence and the Logic of Emotion," in Amélie O. Rorty, ed., *Explaining Emotions* (Berkeley: University of California Press, 1980).
"Emotions without Essences," presented at the March 1985 University of Cincinnati Philosophy Colloquium, and ch. 2 of *Emotions and Reasons* (New York: Routledge, 1988).

Emotions and Reasons (New York: Routledge, 1988).
Practical Guilt (New York: Oxford University Press, 1995).
Guntrip, Harry, *Schizoid Phenomena, Object Relations, and the Self* (New York: International Universities Press, 1969).
Haggerty, Daniel, "Shame," unpublished manuscript.
Hampshire, Stuart, "A Way of Seeing," review of David Sylvester, *Looking at Giacometti*, *New York Review of Books*, 42, no. 12 (July 13, 1995) 46–49.
Hare, Richard M., "What Makes Choices Rational?" *Review of Metaphysics*, 32 (1979) 623–637.
Hardin, Russell, *Morality within the Limits of Reason* (Chicago: University of Chicago Press, 1988).
Haugeland, John, "Understanding Natural Language," *Journal of Philosophy*, 76 (1979) 619–632.
Hegeman, Elizabeth, "The Development of a Worker Elite in a Cali Barrio," in Elizabeth Hegeman and Leonard Kooperman, eds., *Anthropology and Community Action* (New York: Doubleday Anchor Press, 1974).
"World View As Cultural Parataxis," *Contemporary Psychoanalysis*, 30 (1994) 424–441.
Hurka, Thomas, *Perfectionism* (New York: Oxford University Press, 1993).
Husserl, Edmund, *Ideas* (New York: Humanities Press, 1967).
Jacobson, Edith, "The Psychoanalytic Theory of Affects," 1951, unpublished manuscript.
"The Affects and Their Pleasure-Unpleasure Qualities in Relation to the Psychic Discharge Processes," in R. M. Lowenstein, ed., *Drives, Affects, Behavior* (New York: International Universities Press, 1953).
Depression (New York: International Universities Press, 1971).
James, William, "What Is an Emotion?" *Mind*, 9 (1884) 188–205, reprinted in K. Dunlap, ed., *The Emotions* (New York: Hafner, 1967).
The Principles of Psychology (New York: Holt, 1896).
Kernberg, Otto, "Factors in the Treatment of Narcissistic Personalities," *Journal of the American Psychoanalytic Association*, 18 (1970) 51–85, reprinted in Andrew P. Morrison, ed., *Essential Papers on Narcissism* (New York: New York University Press, 1986).
Borderline Conditions and Pathological Narcissism (New York: Jason Aronson, 1975).
Klein, Melanie, *Love, Guilt and Reparation, and Other Works, 1921–1945* (New York: Delta Books, 1977).
Envy and Gratitude and Other Works, 1946–1963 (New York: Delta Books, 1977).
Kleinman, Arthur, *Patients and Healers in the Context of Culture: An Exploration of the Borderland between Anthropology, Medicine, and Psychiatry* (Berkeley: University of California Press, 1980).
Kohut, Heinz, *The Analysis of Self* (New York: International Universities Press, 1971).
The Restoration of the Self (New York: International Universities Press, 1977).
Krystal, Henry, "Aspects of Affect Theory," *Bulletin of the Menninger Clinic*, 41 (1977) 1–26, reprinted in *Integration and Self-Healing: Affect, Trauma, and Alexithymia* (Hillsdale, N.J.: Analytic Press, 1988).
"Trauma and Affect," *Psychoanalytic Study of the Child*, 36 (1978) 81–116, re-

printed in *Integration and Self-Healing: Affect, Trauma, and Alexithymia* (Hillsdale, N.J.: Analytic Press, 1988).

"The Hedonic Element in Affectivity," *Annual of Psychoanalysis,* 9 (1981) 93–113, reprinted in *Integration and Self-Healing: Affect, Trauma, and Alexithymia* (Hillsdale, N.J.: Analytic Press, 1988).

Integration and Self-Healing: Affect, Trauma, and Alexithymia (Hillsdale, N.J.: Analytic Press, 1988).

Landauer, K., "Affects, Passions and Temperament," *International Journal of Psycho-Analysis,* 19 (1938) 388–415.

Lawrie, Reynold, "Passion," *Philosophy and Phenomenological Research,* 41 (1980) 106–126.

Lazarus, R. S., *Emotion and Adaptation* (New York: Oxford University Press, 1991).

Lazarus, R. S., A. D. Kanner, and S. Folkman, "Emotions: A Cognitive–Phenomenological Perspective," in R. Plutchik and H. Kellerman, eds., *Emotion: Theory, Research, and Experience* (New York: Academic Press, 1980).

Leighton, Stephen, "A New View of Emotion," *American Philosophical Quarterly,* 22 (1985) 133–141.

Leventhal, Howard, and Deborah Everhart, "Emotion, Pain, and Physical Illness," in Carol Izard, ed., *Emotions in Personality and Psychopathology* (New York: Academic Press, 1970).

Lewis, Helen Block, *Shame and Guilt in Neurosis* (New York: International Universities Press, 1971).

Lloyd, Antony C., "Emotion and Decision in Stoic Philosophy," in John Rist, ed., *The Stoics* (Berkeley: University of California Press, 1978).

Luper-Foy, Steven, Review of Justin Oakley, *Morality and the Emotions, Philosophy and Phenomenological Research,*54 (1994) 725–728.

Lycos, Kimon, "Aristotle and Plato on 'Appearing'," *Mind,* 73 (1964) 496–514.

Maccoby, Michael, *The Gamesman* (New York: Bantam, 1978).

Marshall, Graeme, "On Being Affected," *Mind,* 77 (1968) 241–259.

Matthews, Gareth, "Ritual and Religious Feelings," in Amélie O. Rorty, ed., *Explaining Emotions* (Berkeley: University of California Press, 1980) and, in an earlier version, "Bodily Motions and Religious Feelings," *Canadian Journal of Philosophy,* 1 (1971) 75–86.

McDougall, Joyce, *Theaters of the Mind: Illusion and Truth on the Psychoanalytic Stage* (New York: Brunner Mazel, 1991).

McDougall, W., *An Outline of Psychology* (London: Methuen, 1923).

McDowell, John, "Are Moral Requirements Hypothetical Imperatives?" *Aristotelian Society Proceedings,* 52 (1978) 13–29.

"Virtue and Reason," *Monist,* 62 (1979) 331–350.

"Values and Secondary Qualities," in Ted Honderich, ed., *Morality and Objectivity* (London: Routledge and Kegan Paul, 1985), reprinted in Geoffrey Sayre-McCord, ed., *Essays on Moral Realism* (Ithaca, N.Y.: Cornell University Press, 1988).

Mind and World (Cambridge, Mass.: Harvard University Press, 1994).

"Two Sorts of Naturalism," in Rosalind Hursthouse, Gavin Lawrence, and Warren Quinn, eds., *Virtues and Reasons* (Oxford: Oxford University Press, 1995).

MacIntyre, Alasdair, *After Virtue* (Notre Dame, Ind.: University of Notre Dame Press, 1981).

Melzack, Ronald, and Patrick Wall, "Pain Mechanism: A New Theory," in K. H. Pribram, ed., *Brain and Behavior 2: Perception and Action* (Baltimore: Penguin Books, 1969).
The Challenge of Pain (New York: Basic Books, 1983),
Merleau-Ponty, Maurice, *Humanism and Terror* (Boston: Beacon Press, 1971).
Miller, Alice, *The Drama of the Gifted Child* (New York: Basic Books, 1981).
For Your Own Good (New York: Farrar, Straus, Giroux, 1983).
Banished Knowledge (New York: Doubleday, 1990).
Millgram, Elijah, "Pleasure in Practical Reasoning," *Monist*, 76 (1993) 394–415.
Milrod, David, "Self-Pity, Self-Comforting, and the Superego," *Psychoanalytic Study of the Child*, 27 (1972) 505–528.
Moore, George E., *Principia Ethica* (Cambridge: Cambridge University Press, 1960).
Moran, Richard, "Impersonality, Character, and Moral Expressivism," *Journal of Philosophy*, 90 (1993) 578–595.
"The Expression of Feeling in Imagination," *Philosophical Review*, 103 (1994) 75–106.
Morrison, Andrew P., ed., *Essential Papers on Narcissism* (New York: New York University Press, 1986).
Shame: The Underside of Narcissism (Hillsdale, N.J.: Analytic Press, 1989).
Moulton, Janice, "A Paradigm of Philosophy: The Adversary Method," in Sandra Harding and Merrill B. Hintikka, eds., *Discovering Reality* (Dordrecht: Reidel, 1983).
Murdoch, Iris, *The Sovereignty of Good* (London: Routledge and Kegan Paul, 1970).
Neu, Jerome, "Jealous Thoughts," in Amélie O. Rorty, ed., *Explaining Emotions* (Berkeley: University of California Press, 1980).
Nussbaum, Martha, *Aristotle's De Motu Animalium* (Princeton: Princeton University Press, 1978).
Love's Knowledge (Oxford: Oxford University Press, 1990).
"Equity and Mercy," *Philosophy and Public Affairs*, 22 (1993) 83–125.
The Therapy of Desire (Princeton: Princeton University Press, 1994).
Oakley, Justin, *Morality and the Emotions* (London: Routledge, 1992).
Olafson, Frederick, "Consciousness and Intentionality in Heidegger's Thought," *American Philosophical Quarterly*, 12 (1975) 91–103.
O'Shaughnessy, Brian, *The Will* (Cambridge: Cambridge University Press, 1980).
Owen, Gwilym E. L., "Aristotelian Pleasures," *Aristotelian Society Proceedings*, 72 (1972) 135–152.
Parfit, Derek, *Reasons and Persons* (Oxford: Oxford University Press, 1984).
Perkins, Moreland, "Emotion and Feeling," *Philosophical Review*, 75 (1966) 139–160.
Person, Ethel Spector, and Howard Klar, "Establishing Trauma: The Difficulty Distinguishing between Memories and Fantasies," *Journal of the American Psychoanalytic Association*, 42 (1994) 1055–1081.
Piper, Adrian, "Higher Order Discrimination," in Owen Flanagan and Amélie O. Rorty, eds., *Identity, Character, and Morality* (Cambridge, Mass.: MIT Press, 1990).
Pitcher, George, "Emotion," *Mind*, 74 (1965) 326–346.
"The Awfulness of Pain," *Journal of Philosophy*, 67 (1970) 481–491.

Plato, *Symposium*.
Republic.
Philebus.
Phaedrus.
Putnam, Hilary, *Mind, Language, and Reality* (Cambridge: Cambridge University Press, 1975).
Racker, Heinrich, *Transference and Countertransference* (New York: International Universities Press, 1968).
Rapaport, David, *Emotions and Memory*, 2nd unaltered edition (New York: International Universities Press, 1942).
"On the Psychoanalytic Theory of Affects," *International Journal of Psycho-Analysis*, 34 (1953) 177–198, reprinted in Robert P. Knight and Cyrus Friedman, eds., *Psychoanalytic Psychiatry and Psychology: Clinical and Theoretical Papers, Austen Riggs Center*, volume 1 (New York: International Universities Press, 1954), and in *The Collected Papers of David Rapaport*, edited by Merton M. Gill (New York: Basic Books, 1967).
"Some Metapsychological Considerations concerning Activity and Passivity," *Archivos de Criminología, Neuropisquitaría Disciplinas Conexas* (Equador), 9 (1961) 391–449, reprinted in *The Collected Papers of David Rapaport*, edited by Merton M. Gill (New York: Basic Books, 1967).
The Collected Papers of David Rapaport, edited by Merton M. Gill (New York: Basic Books, 1967).
Rawls, John, *A Theory of Justice* (Cambridge, Mass.: Harvard University Press, 1971).
Reisenzein, Rainer, "Emotional Action Generation," in Wolfgang Battmann and Stephan Dutke, eds., *Processes of Molar Action Regluation*, forthcoming.
Reisenzein, Rainer, and Wolfgang Schönpflug, "Stumpf's Cognitive–Evaluative Theory of Emotion," *American Psychologist*, 47 (1992) 34–45.
Rey, Georges, "Functionalism and Emotions," in Amélie O. Rorty, ed., *Explaining Emotions* (Berkeley: University of California Press, 1980).
Reich, Wilhelm, *Characteranalyse* (Vienna: Selbstverlag des Verfassers, 1933).
Richardson, Henry, *Practical Reasoning About Final Ends* (Cambridge: Cambridge University Press, 1994).
"The Emotions in Reflective Equilibrium," unpublished manuscript.
Robinson, Jenefer, "Startle," *Journal of Philosophy*, 92 (1995) 53–74.
Roland, Alan, *In Search of Self in India and Japan: Toward a Cross-Cultural Psychology* (Princeton: Princeton University Press, 1988).
Rorty, Amélie O., "The Place of Pleasure in Aristotle's Ethics," *Mind*, 83 (1974) 481–497.
"Explaining Emotions," *Journal of Philosophy*, 75 (1978) 139–161, reprinted in Rorty, ed., *Explaining Emotions* (Berkeley: University of California Press, 1980), and *Mind in Action* (Boston: Beacon Press, 1988).
ed., *Explaining Emotions* (Berkeley: University of California Press, 1980).
Mind in Action (Boston: Beacon Press, 1988).
Ross, Colin, *Multiple Personality Disorder* (New York: John Wiley and Sons, 1989).
Sachs, David, "Wittgenstein on Emotion," *Acta Philosophica Fennica*, 28 (1976) 250–285.

"How to Distinguish Self-Respect from Self-Esteem," *Philosophy and Public Affairs*, 10 (1981) 346–360.

"Self-Respect and Respect for Others: Are They Independent?" in O. H. Green, ed., *Respect for Persons, Tulane Studies in Philosophy*, 31 (1982) 109–128.

Sandler, Joseph, Ethel Spector Person, and Peter Fonagy, eds., *Freud's "On Narcissism: An Introduction"* (New Haven: Yale University Press, 1991).

Sartre, Jean-Paul, *Being and Nothingness* (New York: Washington Square Press, 1966).

Sketch for a Theory of the Emotions (London: Methuen 1971).

Anti-Semite and Jew (New York: Schocken Books, 1976).

Schachtel, Ernest, "On Memory and Childhood Amnesia," *Psychiatry*, 10 (1947) 1–26, reprinted in *Metamorphosis* (New York: Da Capo Press, 1984; reprint of New York: Basic Books, 1959).

Metamorphosis (New York: Da Capo Press, 1984; reprint of New York: Basic Books, 1959).

Scheffler, Israel, "In Praise of the Cognitive Emotions," *Thinking*, 3 (1981) 16–23.

Scheler, Max, *The Nature of Sympathy* (Hamden, Conn.: Archon Books, 1970).

Formalism in Ethics and Nonformal Ethics of Values (Evanston, Ill.: Northwestern University Press, 1973).

Scheper-Hughes, Nancy, *Death without Weeping: The Violence of Everyday Life in Brazil* (Berkeley: University of California Press, 1992).

Schilder, Paul, *Medical Psychology*, 1924, edited and translated by David Rapaport (New York: International Universities Press, 1953).

Searle, John, "How to Derive 'Ought' from 'Is'," *Philosophical Review*, 73 (1964) 43–58.

Seneca, *De Ira*.

Shapiro, David, *Neurotic Styles* (New York: Basic Books, 1965). *Autonomy and Rigid Character* (New York: Basic Books, 1981). *Psychotherapy of Neurotic Character* (New York: Basic Books, 1989).

Sherman, Nancy, "The Virtues of Common Pursuit," *Philosophy and Phenomenological Research*, 53 (1993) 277–299.

Shweder, Richard A., *Thinking through Cultures: Expeditions in Cultural Psychology* (Cambridge, Mass.: Harvard University Press, 1991).

Sidgwick, Henry, *Methods of Ethics* (Indianapolis, Ind.: Hackett, 1981).

Slater, Philip, *The Glory of Hera* (Boston: Beacon Press, 1968).

Slote, Michael, "Morality and Self–Other Asymmetry," *Journal of Philosophy*, 81 (1984) 179–192.

From Morality to Virtue (New York: Oxford University Press, 1992).

"Reply to Commentators [on *From Morality to Virtue*]," *Philosophy and Phenomenological Research*, 54 (1994) 709–719.

Solomon, Robert, "Emotions and Choice," *Review of Metaphysics*, 27 (1973) 20–41, and in an expanded version in Amélie O. Rorty, ed., *Explaining Emotions* (Berkeley: University of California Press, 1980).

The Passions (New York: Doubleday, 1976).

Spelman, Elizabeth V., *Inessential Woman* (Boston: Beacon Press, 1988).

Spezzano, Charles, *Affect in Psychoanalysis* (Hillsdale, N.J.: Analytic Press, 1993).

Spinoza, Baruch, *Ethics*, in *The Chief Works of Spinoza*, translated by R. H. M. Elwes (New York: Dover, 1955).

Spitzer, Robert, et al., *Diagnostic and Statistical Manual*, III (Washington, D.C.: American Psychiatric Association, 1980).
Sprigge, Timothy, "Metaphysics, Physicalism, and Animal Rights," *Inquiry*, 22 (1979) 101–143.
Stern, Daniel, *The Interpersonal World of the Infant* (New York: Basic Books, 1985).
Diary of an Infant (New York: Basic Books, 1990).
Stocker, Michael, "Morally Good Intentions," *Monist*, 54 (1970) 124–141.
"Intentions and Act Evaluations," *Journal of Philosophy*, 67 (1970) 589–602.
"'Ought' and 'Can'," *Australasian Journal of Philosophy*, 49 (1971) 303–316.
"Act and Agent Evaluations," *Review of Metaphysics*, 27 (1973) 42–61.
"Agent and Other: Against Ethical Universalism," *Australasian Journal of Philosophy*, 54 (1976) 206–220.
"The Schizophrenia of Modern Ethical Theories," *Journal of Philosophy*, 73 (1976) 453–466.
"Desiring the Bad," *Journal of Philosophy*, 76 (1979) 738–753.
"Intellectual Desire, Emotion, and Action," in Amélie O. Rorty, ed., *Explaining Emotions* (Berkeley: University of California Press, 1980).
"Values and Purposes: The Limits of Teleology and the Ends of Friendship," *Journal of Philosophy*, 78 (1981) 747–765.
"Responsibility, Especially for Beliefs," *Mind*, 91 (1982) 398–417.
"Psychic Feelings: Their Importance and Irreducibility," *Australasian Journal of Philosophy*, 61 (1983) 5–26.
"Affectivity and Self-Concern: The Assumed Psychology in Aristotle's Ethics," *Pacific Philosophical Quarterly*, 64 (1983) 211–229.
"Emotional Thoughts," *American Philosophical Quarterly*, 24 (1987) 59–69.
Plural and Conflicting Values (Oxford: Oxford University Press, 1990).
"Self–Other Asymmetries and Virtue Theory," *Philosophy and Phenomenological Research*, 54 (1994) 689–694.
"Emotions and Ethical Knowledge: Some Naturalistic Connections," *Midwest Studies in Philosophy*, 19 (1994) 143–158.
"Some Comments on [Thomas Hurka's] *Perfectionism*," *Ethics*, 105 (1995) 386–400.
"How Emotions Reveal Value and Help Cure the Schizophrenia of Modern Ethical Theories," in Roger Crisp, ed., *How Should One Live?* (Oxford: Oxford University Press, 1996).
"Abstract and Concrete Value: Plurality, Conflict, and Maximization," in Ruth Chang, ed., *Incommensurability, Comparability, and Practical Reasoning* (Cambridge, Mass.: Harvard University Press, 1997).
Strasser, Stephen, *Phenomenology of Feeling* (Pittsburgh: Duquesne University Press, 1980).
Strawson, Peter, "Freedom and Resentment," *Proceedings of the British Academy*, 48 (1962) 187–211, reprinted in Gary Watson, ed., *Free Will* (Oxford: Oxford University Press, 1982).
Striker, Gisela, "Emotions in Context," delivered to the panel on "The Emotions in Greek and Hellenistic Ethics," the 1995 Pacific Division of the American Philosophical Association, unpublished manuscript.
Sullivan, Harry Stack, "A Note on the Implications of Psychiatry, The Study of

Interpersonal Relations, for Investigations in the Social Sciences," in *The Fusion of Psychiatry and Social Science* (New York: Norton, 1964).
Personal Psychopathology: Early Formulations (New York: Norton, 1965).
Tawney, R. H., *Religion and the Rise of Capitalism* (New York Harcourt, Brace, 1926).
Taylor, Charles, "Self-Interpreting Animals," in *Human Agency and Language, Philosophical Papers*, volume 1 (Cambridge: Cambridge University Press, 1985).
"The Politics of Recognition," *Multiculturalism and "The Politics of Recognition"* (Princeton: Princeton University Press, 1992), reprinted in David Theo Goldberg, ed., *Multiculturalism* (Oxford: Blackwell, 1994).
Taylor, Gabriele, "Justifying the Emotions," *Mind*, 84 (1975) 390–402.
Pride, Shame,and Guilt: Emotions of Self-Assessment (Oxford: Oxford University Press, 1985).
Thomas, Laurence, "Rationality and Affectivity: The Metaphysics of the Moral Self," *Social Philosophy and Policy*, 5 (1988) 154–172.
Living Morally (Philadelphia: Temple University Press, 1989).
Thompson, Clara. M., "Development of Awareness of Transference in a Markedly Detached Personality," *International Journal of Psycho-Analysis*, 19 (1938) 299–309, reprinted in *Interpersonal Psychoanalysis: The Selected Papers of Clara M. Thompson*, edited by Maurice R. Green (New York: Basic Books, 1964).
Thomson, Judith Jarvis, "Self-Defense," *Philosophy ancd Public Affairs*, 20 (1991) 283–310.
Thomson, Judith Jarvis, and James Thomson, "How Not to Derive 'Ought' from 'Is'," *Philosophical Review*, 73 (1964) 512–516.
Tomkins, Silvan, "The Quest for Primary Motives: Biography and Autobiography of an Idea," *Journal of Personality and Social Psychology*, 41 (1981) 306–329.
Waligore, Joseph, "The Joy of Torture: The Happiness of Stoic Sages" (Ph.D. dissertation, Syracuse University, 1995.)
Walker, Margaret, "Moral Particularity," *Metaphilosophy*, 18 (1987) 171–185.
"Moral Understandings: Alternative 'Epistemology' for a Feminist Ethics," *Hypatia*, 4 (1989) 15–28.
"Moral Luck and the Virtues of Impure Agency," *Metaphilosophy*, 22 (1991) 14–27, reprinted in Daniel Statman, ed., *Moral Luck*, (Albany: State University of New York Press, 1993).
"Morality and the Emotions: Getting Things Right," unpublished manuscript.
Wallace, R. Jay, *Responsibility and the Moral Sentiments* (Cambridge, Mass.: Harvard University Press, 1994).
Warner, Richard, "Enjoyment," *Philosophical Review*, 89 (1980) 507–526.
Freedom, Enjoyment and Happiness (Ithaca, N.Y.: Cornell University Press, 1987).
Weakland, John, "The 'Double Bind' Hypothesis of Schizophrenia and Three-Party Interaction," in Don Jackson, ed., *The Etiology of Schizophrenia* (New York: Basic Books, 1960).
West, Nathaniel, *Miss Lonelyhearts* (New York: New Directions, 1969).
White, Alan R., "The Notion of Interest," *Philosophical Quarterly*, 14 (1964) 319–327.
Wiggins, David, *Needs, Values, and Truth* (Oxford: Blackwell, 1991).
Williams, Bernard, "Ethical Consistency," in *Problems of the Self* (Cambridge: Cambridge University Press, 1973).

"Persons, Character, and Morality," in Amélie O. Rorty, ed., *The Identities of Persons* (Berkeley: University of California Press, 1976).

Philosophical Papers (Cambridge: Cambridge University Press, 1982).

Woodbridge Lectures, delivered at Columbia University, 1993.

Shame and Necessity (Berkeley: University of California Press, 1993).

Williams, Bernard, and J. J. C. Smart, *Utilitarianism, For and Against* (Cambridge: Cambridge University Press, 1973).

Winnicott, Donald W., "Countertransference," *British Journal of Medical Psychology*, 33 (1960) 17–21.

The Maturational Processes and the Facilitating Environment (London: Hogarth Press, 1965).

Wolf, Susan, "The Moral of Moral Luck," unpublished manuscript.

Young, Charles, Review of Sarah Boadie, *Ethics with Aristotle, Journal of the History of Philosophy*, 31 (1993) 625–627.

Zajonc, Robert B., "Feeling and Thinking," *American Psychologist*, 35 (1980) 151–175.

Subject index

act evaluations, xiii–xiv, 3, 138–68 (especially 152, 159, 160), 307–20 (especially 318)
acting well, emotions and, 152–60
 and affectivity, 154–8
 and dissociation, 156
 and duties, 153, 158–61
 and evaluative frills, 153, 161
 and gratitude, 153, 161
 and guilt, 155
 and narcissism, 154
 and "one thought too many," 156–7
 and remorse, 153–5, 158
 and shame, 153–5
activity, 28, 30, 70, 168, 169–87 (especially 169–74), 189, 192–7, 198–200, 290
 active engagement, 245–6
 active/passive, 255–63
 Aristotelian activities, 139
 contemplative, 288
 and fear, 254–60
 good activities done well, xvii, 11–12, 33–6, 69–71, 169–74, 177–8, 183–6, 294, 297
 interpersonal, 164, 199
 and pity, 261–3
 and pleasure, 12, 36, 169–74, 181–6, 294, 297
affectivity, xviii, 1–2, 6–8, 12–13, 17–55, 69–71, 84–5, 103–4, 107, 112, 128, 158, 160–8, 243–64, 325
 and articulability, 193
 and desire, 19, 20, 25–8, 28–38, 47–51, 52, 53, 54

 and dissociation, 17–55 (especially 17, 35, 51)
 and a good, healthy human life, 17–55 (especially 17, 33, 35, 52)
 and pangs, 53–5
 unconscious, 21
agent evaluations, xiii–xiv, 3, 138–68 (especially 152, 159, 160), 307–20 (especially 318)
alienation, xxvi, 114, 132, 173, 204
anger (and *orgē*), 9, 22–4, 41, 44–5, 52, 57–8, 60, 62, 73–4, 93–4, 101, 109, 110, 113, 120, 141, 223–4, 239, 246–53, 265–322, 324–6
 Aristotle on *orgē*, 265–322
 and closeness, 307–20
 and differential focusing, 251
 and guilt, 22, 101, 217
 and narcissism, 268–86
 and pity, 93, 261
 and pride, 246–53
 and shame, 22, 44, 223–4, 227
 and slights, 286–98
anthropology, xvii, xviii, xxiv, xxv, xxviii, 7, 13, 17, 173, 198, 243, 265, 266, 272, 322
articulability and knowledge, 192–203
attentiveness, 76, 119, 127–8, 136
 and friendship, 278–9
authenticity, 62, 204
autonomy
 and enmeshment, 117–19
 and rigidity, 148

background/foreground, emotions and, 8, 23, 24, 61, 68, 85, 100,

341

background/foreground, emotions
    and (*cont.*), 161, 165, 166, 168,
    194, 196, 263
  and culture, 270
beliefs and emotions, 24, 31–2, 38–9,
    41, 47–52
  and cognitive content of emotions,
    24, 38–41, 49
  and trust, 50

character structures, emotions and,
    180, 209–30, 243–64, 265–
    322
characterological values, 56–87
    (especially 57, 67), 160
closeness, 307–20
  and fear and pity, 253–4
content claim, 26–8, 31, 39, 49, 51, 52,
    113, 123, 136–7, 221, 251–2,
    301
  and the information claim, 86–7
countertransference, xxiv–vi, 113,
    188–9
culture, emotions and, xxiv–viii, 2, 83–
    4, 98, 104, 235, 270
  and magic, 42
  and masculine identity, 113–14
  and shame, 218, 228, 270

desire, 17–55, 61, 65–8, 99–101, 129–
    32, 160–3, 175, 287–91, 293–
    5, 308, 314
  and affectivity, not reducible, 28–38
  and closeness, 308, 314
  the functional-biological account of,
    33
  and narcissism, 268–86
  not reducible to enjoyment, pleasure,
    or pain, 28–38
  for recognition, 286–98
  and self-perfection or preservation,
    32–3
  and spiritual maladies, 244–6
dissociation, xxvi–xxvii, 17, 112–13,
    127–8, 132
  and affectivity, 17, 35, 51
  and intellectualization, 211–13

duties, xxi, 3, 4, 37, 84, 110, 153, 158–
    61, 228

ego ideals, 63, 217–20
  and mania, 276
  and shame, 217–20, 284
'emotional' as an epithet, 95–100
emotions as added perfections, 169–74,
    176–9
  alienated work and, 173
  and idealizing emotionless reason,
    173
  and the information claim, 170
  and pride, 170–3
  and products, producing, 172
emotions as affective, 17–55 (especially
    24–6)
emotions as constituents of value, 169–
    87 (especially 174–7)
  in activity, 169–87 (especially 174–7
    and 182–4)
  in play, 174–5, 179–80
emotivism, 12, 26, 59, 73–82, 107, 285
empathy, 140–2, 214–17
  and enmeshment, 117
  and narcissism, 270
  and "seeing all the facts," 214–17
enmeshment, 109, 116–24, 189, 313,
    316
ethical theory and emotions, xxi, 159,
    228, 323–6
eudaimonia, 166, 243, 277, 279, 292–3
evaluative frills, 153, 161
evaluative judgment, emotions and,
    91–121
  and autonomy, 117–18
  and epistemic failure, 118–19
  and hope, 114–16, 119–20
  and universality, 100, 120
evaluative knowledge, 64–5, 91–121,
    122–37, 188–208, 326
  and "cool reason," 64, 92–5, 99,
    101–2, 104–5

fame, desire for, 294–6
family, emotions and, 61, 108–9, 115–
    16, 117, 164–5, 176–7, 179–

80, 190, 229, 249–51, 302–3, 313
fear, 5, 28–31, 47–9, 144, 167–9, 253–4, 254–8, 259–61, 317, 319
  for another, 253–8
  and danger, 121, 124, 167–9, 236
  and depression, 279
  and epistemic failures, 119
  and guilt, 63
  for oneself, 253–8
  and pity, 259–61, 317
  and shame, 63, 217, 218, 220–30
feelings, 17–55
  awareness of, 21–4
  bodily versus psychic, 17–24
  dispositional, 23–4
  and intensity, 20
  misidentification of, 22
  occurrent, 23–4
flattery, 286–98
  and honor, 286, 288–9, 292–3
  and hopes, 286–7
  and love, 286–7, 292
  and narcissism, 289–98
  and recognition, 286–98
  and slights, 286–98
forgiveness, 320–2
formalistic ethics and emotions, 139–49
  contradictoriness, 142–9
  maxims and their meaning, 143–9
  universalizability, 142–9
  and rigidity, 143–9
  and rule following, 144–9
  and uncertainty, 143–9
friendship, xiv, 60–1, 164, 174, 274, 277–9, 280
  and anger, 247–8, 266–7, 278, 300–1
  and narcissism, 274–86
  and slights, 57, 300–1, 307

going astray and emotions, 95–100
"going wrong" with emotions, 93, 95–100, 157, 266, 294–5
  and action guiding morality, 158
  and pleasure, 294
  and spite, 157–60
  and prima facie wrongness, 157–8

good person (being a), emotions and, 152–60
  and affectivity, 154–8
  and dissociation, 156
  and duties, 153, 158–61
  and evaluative frills, 153, 161
  and gratitude, 153, 161
  and guilt, 155
  and narcissism, 154
  and "one thought too many," 156–7
  and shame, 153–5
guilt, 3–4, 22, 63, 155, 190, 217–19, 221, 228, 283–5, 315–16
  guilt-based morality, 3–4, 190, 228
  and shame, 4, 22, 63, 155, 217–19, 221, 283–5, 315–16

hope, 43–5, 114–16, 119–20, 254–8
  and fear, 254–8
  Pitcher on, 41, 43–5, 114–16

idealizations, xvi, xvii–xx, xxvi, 63, 92, 103–4, 189
idealizing emotionless reason, xvi, xvii, xix–xx, 92, 103–4
ideals, ego, 63, 217–20
  and shame, 217–20, 284
identification/identifying with, 307–20
identification with the aggressor, 108, 215–16
imagos, 63, 217–20, 284
information claim, 82–5, 86–7, 136–7, 170, 186
institutions and emotions, 34, 179, 295, 299, 302–4, 305
  and being a good citizen, 179
  and intellectual interest, 179
intellectualization, 102–4, 109, 112–14, 127–8, 132, 211, 213
interest, 11, 19, 20, 21, 29–30, 33–5, 37, 40, 43, 45–7, 52–3, 54
  aesthetic, 29–30
  intellectual, 29–30, 65–73, 101–3, 179
  interpersonal, emotions as 6, 54, 114, 159, 160–8, 174–7, 199, 200, 219, 226, 307, 325

343

interpersonal, emotions as (*cont.*)
  and anger, 306–7
  and Aristotelian virtues, 164, 166–8
  and closeness, 307–20
  and courage and fear, 167–8
  and *eudaimonia,* 166
  and intrapersonal, 219, 226, 297, 307, 325
  and liberality, 166–7
  and play, 174
interpersonal goods
  and affectivity, 160–1
  and metropolis anxiety, 161–2
  and professional philosophy, 162–3, 164–5
  solidarity and community, 162–6
  versus solitariness, 164

jealousy, 40–51, 85
judgment, evaluative, emotions and, 91–121
  and autonomy, 117–18
  and epistemic failure, 118–19
  and hope, 114–16, 119–20
  and universality, 100, 120
justice, emotions and, 139–49
  administrative or bureaucratic justice, 140–2
  and taxation, 141–2
  and anger, 140, 141
  distributive justice, 140
  equity and empathic understanding, 140–2
  and reactive attitudes, 139
    indignation, 140
    remorse, 140
  and respect, 140
  and trust, 141, 142, 144, 146–9

"looking on" at life, emotions and, 109, 178, 246, 290
love, 136–7, 177, 181, 229, 233–5, 237, 240–1, 268, 279, 286–7, 292
  and activity, 177
  and flattery, 286–7, 292
  and narcissism, 234–5, 268, 279, 287, 292

and painful emotions, 233–5, 237, 240–1

maladies, spiritual, 1–2, 13, 17, 185, 244–6, 247, 252–3, 255, 258, 264, 285
maximization, and nonmaximization, 66, 318
maxims, 143–9
medical treatment, emotions and, 138–9
"mere feelings," 53–4, 55, 186–7, 231
mistrust and rigidity, 49
moods, emotions and, 8, 20, 23, 40, 55, 68, 93, 100, 180–1, 189, 304, 314
  optimism and pessimism, 180–1
moral reasoning, emotions and, 142–9
motivation, xiii, xiv, 1, 3–4, 28–30, 37, 83–5, 96–7, 134, 150–1, 175, 178, 228
  and duty, 228
  guilt and, 155
  shame and, 228
motives, 28–30, 83–5, 96–7, 150–1, 175, 178

narcissism, 147, 229, 234, 265–322
  and Aristotle's angry man, 268–86
    his narcissistic wounds, 268, 270, 283
    his rage, 279–80, 281, 283
  and belief, 269
  and depression (melancholia), 276, 278, 279, 284, 285
  and ego ideals, 276, 284
  and *eudaimonia,* 277, 279, 292, 293
  and importance, 266–7
  and love, 234–5, 268, 279, 287, 292
  and mania, 276–7
  and "mere feelings," 271
  and narcissistic needs/demands, 277, 279–81, 283, 290, 296–7
  pathological, 269–71, 278
  and rage, 279–83
  and self-love, 268
  and self-referential values, 274–6

and comparisons, 274–6
relative and absolute values, 274–5
and self-respect, 269–70
and shame, 39, 154, 217, 229
and solitariness, 281–2
and special or manic entitlement, 276–7, 285, 290, 291
and uncertainty, comparison, and ranking, 272
and understanding/being understood, 280–2,
and self-love, 268
and rage, 279–80, 281, 283
naturalism/antinaturalism, 73–82
an interpretation of Philippa Foot, 73–82
the offense-rudeness claim, 75–82
and overall or prima facie wrongness, 76–82
and rudeness, 74–82
neurotic, borderline, and psychotic formations and epistemic-evaluative distortions, 6, 108–12, 127
alexithymia, 108–12
depression, 108, 115, 119, 185, 204
enmeshment, 109, 117–19
paranoia, 109, 126–7
and philosophical errors about feelings, 112–14
schizoid affectlessness, 109–12

"onlooker at life," emotions and, 109, 178, 246, 290
orgē, see anger
other-induced emotions, 61

painful emotions, 170, 230–42
best of all possible worlds, 232–3, 241
the Good Samaritan paradox, 232–5, 237
and hedonism, 231–2
the justification of, 232–5, 240–1
and love, 233–5, 237, 240–1
and Mr. Spock, 235
narcissism, 234, 273, 278, 282, 287

and organic wholes, 231–2
personally, *see* taking things personally
phantasia, 38–9
philosophy, its professional practices and emotions,
adversarial attitude, 162–3
the claim, "I don't understand," 162–3, 280
departmental life, 144, 162, 164–5
killing other people, just as an example, 209–14
philosophy and strange views about emotions, xv–vii, xix–xx, 91–121, 160–8, 209–42
false truisms, 91–107, 122
the fantasy ideal of wholly positive emotions, 235
idealizing emotionless reason, xvi, xvii, xix–xx, 92, 103–4
neurotic formations and philosophical analyses of emotions, 112–14
pity, 121, 253–4, 258–64, 317–22
and activity/passivity, 258–64
and compassion, 259–60
and differential focusing, 259–60
eleos, 259–60, 317
and mercy, 259–60
other-directed, 262
other-regarding, 258–64
and passive aggressiveness, 261
self-directed, 262, 316
self-pity, 93, 258–64, 283, 316
play, 12, 70, 100, 160, 164, 167, 174–5, 179, 180, 189, 195–7, 199, 212, 306
pleasure, emotions and, 169–87
and activity, 12, 36, 169–74, 181–6, 294, 297
Aristotle on, 169–87
and desire, 28–38
energeiai, 169, 182
good pleasures, 183, 297
and health, 183
identical with value, 174–7
perfecting values and activities, 169–74
and the *phronimos*, 183

345

pleasure, emotions and, (cont.)
  processes, 182
practical knowledge, 192–203
pride, 56, 81, 170, 171–3, 200, 222, 246–53, 291
  and anger, 246–53
  bad pride, 171
  and shame, 222
promise keeping, 142–5, 146–7
  and repaying debts, 142–7
proportionality, emotions and 320–2
psychic feelings, 17–55
  irreducibility to desire, 28–38
  irreducibility to reason, 38–51

rationality, xvi, xvii, xix–xx, 64, 91–107, 122
  "cool rationality" in inquiry, 64, 92–5, 99, 101–2, 104–5
  and "don't be emotional," 95–6, 98
  emotions and "going astray," 95–100
  false truisms about, 91–107, 122
  idealization of, xvi, xvii, xix–xx, 92, 103–4
recognition, 286–98
  and being an onlooker at life/spectatorism, 290
  and desire for, 294–6
  and *eudaimonia*, 292–3
  and fame, 294–6
  and science, 294–6
  and self-concern, 293
rights, emotions and, 150–2
  right of self-defense, 150–2
rigidity, 66, 108, 139–49, 195
  and rule following, 145–9
  and uncertainty, 145–9
role playing, 61
rule-based moralities, emotions and, 190–1

seeing and seeing as, 30–1, 40–3, 46–7, 50, 53
self, 17–55,
  as object of shame, 217–30
  self-preservation or self-perfection, 32–4

and shame 4, 217–30
self-misinterpretation, 147
self-psychology, 163–4
  on solitariness, 129, 164, 281
self-referential values, 250, 274–6
  and comparisons, 274–6
  relative and absolute values, 274–5
shame, 3–4, 22, 30, 39, 63, 84, 107, 153–4, 155, 190–1, 217–30, 273, 283–5, 313–16
  and anger, 22, 44, 223–4, 227
  and culture, 218, 228, 270
  defending against, 155
  and ego ideals, 217–30, 284–5
  and fear, 217–18, 220–1, 224–5, 226
  globalized, 221–30
  and guilt, 4, 22, 63, 155, 217–19, 221, 283–5, 315–16
  and honor groups, 218
  and identification, 313–16
  and imagos, 63, 217–30, 284
  and leftover emotions, 63
  localized, 221–30
  and narcissism, 39, 154, 217, 229
  and object-relations, 30, 39
  and *orgē*, 273, 283–5
  partitionable and nonpartitionable objects of, 223–4
  and pride, 222
  and remorse, 153–4
  shame-morality, 3–4, 190–1
  and slights, 283–5
  "totally not" and "not totally," 225
slights, 246–53, 265–8, 286–98
  and flattery, 286–98
  and friendship, 277–80
  and recognition, 286–98
sociology, 6–7, 13, 165, 173, 243, 265–8, 272, 298, 306–7, 322
specificity, 48, 223, 227
spectatorism, *see* onlooker
spiritual maladies, 1–2, 13, 17, 185, 244–6, 247, 252–3, 255, 258, 264, 285
  and active engagement, 255–7
  and Aristotle's psychology, 244–6
  and being an onlooker at life, 256

and care, 254–7
and concern, 254–7
and depression, 254–7
and interest, 254–7
and loss of value
  in oneself, 255–7
  in the world, 255–7
spite, 1, 157–60, 247, 266, 283, 308, 310
  acting with, 157
  and anger, 247, 310
  for oneself, 308
  and *orgē*, 266
  and slights, 283
Spock, Mr., xv–xvi, 235
structures, emotions, values and, 122–37
  distinction between emotions and their underlying structures, 122–37
  and evaluative knowledge, 122–37
sympathy, 214–17
  and identifying with the aggressor, 215

taking things personally, 44, 45, 47, 109–10, 130, 141, 244, 251–3, 263, 284–6, 298–306
  and anger, 298–306

trust, 50, 58, 64, 94, 105–6, 113, 125, 141–4, 146–8, 149
  and beliefs, 50
  trusting oneself, 146–8
truth, affect and, 58, 64, 94, 105–6, 113, 142, 144

understanding, 47–50
  dry conception of, 48–50
  intellectual and emotional, 49
universalism, emotions and, 318–20, 320–2
universalizability, 139–49
usefulness (instrumental, constitutive, functional) of emotions, 82–6

values, revealed or constituted by emotions, 56–8, *see also* emotions as constituents of value; information claim
valuings versus values, emotions and, 59–64
virtue(s), emotions and, 1, 123, 136, 139, 166–7, 175, 181, 193, 200, 202, 243, 246, 288–9, 291–3, 298

wrongness, prima facie or overall, 76–81, 157–8

Names index

Adams, Marilyn McCord, 220
Adams, Robert, 315
Adkins, Arthur W. H., 257, 277
Adler, Jonathan, xii, 17, 80, 92, 94
Agamemnon, 322
Alcibiades, 303
Alcoff, Linda, 294
Aldrich, Virgil, 256
Alexander, Franz, 9, 10
Alexander, S., 40
Alston, William, xx, 18, 26
Amasis, 253
Anaximander, 191
Angell, Roger, 11, 35, 240
Anscombe, Elizabeth, xx
Aquinas, Thomas, 19
Aristotle, xii, xiii, xxi, 1, 7, 12, 13, 19, 24, 25, 28, 29, 30, 38, 39, 40, 48, 50, 57, 65, 67, 73, 82, 85, 106, 120, 121, 123, 136, 139, 164, 166, 167, 168, 169, 170, 181, 182, 184, 185, 191, 193, 196, 199, 200, 201, 202, 209, 217, 220, 228, 231, 236, 239, 243–64, 265–322, 324, 325, 326; *see also* Subject Index and Index of Aristotelian and Platonic Sources
Armstrong, David, 31
Aune, Bruce, 31
Autenrieth, Georg, 254
Ayer, A. J., 26

Bach, Kent, 17, 38, 268
Baier, Annette, 17, 25, 182
Balint, Michael, 71, 129, 180
Bartky, Sandra Lee, 198, 218, 286

Bateson, Gregory, 198
Bedford, Errol, xx, 41
Benardete, José, 273, 299
Bennett, Jonathan, xii, 318
Benson, J., 19
Berkowitz, Howard L., 261
Berman, Paul, 216, 310, 314
Bibring, E., 9, 10
Block, Ned, 32
Bloomfield, Paul, xii
Blum, Lawrence, xii, xx, 83, 107, 123, 159, 190–2, 259
Blustein, Jeffrey, xii
Bramson, Leon, xxiv
Bratman, Michael, 17
Brenman, M., 9, 10
Brentano, Franz, 39, 107
Breuer, Josef, 110
Brierley, M., 21
Broadie, Sarah, 25, 193
Bromberg, Philip, 127, 128
Bromberger, Sylvain, 17
Buechler, Sandra, xviii, 127
Bürger-Prinz, H., 10
Burnyeat, Myles, 65

Cairns, Douglas L., 266
Callias, 299
Campbell, John, 243
Card, Claudia, 296
Charlton, William, 50
Chasseguet-Smirgel, Janine, 217
Chazan, Pauline, 62, 229, 291
Chodorow, Nancy, 7, 113, 114, 173–7
Cleon, 298

348

Cohen, Marshall, 138
Collins, Mr., 98, 100
Conn, Christopher, 303
Cordner, Christopher, 17
Crick, Francis, 69, 71
Cross, Elizabeth, 196

Dahl, Norman, 243
Daly, Robert W., xii, 139, 198
Damasio, Antonio R., 8, 23, 25
Dancy, Jonathan, 138
D'Arms, Justin, 79, 309
Davidson, Donald, 25, 31
Deigh, John, xii, 25, 39, 142, 214, 217
Dent, Nicholas J. H., 19
Descartes, René, 8, 19, 23, 25
DeSousa, Ronald, xx, 51, 83
Deutsch, Helene, 9, 10
Deutscher, Max, 42, 294
Devereux, George, xxvii
Devitt, Michael, 17
Dewey, John, 19
Dinerstein, Dorothy, xxvii
Dreyfus, Hubert, 17
Driver, Julia, 128, 251
Dummett, Michael, 165
Duncker, Karl, 36, 37

Everhart, Deborah, 170

Falk, W. D., 107, 110
Fanon, Frantz, 198, 286
Federn, P., 10
Fenichel, Otto, 9, 10
Ferenczi, Sandor, 128, 129
Filippi, Ronald, 267
Finnis, John, 138, 150
First, Elsa, 119, 209
Foot, Philippa, 74–7, 80–2
Foucault, Michel, 270
Frankena, William, xi
Frankfurt, Harry, 143
Freeman, Samuel, 138
Freud, Anna, 103, 108, 216
Freud, Sigmund, 8, 21, 22, 110, 204, 217, 230, 234, 245, 268, 277, 319
Fudge, Robert, 76

Gardner, John, 138
Garland, Bonnie, 215
Gartner, Richard, 8
Garver, Eugene, xii, 93, 98, 106, 139, 160, 166, 182, 191, 244, 299
Garver, Joel, 270
Gaus, Gerald, 84
Gaylin, Willard, 215
Gean, William, xx, 19
Genné, Beth, 195
Giacometti, 200, 201
Gibbard, Allan, 79, 309
Gilligan, Carol, 83
Goffman, Erving, 316
Goldman, Dodi, 8
Goleman, Daniel, 28, 83, 164, 189
Gorkin, Michael, xxv, 113
Gosling, Justin, 37, 182
Gowans, Christopher, xii
Grahek, Nikola, 170
Greenspan, Patricia, 39, 71, 83
Guntrip, Henry, 108, 109, 110, 134

Haggerty, Daniel, xii, 191, 217, 222, 225, 228
Haley, Jay, 198
Hampshire, Stuart, 200
Hardin, Russell, 240
Hare, Richard M., 49
Haugeland, John, 18
Hegel, 102, 237
Hegeman, Elizabeth, xii, xvii, xviii, xxv, 12, 13, 58, 261, 284, 326
Heidegger, Martin, 26, 40
Herman, Barbara, 80, 142
Herrin, Richard, 215
Hobbes, Thomas, 164, 182
Horner, (little) Jack, 297
Hume, David, 50
Hurka, Thomas, 92

Illych, Ivan, 62
Iphigeneia, 322

Jackson, Don, 198
Jackson, K. R., 243
Jacobson, Daniel, 79, 309
Jacobson, Edith, 21

James, Henry, 190
James, William, 25, 26, 44
Jankélévitch, Vladimir, 216, 310, 314
Johnston, Mark, 17

Kaila, M., 10
Kamm, Frances, 319
Kant, Immanuel, 84, 142, 145, 147, 177, 181, 182, 200
Karenina, Anna, 38
Kent, Bonny, 285, 308
Kernberg, Otto, 111, 268, 269, 270, 278
Khan, Ghengis, 319
Kim, David, 227
Klar, Howard, 58
Klein, Melanie, xvi, 284
Kleinman, Arthur, 272
Kohut, Heinz, xvii, 163, 219, 268
Kosman, L. A., 17, 243
Kretzmann, Norman, 251
Krystal, Henry, 8, 10, 21, 34, 84, 85, 100, 108, 133

Lamond, Grant, 138
Landauer, K., 9, 10
Larsen, Sarah, 198
Lawrie, Reynold, xx, 18
Leibniz, 232, 233, 235, 237, 241
Leighton, Stephen, 17
Leiter, Brian, 138, 165
Leontius, 37
Leventhal, Howard, 170
Levey, Samuel, 92, 324
Levine, Martin, 138, 141
Lewis, Helen Block, 2, 22, 63, 155, 217, 218, 220, 221, 284
Lewis, Oscar, xxiv
Lloyd, Antony C., 49
Lloyd, Genevieve, 17
Loar, Brian, 243, 248
Luper-Foy, Steven, 2, 84
Lycos, Kimon, 17, 39
Lysenko, Gregor, 295

Maccoby, Michael, 173
MacIntyre, Alasdair, 240

Mackie, J. L., 241
Marshall, Graeme, xii, 17, 36, 92, 113, 177, 243
Marx, 237
Matthews, Gareth, 17, 54
Mayer, Kirsten, 301
McAleer, Sean, 191, 228
McDougall, Joyce, 21, 28, 108–10, 134, 173, 189
McDowell, John, 49, 82, 107, 123, 124, 203
McFall, Lynne, xii, 256, 257
Melzack, Ronald, 170
Merleau-Ponty, Maurice, 296
Mill, J. S., 163, 237
Miller, Alice, 216
Millgram, Elijah, xii, 17, 48, 170
Milrod, David, 260
Moore, G. E., xiii, 4
Moran, Richard, xii, 38, 54, 155, 158, 159
Morgenbesser, Sidney, 177, 310
Morrison, Andrew, 30, 39, 84, 112, 219, 220, 225, 268, 269, 277, 278
Moulton, Janice, 163
Murdoch, Iris, xx, 18, 83, 107, 159, 190, 191, 192

Neander, Karen, 230
Neu, Jerome, xx, 18, 41, 42, 45, 51
Newman, Barnett, 196, 202
Newton, Issac, 8
Nietzsche, Freidrich, 2, 276
Nussbaum, Martha, 39, 49, 83, 107, 123, 139, 190, 191, 192, 202, 214–17

Oakley, Justin, 2, 84
Oedipus, 317
Olafson, Frederick, 40
Ortiz, Dan, 138
O'Shaughnessy, Brian, 36
Owen, G. E. L., 182

Pach, Lleni, 61, 280
Parfit, Derek, xiv
Perkins, Moreland, xx, 18, 19

Person, Ethel Spector, 58, 268
Piper, Adrian, 125
Pitcher, George, xx, 18, 41–4, 87, 112, 114, 170
Plato, 20, 26, 37, 39, 100, 228, 231, 235, 236, 288
Puck, 147
Putnam, Hilary, 8, 21, 31

Rachels, Stuart, xii
Racker, Heinrich, xxv, 113
Rapaport, David, 8, 9, 10, 21, 27, 71, 72, 84, 121, 127, 261, 290, 291
Rawls, John, xx, 144
Raz, Joseph, 138
Reich, Wilhelm, 9, 10
Rey, Georges, xx, 18, 320
Richardson, Henry, xii, 5
Robertson, John, xii, 182, 298
Robinson, Jenefer, 39, 217
Roland, Alan, 272
Rorty, Amélie O., xx, 6, 17, 18, 123, 298
Ross, Colin, xvii
Rousseau, Jean-Jaques, 164, 274
Ryle, Gilbert, 26, 113

Sachs, David, xx, 258
Sartre, Jean-Paul, 22, 26, 40–3, 59, 102, 106, 112, 125, 129, 146, 311, 312, 314
Schachtel, Ernest, 6, 8, 10, 34, 84, 85, 100, 133
Scheler, Max, 18, 20, 214
Scheper-Hughes, Nancy, 322
Schilder, Paul, 10
Searle, John, 79
Seneca, 49, 214–17
Shapiro, David, 66, 108, 112, 126, 127, 130, 131, 135
Sherman, Nancy, xii, 291, 296
Shope, Robert, 17
Shweder, Richard, xxvii, 17, 129, 272
Sidgwick, Henry, xiv
Slawson, David, 138
Slote, Michael, 319

Smart, J. J. C., 239
Socrates, 186, 228, 251, 299
Solomon, Robert, xx, 18, 41, 42, 44, 45, 112
Spelman, Elizabeth V., 214
Spezzano, Charles, 6, 21
Spinoza, Benedict, 32, 34, 36
Spock, Mr., xv, xvi, 235
Sprigge, Timothy, 49
Stevenson, Charles, 26
Stock, Barbara, 278
Stocker, Michael, xxviii, 92, 101, 120, 169, 174, 192, 217, 237, 275, 291, 298, 318
Strasser, Stephen, 18
Strawson, Peter, xx, 18, 85, 106, 107, 158, 176, 234, 235, 323–5
Striker, Gisela, 29
Sullivan, Harry Stack, xxvi, 284

Taurek, John, 17
Tawney, R. H., 4
Taylor, Charles, 85, 107, 163, 165, 274, 291, 325
Taylor, Christopher, 182
Taylor, Gabriele, xx, 18, 40, 218–21, 270
Teichman, Jenny, 34
Thalberg, Irving, xi, 17
Thomas, Laurence, xii, 75, 92, 107, 114, 182, 301
Thompson, Clara M., 109, 246, 290
Thomson, Judith Jarvis, 79, 150
Tomkins, Silvan, xviii, 6, 84, 85, 133

Waligore, Joseph, 2, 49, 60, 170, 233
Walker, Margaret, 83, 84, 107, 240, 292, 296
Wall, Patrick, 170
Wallace, R. Jay, 60, 63, 79, 201, 235
Wallwork, Ernest, 106, 117
Warner, Richard, 36, 138
Watson, James, 69, 71
Weakland, John, 198
West, Nathaniel, 316

White, Alan R., 40
Wiggins, David, 67, 131
Williams, Bernard, 4, 7, 156, 157, 191, 218, 219, 228, 239, 268, 273, 283, 294, 295, 319, 322
Winant, Terry, 163, 236
Winnicott, D. W., 113

Wittgenstein, Ludwig, 26, 112–13, 191
Wolf, Susan, 296
Wolff, Jonathan, 138

Young, Charles, 25, 107, 243

Zajonc, Robert, xviii, 18

Index of Aristotelian and Platonic Sources

Aristotle
  Nicomachean Ethics
    I.1, 1095b24, 220
    I.5, 1095b27, 288
    I.6, 1097b10, 277
    I.8, 1099a5, 136, 181
    I.11, 1101a32, 50
    II.5, 1105b21, 28, 170
    II.9, 1109b7, 297
    III.1, 1110a23, 320
    III.2, 1111b20, 255
    III.6, 1115a22, 253, 317
    III.6, 1115a35, 254
    III.6, 1116a1, 258
    III.7, 1116a3, 258
    III.11, 1119a12, 67
    IV.3, 1123b17, 292
    IV.3, 1124a5, 292
    IV.3, 1125a19, 247, 292
    IV.5, 1125b32, 266
    IV.5, 1126a6, 247
    IV.5, 1126a8, 266
    VII.5, 1149a5, 258
    VII.8, 1151a13, 67
    VIII.8, 1159a13, 220, 286
    VIII.8, 1159a19, 286
    VIII.8, 1159a22, 286, 293
    X.4, 1174b25, 183
    X.4, 1174b32, 169
    X.4 1175a18, 171
    X.5, 1175b3, 185
  Rhetoric
    I.2, 1356a5, 106
    I.11, 1370a27, 169
    II.1, 1378a20, 29
    II.2, 1378a31, 24, 29, 57, 73, 247, 266, 282
    II.2, 1378a34, 298
    II.2, 1378b2, 278
    II.2, 1378b8, 278
    II.2, 1378b10, 266
    II.2, 1378b13, 247
    II.2, 1378b14, 266
    II.2, 1378b27, 273
    II.2, 1378b31, 266
    II.2, 1378b35, 267
    II.2, 1379a1, 267
    II.2, 1379a7, 267
    II.2, 1379a10, 279
    II.2, 1379a19, 279
    II.2, 1379a36, 272
    II.2, 1379b13, 277
    II.2, 1379b28, 267, 306
    II.4, 1382a4, 299
    II.4, 1382a6, 282
    II.4, 1382a8, 282
    II.4, 1382a15, 314
    II.5, 1382a22, 29
    II.5, 1382b26, 253, 317
    II.5, 1382b30, 257
    II.5, 1383a3, 254
    II.6, 1385b7, 317
    II.8, 1385b12, 253, 317
    II.8, 1385b27, 317
    II.8, 1386a17, 253, 254, 317
    II.8, 1386a19, 253, 317
    II.8, 1386a27, 253

Plato
  Apology
    30c, 251
  Phaedrus
    253, 100
  Republic
    439, 37
    580, 100

Printed in Poland
by Amazon Fulfillment
Poland Sp. z o.o., Wrocław